Why Men Hate Women

What makes a man like John, in every respect a cultured and charming man, successful in his career and liked by his friends and acquaintances, behave violently towards a woman he says he loves? Is he sick? Is he different from other men? Is it, as he says, Jane's fault? Does she like being beaten? Otherwise why would she go on doing what she knows upsets him? Adam Jukes hopes that by the end of his demanding but gripping book, the reader will be able to answer these questions.

ADAM JUKES works with men who are abusive and violent to women. In the last five years he has been involved in the London Men's Centre, which offers dedicated programmes to men who are violent.

This is a shocking book. Its thought-provoking view of the issues will be of great interest to mental health professionals and all concerned readers.

WHY MEN HATE WOMEN

ADAM JUKES

FAB

'an association in which the free development of
each is the condition of the free development of all'

Free Association Books / London / 1993

Published in Great Britain in 1993 by
Free Association Books Ltd,
a company jointly owned by
Process Press Ltd and T.E. Brown,
26 Freegrove Road
London N7 9QR

A CIP catalogue record for this book is available from the British Library

ISBN 1-85343-195-8 pb
1-85343-300-4 hb

Typeset from author's disc by Archetype

Printed and bound in Great Britain by
CPI Antony Rowe, Chippenham and Eastbourne

To Tamsin Furby and Leda Betti, from whom I learned the difference between theory and practice, and to my son, Thomas Adams-Jukes.

CONTENTS

ACKNOWLEDGEMENTS

Whenever I have read the Acknowledgements page in books I have always been mildly sceptical that any such solitary enterprise could depend on so many people. I now find, to my surprise, that at this stage the list of those without whom this book would either not have been possible, or would have been very different, is very long. In the first place, my gratitude to my parents, Lilly and Ted. The list of those who, with forbearance and occasional enthusiasm, took part in discussions and arguments at staff meetings, dinner parties and other social gatherings, where I aired my latest thoughts, is unending. Special mention, however, is due to Anne Dickson, Tom Feldberg, Anne Koch, Tony Nicholls, Tom Ryan, Howard Tumber and Heather Wood, whose encouragement and wise feedback at difficult moments of self-doubt spurred me on. Special thanks are due to my colleagues at the Men's Centre – Marc Pigeon in particular – and to the hundreds of men who had the courage to give me the privilege of endless opportunities to test out my thinking. All names have been changed to preserve confidentiality.

The informed criticism and dedication of my editors, initially Selina O'Grady and latterly Ann Scott, and of my copy-editor, Gillian Beaumont, made this a much better book than it would otherwise have been. My thanks to my researchers, Belinda Pratten and Barbara Rendall, for the many lonely hours they spent in libraries. Stephen Frosh provided much-needed reality-checking. Professor Ischa Bloomberg, David Malan and Margot Waddell will know how much they contributed. To all them, and to many more who are not named, I owe a debt of gratitude. Responsibility for any opinions and ideas expressed here is, however, entirely my own.

John

I first heard of John when his partner, Jane, phoned in a state of great distress. She informed me that he had beaten her very badly the night before, and that she was leaving him to stay in a refuge for battered wives. She did not want the relationship to end; she had three small children and no other source of support. She wanted John to get some help and stop beating her. He had been inflicting this violence on her since they were married ten years ago. She described him as very quiet and a good father when he was not being violent. Her family and friends would not believe that he was battering her because it was so out of character with the person they saw.

It is the rule rather than the exception for the victim to contact me. Most men who batter their wives do not believe that they have a problem. They genuinely believe that the problem is the woman's, and that if she got some help with the things she does which 'make him violent' he would stop. I informed her – as I usually do under these circumstances – that she had a problem, but that the problem was her husband. His problem was that he was violent and abusive, and was not taking responsibility for it. If he wanted help, he would have to contact me directly.

Later that same day, John phoned. He cried as he told me that Jane had left him and taken the children. He had no idea where she was. He agreed to come and see me later that week. He turned out to be a mild-mannered, softly spoken, well-dressed man in his late thirties. He is a senior executive in a large multinational corporation, and a graduate of Oxford University. I discovered that he had first been violent towards Jane three months after their marriage. Since that time, the attacks had become both more frequent and more violent even by his own account. He told me, however, that he did not understand why she had taken such extreme action as to run off to a refuge. He was very sorry for what he had done, and promised that he would not do it again. I asked him if he had made this promise before. He grudgingly admitted that he did so every time, and that he always meant it. I did not question his sincerity, but asked him if he thought Jane might be afraid of him and could no longer trust his remorse. With some difficulty he agreed that might be so. I asked him to tell me about the last attack, details of which I had already had from Jane.

I knew that he had begun hitting her late at night after she took too long in coming to bed. When she did not hurry up after his first comment, he began to get frustrated and angry, and abused her verbally. When she told him that it was up to her how long she took to get ready for bed, he began to shout at her and call her names. She responded to this by asking why he got so angry with her over such a simple thing. At this point he slapped her, and Jane called him a bastard. He then hit her in the face with a clenched fist while she screamed at him to stop. After three or four punches he did stop, and stormed angrily out of the room. In what he described as an attempt to calm down, he went to the kitchen and made a cup of coffee.

As he sat drinking it, he felt overwhelmed with rage at Jane. He decided to go and try to talk to her and 'sort it out'. Jane was lying on the bed, crying. He asked if they could talk it over. Jane remained silent. John made repeated attempts to get her to respond, with increasing frustration, until he pulled her up and forced her to look at him. Jane closed her eyes. This was too much for John. He began hitting her again and again, with no thought of how much damage he might do to her. This went on for about four hours. Jane had not been able to remember, but thought he had repeated his attack on four occasions with a variety of slaps, punches, kicks and hair-pulling as he dragged her around the room. Jane had described him as demented during these batterings, and said that the more she protested, the more violent he seemed to become. He finally ripped all her nightclothes off, and was threatening to rape her for 'the whore she was'.

Eventually, a neighbour became alarmed by Jane's screams, and called the police. John was taken to the station and charged with grievous bodily harm – a charge which was, in my experience, unlikely to be pressed or proven. The police took Jane to the hospital, where it was discovered that she had broken ribs, cuts and contusions. She was also mildly concussed. The police arranged for her to be taken to a refuge.

John's account of these events is fascinating. He told me that he had lost control and hit Jane once or twice. He could not understand why the neighbour had called the police, as there was no particular disturbance. He loved Jane and his children deeply. He remembered that he had always felt frustrated by her slowness, and said that this had always been the main – if not the only – cause of 'fighting' in their relationship. He felt that he was always waiting for her. He knew that he was an impatient person; he could get very frustrated with his subordinates at work. I asked him if he lost control and hit them. 'Of course not,' was his reply.

John thinks that Jane is the cause of his violence – that she provokes it by behaving in ways which she knows upset him. His back-up to this justification is that he believes he has a problem with his temper. He describes his father as quiet and easygoing. John got on well with him. He found his mother a bit difficult, and thought his father had allowed her to be too dominant in their relationship. His parents had not rowed, his father had never hit his mother, and John had an older married brother who did not hit his partner.

What makes a man like John – a cultured and charming man in every other respect, successful in his career and liked by his friends and acquaintances – behave in this way towards a woman he says he loves? Is he sick? Is he different from other men? Is it, as he says, Jane's own fault? Does she like being beaten, as he unconsciously assumes? Otherwise, why would she go on doing what she knows upsets him? I hope that by the end of this book we shall be able to answer these questions.

PREFACE

> The notion of human progress involves a distortion of the truth of human nature.
> (Saul Bellow)

My central thesis is that men exist in a state of perpetual enmity towards women which they express overtly and covertly, by controlling and dominating them. In this book my focus is on psychological life and psychotherapy, but I am all too aware of the context in which the problem of male violence is set.

Women make up more than 50 per cent of the world's population. They do, on average, twice as many hours of work (largely unpaid) as men. They legally own less than 2 per cent of the world's wealth. In most countries wealth passes through the male line. This ensures that any wealth the woman brings to a union with a man eventually goes to the sons, not the daughters.

Between 1970 and 1980 the proportion of women representatives on National Legislative Assemblies worldwide decreased from 16 per cent to 13 per cent.

In the UK the penalty for sexual abuse of a male minor is twice that for abuse of a female minor.

It is estimated that only 25 per cent of women raped in the UK in 1978 went to the police. Of these, only a third were taken seriously enough for the crime to be recorded, and only 3 per cent of the men were successfully prosecuted. Fifty per cent of rapes are carried out in the home environment by someone known to the victim.

It is estimated that at least half of all rapes, worldwide, are never reported and that as many as one in six women have been raped.

A hundred men are charged with sexual offences for every woman so charged.

In a random sample of 930 adult women in San Francisco in 1978, 16 per cent reported that they had been sexually abused by a relative, and 31 per cent by a non-relative, before the age of eighteen.

80 to 90 per cent of incest is with girl children.

The more attention is paid to the problem of child sexual abuse – which generally means the abuse of girls – the more the figures for its incidence rise. Recent research indicates that a girl child has a one in five chance of being sexually abused by someone during her childhood. Many workers in the field believe that this may underestimate the real scale of the problem by a half. The guideline that one should not take sweets from a stranger seems rather ironic, given that the greatest risk of rape for a girl is by a man she trusts. This is also true for adult females.

In the UK 72 per cent of divorces are granted to women on the grounds of their husband's unreasonable behaviour.

In the USA the physical abuse of women, by male intimates, is second only to male–male assault as a source of serious injury to adults. It affects 3–5 million women a year.

The FBI believes that wife-battering is the most unreported crime – being as much as ten times more unreported than rape.

Scottish police records show that wife assault is the second most common crime of violence.

In the UK 11,000 women go to a Women's Aid Refuge every year with their children.

1,786 dowry deaths were officially recorded by the Indian Police in 1987.

Substantial numbers of women have undergone some form of circumcision, usually carried out to curtail their sexual pleasure and drive. It is still widely practised in some cultures.

Women who marry live shorter lives than women who stay

single, whereas men who marry live longer lives than men who stay single. It has been suggested that marriage kills women.

During pregnancy, two out of three women in poor countries are anaemic and have no access to a trained health worker.

Fifty-one per cent of world births are delivered by untrained attendants. Infanticide – which is reliably reported from China, and rumoured in India – always means the killing of girl children. In poor countries girls are more likely to die or be undernourished than boys. Infant mortality for females in India is 30 to 60 per cent higher than it is for boys.

Women are particularly likely, in rich countries, to suffer from mental illness, to be admitted to mental hospital, or to take psychotropic drugs designed to calm them down. It has to be said that the diagnoses are usually made by men. Women attempt suicide about twice as often as men.

Two-thirds of Asian women, one sixth of Latin American women and half of African women are anaemic.

In Latin American countries, the most prevalent cause of death in women aged fifteen to thirty-nine is complications following illegal abortion.

Abortion laws, or laws outlawing abortion, are always made by men. They have the support of the world's – entirely male – religions.

Official figures from the International Labour Office put the proportions of women in the labour force at:

USSR 48%
USA 38%
Europe 34%
Asia 34%
Oceania 33%
Africa 32%
South America 24%

These figures do not include 'domestic' work.

Two-thirds of officially employed European women work in the service sector, which is usually seen as an extension of domestic work. In industry there are three times more men than women. Worldwide, there are between three and six times more men than women in administrative and managerial posts, and up to six times more women than men in clerical and secretarial jobs. In Britain, whilst 70 per cent of office workers are women, 99 per cent of them are typists and secretaries. Only 14 per cent of office bosses are female.

While it is officially estimated that one-third of all households are headed by a woman, the assumptions that underlie the employment of women are: (1) they want to work only temporarily; (2) they are secondary, not primary, earners in the family. Most countries' tax and social security policies, where they exist, are based on these assumptions.

Throughout the world, women in paid employment tend to be in part-time, low-paid jobs even after their childbearing days are over.

In the UK, women's projected earnings for 1993–94 are 70.3 per cent of men's. This is a drop from 75 per cent in 1979 because employers (with the collusion of trade unions) arranged that women were not doing the same work as men, which at the time was the basis for claiming equal pay. The government was forced by the European Community to amend the Equal Pay Act so that women could claim equal pay for work of equal value instead of only the same work. It is now very difficult for women to increase their earnings because employers have ensured that they are not doing jobs which can be so evaluated.

Contrary to expectations, there is little real difference in occupational discrimination against women in the former Soviet Union and China, where most of the trends, familiar in the rest of the world, prevail – lower earnings, shorter hours, more service occupations, higher unemployment.

In the USSR, after the Second World War, the shortage of men meant that women took up many previously male-dominated occupations. Medicine, in particular, used to be a high-status, high-pay profession, dominated by men. Since the war the profession has become dominated by women, who now constitute nearly 100 per cent of doctors. At the same time, the status of medicine has declined to the point where doctors earn only 70 per cent of average earnings.

In 1978, twenty-eight countries had Equal Pay legislation. By 1983 this figure had risen to 90. Such countries tend to be developed. A study conducted in 1975 showed that women in paid employment in twenty-four countries earned 70 per cent of male earnings. In 1982 this had increased only marginally: to 73 per cent. There are also enormous regional differences – in Japan, for example, it is 50 per cent; while in Sweden it is 80 per cent.

None of these figures takes into account the enormous amount of unpaid work done by women – and not only housework. World Report (1985), for example, shows that women, working unpaid, produce 50 per cent of the world's food, despite the fact that official surveys show that it is men who do the work. This happens because the surveyors define women's work as domestic work, even if it is work in the fields. In addition, the figures do not take into account those many millions of women who are not covered by Equal Pay laws in the developing countries, or are homeworkers in the developed countries and are not, therefore, covered by any employment legislation.

In the rich world, women do an average of three hours less paid work and seventeen hours more unpaid work than men.

A study of twelve – mostly rich – countries in 1975 showed that:

Men with jobs	do 49 hours' paid work per week.
Women with jobs	do 40 hours' paid work per week.
Housewives	do 1 hour's paid work per week.
Men in jobs	do 11 hours' unpaid work per week.
Women in jobs	do 31 hours' unpaid work per week.
Housewives	do 56 hours' unpaid work per week.
Employed men	have 34 hours' free time per week.
Employed women	have 24 hours' free time per week.
Housewives	have 33 hours' free time per week.

In Italy and the UK, 85 per cent of women with both children and full-time jobs are married to men who do no housework.

In Sweden – where many sexually discriminating practices are illegal, one which is usually held up as a model for the future – only one in five men take up their legal right to maternity leave.

In Kenya, agricultural workers visited men growing cash crops five times more frequently than women growing the same crops.

Ten times more female than male farmers in Kenya have never spoken to a government agricultural worker.

Nicaragua is the only Latin American country to have given land to women in their own names.

In Nigeria, when the price of rice – which was farmed by women as a domestic crop under their control – began to rocket in the 1970s, the men began to take control and claim the income for themselves.

A very large proportion of housewives in rich countries have no idea how much their husbands earn.

Between 1975 and 1985, in rich countries, equal numbers of girls and boys were receiving primary, secondary or further education. In poor countries the discrimination which existed in 1975, with many more boys than girls in all forms of education, still persists today, despite a large increase in the numbers receiving all forms of education.

Studies conducted in rich countries demonstrate that teachers behave differently towards boys and girls in the classroom. Girls are rewarded for being quiet, docile and neat. Boys are rewarded for getting the right answer. Research has shown that boys get twice as much attention from teachers as girls. Even when this is pointed out to the teachers, the subsequent difference is very small: an increase of only 7 per cent in the time girls get. This is true regardless of the sex of the teacher.

In the developing countries, twice as many women as men are illiterate.

Ninety-four per cent of all interruptions in conversation are made by men. Women talk only half as much as men in mixed-sex groups.

In research in a class in which girls outnumbered boys, for every four boys who participated in discussion there was only one girl; boys asked twice as many questions as girls, and three times more boys than girls were praised and encouraged.

Repeated studies have shown that boys dominate the space in school playgrounds: girls sit round the edges as spectators to boys' games.

In children's books, three-quarters of the text and pictures concern males. Only a quarter concerns females. Men are depicted in four times as many occupations as women, and are usually active, whereas women are usually passive, dependent and nurturing.

The trade in pornography is estimated to be worth $8 billion a year.

Perhaps, in the circumstances which these statistics reflect, it is not difficult to understand the Jewish morning prayer for men: 'Thank you, Lord, for not making me a woman.'

Many of these statistics and quotations, which are only a sample of those available, are taken from *Women: A World Report* and relate to the end of the United Nations Decade of Women, in 1985. It is true to say that during this time there were changes in the role and status of women, and equally true that these changes were, on the whole, marginal. It remains to be seen what the effects of the greater spread of birth control methods will be, assuming that this is allowed to take place. (In ten African countries covered by the *World Report*, between 32 per cent and 92 per cent of women had never heard of modern methods of contraception.)

These statistics were compiled in 1987–8.* One would not expect large changes since that time, and indeed there are none. Recent evidence shows that little has changed in the intervening years.

* More recent sources: *Manushi* no. 57 (March/April 1990), for dowry deaths; Inland Revenue, for women's projected earnings 1993–4.

Introduction

I will begin this book with an admission: I am one of the first men this book addresses. In effect, as all books about human nature should be, this book is about me. The idea originated during a difficult period in my life. I was in analysis at the time, and it had begun to be a painful experience as I discovered within myself intense feelings of hatred for women which went beyond what Freud described as 'normal contempt'. I was appalled and frightened by this discovery. As many therapists will attest, such experience tends to influence one's own attitudes and thoughts about work with patients. Over a period of a couple of years I began to see that I was far from unique, and that certain difficulties patients presented, which had previously been obscure to me, were now clarified. As a result, I began thinking about the issues this book addresses and conducting research into the status of women. As the ideas began to take a shape in my mind, and as I saw that many of the men I was working with harboured similar feelings of hatred for women, I began to write in an attempt to order my thoughts.

At the time I had not taken up what has subsequently become my major interest: working with men who are abusive and violent towards women. In the last six years, I have spent most of my time finding ways of dealing with this problem in an organization which offers dedicated programmes to men who are violent – the London Men's Centre. Largely against my wishes, I have also had the opportunity to see for myself, with the victims of these men, the damage abuse can cause. The provision of services for survivors is depressingly inadequate, and increasingly so in recent years as we see the effects of reductions in welfare budgets across the country. In spite of this, dedicated women, working in bad conditions in refuges for little financial reward, continue to provide protection for the survivors, without which the work that I and my colleagues do would become impossible.

I must admit that I have undergone a radical change during those years – in my private life but also, and especially, in my work. After initially training as a gestalt therapist, and subsequently driven (as I then saw it) by the inadequacies (in fact denial) of this method for dealing with my own transference neurosis into a long analysis, I entered analytic supervision. I began my work with abusive men as an avowedly psychodynamic therapist, with all the attendant implications for modelling human behaviour and distress. I was not unaware or uninfluenced by the debates in psychoanalysis about the relationship between internal and external reality (Kovel, 1985), and I identified strongly with the Middle Group approach and attitude, which is more aware of the influence of external reality (see Kohon, 1986). As my work progressed, I was exposed to ways of thinking about abusive behaviour which simply did not accord with an analytic view, however liberal. The work of feminists in the refuge movement, and the 'speaking bitterness' of women's writing simply could not be ignored. Their experience and understanding of male violence towards women presented me with concepts and tools which – simply – were much more effective in confronting men's behaviour than anything possible within an analytic approach or understanding. I have attempted to integrate that knowledge with what I brought to the work, but where there is a conflict, I now privilege feminism. This book is a statement of where this development has taken me – often reluctantly.

It has become increasingly clear to me that violence *qua* violence is simply the most visible pole of a continuum of abusive treatment which men inflict on women, designed to establish and maintain control of them in both institutions and personal relationships. I have frequently come across intense and seemingly intractable hatred. Before working with men's violence I had grown used to encountering 'normal contempt' for women, and it was in the attempt to link this 'contempt' with such intense and undoubtedly serious hatred that this book was conceived.

This book is not intended as an explanation of how men achieve and maintain their pre-eminent position in human affairs, although this issue will be addressed. The problem of attempting to explain male sexism and misogyny is that of trying to find an explanation which does not assume the existence of gender identity. The importance of this is that identity, for both men and women, is gendered – that is to say: we all see ourselves first and foremost as sexed beings. It seems, for most of us, to be part of the taken-for-granted, always-already-there world. It is not, in the most important respects, an aspect of subjectivity or selfhood which is accessible to perception. I will argue that it does not fall into the individual's cognitive/perceptual field as an object of knowledge, but is actually the most important principle of meaning by which we order perception and make sense of the social world: that it is actually the basis of perception, not an object of it (Frosh, 1989).

Masculinity is predicated on the assumption of male superiority. Sexism seems to be a function of gender division or differentiation; therefore one is, to some extent, trapped into attempting to account for this. On the whole, that may be a task for an anthropologist, sociologist or political scientist. However, one of the basic assumptions of psychoanalytic thought, as espoused by Freud, is that ontogeny, the development of the individual, reproduces phylogeny, the development of the species. With this in mind, I shall attempt to explain gender division and men's dominance. I am always slightly surprised that the current emphasis in feminism on the construction of gender is presented as a radical departure from orthodox thinking (for example, Gayle Rubin: 'no aspect of sexuality' – especially heterosexuality – 'should be taken for granted as natural': 1975, p. 179). The fact is that Freud's essential radicalism consisted precisely in his theory that the attainment of a gendered identity was the central problematic of psychoanalysis, however much this might be forgotten by modern analysis or denied by feminists.

This book is intended primarily to address the question of why men wish to achieve and maintain this pre-eminence. The conclusion is that male motives are intrinsically connected with their hatred of women, whether or not this is a defensive position, and that so-called 'normal contempt' is the tip of an iceberg of misogyny. Much of what I have to say has already been widely debated in the feminist literature. I have introduced it where it is especially relevant to my own thinking. Feminist thinking is complex and varied, and a comprehensive overview is not germane to my thesis. In any case, such overviews are already available, and are presented far more competently than anything I could provide.

It has frequently been observed that men, on the whole, do not seem to be interested in examining the relationship between the sexes in the way that feminists have been doing since the seventeenth century. At a more personal level, one hears from women that men will not initiate any dialogue about feelings in relationships. By and large, this is true. Men have published remarkably little compared with women. Esther Saraga and Mary Macleod suggest (1989) that it is difficult for men to challenge the orthodoxy in dealing with male abusive behaviour because we would have to ask painful questions about the relationship between violence, vulnerability, helplessness and male sexuality. Not that men have entirely avoided these questions. Bob Connell (1987) and John Rowan (1990) have made important contributions to understanding men's investment in the oppression of woman (see also, Jukes, 1993a).

There has always been a small proportion of men willing to ask the questions, and this has increased in what is reactively known as the men's movement. This movement is strong in the USA, and has made faltering steps in the UK. I would like to make it clear that I do not belong to any such movement, and I am profoundly suspicious of it as it exists in the UK. From what I know of it, from the magazine *Achilles Heel* – for example – the dominant influence is re-evaluation or co-counselling – a method of counselling in which there is no formal power relationship between client and counsellor. Indeed, they switch roles. Such a method abjures authority and power, and stresses the importance of insight (re-evaluation), support and unconditional positive regard, but with the addition of the cathartic theory of the early Freud of *Studies on Hysteria* (Freud and Breuer, 1895). Although its founder, Harvey

Jenkins, explicitly warned against it, it seems that in practice catharsis has become the *sine qua non* of co-counselling.

The men's movement, like re-evaluation counselling, seems to me to be preoccupied, in the main, with men as victims of gender, and particularly of role expectations (Barker, 1992). As a result, it seems largely to attract men who have failed to confront their unresolved Oedipal problems, and are trying to circumvent the necessity to do so. Paradoxically, I now see, some years afterwards, that this book arose as a result of my attempts to resolve my problems with my internal father, my own Oedipus complex. I do not believe it is possible for men to find alternatives to present gender arrangements from a position either of guilt and defensiveness or of narcissistic pride in their maleness. I hope I can clarify what I believe to be an alternative.

In the Preface is a series of statistics relating to the status of women the world over. Anyone who doubts that there is a serious basis for asserting men's superior social status, or their social and private dominance of women, should study these statistics. It goes without saying that class-related poverty and racism are responsible for many of the worst symptoms of women's oppression, but this should not be allowed to obscure the fact that where resources are scarce, it is women who are relatively deprived. In rich countries the symptoms of oppression may be more subtle, but they do exist; the major difference with poor countries is that the consequences are less physical and more moral, economic and psychological.

The use of the word 'oppression' betrays my own orientation to the statistics. There is little doubt that the perspective which informs my judgement is a product of twentieth-century values and ideologies. Nevertheless, my thesis may appear monolithic and ahistorical in that it asserts that men may well always have treated women in this way, and I am implying a belief about some essential difference between men and women which runs contrary to my expressed understanding that sexuality is never given but is actually constructed. I can only hope I succeed in showing that I do not believe this. In any case, I believe that constructionism and essentialism require each other, and are not actually the diametrical opposites they appear to be (Fuss, 1989). I do, however, believe that sexual division is prehistorical, and that such historical differences as are evident are easily understood within the terms of the debate which follows.

I realize that this book could be used by supporters of essentialist thinking – I can anticipate how. However, I am not an essentialist, even though I cannot say how a fundamental change in present gender arrangements might be brought about. I do not believe that biology causes gender, but that gender provides significance to biology. Lynne Segal (1986) criticizes Andrea Dworkin for expressing a belief in the social construction of gender while implicitly writing as an essentialist, and encouraging a politics of despair. I agree with Diana Fuss (1989) that this is inevitable. Whatever form – or forms – feminist politics takes, I am certain that it will finally rest on the activity of women. Although many men are pro-feminist, and struggle for equality in their private lives as well as public policy, they cannot (notwithstanding the embryo men's movement, about which I will say more), in the last instance, give up the power to determine who has power. In any case it is not my place, as a man, to be prescriptive.

For those feminists who are worried about the despair of essentialist thinking, I can say only that years of working with men who are violent towards women have taught me that abusers will use any uncertainty about the responsibility for their violence to support their denial, and continue to abuse. The socialist understanding of violence (for example, Wilson, (1983) maintains that it represents the failure of male power) is of little use in such work, and may even be counterproductive. I cannot say I am happy about the conclusions to which my work with abusive men has led me; only that they are based on experience, not abstract theorizing. I cannot find another way of explaining or working with abuse which satisfactorily achieves results and simultaneously accords with the thinking of those feminists who first drew attention to male abusiveness and its pivotal importance for any attempt to change prevailing conditions, whether individually or collectively. This seems a good moment to state the central theme of this book: the trauma of the birth of the individual subject, the self, in the separation from the primary object, the mother, leads to the development of what I think of as a gendered psychosis which is encapsulated (Hopper, 1991) by primitive internalized sadomasochistic objects. I believe that this gendered psychosis is the source of male misosgyny. In this book I hope to explain this highly condensed statement so that the reader may come to an independent conclusion.

Comparative wealth undoubtedly allows feminism a space in which to emerge. It allows a breakdown in traditional patterns of sexual differentiation, where work is less directly linked to survival, and calls for an intellectual framework in which to construe changes. Even so, the statistics in the Preface reflect a major aspect of social organization and raise questions which, under any circumstances, require explanation.

The question of the origins of women's oppression has always been important to feminist scholars. Anthropologists in particular have played a major role in exploring this issue, although historians, philosophers and others have also participated. Perhaps the most important interdisciplinary contribution is Gayle Rubin's 'The traffic in women' (1975); see also Hubbard, 1979; Lane, 1976. Kate Millett's *Sexual Politics* (1977) is often regarded as the ground-breaking populist analysis. The explanation offered here will be entirely psychodynamic in that I will attempt to account for the phenomenon of the sex-gender system in terms of human psychic conflicts, and in particular men's relations with – and the deep-seated myths which we hold about – women and men. I shall place this psychodynamic account within a sociopolitical context.

This is not the first time such an attempt has been made (see Benjamin, 1990; Chodorow, 1978; Dinnerstein, 1976). There are similarities in the way in which Jessica Benjamin, Nancy Chodorow and Dorothy Dinnerstein reduce women's oppression to mothering practices, although Dinnerstein's account is closer to mine in the way she explains the structuring of men's expectations of women as the root of their impulse to oppress. There is little I would disagree with in these accounts, to which I will return. The whole mothering debate in feminism, however, can be understood in terms which are outside its content. The interest in the daughter's relationship with the mother in the last twenty years parallels developments in analytic therapy in the last forty. I believe that the 'mothering' debate in feminism has encouraged this development; I also believe it has gone too far. The limits of subjectivity are set by the Oedipus complex and the relationship with the father, not the mother, as both reality and symbol. Within the terms of this debate, although contributors like Dinnerstein and Chodorow address the reproduction of gender, none of them regards heterosexuality as a problematic, and this led to some criticism within feminist circles. Adrienne Rich (1980) argues that both Dinnerstein and Chodorow have failed to account for why, if women are the source of nurturing and caring for both boys and girls, little girls should redirect their search for attention to men. The criticism of the assumption of 'natural' heterosexuality was one of the main factors in opening the debate around recognizing heterosexuality as a political institution; ultimately it led to serious fragmentation within feminism.

Feminist theorists frequently assert that the root of women's oppression is that it is wilfully imposed by men (see Chapter 6 below). They often go further and assert that the problem is that men are misogynous – that they hate women. This assessment of the situation seems sound in so far as that men's investment in maintaining the status quo seems to go far beyond the need to protect the advantages it so clearly confers on the vast majority of them. The extent to which their motivation exceeds this need is a function of fundamental ambivalence in men's feelings about women. I do not know – and doubt whether anyone ever will – if the complex of feelings which are described in this book are the egg or the chicken – the cause or the result – of the evolution of a social system which allows and enforces the subjugation of women on a worldwide scale. It is clear, however, that the social reinforcements and syntonic psychology which perpetuate the situation evolved together in a complex interaction. In any case, given the universality of internal psychic conflict, it is possible to assert that men hate women without remotely attempting to deny that we also experience feelings of attraction to them, and are compelled to seek them out and form relationships with them.

I shall examine the evolution of this masculine psychology in the development of male children, and attempt to show that it is misogynous. The hatred of women may be, in most cases, a deeply repressed facet of the male character. At one extreme is the rapist or sexual murderer; at the other extreme is the apparently ordinary man who does not rape or murder, and feels mild and hidden (at least socially) contempt for women, or expresses it only in the privacy of his own home. He does not question his chauvinism, whether he reveals it in the way he regards women as sexual objects and can quite cheerfully buy a pornographic magazine, or in the fact that he regards the money he earns as his own and his wife as a dependant. Many of the men with whom I work – and the majority are extremely violent – are simply not identifiable as more than ordinarily misogynist or sexist outside the home.

It is crucial, of course, that one should be able to demonstrate that these people, at these extremes, are expressing the same feelings, and that the differences between them are quantitative rather than qualitative. It is also important to add that although this book asserts that men are misogynous, this does not mean that they are in a constant state of hatred for women. What it means is that misogyny exists as a potential in all men until particular circumstances call it out. The control of women is, perhaps, the area where misogyny is most visible. I hope to show that so long as men feel in control of women they are able both implicitly to express and at the same time to repress their hatred of them. The most important questions concern the circumstances in which men are misogynous, and the way in which this misogyny is subjectivized. It is interesting, in this context, that although Freud addressed the problem of women's status, he never did so more than peripherally.

It would, of course, be a nonsense to ignore the role of biology in determining sexual roles. Obviously women are more fitted for certain tasks than men, and vice versa, but there are only a few of these tasks. Some writers go further in their assessment of the importance of biology – for example, the psychoanalyst Anthony Storr (1965):

> It is a sad reflection upon our civilization that we should even be concerned with such a problem (sexual equality), for its existence demonstrates our alienation from our own instinctive roots. No doubt it is important that men should reach the stars, or paint the Sistine Chapel or compose nine symphonies. But it is equally vital that we should be cherished and fed, and that we should reproduce ourselves. Women have no need to compete with men; for what they alone can do is the more essential. Love, the bearing of children and the making

> of a home are creative activities without which we should perish; and only a civilization in which basic values have become distorted would make these sterile comparisons. (p. 62)

It is easy to agree with the general theme and sentiments of Storr's remarks, particularly the value of women's essential contribution. Their contribution, however, goes far beyond what he sees as their unique capacities, and it is not true (as the statistics in the Preface show) that women are simply asking for equality, or to compete with men. The problem, rather, is that in comparison with men, women are treated unjustly the world over and, seemingly, solely because they are women. This is particularly true in those activities which Storr thinks are paramount, such as giving birth, in addition to those which, according to him, might be more appropriately performed by men. I realize that many men would take issue with this. In particular, there is a strand of the emerging men's movement - well established in the USA - which believes that, on the contrary, it is men who are the victims of women's power. The psychological suffering which the possession of a penis imposes, however, cannot be compared with the psychological and physical damage which men actually inflict on women. Men cannot compare their position as passive victims of gender with women's position as victims of men's rage.

There seems little doubt that from the point of view of survival the female is the more important member of a species, and this is particularly so where there is a long period of childhood dependency. It is also interesting to note that in those species which are not always sexually dimorphous - where there are not always two distinct sexes - and are capable of being single-sexed when the environment is particularly rich in resources, the female is the surviving sex, and is clearly more important than the male. No doubt most men appreciate this in the depths of their being, and we are all a little afraid of and envy the strange and mysterious power to create and maintain life, which we can never fully understand. Adam's rib is paltry consolation for our impotence.

Many readers will find unpalatable the passivity I attribute to women. It is important to point out that I believe this represents the actuality of their position in the world, and that this position is forced on them, both actively and subtly, by men. I do not believe that women are innately passive or submissive; simply that the range of choices offered them is determined by their (male)-prescribed gender and sex roles, and that these choices are essentially reactive to men's activity. Also, I have no doubt that the way in which I present men will cause distress to those men who experience their masculinity as a burden – and which of us, at some time, does not? I will not go so far as to suggest that men are prisoners of gender. I believe that men have available to them in their lives a range of choices – in sexual behaviour, occupation, power and control over resources (including women) – which is simply denied women. Discourses of economics, class, race, power and so on, define and set limits to the boundaries of people's choices as agents in public affairs. This is as true for men as it is for women. Gender, however, is not one of those limiting factors for men as it is for women. On the contrary, maleness is a permission; whereas for women, gender is the most powerful and wide-ranging limitation of all.

In Chapter 1 I argue that misogyny, the hatred of women, is an inescapable element in the development of masculinity. This chapter deals largely with feminist constructions of male violence and dominance. The reader who is already familiar with feminist thinking on these issues may wish to skip to Chapter 2, where I begin to present a psychodynamic perspective. In Chapter 3 I examine the relation between misogyny and love. Chapter 4 traces the development of male gender identity. An explanation in Chapter 5 of the extreme variety of apparent desire for women, Don Juanism, is followed in Chapter 6 by an exploration of the linked theme of men's relation to pornography and rape. Chapter 7 traces the development of female gender identity, with particular emphasis on the meaning of masochism for women and its place in the female psyche. Chapter 8 describes how men maintain their superiority over women through the systematic inflicting of abusive and controlling behaviour. This chapter takes an especially close look at male violence towards women, and attempts to illustrate how the model of misogyny described here is applied to an intervention programme to stop male abusiveness.

I believe that this is a shocking book. Reluctantly, I admit that I hope so. Many of the men I work with inflict shocking suffering on women, and I have come to believe that this is representative of a widescale male abusiveness which ordinary men the world over regard as normal in their relations with women. Finally, to those who will say that this book contains the thoughts and feelings of a self-hating man, I confess that this is partly true – I do not like some of those aspects of myself which are reflected here; but I do not hate either men in general or myself. It will become clear that I am profoundly suspicious of the concept of the New Man.

Many men – including me – may struggle with the sentiments, attitudes and behaviour described in this book. This is the limit of what I believe to be possible for most of us – that we will continue to struggle, rather like non-drinking alcoholics who have to decide that every new day is another one in which they will not drink. I am convinced that any man who denies that he has these feelings or impulses towards women is self-deluding. Feminist suspicion of New Men is well founded. Although I believe that masculinity is an impoverished character structure and can be limiting and damaging, I also agree with Lynne Segal (1990, p. 289), who approvingly quotes Bob Connell, that it is more of 'a richness, a plenitude . . . ' which is, unfortunately,' founded on and enforcing the subordination of women'.

1 The Hatred of Women

INTRODUCTION: MISOGYNY – INNATE OR SOCIALLY CONSTRUCTED

Do all men hate women? My central contention is that they do. Of course this statement will be qualified and expanded, but in its essentials it will remain unchanged. My aim is to examine – and perhaps to qualify – the nature and origins of this hatred and the means by which men express it, whether explicitly or otherwise.

I hope to be able to show that misogyny is universal, and that it has profound effects on men's and women's capacity for creative and healthy living. The universality of misogyny consists in the fact that it is not only a facet of the male character but also an aspect – albeit a less debilitating one – of the female character. The origins of misogyny in both sexes will be examined, but its male manifestations are my central concern. The vicissitudes of misogyny in the female will be alluded to and, to some extent, traced in the context of the female contribution to the oppression of women. There is no great novelty in the idea that women collude in their own oppression. There are, however, serious questions about the origins of this collusion – whether, in essence, it is natured or nurtured by men, and whether it is even valid to describe women's apparent passivity in this way; these questions are not so very different from those concerning the origins of misogyny in men. I use 'apparent' in describing women's passivity in order to make explicit my belief that it is possible to be subordinated without being passive, and that this subordination is then rationalized by the oppressor as the victim's passivity.

My assertion that misogyny is universal presupposes the existence of the unconscious. The idea of an unconscious mind is an ancient one. Fables which show an exact understanding of the defence mechanisms which we humans use to prevent the emergence of uncomfortable feelings and thoughts have been extant for centuries. For example, the fable of the fox who decided that the grapes were sour after he had tried, in vain, to reach them on the vine illustrates one way of rationalizing failure. Hartmann (1869) and others had written about the unconscious long before Freud first made use of the term (Freud and Breuer, 1893, p. 76) and expanded on and universalized it. It was a shocking notion in its day, but mainly, one suspects, because of the qualities with which Freud endowed it; and it still cannot claim consensual status.

Freud's ideas, however, are now widely disseminated, and most people are familiar with the idea that our conscious self is not necessarily in control of our behaviour, feelings or thoughts. None the less, there are still many unresolved logical and semantic difficulties with the idea of the unconscious, even though it is generally accepted as a daily demonstrable fact of life. Still, it will be very difficult for any reader who rejects the idea of an unconscious self to feel any sympathy with my theme. Not that such a reader will be alone with his or her discomfort. As I said in the Introduction, this is intended to be a shocking book. I do not believe it is possible to examine the basis of male–female relations critically without causing anxiety. Nor is it possible, without considerable defensiveness, to remain utterly detached when one is made aware of the plight of women. This was certainly true for me as I wrote, and even now it is not clear how far I have succeeded in standing aside from my own infantile perceptions and expectations of intimate sexual relationships, as well as from any biases introduced by my masculinity.

Rather than take up the philosophical and semantic difficulties of the concept of the unconscious, I will briefly describe unconscious functioning and its consequences for our everyday lives.

It is important to distinguish between different sorts of unconscious material. We would all agree that there is a great deal of knowledge and information which we know, and know that we know, and which can be called up when needed. It is as if we have in our minds a sort of databank which we can access as necessary. This databank has the primary quality of unconsciousness: it is out of awareness. There is another sort of unconscious material, however, which cannot be accessed at will. This material is actually being kept unconscious. It is material which we do not want to know. Psychotherapists call this not wanting to know resistance.

There are major differences in the way these two types of information are processed in the mind. The readily available databank obeys all the usual rules of thinking. It is logical, it is reality-tested, it is linear in time and causality, it is not internally contradictory – we do not think that A, which is opposite to B, is true when we also believe B to be true. These rules, which are essential for everyday living, are known as the rules of 'secondary process'. We all learn them with our acquisition of language and they are employed, for most of the time, by the conscious 'self'.

The second type of unconscious material – which we resist knowing, and actively 'unknow' – obeys quite a different set of rules: the rules of 'primary process'. This part of the mind is almost a separate person inside all of us – a structurally separate part. It has a life of its own in which people and information are treated without regard for secondary-process rules. Contradictions abound. Mutually exclusive truths coexist. Time is at a standstill. Causality is not linear. Information is not reality-tested; internal reality rules. Something is true because we believe it to be true (Brenner, 1974, pp. 1–15). I believe that these processes are equally true of society and culture. Although at times I present what seems to be a monolithic picture of men and women – and indeed of history – I am well aware that no form of hegemony – whether in Hitler's Germany or in a 'man's world' – can mean the total control or end of alternatives in theory or practice. Even the winner's definitions of reality are an achievement – they are never complete, and they are always contested. So it is with gender relations.

These distinctions, and the existence of these two parts of the self, are not always so clear in our minds. At one extreme is mental illness, in which the conscious is overwhelmed by unconscious material. To an external observer this can be quite bewildering, particularly if one is talking to a floridly psychotic person in whom delusions and hallucinations alternate with moments of lucidity. Less extremely - and far more common - even most ordinary people will have experienced similar processes at times in their lives. In states of jealousy, for example, we are all capable of thinking the most appalling thoughts and having frightening impulses about someone we love. This temporary insanity seems bizarre when we later recover our equilibrium. Perhaps even more common are states of grief or mourning which can seem, to the sufferer, so similar to states of pathological depression. Normally optimistic and robust dispositions can be overcome by feelings of loss and despair which border on the suicidal.

One of the most common signs of the danger of a breach of the boundary between our unconscious and conscious selves is anxiety - we all experience anxiety. It does not always imply the danger of an incursion of the unconscious into the conscious self - clearly, there are many realistic sources of anxiety. These, however, can be employed by the unconscious and cause an excessively anxious response to quite ordinary sources of worry. This happens when an everyday event evokes in the unconscious mind echoes of situations which seem similar. All events are processed by the unconscious. The barrier works, in the main, in one direction only: from the unconscious to the conscious. The unconscious mind is primitive, infantile and dominated by passions. If it were to overwhelm the conscious self, normal functioning would be impossible. Anxiety is a signal that this might occur, and that the conscious self had better take avoiding action. Everything contains the potential for evoking primitive responses from us. Clearly, however, some of us are better defended than others against this possibility. What makes this so is an important question in so far as it is probably a major determinant of the extremity and intensity of expression of each individual man's misogyny, whether violent or silently contemptuous.

This - admittedly simple - description of the unconscious mind will be amplified below. Accepting the existence of the unconscious will simplify my task considerably. It enables me to introduce a qualification to the original statement about the universality of misogyny. If there is an unconscious mind, it is tenable to assume that it is quite possible for a man to hate women without being even remotely, consciously, aware of it. In fact we can go further towards those who might accept the unconscious but find universal misogyny a little more difficult to swallow by adding that this hatred may vary in intensity from mild to extreme. I realize that statements like these go right to the heart of a major methodological problem with the concept of the unconscious. If it is asserted that there is something about you which is unconscious, and which you deny, it could be said, with conviction, that you are bound to deny it because it is unconscious. This is a double bind. You could equally well reply that if it is unconscious, it is impossible for either of us to perceive it. This is a major dilemma for dynamic psychotherapists, but I hope to achieve some resolution of it.

If I can demonstrate that misogyny is universal, I hope then to examine its consequences – not only for you and me as individual men and women, but for society as a whole. In my opinion, men's struggles with their misogyny and its emotional consequences are responsible for most acts of male creativity, from the most sublime to the most destructive, in that this struggle involves extremes of emotion, from intense hatred to passionate idealization. It is difficult to think of an aspect of the male psyche which does not in some way, however obscurely, reflect these extremes of feeling in relation to women.

Collins English Dictionary defines misogyny as 'hatred of women', and it should be stressed that it is 'hatred' of women, not simply anger with them, which is my concern here. Although there may not commonly be many differences between the observable behaviour of an angry person and a person who is in a state of hatred, there are fundamental differences between hatred and anger. Our own integrity is not particularly discomfited when we are angry with another person. Subjectively, therefore, the experience of hatred is that it is a threat to the physical and psychological well-being of the subject, ourselves, and the object. Most people, on the other hand, experience anger as a threat to the object only. It seems to me that when I work with hatred in my patients – or, indeed, struggle with my own – that it has a quality of endurance, and it is often difficult to analyse because it has a thought-stopping effect. It involves the inability to see any good or redeeming features in its object. Anger, on the other hand, is usually easily identified as having been caused by particular circumstances. It has a more immediate reactive quality, and does not involve the kind of splitting of good and bad, with the subsequent denial of good, which we see in hatred. Hatred is essentially a state of enmity for an object, with its attendant wishes to dominate and control it. In most cases these impulses are reinforced by a – not always unconscious – desire to exterminate – that is, kill – the object if one fails to dominate it.

It is true to describe men's relations with women as being founded in hatred and a state of enmity. Naturally, this calls for major qualification. In all fields of human relations one finds that enmity and fear are handmaidens. Nobody would dispute that relations of enmity are based on fears of the other's intentions. The history of superpower relations, until the recent apparent end of the Cold War, is a good demonstration of this. Equally, it would be difficult to deny that these fears are paranoid – projections on to the 'enemy' of one's own hostile impulses towards them. There is an old American joke which was invented after a well-known Civil War general said that he had 'seen the enemy and it was ours'. A wag coined the immortal phrase: 'I have seen the enemy and it is us!'

There is a direct parallel here with the origins of male misogyny. In the final analysis it is difficult to judge the exact contributions made by, on the one hand, paranoid projection and, on the other, reality in one's final perceptions because of the necessity of determining the enemy's intentions in the absence of unambiguous information. Often the only information available is one's own fantasies, and in conditions of uncertainty one's worst fantasies prevail.

It is the hatred and fear of woman which lies behind the male need, and its praxis: to dominate and control her. That men actually dominate and control women is amply demonstrated, I believe, by the statistics in the Preface. In many instances – but, tragically, not always – this need stops short of the woman's death or serious injury. The need to dominate and control none the less allows expression of the hatred behind that desire, as well as preserving some vestiges of relationship within which to express love, in however limited a way. Sadly, for a great many men, the only means left for this expression is a distorted sexuality which might be described as exclusively male. It tends to be of a highly circumscribed and limited nature which allows for very little intimacy and closeness. It regards every woman as a sexual object, not a whole person. She becomes 'fair game' for a male predatory sexuality which is driven by a need aggressively to penetrate and possess. The subject, woman, becomes object. Aspects of the male self which yearn for intimacy and mutuality are split off and discounted. It was thought that the anxiety about AIDS had induced many heterosexuals to change their sexual behaviour, and this may indeed be true in the long term. Surprisingly – to me – however, it seems that massive publicity campaigns are having little effect, and the spread of HIV amongst heterosexuals now seems to be causing greater alarm than did its earlier appearance in homosexuals and drug users. I will return to this issue when I discuss the politics of homosexuality.

I can now restate my central thesis. *Men exist in a state of perpetual enmity towards women which they express overtly and covertly, by controlling and dominating them. Whether by attrition or violence, women are ultimately controlled or destroyed by men.* This destruction is usually carried out on women's psyches and their self-esteem, although as we see with each passing day, and as the evidence in the Preface shows, it all too often involves physical damage in addition. Of course, this damage varies: not all women are destroyed spiritually. However, as Rowan (1990) states, the introjection, by women, of what he calls the 'patripsych' is inevitable.

I believe that there is conclusive proof of the damage men inflict on women. This damage is visible and measurable. There is also damage of a sort which is not so evident: the spiritual damage to women – the destruction of their unique individuality and strength, self-esteem and freedom from fear, which comes from the limitations imposed on their development by men's use of their physical superiority.

Why do women put up with it? Can it, after all, be simply a consequence of men's physical superiority that they are, and seem always to have been, in the dominant position? The literature is not crammed with tales of big women battering small men. Although this is not entirely unheard of (see Straus *et al.*, 1980) it is stretching the bounds of credibility to use such examples as there are to assert that violence is interactive or relational, not gender based. Surprisingly, there are still respectable researchers and clinicians (for a good example of this in clinical practice see Bowlby, 1988, p. 77ff.) who maintain this position despite the fact that society markedly discriminates against women who are violent towards their husbands. Often this discrimination takes the form of the most extreme applications of medical technology or the law (take the case of Sara Thornton in the UK in 1990. She was given a draconian sentence for killing her husband after suffering years of physical and emotional abuse. Fortunately, there is evidence that the battering defence is beginning to gain credence in such cases.) In comparison, society's response to men battering women is at best mildly disapproving and at worst explicitly collusive and outrageously encouraging. In 1989, out of 100,000 calls to the London Metropolitan Police from women who were victims of male violence in the home, fewer than 5,000 men were put on report. An even smaller proportion were prosecuted, although the figures are not centrally collated and precise numbers are impossible to come by – in itself a telling state of affairs. It is a well-documented fact that the police are less likely to act if an assault occurs in the home between intimates (Stanko, 1985). The evidence for society's differential response to female violence is overwhelming. Susan Edwards (1984) documents differential responses to women who 'maltreat' men.

Feminists debate whether 'women's putting up with it' is entirely men's responsibility – that women have no choice, or that there may be a masochistic element in women which colludes with men. Elizabeth Wilson (1983) argues that women have no choice; Dee Graham and her colleagues (1988) suggest that this apparent masochism is an adaptive response to men's behaviour. In Chapter 7 I will examine these different ways of construing female behaviour in an attempt to understand whether female masochism is a figment of the male imagination.

The notion of universal male misogyny will come as no surprise to the more radical strands of the feminist movement in that it simply states what they have asserted for many years. The movement may be happy that support is coming from a man, and yet it is difficult to avoid a feeling of guilt that a man is once again trying to define the issues.

One of the major theoretical planks of feminist thinking is that patriarchy, the institutionalization of masculine dominance, persists and thrives precisely because men have always assumed responsibility for defining the world and, in so doing, have taken possession of it. The notion of patriarchy, though it is much used in feminist thinking, is often not defined or critically examined. The Dobashes clearly indicate their belief in its centrality by subtitling their important book *Violence Against Wives* (1990) 'A Case Against the Patriarchy'. They define it as 'the long tradition of belief . . . that men had the . . . natural, sacred and unproblematic . . . right to dominate and control women, and that (this belief) is explicitly established in the institutional practices of both church and state'. Bob Connell, who was to attempt to develop a comprehensive, integrated theory of the relationship between gender and power (1987) had earlier questioned 'what entitles us to talk of a unity, a coherence, and system and hence "patriarchy" at all?' (1983, p. 51).

The literal definition of a patriarch is 'the father and ruler of a family or tribe', and this has some resonance in recent theoretical developments in some strands of feminist thinking. David Morgan (1985) argues that this conception of patriarchy is still useful. Jan Horsfall, however (1991), thinks that Morgan fails to make explicit the fundamental importance of gendered power relations, which is central to feminist thinking. Although patriarchy, as a concept, resonates with most feminist experience, it none the less remains murky. I will take up this issue in Chapter 8, in the context of a discussion of male violence.

One common male response to criticisms of our monopoly of reality definition is that it arises because of our innate intellectual superiority and the biological determinants underpinning women's intellectual passivity. This is an apologist's way of politely accusing women of mental incompetence. Perhaps the one 'problem' or 'frame of reference' owned by the women's movement – and why not? It wouldn't have been in men's 'interests' to define it – is the issue of *male* misogyny. It does rather seem to be adding insult to injury for a man to question whether misogyny is the exclusive possession of the male. It implies that women cannot be absolved from a share of the responsibility for the continued oppression of their own sex, and does rather smack of the 'She asked for it' defence of the rapist. In asserting, here, that women participate in their own oppression, and may even be active in it, I am not anticipating the later discussion of female masochism. I shall soon make it clear that this is not the basis for my current asssertion.

Majorities, of course, have always defined the 'problems' of oppressed minorities. As the feminists assert, this capacity is one of the most powerful expressions of men's control – if we assume that defining actually gives control. The irony is that men do not actually constitute a majority, and yet both men and women behave as if they did: women, I would argue, because they have no choice; men because they refuse to exercise choice. When minority problems are defined in this way, by the majority, they are simply extensions of the consensual frame of reference; they cannot be expressed in a way which directly challenges that frame of reference. This is one of the main reasons why so few men have addressed themselves to misogyny as a political issue, for to do so would involve a challenge to a whole way of thinking about and perceiving the world, and must ultimately involve real efforts to induce change. Perhaps the task is simply too much for most of us. It seems that we either sink complacently into the welcoming bosom of the uncritical patriarchy, or live uncomfortably as closet chauvinists who espouse the causes of feminism yet covertly practise chauvinism in our private lives.

Not that men have not addressed this problem (see Connell, 1987). The difficulty, for heterosexuals, is that most of the male theorizing about male sexuality and dominance has been conducted by gay theorists, because – superficially – they have most to gain by deconstructing male sexuality (see Jeffreys, 1990). Unpalatable as this may be, its origins in the gay community make this theorizing less acceptable not only to heterosexual men but also to some feminists (Jeffreys, 1990). Also, because gay oppression derives from sexuality, there is more pressure on gay intellectuals to theorize about sexuality. For whatever complex historical and social reasons, gay sexuality is now more public. This makes it easier – and more necessary – for gay men to theorize about issues which would be threatening to heterosexual men. Here I am thinking, in particular, about issues concerned with dominance and submission – issues which, as we shall see, have caused heated and destructive debate within the feminist movement.

Laziness, or fear of changing, are not the only significant reasons why most men fail to confront their misogyny. The main reason lies in the dynamics of the misogyny itself. Misogyny is self-perpetuating. There is no motivation, within a misogynistic frame of reference, for change. If I believe I have good reason for hating you, what good reason could I have for wishing to love you, especially if, as is the case, my hatred of you bestows upon me entry to an exclusive club which offers me many benefits – a sort of freemasonry of misogynists? This sounds rather extreme. Yet this freemasonry exists, and the only qualification for membership is the possession of a heterosexually inclined penis. It would not be true to say, either, that men are motivated by conscious malevolence in clinging to their misogyny – that they are innately evil. Rather, misogyny is as natural to men as the possession of a penis – its development is inevitable, and men are no more capable of fighting it as children than they are capable of being little girls.

Although all this sounds very pessimistic, I hope to avoid any crude Darwinistic sociobiological arguments that the interaction between culture and biology has produced imperatives which, if threatened, will undermine the fabric which is intended to ensure the survival of the human race. While I harbour profound doubts about the possibility of any widespread change, I have no such doubts about the possibility that individual men can change. Regrettably, I believe that even this individual task is so daunting that too few men will make the effort – there will be no noticeable difference in the position or prospects of those women who define such change as necessary.

In any case, the issue of whether it is possible for men to change seems, rather, to beg the question why they should. In terms of our personal lives, men will have the motivation to change only when misogyny ceases to be rewarding. Who, one might ask, provides these rewards? The surprising answer is that they are not provided solely by other men, but also – and mainly – by women. Why women go on providing all the rewards which accrue to men is a profoundly important question. In general feminists agree that men dominate and oppress women, by force and by the ever-present threat of force. Indeed, this is the defining criterion of feminism. There is no such agreement, however, about whether women might have an investment in supporting their own oppression which cannot be presumed to be based entirely on highly questionable biological imperatives, or even more questionable feminine masochism.

One aspect of sexual relations which must be raised briefly, pending a fuller consideration later, is the positive feelings of attraction between men and women. We may reasonably ask why, if men hate women, we spend so much time in pursuit of them?* My provisional answer to this is that human behaviour is not a product which can be totted up on a balance sheet. We are so much more complicated than simple debits and credits. We can live relatively comfortably with quite staggering contradictions and conflicts – for example, smoking when we know it will probably cause illness and early death. The average human being is not possessed of a seamless personality in which every part is consonant with every other part. We are full of conflicts and contradictions, and most of us probably live closer to the edge of insanity than is comfortable for much of the time. To repeat what I said in the Introduction: the universality of internal psychic conflict is what makes men hate women and desire them at the same time.

All human behaviour is a compromise between conflicting and competing impulses, needs, feelings and thoughts. Whereas competing impulses usually involve relating to different objects in the same or different ways – Do I go to the concert or stay at home

* A general apology is due here for the heterosexist bias of this book. It does not reflect a lack of awareness of the importance of homosexual issues, and some of these will be addressed, however tangentially, as we proceed. My main concern, however, is with the origins of heterosexuality and heterosexual relationships.

and watch television – conflicting impulses involve relating to the same object in different or mutually exclusive ways – I am afraid of my boss, and angry with him too. I want to express my anger and placate him at the same time. In his later writings, Freud, in his attempts to explain these apparently universal and chronic conflicts, was led to the conclusion that there is a fundamental human conflict between a life instinct (Eros), which is creative, and a death instinct (Thanatos), which is destructive; and that this opposition is the source of human ambivalence (Freud, 1920, pp. 38–41).

On the face of it, it seems rather absurd to assert that there is an instinct for death, and the notion has caused – and still causes – furious debate among theorists. In clinical practice, however, it is relatively common to come into contact with a level of destructiveness of such intensity that it could readily be interpreted as a death instinct. It can seem to resemble an anti-life force in the vigour with which someone in its grip will systematically destroy any hopes, aspirations, good feelings, and so on, in himself and in others. There is no doubt that my essential thesis in this book can be partly explained by resorting to the idea of a death instinct. One could take it a step further and relate it to a universal urge to return to the safety and security of the womb – to a period in one's life when passivity reigned; when no response was required, no demands were made. The hypothesis is that the loss of this paradise evokes such rage as to engender the wish to destroy anything which represents its absence – life, consciousness, reality itself. This would imply that aggression or destructiveness is a fundamental hostility to otherness and separateness.

There are two major flaws in this argument. One is that a universal death instinct would be as evident in women as in men, and the crucial fact is that every index one examines shows that men are responsible for most of what we would define as destructiveness in the social sphere. The other is that it leaves an elision between this instinct and misogyny. One still has to account for the relationship between a death instinct and the hatred of women. The one does not follow from the other. Misogyny is gender-based; a death instinct must, presumably, be gender-blind. Unless we can show that the death instinct or – less controversially, the instinct to destroy – undergoes different influences in women than in men, whether biological or cultural, we must conclude that it has no bearing on the origins of misogyny.

This is really an acid test of any explanation of men's behaviour towards women which lays responsibility for it anywhere except on men themselves, and on masculinity. If any explanation other than one based – however broadly – on gender is to be acceptable, it must be applied to women in the same circumstances to see if it produces the same results. If it does not, then it is essential to account for why similar circumstances cause different behaviour in men and in women. For example, it is often asserted by men who beat their partners that they do it only because of the effects of alcohol. However, women who get drunk do not beat their husbands. To take another example: Maria Roy (1989) argues that battering, which she defines as symptomatic of uncontrollable rage, may be triggered by food allergies. Her research showed that once the allergies of a group of batterers were identified and the toxic food was withdrawn, the offenders stopped their violence. It singly failed to account for the fact that the sample of batterers was almost 100 per cent men. The notion of a death instinct which fails to meet this criterion as an explanation of misogyny simply does not stand up unless one can explain what women do with it, and why their expression of it is different from men's.

Feminists of different schools (see Wilson, 1983) get into quite complex cognitive knots when they assert that misogyny derives from cultural and/or economic processes which can be undone by social engineering. Many feminists think that definitions of gender – the sex one is assigned – and sexuality – the way one expresses it, are cultural, and have no biological origins. If this were true, any change towards true sexual equality would involve a redefinition of these concepts. Where would all the aggression go, given the indisputable links between male sexuality and gender and aggression? If it is culturally constructed, would it have to 'go' anywhere? Without male sexuality as it is currently learned and practised, would the aggressive, misogynistic male become extinct along with the passive, submissive female?

Although I have great sympathy with the culturalist feminist perspective, I believe it is incomplete on the origins of gender and sexuality. I have no doubt that they are socially constructed, but social construction cannot originate anywhere except in the minds of people. Society has a mind, but not a mind of its own. The individual organism (*not* the subject) existed before the horde. The optimistic prognosis offered by social construction theories makes them attractive to advocates of change. This can blind them to the real difficulties of attempting to evolve a social psychology which adequately accommodates the interaction between individual and group.

Feminists cannot have it both ways. If male aggression and dominance, and female passivity and submission, are culturally derived, any change of the sort we desire will inevitably lead to a more aggressive woman if, as I believe, the conditions under which aggression originates in men apply equally to women. In this case the crucial difference is in the social construction of gender which enjoins, and gives permission to, men to act aggressively while simultaneously forbidding women to do so.

Any assumption that the social deconstruction of gender would reduce the overall level of human destructiveness is simply unfounded. The idea that women are not as innately destructive as men is, from this point of view, sexist. I realize that this is a somewhat simplistic presentation of the case. It could be argued that male aggression is actually caused by our present social arrangements, but I do not find this view credible. The idea that social arrangements can have their origins anywhere except in the minds and biology of humankind is an abdication of personal responsibility and intellectual integrity in favour of street credibility. At best, individual and group interact systemically, not in the linear fashion implied by social theory.

Whatever one's views about the death instinct, it is undeniable that humanity (at the moment, mostly the male of the species) is equipped with a large capacity for destructiveness and creativity. However, it is often very difficult, at least from a moral perspective, to determine which of these motives is in operation in any particular case, especially when one is attempting to determine which of two activities is the lesser evil or the greater good, or where 'good' ends can be achieved only by 'bad' means. This problem is even more difficult when we attempt to evaluate history, because victorious –

or surviving – perspectives have an influence on the way succeeding generations think about moral issues. 'Winners' tend to define history, and it would be most unusual if they painted themselves in a bad light – 'justice' always wins. Only with the passage of time and the emergence of different frames of reference can a different view be formed. This power of dominant points of view to suppress dissenting or alternative perspectives is overwhelmingly in evidence when we examine the representation of women in accounts of the development of human culture. A visitor from outer space could be forgiven if it were unable to deduce the existence of women from such accounts. Nothing speaks more eloquently of man's oppression of, and supposed supremacy over, women. Not until recently, and at the instigation of feminists, could women be seen to have any historical existence at all (see Spender, 1980).

The oppression of women by men, however the genders may have been variously and historically defined, is transhistorical. I believe that it has existed for all time, even though its nature may have varied according to cultural and historical conditions (see Bamberger, 1974). Feminist academics are acutely aware of women's absence from history, and in the last twenty years feminist theory has had a substantial impact in some areas of academia (for an assessment and interesting disciplinary cross-section of readings, see Dubois *et al.* 1987). It must be said that the view of the transhistorical nature of women's oppression is not without its critics. There is clearly a danger of paralysis in the face of such magnitude: the problem can become unmanageable.

Socialist feminists in particular are interested in the materiality of women's oppression and the ruptures in the apparently seamless fabric of male dominance. Feminist scholars have worked to refine its dimensions and its historical transformations in order to see what can be learned about the prospects and strategies for change. Men point to the relative absence of feminine marks on history. Often this is rationalized by reference to women's biological fitness for non-historical roles. I think we should see this for what it is – an expression of an oppressive ideology. It is of no concern to me that women have made little public contribution to the outcome of those affairs which men value. This is symptomatic of their oppression. It should be seen in the same light as the assertion by men that we do the work while women look after the children – that is, do not work. Even there, women have been denied a role in their own history, and have had the power to define and control those aspects of history most rightfully theirs – for example, childbirth – stolen from them.

The relationship between midwifery and the oppression of witchcraft is most illuminating. It has been shown that this was largely an attempt by men to gain control of the practice of medicine, at which many so-called witches were substantially more skilled. Many women were called witches when their only 'crime' was that they attended births and acted as midwives. (Miles [1988 p. 110] suggests – very much as I do in Chapter 8 below, on violence – that the gynicidal attacks on witches coincided with the significant rise to power of a number of women.) It is a commonplace finding in media research that women are relatively nonexistent in news coverage. The triviality of most specialist women's magazines, and their increasing number, reinforce women's irrelevance to men. Not surprisingly, men have devoted scant attention to the study of their relations with women, and if they have studied them it is not from the point of view adopted here: as a war being waged by men upon women.

The battle of the sexes, which has more the appearance of a rout, is no mere abstraction, any more than misogyny can be said to be the product of feminist imagination. The battle is not fought with swords or guns. In spite of the data in the Preface, there are doubtless many people to whom it would be difficult to present evidence with sufficiently high validity to demonstrate conclusively the existence of universal male misogyny. *Prima facie* evidence such as wife-battering or rape is presented and seen, by men, as marginal, and as indicative of individual emotional disturbance. 'Wife-batterers' are represented as being in some way qualitatively different from all other men whereas – other things being equal – I would assert that the difference is quantitative only, and that such people's behaviour differs from other forms of misogyny only in its dramatic consequences, and in the opportunity it affords other men to condemn and distance themselves from it.

An incident involving a man with whom I worked in a batterers' programme illustrates this. The man's partner and victim had disclosed to her closest friend that my client had been abusing her. The friend disclosed in turn that her husband had been doing the same to her for many years. A little later, the friend's husband appeared at my client's house and threatened to 'beat him up' if he persisted with his abuse. It emerged that in an attempt to get her assailant husband to seek help in the programme she had told him about my client's behaviour, in the hope that he would identify with him. During this conversation she did not articulate that she defined him as abusive too. Apparently her husband became enraged because he believed that my client's behaviour was appalling, and should be punished. He was unable – or unwilling – to see any similarities to his physical attacks on his wife, and did not see himself as abusive in any way!

The psychological and social conditions which germinate and perpetuate such 'extreme' behaviour appertain to all men. I hope I can demonstrate this existence and reveal their nature; examine their origins and consequences; and finally look to the future of relations between the sexes.

THE ORIGINS OF MISOGYNY

How can it be that 'Nature', even a socially constructed one, could be so blind as to allow in men the existence of a feeling which, if it were expressed without restraint, would lead to the extinction of the species? It has been said that Nature is a blind designer – a force without a plan. We have no way of knowing its real qualities, except through our constructions of it. Nature is the name we give to the process in which events and their consequences endure until stronger events eradicate them (it has often been remarked upon that nature – primitive, wild and anarchic, red in tooth and claw – is seen as a female which masculine science, against which it is opposed, attempts to dominate and control). Evolution is a random process in which the strongest members of a species, and the strongest species, survive. Survival is no guarantee that all the characteristics of a species are useful in their environment; it is clear that many species possess qualities which are of no present value.

Qualities which are of value will survive, but this has no bearing on the fate of qualities that are irrelevant for survival. Survival is never assured – it is constantly threatened, and humankind's is by no means certain. Technological acumen is no guarantee of survival. In fact, for the past forty years humankind has lived with the threat of self-extinction because of our technological skill. Humankind's dominance of Nature is unquestioningly man's dominance, not women's. Scientific advancement is male-initiated.

In fact it is not difficult to conceive of a satisfactory biological theory which might go some way to account for the origins of misogyny – at least the need to control women – as a characteristic which would improve the chances of species survival. We simply need to allow that there was a time in humankind's prehistory when the male of the species, driven by a biological imperative, made every effort to ensure that his genes were passed on – not such a large assumption – and that he took extraordinary precautions to ensure that no other male had access to his ovulating or already impregnated female. With the development of culture and the male need to ensure his line of descent (which we will examine below), it is easy to see that this may be the basis for men's need to control women. The evolution of the role of 'mother' and the addition of successive injunctions, based on spurious biology, to the effect that women possess natural qualities of mothering and primary caring, ensured that a man's control exceeds that needed to ensure his fatherhood of his female's children. At this point, biological imperatives are superseded by men's psychological needs to control and dominate. There is a famous and serious Japanese poem which speaks of 'the joy of housecleaning' and the ecstasy of the woman of the house in the rituals of cleaning (Ukiyo, 1978).

In these circumstances, however, one would expect that women who have these natural qualities would be accorded a special place in men's regard, yet this is not so. There is little doubt that masculine ire 'seems to be' particularly directed at women who do not meet these criteria. As the journalist Katherine Whitehorn wrote (1984): 'men when professionally threatened by women operate from the basis that "one is a freak, two are an outrage and three are 'they're taking over'"'. But the fact is that women who meet the criteria are more overtly oppressed than those who do not. They are the ones who suffer the battering, marital rape (Finkelhor and Yllo, 1985) and severe emotional abuse from which there is little escape because of their economic dependency. It is well known that many marriages break down within the first year of the birth of a child. How much hidden abuse is there?

To account for the hatred and fear that men feel towards women, we must look closely at the biological and social beginnings of the human infant and its relations with the external environment. In locating the source of misogyny during this period of human life, this explanation is – with minor differences – in agreement with some feminist analytic theorists (Benjamin, 1990; Chodorow, 1978 and 1989; Dinnerstein, 1976), although Benjamin is more concerned with 'why women submit to the power and domination of men' (p. 5). I would like, therefore, to look briefly at the three main strands of feminist analyses of male dominance before returning to the main argument being presented here.

Feminist Explanations: An Overview

I am daunted by this subheading. The reality is that there is no such thing as feminism, although there are many feminisms. Feminism is not a unitary concept, although there there are fundamental concepts, values and concerns which all feminists share. In particular, there is a consensus that the central problematic of feminism is the subordination of women by men.

Feminist thinking has undergone profound changes during the last twenty years, some of which bear directly on the thesis of this book. There are various theoretical positions within feminism, and these tend to be grouped into general categories like cultural, socialist, radical, liberal, revolutionary, and so on. The distinctions between theories in these categories are not always clear, but generally speaking they reflect positions on the issue of the nature of men's dominance, and in particular whether it is transhistorical, monolithic and basically innate, or a variable function of – that is, caused by – particular historical, material and cultural conditions. As is well known, socialist feminists incline to the latter position and, in general, tend to be more sanguine about the possibility of fundamental change in the distribution and organization of power between the genders. Radicals and revolutionary feminists (paradoxically referred to as culturalists in the USA) are more inclined to the former view, and generally argue for separatism. Liberals are more identified, in particular, with a permissive position in relation to pornography and censorship. More recent thinking – or at least, the most influential – tends to be of the revolutionary, radical sort which might be called apocalyptic. It propounds the idea of fundamental irreconcilable differences (of essence – hence essentialism) between male and female, to all intents and purposes innate differences.* My description of feminist theories should not mask the fact that few feminists fit neatly into these categories – indeed, many agonize about the contradictions between lived experience, desire and theory.

Although the essentialist view has been gaining ground in recent years – mainly as a result of the efforts of activists working with survivors of male violence – it does not go unchallenged (L. Segal, 1987). Nor, indeed, was it the starting point for much of today's feminism. Old-style (1960s–1970s) feminist thinking found the notion of innate differences unappealing. Then, feminism, although it was most explicitly concerned – indeed coterminous – with sexual liberation for women (a view which has subsequently been widely – and, I think, decisively – debunked: see Jeffreys, 1990), was implicitly about the social construction of gender differences. It held out the possibility of real change through social engineering, and the emergence of a new man and woman. This kind of thinking largely mirrored the growing challenge to the widespread academic consensus about the innate nature of sexual difference from an increasing body of research showing no significant innate differences between men and women. The argument which developed between constructionists and essentialists, which is of

* Some radicals can seem to get into quite intricate knots in arguing that gender is socially constructed, while at the same time they espouse the view that change is impossible because it is constructed in such a way that it may as well be innate. I agree, even though I also believe in the possibility of significant – albeit limited – change. The radicals argue that unless women become more powerful, men will eventually destroy the world because of our innately greedy, violent and terrorizing natures.

far more significance than the debate about the influence of nature compared with nurture (Frosh, 1989), seems no nearer resolution than it ever was (for an innovative and exacting analysis which attempts a new synthesis, see Fuss, 1989), but there is a new kind of consensus about the interaction between biology and culture.

I will take a broad look at both socialist constructionist feminism, as exemplified by Lynne Segal (1987), and the later 1980s feminism which stresses innate sexual differences but emphasizes the superior virtues of femininity – the so-called apocalyptic or essentialist theories. As Segal (1987) argues, the concerns of present thinkers seem very narrow compared with those of the earlier period. She points to the almost exclusive concern with and concentration on male violence in all its manifestations, seemingly at the expense of political campaigning around specific issues which are of concern to women and might be easier to effect. She does, however, make the point that this newer feminism is based more on an appreciation of trends within politically activist feminism, and goes to great pains to analyse the hold of essentialism on modern feminism and its origins in the concerns about male violence towards women. Academic feminism is alive and kicking and, as Ellen Carol Dubois and her colleagues (1987) point out, is making real and radical contributions to the human sciences.

It must be said that it seems as hard for feminists to agree on theories which might explain men's power and dominance as it is for psychoanalytic thinkers. This does not in any way detract from the almost universal unity and unanimity among feminists that men's dominance is the central concern, both theoretically and politically. The divergence is in the analysis of the origins of male dominance. What follows is based on only one strand of feminist argument. Some feminists are psychoanalysts or influenced by psychoanalytic thinking, and later sections of this book are greatly influenced by such contributors. Here I focus on a particular feminist position, one not dominated by analytic discovery or thought, to illustrate my argument.

The position I adopt here could, in most respects, be described as apocalyptic or essentialist. Fundamental differences, however, between apocalyptic feminism and this account of misogyny will emerge. In particular – and fervently – I do not subscribe to the argument that women are in some way innately superior to men in being non-violent or more caring. The corollary to this view of women, of course, is a perception of men as being innately – that is, biologically – violent. 'Women's sexual desire for the penis has been inflicted on us by the male-dominated culture' (Lesbians Against Pornography, 1984) and 'Heterosexuality [may] have been composed, managed, organized, propagandized and maintained by [male] force' (Rich, 1980) clearly illustrate how lesbian separatist feminists, among others, have contextualised and understood the 'problem' of male violence. For them, it is the ultimate weapon in the battle to control female sexuality.

These quotations may make sense only if the reader has any familiarity with a feminist understanding of sexuality. Through a series of changes in focus during the last twenty years, the emphasis on family, marriage and mothering – pioneered by the feminist magazine *Red Rag* since 1972, and theoretically elaborated largely by the work of Nancy Chodorow (1978, 1989) and Dorothy Dinnerstein (1976), and the debates these books generated – has shifted to the institution which underpins them. Heterosexuality has become a central problematic for feminists in the way it has always been (or, at least, Freud intended it should be) for psychoanalysts. The vast majority of people go about their daily lives without ever thinking that there may not be something 'natural' in the seemingly universal truth that men and women are made for each other. The idea that heterosexuality may be 'man'-made seems, on the face of it, absurd. After all, women and men are anatomically compatible – necessarily so – in order to reproduce the species. This is the way God – or Nature – made us. Therefore – or so the common-sense (essentialist or natural) argument runs – heterosexuality is the natural order of things. This argument, however, confuses anatomy with psychology. Desire, whether sexual or any other kind, is socially constructed. We desire what we learn to desire.

Thinking of this sort is now consensual in the social sciences. Heterosexuality is no longer taken for granted. It is part of most individuals' core identity – that part known as gender identity, the sex we think of ourselves as being – but it is learned, not innate. There seems to be little doubt about this. Studies of individuals with 'faulty' gender identity – transsexuals, for example – confirm that the sense of whether one is masculine or feminine, and whether one is attracted by the same or the opposite sex, is learned, in the first instance, from the parents (Sheila Jeffreys (1990) makes the telling point that male-to-female transexuals, in acting out their desires, almost universally act out a caricature of stereotypical femininity). Sex and gender are not the same thing. Sex is anatomical and biological; gender is psychological (Stoller, 1968). There can now be little doubt about the cultural construction of gender and sexuality, though even Stoller, that incomparable sex researcher and psychoanalyst, presumes that which he sets out to explain, the existence of gender, when he places responsibility for its origins on the mother–infant dyad. The contention concerns the origins of these cultural constructions. For cultural feminists it seems there is no doubt: heterosexuality is imposed on women by men. It is the *raison d'être* of male dominance and female subordination.

It is less clear why men should want to impose heterosexuality. The argument runs that it is through controlling women's sexuality that men control women. Lynne Segal asks:

> Is sex not, in the intimate last instance, the solid base from which men's social control over women is built? . . . Is it some overpowering all conquering male instinct to be sexually aggressive and assertive or . . . some need for power somehow restricted to men? (1987, p. 72)

> . . . the universality and tenacity of men's dominance . . . the rise of the political right . . . and decline of radical movements led to . . . more feminists being drawn to an analysis which . . . stresses men's transhistorical primordial drive for power rather than one which explores how changing social arrangements and their ideological articulations institutionalise men's power. (1990, p. 207)

What the essentialist argument boils down to is that men have an innate need to dominate and oppress women. This stands in sharp contrast to the essentialist view of women's innate capacities and virtues. As I said above, these are little different from those qualities which were once regarded as having been imposed on women by patriarchal culture – that is, by men.

Some essentialist feminists, urging that women should develop their innately feminine virtues in order to save the world from male destructiveness, seem to contradict everything the feminist movement once stood for. It seems to reinforce precisely those qualities which men have asserted to be uniquely feminine, and cultural feminists have struggled to establish as the product of patriarchal/male chauvinistic culture. The social constructionist feminists – including British socialists like Lynne Segal and Elizabeth Wilson – can, with some justification, accuse the essentialists of sexism. This is not to say that essentialists are any less radical than socialists. On the contrary, they tend towards the revolutionary. Biologically essentialist, apocalyptic feminism is separatist in the extreme, and tends to be espoused by lesbian women. If the differences are effectively biological, then women will be freed from male domination only when they sever all contact with men. This is not so ridiculous as it sounds. In apocalyptic thinking, firmly focused on male violence, the world will never be free of aggression and war so long as there are men in it, or so long as men remain in control. A world controlled by women would reflect the fundamental feminine virtues of co-operativeness, sensitivity to others, tenderness and non-violence.

Whether this could happen remains to be seen, but the idea that such a world would be free of aggression, violence or war seems wish-fulfilling, to say the least. Where would women be in a world without men into whom to project their violent impulses (see Temperley, 1985) if, indeed, this is what they do? According to Freudian and Kleinian analysts, the source of these impulses is universal. They derive from the earliest relationship with the mother, and women are no less subject to them than men are (H. Segal, 1973, pp. 54–67). Although I share the view that the source of these impulses may be universal, I believe the impulses themselves are structured, not innate. Here I am broadly in agreement with Alice Miller (1979): parental narcissism is the source of much of this impulse to violence. This argument fails to take into account the fundamental importance of gender differences in the psychological structuring of infantile trauma.

If any proof were needed that a world run by women might be lacking in the essential feminine virtues so beloved of the apocalyptics (Mary Daly, Gayle Rubin, Susan Griffin, Andrea Dworkin and Adrienne Rich are good examples), one could simply take a close look at the history of the feminist movement in Britain (L. Segal, 1987). Since the emergence of anything resembling a movement it has been riven by splits as severe as any suffered by any male-dominated institutions. The fragmentation of feminism is saddening for feminists. It is also illuminating – not because of the rich divergence of opinions, but because it shows that women are no strangers to the urge to power which is so central to masculinity. We should not be surprised that the differences between women can sometimes seem greater than their differences from men, nor at the intensity of feelings these differences generate. I do not believe this is due in any way to the fact that feminism is a movement of women, but I certainly think it is due to the fact that women are people, with the same capacities as men. This fragmentation gives the lie to any claim that women are inherently more co-operative, or that hostility is the antithesis of femaleness.

The fragmentation of feminism seems to owe its origins to the qualities of activist feminists. They are not like other women. They have freed themselves from adaptations to many of the social and psychological expectations to which they were subjected. They are the antithesis of the female object of desire which they are raised and educated to be. There is something (it is not difficult to see what) frightening to men about the psychology of these women which has enabled them to be more aggressive, forceful and sexually independent than the majority of their peers. In these circumstances, the 'essential' feminine virtues can be seen as the chimera I believe them to be. We can learn much from this. I explore it more fully in Chapter 7.

There are differences between men and women which, as a reluctant apocalyptic, I believe are ineradicable on any meaningful scale. These differences, however, arise from the interaction between anatomy/biology and culture, which is both a product of and mediated by individual psyches. Gender differences are transmitted – largely in ignorance – by mothers and fathers to their children, and – less in ignorance – by mass media with a vested interest in reproducing and reinforcing these differences. They are no less permanent, rigid or rooted by virtue of being mediated by and partly derived from culture. I realize that I risk establishing myself as a full-blown culturalist if I assert that individuality is determined by language – culture or symbolic order – unless I also assert that there is something uniquely individual about each pre-human being, and that this something is not predicated simply on language. The risk evaporates, however, if we do not assume linear causation, and also if we realize that one of the essences of essentialism and constructionism is that each depends on the existence of the other. The question of which came first, the person or the group, may be a meaningless one. Far more likely is that they developed hand in hand in a feedback loop.

I would not object to being labelled a psychic rather than a biological essentialist. To that extent I have more in common with Lacan-influenced feminists like Juliet Mitchell, although there is much about the Lacanian-derived analysis which is unpalatable and inaccessible. Apart from its rather questionable linguistic basis, which has been widely criticized, my main criticism is its utter lack of passion as it is used and understood by feminists. One could not accuse Mitchell of this, but in the hands of feminists such as Luce Irigaray (1985) and Julia Kristeva, Lacanian theory speaks a language which in my view does not relate to people's lived experience, one in which signs become mere signifiers in a world of signifiers. We are, more than anything else, feeling animals. This seems to find no place in Lacanian analytic thought as used by feminists, which appears to have reached the apogee of a certain kind of masculine intellectual rigour in the extent to which some intellectual feminists have misplaced the object of its inquiry, women, in their analysis of women's oppression. Thought seems to have become self-sufficient: 'It tears speech out of history; the word possesses no virtue, no weight of its own' (Heaton, 1976).

This may be all very well for academic feminists, but of what value is it for the vast majority of women who may be feminists with a small f, in that they have feminist attitudes but no commitment to political action for widespread social change, or for the activist working in women's refuges or advice centres? I understand that a discourse may be in progress, but what is its value if it excludes and mystifies the vast majority of its intended participants?

If I have any quarrel with cultural feminism on the other hand, it is not with its lack of passion, or with the obscurity of its discourse or its intentions. During its recent history, feminism was a source of optimism for the many women engaged in the struggle. They offered a vision of a world in which the oppression of women was determined, caused and reinforced by social and political processes. In the heady days of the left-dominated 1960s and 1970s, utopian thinking was the order of the day. Men and women, so the argument went, were really no different from each other. The feminist socialist utopia was just around the corner, the pinnacle of a social process which began after the war, when the political consensus shifted radically left. As we now know, these dreams were short-lived and the increasing worldwide dominance of the political right may consign feminism to a footnote in history. However, the ghost lives on. The feminist analysis of female oppression has gone through many final causes during the last twenty years. It began with sexuality, made detours through birth control, equal pay, and gay liberation – among other issues – and, as a cohesive movement, finally came to grief on the rock of male violence and sexuality. My quarrel with cultural feminism is precisely its optimism. Community solidarity – which is, no doubt, of crucial importance in breaking down individual alienation, for men but particularly for women – is no serious threat to male cultural dominance.

I have already described the apocalyptic perception of male violence and aggression – or, more accurately, sadism – as an (the?) essential element of masculinity or – more accurately – maleness. How do cultural feminists understand it?

In general, cultural feminists, like their essentialist sisters, link male violence and sexuality in a seamless symbiosis. The major difference is that culturalists see masculinity, and therefore sexuality and violence, as socially constructed rather than innate. The cultural feminists (e.g. Wilson, 1983) accuse the essentialists of being blind to the historical context of female subordination, and to the variability in the conditions and forms of women's oppression. Although they agree that male violence is the essential underpinning of this oppression – 'force and its threat is never . . . residual or secondary . . . rather it is the structural underpinning of hierarchical relations' (Hanmer, 1978, p. 229) – they contend that the causes of this force and its threat are historically variable rather than universal, and can be found, for example, in political and material conditions. There is agreement that male violence is the source of women's oppression, and that in connection with sexuality it serves the interests of male dominance. For the culturalists the essential question concerns the social construction of violence, sexuality, heterosexuality and male power (Edwards, 1987). Essentialism, they argue, is a politics of despair. It obviates any necessity for women to analyse and understand the ways in which oppression is enforced and maintained on an ongoing basis in institutions such as marriage, the family, the law, medicine, education and, ultimately, the state, and to challenge and confront these manifestations of male dominance. For example, as Anne Edwards points out:

> The feminist analysis of the legal and judicial systems and of the state in general . . . can be read either as a warning against any strategies that assume the system will ever do anything against men as a group and for women, or as useful information which helps us locate the places and ways in which structural contradictions can be exploited to women's advantage.

This debate about whether or not women's oppression is universal and trans-historical is far from resolved. It was Engels who set the terms of the materialist debate in his seminal work on the relationship between capital and the family (1884). His famous statement that 'at some point in human history men took power away from women' is now widely discounted. The common-sense belief that men have always held power and women have always been oppressed is very difficult to discount or disprove, even though it may be possible to demonstrate variations in the nature and patterns of that oppression. I believe that this also applies to the concept of masculinity. What constitutes maleness at any point in time is determined by the discourses which have most relevance at that time. Honour, for example, was once a central discourse in the construction of maleness. Now it is largely irrelevant. Like Lynne Segal, I believe it is important to understand the relevant discourses which construct gender, and the context of these in their social, historical and material dimensions. For the purposes of my argument here, however, it makes little difference. Whatever is constructed as masculinity will not have a bearing on the construction of femininity as the excluded and secondary other.

For a Freudian psychotherapist or analyst, sexuality cannot be a 'natural' given. Only anatomy is given, and even then we cannot assume that the body or our experience of it is an essential quality in an otherwise constructed universe. The human subject – I, including the body – is psychosocially constructed. In Freudian theory, this construction takes place as a result of the Oedipus complex (which we shall examine in detail). At the core of this complex is the child's relationship with Mother and Father (themselves social constructs). The child is father of the man. Only relatively recently, in the 1970s, did feminist theorists turn their attention to the family, and in particular to the relation between women's oppression and the apparently universal role of women as mothers or primary carers. They have been relatively slow to realize the crucial importance of 'mothering' as the dominant social institution for the rearing of infants and the teaching of gender identity (Chodorow, 1978; see also Dinnerstein, 1976). Post-Freudian psychoanalysis, however, has long recognized the centrality of the child's relationship with its mother as a determinant of its future identity, even if it can seem more prescriptive than descriptive in its elaboration.

Most theories which address mothering and the social reproduction of gender assume the existence of gender differentiation – that is, a society divided into men and women. This is not entirely to everyone's liking, in that gender differentiation is therefore assumed to precede role differentiation. Role differentiation, however, is not possible without gender differentiation. Although I believe that gender difference is ineradicable, it is none the less necessary to explain how gender differentiation comes about when we are accounting for its reproduction and maintenance (Cucchiari, 1981). No attempt to explain misogyny can avoid this issue. Misogyny assumes a gender system. There will be no full and detailed attempt here to explain how it developed socially or anthropologically; instead I attempt to explain its psychological origins. It is for the reader to decide the success of the enterprise.

In a sense, this limitation of 'mothering' explanations, the assumption of gender differentiation, goes to the heart of my main criticism of the culturalist feminist view of male violence and the domination of women. My criticism applies also to certain mother-centred psychoanalytic theories to the extent that they, too, assume a gender system to explain the infantile roots of neurosis in the relationship between mother and child. In my view, the gender system and misogyny are inseparable. We have to explain how every child comes to perceive that men and women are different, and the nature of these differences. Freud believed that every individual human infant reproduces the history of the human species in becoming a human individual, a subject or an 'I' – 'ontogeny recapitulates phylogeny' (Freud, 1916, p. 199).

As we shall see, Freudian psychoanalysis does not contend that the human infant is born with an innate sense of self (which is, of course, almost synonymous with gender or sexual identity). The sense of self is learned. The objective of psychoanalysis is to reconstruct how the individual became him- or herself. Subjectivity is not taken for granted. I should make it clear that many Freudian or neo-Freudian analysts do not subscribe to this view. There has been a great shift within the analytic movement, paralleling the rise of humanism during the twentieth century, towards regarding the individual as somehow being born innately human. In fact, all developmental models of humanity implicitly assume this in that they see subjectivity as the inevitable consequence of a progression through a graduated series of preordained stages. Although this may be true in a biological sense, for a Freudian it can never be so in a psychological sense. This undoubted strength of Freudianism is marred, to my mind, by the almost universal assumption, in analytic explanations, of a two-parent, two-sex family.

Bearing in mind this limitation of mothering explanations, I begin with the relationship between the unformed human, the infant, and his first teacher or guide in the assumption of his identity, the mother. Whatever one's views on the origins of sex roles, one cannot doubt that since the human race began to evolve, there has been a necessity to provide for the care and protection of infants. Although this is not debatable, it in no way explains how it has come about that this is a role now performed almost exclusively by women. I am afraid that woman's role as mother will have to be taken as a given until the end of this book. By that time I hope to be in a position at least to offer a hypothesis to account for its emergence.

To account for the emergence of the subject 'I' one must begin by exploring the infant's earliest relations with the external environment. In all crucial respects the word 'environment' in relation to the infant means 'Mother'. 'Mother' refers not to the woman who bore the child but to the role performed by one or more persons of either sex in guarding the health and welfare of the infant, and in providing the psychological and physical necessities to ensure its survival and growth. Mothering, in this context, is a functional relationship to a child or infant rather than a socially prescribed sexual role. In fact – in line with our conjectures about the construction of the subject, especially in connection with sexual difference – we must assume that the infant has no knowledge of the mother's sex. It is an answer for which there is, so far as the infant is initially concerned, no question. There is intense disagreement about the time at which the infant becomes aware that there are differences between people, especially that some have breasts and some do not, and what it makes of these differences. For the unreconstructed Freudian this awareness can only ever be retrospective. It is a historical revision which arises during the Oedipus complex when the questions, to which the infant has long had the answers, evolve. For other schools of analytic thought – in particular Kleinians and other object-relations theories – this awareness occurs during the breastfeeding phase, in which there is an oral precursor of the later genital Oedipus complex. Of special significance is the Kleinian belief in an innate awareness of sexual differences: of the existence of the penis and the vagina.

It is hard to know precisely what practical differences there are between these different schools of thought. There are very few analysts or therapists who do not pay particular attention to the patient's earliest relationship with the mother. Whether this is a reconstruction or an actual memory probably makes little difference to the outcome, according to available research. The particular school of thought to which the therapist belongs seems to be unimportant as a determinant of therapeutic outcome. What we can say with certainty is that very few people who enter therapy do not re-enact with the therapist what therapists believe to be – and therefore construct as – their earliest relationship with their mother.

These days there is an influential feminist argument (Chodorow, 1978; Orbach, 1981) that because mothering is almost always performed by women, children grow up with a limited set of perceptions of the nature of women and a distorted view of female sexuality. This culturalist view regards all the ills that befall women as the result of the social reinforcement of a prescribed role for women, including the most basic of all: heterosexuality. This reinforcement is carried out by men acting in the interests of patriarchy – a sort of male Mafia whose sole interest is in continuing to oppress women in order to retain power and privilege, and ensure continuous servicing. It is obvious why this view is so popular with feminist thinkers. Clearly, if misogyny and the oppression of women are the results of social processes, such as mothering, then the task of changing becomes that much easier, in that these things are visible and relatively easy to control through changes in social policy. To the extent that behaviour is learned or acquired, rather than innate, it is amenable to change – it can be unlearned or taught differently. For example, it has been expressly stated by Chodorow, and by Orbach and Eichenbaum, that we ought to stress *parenting* of children rather than *mothering* and encourage men to share the burden as well as the joys of care. These writers believe that this is the most significant change that could be initiated in the interests of reducing sexual inequality and sexism. The assumption is that if the child grows up being cared for jointly by male and female parents, and the responsibility is equally shared, that child will not come to regard women exclusively as caretakers, or as the sole source of tenderness and femininity. In this way, women could break out of their sexually defined roles and begin to aspire to roles historically assigned to and performed only by men. I shall attempt to show that this account is, to say the least, flawed in its understanding of the construction of male psychology.

There are good reasons why feminists place such stress on woman's role as mothers. In simple terms, the argument is that because women are seen as being predominantly caretakers in relation to children, they are forced into fulfilling that same role for adult men – in other words, female labour is seen as an extension of the role of mothering, so that women are assigned the task of looking after men as adults just as they looked after them as children. Marxists believe that mothering also plays a major part in maintaining capitalist economies – not only because women take on the reproductive function of providing the state with a trained, tame labour force, but also by virtue of the unpaid labour they provide to service the material production of other goods and services which contain added value. It was largely as a result of this thinking that the Payment for Housework movement gained support during the 1970s, although it did not go unopposed by feminists. The controversy generated prevented it from gaining the widepread support necessary to become a national campaign (see Kaluzynska, 1980), although it was later generalized into a more widespread campaign about wages for women.

To the extent that we believe sexism to be a learned behaviour which is socially acquired and reinforced, this is a powerful argument. It is undeniable that sexism is socially reinforced. Women are represented everywhere as secondary, sexual objects who exist for the titillation and gratification of male needs – despite twenty years of high-profile proselytizing by the women's movement and the appointment – no doubt token – of women to what were previously exclusively male strongholds: the Stock Exchange and the Bench. Interestingly – and unsurprisingly – women who have achieved positions of some authority in what were once thought of as exclusively male domains have coined the new expression, 'the glass ceiling', to describe the invisible limits to advancement which are imposed on them by men.

While it seems clear that sexism – and its progenitor, misogyny – are socially taught and reinforced, it seems questionable, at the very least, to reify social structures by asserting that they also originate in culture. Where else can social structures originate? I do not wish to deny that the group is greater than the sum of its parts, but this is simply because gatherings of individuals make for greater complexity of interactions. These interactions require the evolution of structures and roles, society or the social system, but the group itself has no mind other than the system of shared meanings of its individual members, whether or not such meanings are conscious.

Members of women's consciousness-raising groups in the 1970s found that although their awareness of women's issues was heightened, such groups had little or no effect on the way they felt and behaved, particularly in terms of their sexuality. Some turned eventually to Freud and psychoanalysis to gain insight into the deeper psychological processes which led to the development of their femininity and sexuality. They needed to explain the tenacity of their desire for men, and the consequences of this for the further development of their consciousness of sexual politics. This interest had wider repercussions for heterosexual women in their relations with revolutionary lesbian feminists, who often accused them of betraying the cause by continuing relations with men. I have worked with some women who have articulated their defensiveness, anxiety and guilt about their heterosexuality in their relationships with lesbian friends. There is little doubt that adherence to radical feminist thinking can cause real distress to heterosexual women.

The greatest flaw in the culturalist feminist view is the belief that the social reproduction of sexism and gender identity can somehow be reduced to observable interactions or institutional practices. Without wishing to minimize the significance of such processes, or their importance in providing a focus for social action on the lines recommended by Rodgerson and Wilson (1991) or Lynne Segal (1987), I would argue that this view fails entirely to account for unconscious processes – not only of transmission but also of reception of social expectations. Although many significant differences can be observed in sex-comparative parent–child interaction between parents' handling of boy and girl infants, it is impossible to know the significance of these differences without an understanding of the unconscious mind. Additionally, it is not possible directly to observe the child's or the parent's understanding of this, or to relate it to the child's eventual behaviour. I cannot be persuaded that little people are blank screens.

We simply cannot understand how we become people without examining the unconscious. Many feminists understood this when they began to appreciate the intensity of resistance to their efforts to change not only men's behaviour but, more importantly, their own. Hoffman Baruch and Serrano (1990) point out how many theorists (Chodorow is one) who have set out to explore psychoanalysis for its feminist possibilities have since entered psychoanalytic training.

Apart from the consideration of women's efforts to change, there is the entirely separate issue of how men may be induced to do so. The belief that misogyny can be eliminated from social relations by social engineering seems to me entirely mistaken. This is not an argument for passivity – individual women and men will continue to forge their own arrangements – but the scale of change required is beyond comprehension. On the one hand there is massive institutional resistance; on the other, men's behaviour is so predicated on the idea of women as an excluded sex and as providers of services that the idea of a society differently ordered is beyond my imagination. My pessimism derives from my understanding that heterosexuality is predicated on the notion of woman as an excluded and inferior sex. Change of the sort envisaged would therefore require nothing less than the breakdown of this most primary form of differentiation. Can anyone imagine a world which is not predominantly heterosexual?

Even if one were sure precisely what needs changing, such change would require more than significant changes in social structures of the sort recommended by Lynne Segal, and Rodgerson and Wilson, essential as these are. Such an upheaval will be impossible unless men face the emotional and psychological roots of their relations with women; this is initially more important than the need for women to examine their contribution to their own oppression. The unpalatable fact is that men have the power to change what is changeable (Lysistrata notwithstanding) in the situation, while women do not. Men will never willingly give women what feminists assert is theirs by right unless they first face up to their unconscious attitudes and feelings about women. Experience has shown that laws do not change attitudes – resistance becomes covert and less amenable to external influence (since the enacting of Equal Opportunities legislation in Britain, women's earnings have actually declined as a proportion of men's). Women will not change men without their co-operation, and unless men are convinced that the changes will be to their own advantage or, at worst, will not disadvantage them. This requires that men must be convinced of the limitations that misogyny sets on their own emotional and psychological growth and well-being, and their overall satisfaction with life. Apart from the difficulties – perhaps the impossibility – of giving up gender identity, this seems an awesome task when it is set alongside the distinct advantages men derive from women's subordination, and the cultural acceptance and encouragement of men's normative expectations of women.

In all feminist schools of thought, the notion of patriarchy occupies a dominant position. Whilst it is undoubtedly true that patriarchy – institutionalized male dominance – possesses all the power attributed to it by women, cultural theories fail entirely to account for its existence, even though materialist theorizing – largely based on Marxism – accounts, in analysis of its importance in particular aspects of the socioeconomic structure, for some of its inertia and the constraints against change. (For example, even though it may be very difficult for feminists to reach agreement about the complex nature of the relations between the division into public – 'work' – and private – 'domestic' – spheres of activity and the capitalist organization of production, the debate problematizes and defines the importance of this relation, and raises crucial questions which otherwise go unasked by economists.)

Feminist theorizing about the nature and causes of women's oppression, the origins of male dominance, is not new. Implicitly or explicitly, this project underlies all feminist scholarship. After Engels and Marxist analysis, which locates women's oppression in economic conditions, and Simone de Beauvoir's (1949) and Shulamith Firestone's (1971) emphasis on women's childbearing capacities, the newest perspective focuses more on the notion that there is a separate system of sexual and gender relations which is distinct from either economics or reproduction – a view with which I am in complete agreement. Indeed, I believe this system to be the fundamental one, more important than economics, class or race as an ordering principle of meaning. I would go so far as to say it is the organizing principle of meaning. The question, as I have already pointed out, is whether this sexual and gender system represents something innate in 'male' and 'female', or whether its origins can be found in historical developments. As Gayle Rubin put it:

> The question of the nature and genesis of women's oppression . . . is not a trivial one, since the answers given to it determine our visions of the future and our evaluation of whether or not it is realistic to hope for a sexually egalitarian society.(1975, p. 157)

I would add only that it determines women's individual strategies for change, and whether they begin from hope, or from resignation and despair.

Why do men hold this pre-eminent position in defining and controlling reality and social events? How did it come about in the first place? Those who argue that the existence of a patriarchy is a figment of the feminist imagination – and there are many, including women – who maintain this, are clearly flying in the face of overwhelming evidence. Even the most cursory examination of social statistics shows that women are massively disadvantaged in relation to men. It rather begs the question to state that men are in this position because they conceived of, built and run the institutions which make such decisions, although this is undoubtedly true. One must account for the fact that they are still in a position to do this without any concerted opposition from women who, in most instances, cannot fail to be aware of their exclusion from such institutions. Men rarely ask themselves why women are excluded in this way; indeed, one might wonder if they are even aware of it. The inferior status of women is such an integral part of the environment that it is quite taken for granted, rather like the air we breathe.

This is poignantly and tragically illustrated in Gordon Burns's book (Burns, 1986) about Peter Sutcliffe, the 'Yorkshire Ripper', where the tragic consequences of uncontrolled misogyny are disturbingly spelled out. According to Burns, it was Sutcliffe's inability to live up to the demands of his maleness which led to his destruction, and that of his victims. This is the kind of thinking which informs much of the men's movement. I believe it is profoundly mistaken, and that much of men's suffering derives from our beliefs about, expectations and *treatment* of women. I would go further and assert that from my experience of abusive men, this kind of thinking is dangerous to women. It reinforces many of the abusers' justifications for their abuse. Sutcliffe was not a victim of gender expectations; his victims were. Lynne Segal, perhaps unintentionally, makes this disturbing inference in her analysis of the Sutcliffe case (1990, pp. 251 ff.). While I agree with her general message – that we need to know more about what makes particular men abuse at particular times and in particular ways – I believe we must begin with a clear commitment to a pro-feminist analysis. Segal comes dangerously close to the kind of thinking, long associated with psychotherapy and analysis, which she earlier (p. 55) criticizes as a dangerous 'orthodoxy'.

The Qualitatively Different Beast?

It would be helpful to digress here and examine the way in which Peter Sutcliffe was presented in the male-dominated mass media. He was commmonly described as 'a beast', 'evil', 'a vicious animal', and so on. Such epithets – while they no doubt express and reflect the universal revulsion and repugnance his actions generated – do little to help us understand either Sutcliffe or the circumstances which helped to create him. In fact they generate exactly the climate which prevents such a critical examination. To some extent this is understandable, given the horror his actions evoke, but by presenting him in this way, the media also imply another more sinister motive. The unstated but intended consequence is to define his actions as so outrageous that no 'normal' frame of reference can be applied in his case. As an 'animal' his actions can tell us nothing of the relations between men and women, or of media attitudes to women. He was defined from the outset as 'qualitatively' different from all other men, not merely 'quantitatively' different – not as an extreme example of men in relation to women, as I would maintain, but as a separate case, entirely in a category of his own. In much the same way, men who batter their wives are stereotypically seen as sick or different, despite the fact that as many as one man in four is regularly violent towards his partner, and that 40 per cent of men acknowledge using violence on their partners at some time, and express belief in their right to do so (Andrews, 1987). This is not to say that Sutcliffe is not insane, but that insanity is not a qualitatively different state from normality – rather, it represents the extreme end of a continuum of largely explicable processes. An interesting feminist analysis of the 'ripper' mythology suggests that it serves the unconscious purpose of reminding women that they are in danger from men, and sanctions the expression of male violence towards women (Walkowitz, 1982).

This sort of hypocrisy masquerading as outrage is also evident in media coverage of rape (all too often such stories are positioned next to 'girlie' pictures in the popular British press). Again, rapists are presented as animals, yet if we take a woman's definition of rape rather than a man's – where she has been made to have sexual intercourse without her full consent – we find that most rapes occur within marriages or other long-term relationships (Kelly, 1988). Sir Matthew Hale's now infamous eighteenth-century ruling – 'a husband cannot be guilty of rape upon his wife, for by their mutual matrimonial consent and contract the wife hath given up herself in this kind to her husband, which she cannot retract' – has recently been dramatically overturned after decades of struggle by feminists in the UK. Lord Justice Lane's 1991 ruling 'that the idea that a wife by marriage consents in advance to her husand having sexual intercourse with her whatever her state of health or however proper her objections is no longer acceptable' was a significant one for women and, indeed, for men. Within weeks, the first man was convicted and jailed for raping his wife, from whom he had recently separated. This ruling, however, will have little or no bearing on rape in ongoing marriages – still the most common type – rather than those where separation has already occurred.

Apart from the significance of this change for some women, it explicitly recognizes the serious and common experience of rape within marriage rather than from a stranger. It acknowledges what activists have been saying for many years: that the man a woman has to be afraid of is the one in her own home. It gives the lie to the myth of the qualitatively different beast. Socialist feminists who disagree with this monolithic representation of men – first mooted by Susan Griffin (1971) and so vividly taken up by Susan Brownmiller (1976) in a way which was to place male violence and rape at the centre of feminist politics – argue that it is a politics of despair, and fundamentally not useful, to see men in this way. Lynne

Segal (1990), for example, argues that not all men are potential rapists, as Brownmiller insists, and that it is crucially important to discover why some men rape while others do not, and in what circumstances they will do so. However, there is a familiar note of doubt in Segal's thinking when she adds: 'Although not without justification, it is a politics of the profoundest pessimism' (p. 240).

Once Peter Sutcliffe (or a batterer or a rapist) has been defined as an 'animal', other men do not fall into his shadow. It is not necessary for us to question the origins and nature of our violent feelings, and actual violence, against women. This does not imply a conscious plot within the media to produce such a consequence. It seems to be simply one more expression of male misogyny and its patriarchal power – the sort of 'knee-jerk' response one would expect from a freemasonry which wanted to disown one of its members whose actions might lead to critical attention being focused not on him but on the institution he represents: masculinity. As the Preface to this book illustrates, men the world over are committing – or having committed in their name – violence against women on a catastrophic scale (see also French, 1991). There is little difference between arguing that Sutcliffe, or a rapist, or a child molester, or a wife-batterer, is sick, and arguing that masculinity – at least in some important respects – is a form of sickness. (This is an intriguing and not altogether undiscussed possibility. Jessica Benjamin [1990] virtually says this when she discusses – in terms not too dissimilar from mine – the basic 'fault' which, she believes, underlies maculinity.)

Childbearing

One might – and many writers on feminist politics and the sexual division of labour do – account for the strength of the patriarchy and its existence by pointing out that women bear children, and this makes them physically dependent on men for protection. It is undoubtedly true that this single biological function of women provides – and has always provided – men with a ready-made and seemingly cast-iron justification for their continued oppression of women. No doubt most men who have used it do so sincerely and partly out of concern, however ill-judged, for the well-being of children. Women have always been beaten with the stick of motherhood. Evidence that motherhood must be an exclusive preoccupation of women, however, is non-existent. On the contrary, as we have seen, the assumption of 'womanhood' rather begs the question of sexual differentiation. It simply will not do to believe that it is natural. It may seem to be the most natural alternative, but I argue here that each individual still has to grow into it.

It is certainly true that babies are totally dependent on stable and 'good-enough' parenting, and on the emotional bonding of this relationship, but it does not have to be with a woman (see Chapter 2). There is no reason to believe that an infant would be aware of the difference if it were bottlefed by a man or that any perceived difference would have any significance. Nevertheless it is a fact that the biological make-up of a woman makes her the most efficient and effective feeding parent during the early stages of an infant's life. In addition, it seems that mothers form with their babies an emotional and psychological bond which will withstand the most severe environmental traumas. Witness, for example, the studies of Hiroshima after the atomic bomb – the only emotional bond which seemed to survive was the mother–child bond. While this bonding undoubtedly helps the species to survive, there is no evidence that it is biological. The social pressures on women to form such a bond are extreme. There is no readily apparent reason, however, why the mother's bonding behaviour towards the baby should not be a male function (Sander, 1975).

A major caveat must be given here about most baby research. It almost always assumes what – at least in theory – psychoanalysis attempts to explain: the existence of Mother and, with her, the two sexes. Additionally, research shows that where the infant–mother relationship is interfered with – for example, when the mother is not able to feed or hold her baby at will – maternal bonding and attachment behaviour are reduced (Barnett *et al.*, 1970). Of course one should be wary of the conclusions one draws from research of this sort. Most interpretations tend to be rather sexist. This research, for example, has been interpreted as showing that there is a natural bonding instinct in the mother which peaks after the birth, and if this is delayed, the instinct, which is phased to the birth, will weaken. Apart from the difficulty with the concept of instinct, it makes just as much sense to interpret the results as indicating that there is no bonding instinct (Lichtenberg, 1981). Proximity and frequency of contact – even without the massive role expectations and sanctions for failure placed on new mothers surrounded by 'experts' – will lead to attachment behaviour.

As I hope to show later (see Chapter 7), women can be 'interpreted' as colluding with men in their oppression, and the emphasis that most women attach to bonding is more easily understood, in this context, as a psychological rather than a sociobiological process, and as an adaptation to men's demands and expectations. It should not, however, be taken to mean that for this reason it is easier to modify the mother–child bonding process, even if one were to conclude, as one might, that it is necessary and desirable. It is in our understanding of the psychological significance of the baby for the mother that we can account for women's apparent collusion with the male notion that men are in charge because of women's childbearing and rearing functions. Of course, the vast majority of men have no motivation to take over the mothering role from women – not only because it can be burdensome and a chore, however rewarding it may be, but perhaps – more importantly – because the process of becoming a man makes men ill fitted for such a role. As we shall see, the exorcism of all one's identifiable 'feminine' or 'mothering' qualities is essential to assuming masculinity (a point also made by Chodorow, 1978, although she emphasizes maleness as all that is not mother). Freud (1905) made the same observation although his explanation was different. I prefer to stress the advantages of becoming male rather than – *pace* Chodorow – the advantages of becoming 'not female'.

The social or constructionist explanation of the origins of misogyny fails to account for the existence of the patriarchy. Women's childbearing and child-rearing function is not the basis of male power over them – not, at least, in quite the way that some feminists think. Such thinking ascribes far too much importance to the male's need to guarantee the survival of the species, in that it assumes this as the motive for men's oppression of women. This is not an irrelevant consideration and it is one which contributes to a justification for keeping women in an oppressed position where they can concentrate on raising children. Women's capacity for being made to feel guilty by men in connection with their mothering capabilities should not be underestimated. The power of the childbearing explanation is limited, however, in that it accords too much status to men's conscious intentions. The fact that women have children is a crucial source of men's hatred of them, but for less altruistic and more unconscious reasons than those connected with species survival.

How, then, are we to account for the universal phenomenon of male dominance?

2 Child Development

MOTHER: PRINCESS AND WITCH

Let us return to the examination of the social beginnings of the human infant. 'Mothering' has been defined as a functional relationship with the infant rather than a biological gender role which is exclusive to the biological mother. This is a basis for optimism for those who hold to the constructionist or cultural theory of male dominance or – as I call it, misogyny.

Influential thinking in developmental and object-relations psychology has led to the conclusion that a mother's role in child-rearing is to encourage independence in the child, and to produce it faster than it would otherwise develop (Winnicott, 1949). It has also been suggested that the human child is adapted to cope with the frustration this causes, and that while this frustration is unpleasant, it provides the impetus to cognitive and physical growth and autonomy by encouraging the utilization of the child's own innate potential. The mother, therefore, has to possess the capacity to reject her offspring. It is undoubtedly true that the child's physical development is towards independence; the evidence for a similar emotional urge is less clear. It may well be, but it certainly does not follow, that this necessitates a graduated rejection by the mother. There is a clear implication here that the child experiences infancy and dependency as such a rewarding experience that it will never willingly relinquish them. The fact of physical growth is proof, if it is needed, of an inbuilt pressure towards maturation of a kind. The maturation process involves a gradual shift from the position where the infant requires the world to organize the satisfaction of its needs to a position where it can organize this itself. Independence and dependence are relative terms in this context - complete independence is not possible.

At some point in human history it clearly became necessary for the male infant to be thrown from the nest - for biological or social reasons or, more probably, a combination of the two. The eventual synthesis of these developments, in incest taboos, is universal. All human societies have moved sexuality from the realm of Nature to a cultural ordering principle. It is also clear that whether or not there is an emotional drive towards separation from the mother, such separation becomes a necessity for boys under the pressure of the conflicts which the incest taboo causes him. These conflicts are, in their turn, a product of social pressures and expectations which have, no doubt, evolved over aeons. I will show later that these pressures work differently for girls. Although much of what follows applies to both male and female infants, I will use the male pronoun to indicate my primary focus.

At the time of his greatest dependency, after he passes through Nature's original one-way street, the infant experiences his mother in two ways: as both 'environment' and 'object' mother (Winnicott, 1963b, p. 182). As environment mother she constitutes the whole background world in which the infant exists - the air he breathes, the force of gravity that holds him to his crib, the emotional climate in which he feels, and so on. As the object mother she is the mother with whom the infant interacts in response to all his needs and drives, 'the mother who feeds him, the mother he cries to have come, the mother whose face he explores, the mother against whom his rage is directed' (Winnicott, 1963a). Experiencing the mother as environment is the paradigm of the tendency to generalize; experiencing the mother as object is the paradigm of the tendency to particularize - hence the psychotherapists' assertion that a patient's anger with the world is an expression of his early anger with his mother.

I would add, without contradicting this, that in my experience with adult males the tendency to perceive the environment as Father, and the escape from this, is far more important. I greatly regret the slow erosion, in most psychoanalytic theory, of Freud's emphasis on the genital Oedipus complex in favour of the early relationship with the mother. What might be the unconscious reasons for this, whatever truths are being expressed about early emotional development? It is my personal experience, as well as my experience in work as a therapist, that castration anxieties connected with, for example, success or sexual potency are at least as terrifying, if not more so, than their pre-oedipal progenitors. I have often wondered if it is not the desire to avoid these anxieties which motivates much of the men's movement. For example, Charlie Kreiner, the 'reference person' for men in re-evaluation counselling, asserts (1991, p. 6) that men have to be forced to separate from Mother. I find it interesting that he says: 'Men have to be humiliated . . . or . . . they would never choose to split from their mothers . . . that's why all the Freudian Oedipal thing is largely nonsense'. He does not specify precisely which aspects of 'the Freudian Oedipal thing' are 'largely nonsense'. It is hard to imagine this statement being made by a man who had been analysed. Unfortunately, the re-evaluation counselling model has quite a hold on men's consciousness-raising efforts, and professional work with men, in the USA and the UK. This depiction of men as victims of gender is all too depressingly familiar from some programmes with abusers in which the real victim, the woman, disappears in a major feat of prestidigitation.

The human infant is notable for its absolute dependency on the mother – without her it would not survive. This dependency, which persists for longer in humans than in any other species, is at the core of any assertion of the masculine fear and hatred of the feminine. All dependency involves the potential for fear and hatred: to the extent that the dependent person is unable to meet their own needs, or has to sacrifice the ability to do so, or that the dependency fails (as it does for all humans), the provider has power over them. For the infant the power of the mother is total – she can literally decide whether he will live or die.

This period in the infant's life seems to generate two opposed representatives or internal images of the mother as both environment and object. The one is nurturing and loving, providing all life's essentials with the maximum of security and care, responsive to the infant's needs and expressions of discomfort – she seems almost to possess the magical power of knowing what the infant needs before the infant knows himself. This, of course, is true to the extent that the very young infant cannot differentiate between various states of discomfort – he does not know whether he is wet, cold or hungry. The mother has to think for the infant and make appropriate responses by using her identification and empathy with him to differentiate between the various signals of distress. The infant could be forgiven for fantasizing that he has total control over this mother who responds to his every wish. This image of the 'ideal mother' is the essential basis for healthy adult life in that it provides the foundation for the later development of the 'good-enough mother' (Winnicott, 1960a, p. 145) who can 'meet the omnipotence of the infant and to some extent make sense of it'. Without Mother, no infant can survive.

Opposed to this 'ideal' mother or 'princess' is the 'witch'. This is the mother over whom the totally dependent infant has no control; she either does not respond to distress signals, or she responds badly. Whereas the good mother provides what is needed, the bad mother either takes it away or fails to provide it at all. This 'witch' may even, in extreme cases, really behave in an actively life-threatening manner. Even if she does not, the infant will experience these objects as being life-threatening:

> The child conceives of them [objects] as actually dangerous – persecutors who it fears will devour it, scoop out the inside of its body, cut it to pieces, poison it – in short, compassing its destruction by all the means which sadism can devise. (M. Klein, 1935, p. 262)

One really cannot overemphasize the terrifying quality of this internal 'witch'. She will be recognizable to anyone who is not completely cut off from their childhood as a familiar figure from fairy tales, where she appears in many guises. One of the most familiar and terrifying (certainly for me) appears in *Hansel and Gretel*, where she fattens up Hansel so that she can eat him. She appears in many other stories as a vicious, neglecting, depriving stepmother whose only opposition is the child's fairy godmother. The dramatic quality of these stories is provided by the uncertainty as to whether the child will be saved or the 'witch' will triumph.

The universal popularity of these tales and variations on them is well documented by Bruno Bettelheim (1972); in Jung's work such figures or imagos are seen as universal archetypes. The fact that each culture has its own version is testimony to the very deep resonance of these characters within the human unconscious.

THE SPLIT IN PRACTICE

I will now illustrate how these opposing images can (in my opinion, do) influence men's behaviour. One of my clients, a man in his fifties, has had two long-term relationships with women: one a fifteen-year marriage which produced two children; the other a live-in relationship which lasted seven years. He is a moderately successful small businessman. His present partnership is with Kate, a nurse, whom he met in hospital while he was a patient with a non-threatening but painful illness. She had a child from a previous marriage. They fell deeply in love (his description) and within a matter of weeks they had set up home together. After about eight months of what he described as 'bliss' he came to me for a consultation after a night when he had twice viciously attacked his partner. He had no history of violence in his previous relationships, although it was clear that he had expected – and been given – complete control in both of them. He jokingly described how his last partner had given up three jobs because he had told her to. He admitted that he had liked the control and her submission, but that he had been bored by her. Kate could not have been more different. He described her as beautiful, vivacious, lively, independent and sociable – all the qualities which attracted him. He said that he was besotted with Kate, that he idealized her. His attack on her had been precipitated by his feeling jealous at a party where he had seen her laughing with another man.

He confirmed that he had often had jealous fantasies and anxieties about her active social life, from which he excluded himself. His account was that he enjoyed being with her so much that he did not want to be with other people and could not understand, if she loved him, why she did. He said that he had been increasingly depressed during the relationship, and unable to understand why, but wondered if it might be something to do with his intense possessive feelings, and the fact that he loved her too much. To my inquiry about his possessiveness he said that he always asked her where she had been and what she had done, but only because he loved her and was interested in her life. He volunteered that he told her everything about his life. When I suggested that this sounded like an interrogation, he replied that this was what Kate said it felt like. I asked if he had experienced other feelings about her which, perhaps, were not so easy to face, and might be connected with his depression. He was confused by this question; he maintained that he had never felt resentful towards or angry with her, and that he had never tried to restrain her social activities (this subsequently turned out to be untrue: he had, in fact, made several what he described as 'snide comments' about Kate's activities, which had the effect of making her feel guilty and spoiling her enjoyment). Apart from his depression, he had felt really happy until now.

His attack on Kate had been brutal. He had knocked her out with a full-blooded blow to the jaw, and attacked her again when she later attempted to escape from the house. He remembered that at the time of the attack he had been overwhelmed by hatred for her, and experienced her as very dangerous to him. He was alarmed – even terrified – by these feelings, which he had never had before; and, not surprisingly, wanted me to do something 'to take them away'. He made it clear that he felt very much a victim of Kate's independence and her capacity for enjoying herself without him: it 'makes me feel unloved and rejected', he said. In my experience, this is normal. All abusive men feel like victims, and erect complex mental structures to maintain denial of their actual sadism, hatred and rage. In fact he is a victim of his own expectations and Kate's unwillingness to adapt to them. In our subsequent work together we painstakingly built up his awareness of all the resentment, rage and hatred which he had felt and pushed away every time she did something which did not involve him. Of course he also felt guilt and fear of abandonment, but I believe these were as much consequences of the rage and hate as causative of his violence. He finally found a moment when he believed he had proof of his fantasies. It gave him the opportunity, without guilt, to act out all the feelings he had accumulated during the previous months. He felt that he was now justified in using violence, and implicitly letting Kate know that she could not do as she wanted with impunity.

I realize that, even from these few details, much more could be said about this man. The point I am stressing here is the split between the woman he consciously adored and the emergence of the woman he attacked, and the lengths to which he went for many months to keep these images and feelings separate. In groups with abusers I frequently have the experience that when they are talking about their victims I see them as crazy or deranged, and feel that I too would want to hit them. I am no longer embarrassed by these feelings, as I used to be, because I know that I am identifying with the man's projections of his partner. When other men in the group are asked to give a member feedback about their perceptions of this woman as seen through his eyes, it frequently arouses real sadness and guilt, and protestations that 'She isn't like that at all, I really love her'. I am convinced that whatever it means, when a man is attacking his partner he is feeling 'crazy' at that moment.

The relative strength of these opposing internal images of the mother will depend on a number of factors – some are qualities of the infant; others are qualities of the mother. For example, there is the infant's innate potential to react aggressively when frustrated, the strength of its needs, its capacity for making a fuss, its need for soothing, and so on (M. and D. Aleksandrowicz, 1976). On the mother's side, there is her actual responsiveness to take into account: how quickly does she react to the infant's distress, or how much does she think about forestalling distress before it occurs? Are her responses adequate?

This splitting of the mother into two parts by the infant is not precisely a psychic phenomenon; it is probably more of a somatic process connected with whole-body states of feeling. It could be said to represent a primitive attempt by the infant to control an uncertain environment and master anxiety, but it is actually more like a reflex. Those who would dispute that such a process of splitting occurs need only look at the way supposedly mature adults think about opposing political views, or at the feelings generated by sports supporters in favour of their own team and against the opposition. This splitting of the world into good and bad is the adult derivative of this infantile reflex, which at one end of the spectrum is unconscious and pathological and, at the other end, is used to bolster 'normality'. It is particularly obvious at times of war – we need only look at the way the enemy is represented. 'Kill an Argie, Win a Metro', the infamous joke during the Falklands War, may have been a spoof, but it reflected much of the sentiment of the time. Apart from such extreme examples, it must be said that a capacity for splitting is essential for psychic health: it is the basis for discriminating between good and bad.

There is evidence that before long these bodily sensations of bliss and distress begin to be organized into mental representations or memories (Carpenter, 1974). How does the infant cope with these contradictory images? In the early stages it is not possible to say that he represses them, because his mind is not organized into a repressing part and a repressed part. Rather, the split is a precursor of repression, and is something like the adult process of keeping things separated in the mind. It is more useful to think of splitting as a whole-body experience. When the infant feels good, all of him feels good. This is the state of satisfaction when his being is not in a state of arousal. His whole being begins to feel bad when he is in a state of need. This can become traumatic if and when a state of need arousal is not met with a response from the mother. At this stage of his development the infant could be said to be pre-ambivalent. There is no mixing of these opposing states. The mixing occurs when he begins to be aware that the good and bad states are related to the same person: his mother. However, it is probably at the point of first failure (the failure of his basic unity with his carer) that the infant develops feelings of dependency, as distinct from actual dependency, and ontological insecurities and anxieties connected with the absence of Mother or primary carer. Anxieties about death, fragmentation and dissolution connected with the absent and needed object survive with us throughout life in an encapsulated and unconscious form. It might be said – indeed, I believe it is true – that we all suffer from a hidden psychosis in which these most primitive infantile experiences and responses are encapsulated by sadomasochistic feelings.

This awareness that the infant's good and bad states are related to the same person – ambivalence – cannot be said to exist without some intrapsychic structure, whose establishment is regarded as a milestone in the humanizing of the infant (M. Klein, 1935), although there is marked disagreement not only over the time at which this intrapsychic structure can be said to have been established, but also over what it means (Sander, 1975, p. 131). I believe, with Dinnerstein (1976), that one of the inevitable consequences of the establishment of ambivalence is that the infant decides he will never again allow a woman to have such power over him. Even in a relatively healthy mother–child relationship this 'bad' mother is terrifying. The conflicts she provokes in the infant arouse his fear and hatred, and are very difficult to cope with. This decision – never again to allow a woman such power over him – is a momentous one. I believe it is made by all men, whatever the particular form, or intensity, it adopts in adulthood. It is the individual psychological root of misogyny, whatever its social or biological significance, and the basis of the masculine rejection of the 'feminine' qualities of tenderness, loving, and so on, which we are all capable of possessing.

Such contentions about the existence of 'good and bad mothers' are, by their very nature, impossible to prove in infants, despite the fact that any therapist sees them acted out and writ large in the consulting room every day of their professional life as their patients re-live infantile experiences. It is not difficult, however, to show that splitting, for the infant, represents a creative – almost biological – attempt to deal with his aggressive impulses. Given that he does not yet possess the intellectual integrity and strength – as adults presumably do – to integrate powerful conflicting emotions and needs, splitting off the 'bad' feelings and 'bad' mother while relating to the 'good' enables him to continue to survive. Consider the difficulty of feeding from someone you hate and imagine to be bad – someone who, *in extremis*, wants to kill you. It is not hard to see that this may be the origin of all difficulties in taking anything from anyone. Such a situation would be impossible. The child would either feed and vomit, or simply refuse food. In the very early days of life this situation would not be so acute, as the mother's need, in most cases, is to be constantly responsive to the child, and most mothers are intuitively 'good' enough. With increasing development, however, the mother becomes less responsive as the infant is gradually weaned from his dependency.

It might be argued that this scenario is based on a false premiss, and that the child does not have internal representations of external objects and people. From this point of view the infant's activity consists of feeding when the opportunity presents itself, and any speculation about its state of mind is both unnecessary and complicating. It might be said that the infant is not psychologically active enough to develop what, at first sight, seems a highly sophisticated mental process. This may well be true of the pre-ambivalent stage. However, the bodily experience which will later lead to internal representations dominates the infant's life at this point. Any assertion that the older child – say at six months – does not have internal relations with objects would fly in the face of all the evidence concerning the discriminating model-building activity observable in even very young infants. Although it is difficult to interpret, it is well established, for example, that even two-week-old infants react differently to pictures of people and to pictures of inanimate objects, and to Mother's face differently from the face of a stranger (Carpenter, 1974). How can one interpret this, except as evidence of some form of mental activity on the infant's part?

In so far as the ability to think is precipitated by experiences with the external environment, the most important precipitators are the states of distress which the infant experiences associated with various physical discomforts such as cold, hunger, wetness, and so on. Without becoming involved in arguments about whether the infant experiences his own body as internal or external, or whether he has the capacity for making such distinctions, one can state categorically that infants experience distress, and that this is communicated to the external world. What is more natural than that stress should lead to the development of coping strategies even in infants, or that it should evoke innate responses for dealing with it? Something which is within the capacities of a simple amoeba is certainly not beyond a much more complex multicelled organism.

From the stress induced by the experience of coping with the conflicting images of the 'princess' and the 'witch' the infant develops conflicting views of the world – one benign, responsive and safe; the other life-threatening, fearful and dangerous. All other things being equal, he will struggle to keep the good world around him against the omnipresent threat of being overwhelmed by the bad. In this context, the distinction between external and internal is probably a meaningless one for the infant – not only because he is incapable of differentiating, but also because the strength of the 'witch' is a product of the mother's actual failings and, perhaps more importantly, the infant's own characteristics: the strength of his needs, his reaction to frustration, and his propensity for aggression. If the 'witch' takes over, the whole world will seem to be bad, both inside and outside. The more intense the feelings of fear and hatred generated by real frustrations, the more 'bad' the 'witch' will be. It is as if her sadistic impulses towards the infant are in some way fed and intensified by the infant's own feelings. If you have had the experience of hating and fearing someone (and which of us has not?) you may have noticed how these feelings have a circular quality. The more you fear, the more you hate; consequently, the more you fear. In extreme instances this can become paranoia.

In a sense, the bad image of the mother is fed by the infant's feelings in that one way for the infant to cope with them, apart from splitting, is to project all his own aggression into the 'bad' mother. The intensity of this aggression will reflect the mother's actual inadequacies. It is probably true that the infant feels these as attacks on him – at the most primitive level, all deprivation and frustration is experienced as an attack by the frustrating object. The more intense the frustration, the more malign the mother's intentions. This defence – of projecting on to the external world feelings which properly belong inside the self – is another primitive coping mechanism which, to some extent, we all carry into our adult lives. Indeed, it could be argued that all perceptions of others are projections of aspects of the self, whether or not such perceptions are accurate reflections of the other's character. Projection is the infantile basis of the adult capacity for empathy.

These processes, splitting and projection, do not occur only in people who will later become neurotic, psychotic, or emotionally disturbed. They are universal. The outcome of the conflict between 'princess' and 'witch' will be a major determinant of the future health of the adult individual. The conflict itself is one which must be faced, at some point, by all of us in our natural striving for emotional maturity.

THE DEVELOPMENT OF INTERNAL IMAGES

Everyone must be familiar with the process of identifying with another person, and with the act of imitating desirable characteristics and qualities which we perceive they possess while we do not, but would like to. In its mature form, such behaviour can be wholly constructive. Although our understanding of it is confused, a more primitive form is presumed to occur in infancy, with the same motives that prompt it in adulthood. One such motive is the desire to be like the admired person, but underlying this are mixed feelings of insecurity, fear and powerlessness. The act of identification gives some illusion of control over – and helps to reduce conflict with – the admired person.

It is thought to be part of the normal process of growing up that a child should internalize and identify with his parents. This process is encouraged in many ways in every culture, even though such encouragement is hardly necessary. Very few little boys and girls do not learn to want, at some stage, to be like Daddy or Mummy. For the infant, the internalizing of the 'good' mother, which will occur through the experience and satisfaction of his needs, and his eventual identification with her, will lead to the formation of a strong ego, or sense of self, of his own. All children want to internalize the 'good' and reject the 'bad' – or, as Freud put it, 'to eat the good and spit out the bad' (1925c, p. 237). The experience with the 'good' mother becomes the core of the sense of self, and of feelings of self-esteem through identification. Her reliability and goodness provide an organizing principle of meaning which will eventually give sense to the world – or, at least, motivate the infant to make sense of it. This identification will be a bulwark of hope against despair, of self-worth against inadequacy, and of optimism against hopelessness.

The continuity and reliability of the rhythm of 'good enough' caretaking will assure the infant of his own 'continuity of being'

(Winnicott, 1960b, p. 52) in the face of fears of death at the hands of the 'witch', who may be present or absent. My clinical experience with violent men leads me to believe that a real and present witch is more likely to lead to paranoid anxieties, and an absent witch to a mixture of these with ontological anxieties derived from the first experience of the failure of unity with the primary carer and the development of dependency. These ontological insecurities later become confused with paranoid ones after the infant intuits that the absent object is also the present one into whom he has projected his hatred. Not that security of continuity of being is automatic. The infant will have to go through many struggles to achieve this psychic safety, and few of us achieve it with any stability. In very unfavourable cases the 'bad' is split off and denied, through projection, and forms no part of the ego or self. Unfortunately, the child is unable entirely to spit out or reject the bad, because the 'bad' mother is as much a product of his own aggressive feelings as she is of the real mother's actual failings, in that she is a container for the projections of those bad feelings which he wants to disown. In a very crucial sense, he needs the 'bad' mother as much as he needs the 'good' mother in that the 'bad' leaves the 'good' free of both the infant's aggression and the real mother's failings – she is therefore good enough to eat (from). We will have to examine what the infant requires if he is to integrate those sadistic aspects of his 'self' and 'mother' which will mitigate the necessity of continuing to split off and deny them. As I said above, this is not something that any of us can fully achieve. However, every survivor does it to some extent. To the extent that men fail, women will remain, in our unconscious, objects of hatred and fear whom we need to control and oppress just as we did, in fantasy, as infants.

Apart from any other motives, the child uses the basic defences of denial, splitting, projection and its opposite, introjection (a psychic equivalent of eating good things) to ward off anxiety – the anxiety that the bad will destroy the good, which would, of course, result in his death. With the increasing strength of his own capacities for testing reality – the so-called ego functions – the infant begins to realize that the opposing images and the feelings connected with them are part and parcel of the same real person.

To some extent this reality-testing leads to an adaptation of his fantastic conception of the mother so that it accords more with his newly acquired information about her. This does not, however, lead to the total destruction of the 'witch', or to the complete mitigation and integration of the sadistic feelings which belong to the infant. Even in the most favourable cases (where the mother is very responsive to the child and the child's needs, desires and impulses are not overwhelming or uncontrollable) the 'witch', and the sadistic feelings which in part give rise to her, are driven into the deep unconscious. There they find a soul mate in the residues of the 'princess', which are also repressed after a large part of the love and desire which gives rise to her have formed the conscious basis of the ego or self.

It is not possible for the infant totally to resolve or reconcile these opposed images through the means which are normally available to adults – thinking, and the tolerance of conflict and psychic pain. In so far as they become resolved, they become resolved through a process of emotional reconciliation. To some extent a 'bad' mother containing much of the child's own fear and hatred, and still an unconscious focus for these destructive feelings, is repressed at this stage of development – with significant implications for the child's adult relations with women, and his feelings about himself and his internal world. Whatever the residues, the relationship between the child and the 'witch' persists into adult life and operates largely internally, in most cases, rather than externally. This is a somewhat tentative statement, as we shall see from later evidence about the scale of partner-battering by men (see Chapter 8). We could interpret it as meaning that such an internal relationship is actually acted out by a great proportion of men, but I will argue that this would result in far more spouse murders than there actually are.

To the extent that the infant can cope with these contradictory images and tolerate the pain involved in coming to terms with the harsh reality that the mother whom he loves and who keeps him alive through her love is also the mother whom he hates and fears (Benjamin [1990] calls this the *rapprochement* phase) and is felt to hate him, his identification with her, both conscious and unconscious, will be more reality-based. The good loved one will be associated with less desperation and idealism, and the hatred of the bad one will be less fearful, enabling him to be on better terms with his own aggressive feelings – less fearful because he will realize that she can survive an attack of his anger, and – perhaps more importantly – so can he. Such an outcome is possible only if the love is stronger than the hate – if the 'good' mother is more powerful than the 'bad' mother. Whatever the particular circumstances, every individual has eventually to face the loss of the idealized 'good' mother or 'princess'. The reaction to this loss is crucial for the future integrity of the individual. We can, however, be sure that this is an extremely painful experience for everybody and leaves a lifelong potential, which can vary from mild to totally debilitating, for reacting badly to loss and separation.

The continuing process of development provides ample opportunity for the child to test the reality of his image of his mother, and his increasing capacity for thinking enables him to relate to her as a real person. One crucial consequence of this capacity is the severe blow the child receives when he realizes that his omnipotence is, after all, a fantasy, and that he cannot actually control his mother. Such crises – and there are others, as we shall see – threaten his fragile ego with eruptions of 'witch' and 'princess' from his unconscious, but his increased capacity for integrating information is a resource which he did not possess when he was first confronted with these primitive and powerful images. In fact, it is the repeated struggles between his fantasy and reality which enable him eventually to complete the process of repression and begin coming to terms with the feelings of rage and grief which are provoked by the loss of the 'princess' and his growing awareness of his own impotence.

Psychologically, the process of development can be seen as a sort of steeplechase which is run against the clock. Along the way there are a number of hurdles to clear if we are to reach the finishing line. To some extent all of us who survive clear all the hurdles but, equally, not all of them are cleanly overcome. In psychological terms this means that these stages leave various marks on the personality. For example they influence the way we later deal with problems (what might be called character traits), but – and perhaps more importantly – they also become, in so far as they remain unresolved or incompletely overcome, 'places' to which we can return under certain conditions of stress. For example, the splitting stage – technically known as the paranoid–schizoid position – if regressed to under stress, would lead signs of a so-called schizoid illness. The stage where the 'witch' and 'princess' are tested against reality – the depressive stage – when the child realizes that they are one and the same person, would, if regressed to, lead to the development of a depressive illness. Each of these stages leaves behind it the feelings and desires which are appropriate for a child at this point in his development, and their intensity cannot be overestimated. We shall look at other important stages later, but for the moment it is necessary to comment on one in particular: the oedipal phase of development.

THE OEDIPUS COMPLEX IN THE LITTLE BOY

Freud and others have shown that from the age of about three the child begins to experience his love for his mother – or, more generally, his sexuality – in a rather more specifically genital way than hitherto. The child, in fantasy, wants to be the father of her children. In the simplest possible terms, this desire brings him into direct rivalry with his father. Little boys of this age express their great desire to 'marry mummy when I grow up'.

Schematically – I will go into more detail below – this Oedipus complex is resolved – or dissolved, as Freud (1925) puts it – when the child discovers that his mother does not possess a penis. This discovery terrifies the child because he imagines that this is what will become of him – that is, his father will cut off his penis – if he does not relinquish his desire for his mother. Partly, of course, this is a projection of his own sadistic wishes, and of aspects of the 'witch' into his father.

The crucial factor is the child's knowledge that his mother lacks a penis, and the wholly mistaken deduction that this lack is due to his mother's having been castrated by his father during lovemaking. Of course, when the boy makes this deduction he is totally ignorant of what this act involves; he simply knows that something interesting and exciting is going on between his parents, and he has an idea that it involves violence on the part of his father towards his mother. This fantasy of violence in the primal scene is a product of the boy's own violent feelings towards the couple derived from his feelings of rejection, betrayal and jealousy. This is not to ignore – and Freud (1925) pointed it out – that the actual sight of parental intercourse could lead to this perception. On this faulty premiss the boy builds the conclusion that if he adopts the passive/female position with his father he, too, will be castrated. Whatever the actual physical reality this involves, for the child it symbolizes a massive paralysing loss – not only of physical capacities but also of intellectual and cognitive functioning.

As a result of this anxiety about losing his penis – castration anxiety – the child begins the process of identifying with his father and relinquishing his mother. During this process the child increasingly sees his mother as a castrated man, and she becomes an object of contempt because she lacks a penis which, by this time in his development, has become an object of veneration: the phallus, which is more than just his penis. It also stands for his father's power over his mother, and his position in the outside world.

This account of the boy's sexual development has a great deal to recommend it. Functionally, the boy's contempt for the castrated woman paves the way for his final development as a male by enabling him to identify with his father. This identification (during what Freud – wrongly – supposed to be a sexually quiescent latency phase) allows his fragile 'gender identity' to become more firmly established. Gender identity is the individual's sense of themselves as belonging to a particular sex. Boy children seem to go through three different phases of developing such a crucial aspect of the self: the first when they identify that they are, say, John; the second when they identify that they are a boy; and the third when they discover that being a boy means liking to do certain things with people they know to be girls. The most important phase, in terms of heterosexual behaviour and for relations with the opposite sex, is the third (Greenson, 1964). A crucial question which remains is why the child should choose, from all the potential reactions, to feel contempt rather than, say, sorrow or concern for his mother because she lacks a penis.

This contempt has its roots in the boy's earlier relations with his mother. As I pointed out above, during the period of development up to and including his realization that the 'princess' and the 'witch' are the same person, the child lives with the experience of his omnipotence in relation to his power to conjure up the 'princess' at will, on the one hand, and his total impotence at the hands of the 'witch' on the other. The loss of his omnipotence with the onset of reality-testing is a more or less cruel blow as he learns to struggle with the reality, to all intents and purposes, of his parents' omnipotence. It seems to me that the boy's contempt for his 'castrated' mother, whatever its functional value for his masculine development, rests on a reversal of his earlier feelings of impotence in relation to her. She is now impotent because she lacks the all-powerful phallus – she is castrated. Whereas she once possessed all the 'good' things of life and frustrated him by keeping control of and withholding them, he now reverses the situation by seeing himself, a male, as having the 'good' thing – the penis – and her, a female, as being deprived. In a reversal of an earlier state of affairs the penis, therefore, inherits all the power of the breast.

Stoller (1975) describes how this reversal from impotence to omnipotence and disaster to triumph, or masochism to sadism, can influence sexual fantasy and, in particular, perversion. His highly readable and scholarly work does not, in my opinion, go far enough. Stoller does say that he believes no man ever has sexual intercourse, even with someone he loves, without hostility, but he still confines himself to a description of sexuality and perversion without taking too close a look at 'normal' sexuality and heterosexual relations. My Preface and the case studies I shall present in Chapter 8 show quite clearly that even normal heterosexual relations are characterized more by sadism inflicted by men on women than by love.

The stage is now set for the boy's initiation into the penis-based hierarchy, and needs only the identification with his father to complete the process. Thus the basis of the Oedipus complex, with the attendant splitting, is already established when the complex proper arises with the boy's desire to possess his mother genitally. This first develops during the earliest period of the child's relationship with his mother when he wishes to possess her orally. He wishes to devour her and keep her inside himself, so that he can control her and never suffer the pain of separation or deprivation.

His realization that he cannot do this, and the development of the internal ' witch' object as a repository for his own destructiveness, lead to feelings of homicidal sadistic rage (although Melanie Klein believed that this is derivative of primary envy and the death instinct). The inevitable frustration of his oral desires, and his fear of this internal witch and his own destructiveness, provide the basis for his eventually relinquishing his mother, and for his perception that in any case she is not worth the pain of so much desire. In effect, he cannot tolerate the pain of his failed symbiosis and later dependency, and he devalues the object to avoid both the envy and the pain of the failure. I believe this is the only way to account satisfactorily for the 'normal contempt' (Freud, 1925) which boys develop for women, which overlays the 'wounds' the child experienced at the hands of the 'bad' 'witch' mother, and his hate-filled destructive impulses towards her.

I hope I have succeeded in showing that misogyny is a ubiquitous phenomenon with deep psychological roots which are common to all human beings in their early physical and emotional development. Every human being has had to confront the most primitive feelings of sadistic destructiveness towards his or her mother during the earliest years, when he or she was least fitted for the task. These feelings are rarely more than partially resolved. This is especially so for men; as we shall see in Chapter 7, women resolve them differently. Before I go on to analyse these roots more closely I must explore one more fundamental issue concerning male attitudes to women: I must describe and account for the role of romance or romanticism in adult sexual life. This is a crucial issue, in that a sustained romantic attitude would be a direct contradiction of the idea of universal male misogyny. Yet literature – particularly fairy tales and mythology – is full of examples of such attitudes.

Now, therefore, I would like to examine the consequences of the infantile splitting of the mother into 'witch' and 'princess' and see how the unconscious good and bad images are developed, and what influence they have, during the male child's growth into manhood, on the adult man's relations with women.

3 Falling in Love

In Chapter 2 I stated my belief that the male infant makes a decision never again to allow a woman to have the degree of power over him that he experienced his mother to have during his early life. Dorothy Dinnerstein (1976), whose views I broadly share, makes a similar point. She also makes the salient point – which I endorse – that men, in making this decision, are actually renouncing the opportunity for the deep feeling inherent in heterosexual love by keeping it emotionally and physically superficial (p. 67). However, she lays far more stress on the ultimate costs of this decision for men, in that she sees escaping from women's – Mother's – dominion as accepting the tyranny of father rule. She also believes (in common with Benjamin, 1990) that women have an active, collusive investment in the present gender arrangements. This is the standard psychoanalytic view, and one with which I profoundly disagree. While I am conscious of the costs I am far more aware of the benefits, for men, of accepting the Law of the Father and the entry into the male freemasonry. It should be clear that I believe the notion of men as victims is profoundly undermining to attempts to help men to change. My experience is that we first need to see our role as oppressors and the power we, as men, have over women. Men are more victims of our expectations of women than we are of the male Law. It may be, as Dinnerstein says (pp. 180 ff.), that for most men acceptance of the Law represents an acceptance of the illusion of freedom based on a fear of it – a point also made by Erich Fromm. I do not, however, think this is an inevitable outcome of the oedipal drama for men. I will explain below how a more positive resolution is possible – one which involves something as close to true freedom as is achievable while we retain the notion of gender.

Unless one attributes to the infant a capacity lacking in a great many adults – decisiveness under great stress – this idea that all little boys make such a decision requires some explanation. Of course the infant does not decide in the manner of an adult. In so far as this decisive process takes place, it is more like a natural developmental process as the infant transfers his attachment to other significant people around him, including inanimate objects. Infant observation studies attest to this process of increasing detachment from the mother in both boys and girls. Such studies also describe pathological states of detachment more akin to withdrawal or infantile depression (Mahler *et al.*, 1975; Spitz, 1965). My fundamental criticism of all such studies is that while they describe, often in exquisite detail, the relationship between mothers and their children, and point up the factors involved in 'normal' development, they all fail to address – let alone account for – the universally oppressed position of women.

This criticism is not limited to child studies; it is also true of most psychoanalytic practice with adults. It is acknowledged that a 'lifelong, albeit diminishing, emotional dependence on the mother is a universal truth of human existence' (Mahler *et al.*, 1975, p. 197). Mother is taken for granted; she is part of the 'ready-to-hand'. Her status and centrality are unmatched in such studies, yet they never take into account the fact that there is a direct relationship between the cult of motherhood and the oppression and persecution of women.

I realize that there is a real difficulty for psychoanalysis in taking feminism on board. How does one integrate an avowedly political perspective into one's clinical endeavour with a suffering person? There are genuine contradictions here, and they have real impact in the consulting room. If a female patient is talking about her difficulty in mothering her own children, is it appropriate to attempt to raise her consciousness by addressing the politics of mothering and the oppression of women? In working therapeutically with a male patient who physically abuses women, is it appropriate to attempt to raise his consciousness by informing him how his behaviour is connected with other forms of men's oppression of women, or to continue passively to wait for him to raise material which affords the opportunity to make links between his male role-learning and his present behaviour? What is most therapeutic may not be dynamic psychotherapy or psychoanalysis.

I am not suggesting that these are impossible tasks or insurmountable problems, but they are not the task of analytic therapy, and even less of psychoanalysis, which aims to alleviate distress through the discovery or reconstruction (some would say creation) of the history of the patient's development (to which I would add: 'as a gendered subject'). It is not part of the therapist's task to make moral judgements, or to parent the patient. This does not, of course, mean that the analyst or therapist does not set limits to acting out at certain stages of the process. This, however, is usually a very carefully considered intervention, and its consequences for the relationship must be thoroughly worked through. Joel Kovel (1981) argues passionately that the issues raised by feminist discourse have never been effectively addressed in the analytic community. He sees psychoanalysis as a discourse which contributes to present gender arrangements rather than simply observing them. Although he agrees that it has been influenced by feminism, he believes it has failed to recognize that 'social practice . . . is a dialectical play of forces within which . . . analytic activity . . . sustains one side or the other. Analysts . . . always seemed to support the patriarchy . . . a nature represented by woman against which the male struggles and dominates' (p. 17).

In this context I believe one can make an even stronger criticism of the efficacy of analysis or analytic therapy. This criticism concerns men's capacities to blind themselves not only to the 'real' intent of their behaviour – a problem with which all dynamically orientated therapists are familiar – but also – and, in my view, more importantly – to behaviour itself. I would like to illustrate this with an actual incident from my practice.

About halfway through his treatment, a highly successful businessman in his mid forties turned up and announced that he had left his partner. I was very surprised to hear this news, as only four weeks earlier he had been suicidally depressed after leaving the house at his partner's request following an attack on her. He had returned two weeks later after negotiating an agreement with her. He told me that he had gone home the previous day, a Sunday, three hours later than he had undertaken to cook the lunch. He said his partner was furious with him and had gone crazy in front of their thirteen-year-old daughter. Finally he had taken as much as he could stand – he packed his bags and went to the flat he had rented during his previous absence. I was suspicious about his account, and questioned him closely about this incident. He was unshakeable in his conviction that his partner was completely in the wrong to shout at him in that way in front of their daughter, although he said he could understand why she was angry, and it was not unreasonable.

Ignoring for the time being his belief that he had the right to define how and when his partner expressed anger, and the right to define what is and is not reasonable anger, I suggested that he should talk to his daughter about the incident to find out how she really felt. It was a measure of the growing success of our work that he came to his next session and informed me that his daughter had 'shocked him rigid' with the news that his partner, her mother, had not been shouting at all, but that my client had been shouting in a very frightening way, and had started to do so almost as soon as her mother had hinted at her annoyance with him for not keeping to his commitment to cook the lunch.

I could give other examples, but they would only serve to illustrate what I now believe is men's almost infinite capacity for distorting, or failing to perceive reality in, their attempts to avoid the truth about their relationships with women. To illustrate how we work with this (see Chapter 8 for a fuller description), I will simply say for now that whatever a man tells us about his partner's behaviour towards him, we ask him to describe incidents when his own behaviour towards her fits that same description. I believe that male therapists are similarly blind; indeed, I have worked with some who abuse their partners in comparable ways.

These questions raise ethical issues for therapists and analysts. Who is the patient or the client, the individual or the community? The questions are even more pertinent when the issue is child sexual abuse. Susan Schechter (1982, p. 238) says that 'in building theories . . . the challenge remains to see violent behaviour as individually willed yet socially constructed'. This is equally true of all forms of male abuse of females. To what extent are men prisoners or agents of gender?

As Joel Kovel says, feminist thinking about the politics of gender is not entirely ignored within psychoanalysis. Recent work by feminists writing from an analytic perspective – particularly Chodorow (1978, 1989) and Benjamin (1990) – take a detailed and critical look at the social and psychological reproduction of mothering. It has also become a focus for British feminists as a result of the popularizing work of Susie Orbach and Luise Eichenbaum (1982). It is fair to say, however, that a common criticism of all this work is that it assumes a gender system; it is precisely this, and its heterosexual underpinnings, that many feminists wish to challenge, not simply the unequal distribution of power between the genders.

To return to the discussion of gender bias in infant research: it is fair to say that such realities are not the express concern of infant researchers, and they all go to great lengths to disclaim any long-term predictive value for their research. Their primary concern is to understand the process of individuation (Mahler *et al.*, 1975) and to seek out the variables in mother–child relationships which might have long-term consequences for mental health. However, one cannot but be dismayed by the failure to acknowledge that, in so many cultures, femaleness is seemingly a sufficient condition for mental ill-health.

The infant does not simply move away from his mother: he also moves towards increasing self-sufficiency. I said above that this could not properly be described as a decision. I believe, however, that his entry into society proper, which involves the recognition that Mother belongs to Father, is predicated on what might be called a decision in the more normal sense. This decision is essential and, as we shall see later, it provides him with a way of dealing with his primitive, infantile sadistic impulses and feelings towards Mother. His attempt to relinquish his infantile dependency – to dis-identify from his mother (Greenson, 1968) – has both defensive and expressive qualities in that it protects him from the pain and anxiety of his primitive feelings and also expresses his pleasure in his own capacities for organizing and controlling his world. It provides the basis for developing both a sense of self as an independent person and the capacity for providing oneself with the necessities for survival without a symbiotic attachment. The evidence is that this this can also be a source of enthusiasm and elation in boys (Mahler *et al.*, 1975, p. 217). All that remains is to learn the skills necessary for this, and here the identification with the father and the educational process can provide what is needed. The decision, *qua* decision, to relinquish his mother as the object of his desire occurs during the boy's resolution of the full-blown Oedipus complex – from around the age of five to early adolescence.

The child's move away from Mother – coinciding, as it does, with increasing cognitive and physical capacities – provides a further push towards ego development and self-consciousness. The long- and short-term benefits of this are obvious. Less obvious are the long-term costs – in particular the repression of the unresolved conflicts and unmet needs of infancy, the 'unrememberable and the unforgettable' (Frank, 1969). To recapitulate, these are: primary fragmentation and chaos resulting from the failure of basic unity which led to the development of his dependency and, ultimately, to the conflict between the 'good' and 'bad' mothers; his fear of the destructiveness of his own aggression and his omnipotent belief in its invincibility; the sense of deprivation of his basic needs caused by the existence of the 'bad' mother – first to the extent that actual deprivation occurred, secondly to the extent that he was unable to feel nourished by the 'good' mother because he was still in the grip of the 'bad' mother; guilt about the destructive feelings he has towards the 'bad' mother and the attacks he carries out on her in fantasy; anxiety that his overwhelming rage will destroy his internal 'good' mother and that he will, in a sense, lay waste to himself. This passively and primarily repressed material constitutes the core of the encapsulated psychosis in the psyche of both men and women (Herman, 1988, p. 152; Mitchell, 1986, pp. 392–3).

Before we take a closer look at what it means to be in love, we must make a slight digression and examine some particular aspects of the unconscious which have a bearing on the adult proclivity to fall into this bewildering state of mind.

DEFENCES

Although some people baulk at the notion of unconscious feelings, many of us can remember instances where we have discovered that we are holding on to feelings entirely without awareness – feelings which have overtaken us with some force when we are reminded of the events which originally precipitated them. How many of us have not been in that bewildering state of anxiety which seems totally inaccessible to thought or understanding, only for it to be relieved by the sudden expression of feeling over an incident which we had apparently forgotten, or told ourselves was irrelevant or unimportant?

I do not intend to represent the unconscious simply as a rubbish bag to which we temporarily consign feelings which we find inappropriate or anxiety-provoking, in order to deal with them later – a sort of 'pending' tray. Although this is true, the unconscious is far more dynamic than such a notion would allow for. Conflicts which undergo repression do not simply cease; they continue to be active in the unconscious, and to generate the same intensity and range of feelings as conscious conflicts. In fact, one could say that the only differences between the conscious and unconscious minds are that the one – conscious – has the power to repress the other – unconscious – and the unconscious is far more powerful and primitive in its functioning. Central to our understanding of the unconscious is the notion that it is governed exclusively by what Freud (1895, p. 312) called the 'pleasure principle', whereby pain is avoided and satisfaction is sought either by acting or by fantasy. The conscious mind, by contrast, is governed by the 'reality principle', whereby wish-fulfilment, whether of a real or a hallucinatory kind, is replaced by behaviour which is adapted to reality. Our ego or conscious self, the 'I', takes reality into account when we are attempting to meet our individual needs.

Another – perhaps the most important – feature of the unconscious is that it functions according to what Freud (1900, pp. 588–609) called the 'primary process'. Freud contrasts this with the secondary processing of the ego or self. Primary processing is what the unconscious does with information about the internal and external worlds. Unlike the ego, which operates according to the reality principle and processes information using grammatical models which are logical and linear, the unconscious operates according to the pleasure principle, which is non-linear and alogical. The primary process is basic. It is older than the secondary process, and is reminiscent of pre-human activity. Its objective is simple: to satisfy any and every impulse arising within the person. Thinking, which is a secondary process, is inhibited action. Primary process obeys none of the laws of reality. Objects can stand for others on the most surprising basis: thoughts may be condensed into each other – they obey no laws of time, space or grammar. Our most familiar encounter with primary process is in our dreams.

One of the most striking features of unconscious ideas, feelings, impulses and processes is that under the influence of the pleasure principle they strive for expression in consciousness. As Freud wrote (1907, p. 35), 'the repressed will always return'. The subjective experience of unconscious material becoming – or striving to become – conscious is primarily one of anxiety. When we become anxious we begin to behave, think and feel in various stereotypical and habitual ways which are technically known as 'defences'. Some of these defences can be clearly diagnosed as pathological in that they seem a bit odd or eccentric, and obviously interfere with the person's capacity for coping with life, especially 'work', which holds a pre-eminent place in society and in the unconscious mind. For most people it represents the opportunity to be creative and to demonstrate, to oneself and others, that one is more 'good' than 'bad'. It symbolizes the constructive defeat of the 'bad world/mother' and the despair, emptiness and depression which would result from her ascendance and victory over the 'good world/mother', which could result in madness or suicide. Work is one of the primary expressions of one's need for and capacity to make reparation for one's destructiveness.

Idealization

A defence of particular interest in the context of men's relations with women, which is culturally syntonic, is idealization: the persistent overevaluation of another person and a steadfast refusal to face facts about them which contradict this overevaluation – or, if those facts are faced, an equally steadfast refusal to accord them their true significance and form a more realistic assessment of the person. A common notable example of idealization is the acclaim accorded to people in public life by their fans – the 'star' syndrome. Another notable example is the state we call 'being in love'. This romantic state is, in itself, idealized in Western culture – it is presented to girls by their mothers (not necessarily overtly) as a state to be sought after, pursued, planned for and envied in others. Against this – one element of the patriarchy's efforts to reproduce heterosexuality and the 'normal' nuclear family – one must set feminist criticism of this aspiration (Radway, 1983; Snitow, 1979) and the evidence of a trend indicating that young women are becoming more orientated to pursuing careers and having children later.

In fact the feminist examination of all works of literature, both historical and contemporary, has always been – and remains – an important feminist agenda. Many of the best-known feminist texts are the product of literary scholars such as Kate Millett (1977). One can see, without much effort, the value which 'being in love' has for the preservation of the species. It brings together members of the opposite sex to procreate and rear children. Set against this, as we have seen, is the view that being in love is one of the most outrageous confidence tricks ever perpetrated by men on women. Romance has been the subject of intense analysis by feminists. It is well known that romantic fiction for women has an enormous market, one that increases every year. Feminists have had to subject the Mills and Boon style of fiction to intense critical analysis in an attempt to understand the grip it exercises on the female imagination. For apocalyptic, revolutionary feminists, 'love' (the construction of female desire) is a foundation stone of the male ideology of heterosexuality, which they see as the fundamental organizing principle of the male control of women's sexuality. This has led many radical feminists to adopt lesbianism as a political statement. Unfortunately for many feminists, the contradictions between their deeply held political convictions and their lived experience of continued 'desire' for men are difficult to reconcile. This is one of the reasons why many turned to psychoanalysis in an effort to understand 'desire'. As we shall see, I have little doubt that historically this too was – and continues to be – shaped by men.

The romantic ideal of love is, in essence, a state of idealization. In a very important sense 'being in love' is, as Freud pointed out (1910), the exchange of two fantasies. Breuer, Freud's co-author, likened being in love to being in a pathogenic, hypnoid state (Freud and Breuer, 1893, p. 118). In Chapter 7 we will look at the fantasy life of women, and at the nature of a woman's fantasy when she is 'in love'. My concern now is to inquire into the origins of the man's fantasy of the woman he loves. Does it spring into being like a newborn child or is it, instead, a long-cherished image to which the adult is deeply attached? Since Freud first made the observation (1910, pp. 179–90) it has become a commonplace to observe that every man is seeking his mother in a prospective partner. This is a partial truth which conceals a deeper one. In the scheme of things presented here, the fantasy the man overlays on the woman is the infantile image of the 'good' mother – an idealized image stripped of any negative characteristics.

This is why 'being in love' can be such a wonderful experience in the early stages. The overwhelming impulse is to break down all boundaries between oneself and the object of one's love. If it were possible, lovers would physically merge with each other. Every separation is a painful experience. How similar this must be to the experience of the infant in relation to the 'good' mother – she appears, and the world is good and secure; she disappears, and it becomes frightening and unsafe because she, who contains all goodness, takes it with her when she goes. Later, of course, a third element enters this equation: the father, to whom she takes all the goodness; a figure for jealousy, fear and hatred. For the infant it really is all or nothing – he cannot, because he does not possess the cognitive equipment, know that his mother may be in the next room and will come back – she is either present or absent.

The desire to absorb – or be absorbed by – the mother arises from both the intensity of the love the infant feels and his fear of being abandoned by her. If he could permanently enrich himself by making her his, by eating her or being eaten by her, then he need never be afraid of losing her. At the same time, this impulse to devour the mother also expresses the infant's oral-sadistic impulses towards the 'witch'. Unfortunately, this wish to devour, which expresses such intense love, also largely accounts for the profound anxieties about being devoured by the 'bad' mother in that it is mainly through the projection of these sadistic impulses, in an effort to keep the 'good' mother safe, that the 'bad' mother, even as an empty space, becomes so terrifying. The idealization of the 'good' mother, which is accompanied by the splitting off of the 'bad' mother and the denial of the source of the sadism, is continued in the unconscious. Adult idealization always involves the denial of intense and terrifying sadism and persecutory feelings, as well as feelings of impoverishment. The more intense the sadism – and it is a natural and universal human attribute – the more intense the idealization. Idealized love has a quality of desperation accompanied by a great fear of anger which might signify the return of the repressed sadism and persecutory anxiety.

One of the inevitable costs of idealization is the loss of self-esteem which follows from projecting into another person all the desirable and good parts of the self. The fear of the loss of this person is therefore magnified in that she will take with her the most valuable parts of the self. It is beyond question that such feelings are primitive and infantile; they are, however, everyday currency for lovers in the romantic stage of a relationship, regardless of the lack of concordance with the real character of the person to whom they are directed. This is quite simply because they are the infantile perceptions of the 'good' mother which have been de-repressed. The 'good' mother is also an idealized image. To some extent, the infant idealizes the mother for the same reasons that adults idealize others – to avoid guilt and depression about destructive feelings towards the object. Infantile idealization, however, is very different from the adult equivalent of love – not only because the infant does not possess the mental equipment to do anything else, but also because there are qualitative differences between adult and infantile love. The latter is essentially devouring and possessive. It lacks concern for the object as a person: the only concern is for the self. Adult love, on the other hand, contains concern for the other, and not simply for utilitarian motives. It is characterized by mutuality, reciprocity and respect for the individuality and separateness of the loved one. Adult love has the potential to survive ambivalence in a way which is impossible for infantile, idealized love.

OMNIPOTENCE

Although it was implied above, it is necessary at this point to amplify that the 'good' mother is, to some extent, a product of the infant's omnipotence. He is unable to distinguish cause and effect in the way that an adult can, and he assumes that he wishes her into existence (M. Klein, 1952, p. 65). It might be more accurate to say that he does not assume that he has not wished her into existence. To the extent that she is good, he creates her by wanting her to exist. This may seem paradoxical, like so many other assertions about the deepest psychological processes, yet it is not so difficult to understand. If the infant experiences a need, and the mother appears and meets this need as a result of the infant's signals, what could be more natural than the magical belief that the infant has control over her? It also seems, at first glance, to contradict all that has been said about the 'bad' mother, for if the infant believes he creates the 'good' mother, why does he not simply create her all the time and keep away the 'bad' mother? Partly, of course, this is precisely what the infant attempts to do as he psychologically takes the 'good' mother in (introjection). To the extent that the real mother is responsive and adaptive to the infant, this internalized fantasy 'good' mother will be effective in warding off the 'bad' mother, for a time, when the infant feels distress. Of greater importance, however, is the fact that the environment cannot ever be totally satisfying to the infant. All babies will be frustrated at some time, and painful experiences are unavoidable.

I should like to digress a little here and take up the issue of whether the infant's sadistic impulses are innate or reactive to frustration and deprivation at the hands of a primary carer who actually does have homicidal and sadistic feelings towards him. This will prove important later, when we look at male violence towards women. We may never know the true answer to this question – in any case, truth is 'man'-made – but whatever position one takes has significant social policy implications with respect to the treatment meted out to women by men and by male-dominated institutions such as the state, and the legal and medical professions. One must also add that it has profound implications for the profession of psychotherapy (see Masson, 1989) which certainly challenge its present forms of practice.

To anticipate the chapter on violence (Chapter 7): if one assumes that male violence is a reaction to frustration, this inevitably dictates that one will see men as being ultimately victims of women – or Mother. This will provide, at best, a justification for men's violence, and at worst a redefinition of male violence in terms of their impotence. In the treatment of such violence this will mean that the violence itself will not be defined as the problem. The impotence will be seen as causative, and treatment outcomes will be defined in these terms rather than in terms of the violence. This is no mere playing with words. Work in the USA shows quite clearly that this is the case (Adams, 1988, pp. 176–200). I would like to state categorically that I believe male violence towards women is primarily an expression of, and the product of, men's sadistic feelings towards them, even though these may be complicated by many other feelings, including impotence. I also believe that these sadistic feelings reflect, in part, actual sadism in the primary carer whom we call Mother, which derives from her own feelings of neglect and maltreatment at the hands of men, and her real powerlessness, as a sex, to effect beneficial changes in her real environment. These issues are too important for psychoanalysts and psychotherapists to protest scientific neutrality. Psychotherapy and psychoanalysis aspire to moral neutrality, but they are not value- or gender-free: this would require that they be a product of something other than human language.

Whether one believes that all aggression is induced by frustration or is innate, the fact is that aggressive – indeed sadistic – feelings, are inevitable, and the infant will split the world into good and bad in order to cope with these feelings. This issue always arises in clinical practice. The client wants to know if he is innately sadistic and bad, or whether his sadism is a response to bad treatment. In my experience this question is largely irrelevant. The fact is that whatever their origins, his sadistic impulses are now as fairly and squarely in his internal world as his behaviour is in the external. The originally bad and frustrating experience is part of him and its continuation, including the internalized sado-masochistic relationship with the 'witch', is his responsibility. The 'bad' mother becomes a product of the infant's fantasies, even though such fantasies are based on real experiences with (perhaps in most cases, of) his mother.

Although we can never know the truth of its origins, the dominant – Kleinian – approach in psychoanalysis and analytic psychotherapy makes the assumption that the intensity of his homicidal, evil impulses will, in the vast majority of cases, be a function of the strength of the child's aggressive feelings. This is not true, however, of all analysts (see the work of Alice Miller); and indeed the so-called Independent or Middle Group of British analysts have long emphasized the importance of the real environment. It is not germane to my thesis to go into this in any detail, but it is important not to minimize the continuing debate in the analytic community about the interaction between fantasy and reality (Masud Khan, 1986; Scott, 1988). Winnicott's concept of the 'good-enough mother' is central to this concern, for she is no mere fantasy, a figment of the infantile imagination. He also emphasized the mother's role as a protective shield for the child against external impingement. Not surprisingly, the mother as primary carer is the main source of impingement, and it makes sense to assume that homicidal feelings actually mirror her own feelings towards the child.

Of course, the child's omnipotence is also at work in his method of dealing with the 'witch'. He attempts to split her off and deny her existence. He assumes the same sort of control over her in fantasy as he has of the 'princess'. In short, the child comes to need the 'bad' mother as much as he needs the 'good' one. She is the container for his own sadistic, homicidal impulses towards the unified mother.

As we shall see, the adult state of 'being in love' quite faithfully reproduces the infantile processes of splitting and idealization, although there are some important differences in consequences. Before we examine those differences, we must explain and account for the de-repression of the internal, idealized 'good' mother which takes place in order to allow the exchange of fantasies which we call 'falling in love'.

THE RE-EMERGENCE OF THE GOOD MOTHER

Biological Pressures

There seem to be a number of forces at work within the individual which predispose him to the re-emergence of his split, infantile image of his mother. The sexual drive is the most obvious, as one of the two most powerful and urgent biological imperatives. In men, as we shall see, this drive can be used or expressed in many different contexts. It is a commonplace observation that men sexualize a great many of their non-sexual needs and feelings, and seem dominated by the urge to conquer and penetrate women. Many men indulge in behaviour which, in a woman, would result in her being stigmatized by a variety of epithets – none of which has any male equivalent – such as slag, slut, nympho, easy lay, and so on. Men may assert that this attitude has biological origins, but it seems far more probable that it is derived from men's need to control women's sexuality, and is culturally produced and enforced. Be that as it may, the sexual drive is imperative, and at the time of its emergence in young adulthood it urges most of us, male and female, towards forming relationships and bonds with members of the opposite sex. By this time the sexual drive has been subjected to intense cultural and psychological pressure. Heterosexuality is, generally speaking, unquestionably accepted as normal, although many adolescents will have quite a struggle with a resurgent bisexuality for the satisfaction of which there will be no support. The ultimate biological aim of the heterosexual bonding process is to procreate, although there are many obstacles to be overcome before this is achieved.

How is it that the biological imperative evokes this infantile imago of the idealized mother, or 'princess'? The adolescent boy's sensual capacities are awakened by the release of hormones, but those hormones are not object-attached. In fact, they are indifferent to the object of satisfaction, and according to the primary process, an inanimate object will do as well as any other. It can only be that this reawakening of his sexuality – this time with the physical capacity for sexual fulfilment – re-evokes the memory of the first object with whom such feelings were originally awakened. This observation is borne out with adult men in the psychotherapeutic relationship. Time and again one hears how a boy's sexual feelings at the onset of puberty were attached to his mother, and of the struggles he went through to find more appropriate objects for satisfaction (for his initial account, see Freud, 1905, pp. 207–30). In my experience with male patients, most of them have as their first masturbatory object, in all consciousness, their mother.

Psychological Pressures

Added to the biological urges are the psychological pressures which are at work in the individual – I will leave aside, for the moment, the extent to which these pressures are responses to the biological imperative. Many writers have commented on the essential 'aloneness' of human existence, and many terms are used to describe what is presumed to be a universal experience: from 'alienation' to 'existential loneliness'. Man is a relating animal. We need other people for a variety of reasons, and will persist in seeking the company of others even if it proves chronically painful and difficult. Most people experience the presence of others as nourishing – other things being equal – and as going some way towards mitigating the quiet despair which all of us, to some degree, experience as a result of our 'existential loneliness'.

Such loneliness is universal. However, people are not born with the experience – it is not innate. What is innate is the predisposition to it, and the universal experience of maturation from infantile fusion precipitates this predisposition into an actuality. The original experience of being a person is not one of existential loneliness – on the contrary, it is one in which we can presume that boundaries between 'I' and 'thou', 'me' and 'the world', or infant and mother do not exist. Strictly speaking, it is not an experience of 'being' at all; to be myself I have to be 'other' than and separate from you, and we can assume that an infant's early experience is one of basic unity with the primary object. From the point in his life when the infant is aware of sensation he probably has what Freud called an 'oceanic' feeling of bliss (1930, pp. 64–72). One would not suggest that this feeling is one of unsullied bliss, but that for most babies the experience of the womb and, later, the experience of being fed and held and cuddled is blissful: the security of never having to doubt that all is in order in the world, and that it will provide what I want and need merely *because* I want and need it. The world must be a blissfully benign place.

Who can wonder that we should want to return to such a state of things, at least in an adult version, when all of us have lost it – a loss which leaves us all in a lifelong struggle with the attendant feelings of anxiety, dependency and vulnerability? We lose it even if we are successful in integrating the 'good' and 'bad' worlds/ mothers – its loss is a precondition of growing up and becoming a person. To make it absolutely clear: the loss of this 'good' symbiotic attachment is universally painful and we all, men and women alike, live with the loneliness that a separate sense of 'self' involves, and with the feeling that it was not always so. We all experience that to some extent our basic needs were frustrated and we all, to the extent to which this is true, had to cope with a 'bad world/mother' whom we cannot acknowledge emotionally to be the same person with whom we experienced those blissful feelings of oceanic oneness. The essential human experience is of 'incompleteness, impairment and loss' (Moberley, 1987, p. 96). The fall from grace is no mere theological abstraction.

When Thoreau coined his now famous remark 'All men lead lives of quiet desperation' (perhaps he had never heard of women) I am sure that what he had in mind was our awareness of our existential loneliness – which comes about as the result of the loss of the oceanic bliss with the 'good' mother and the later oedipal-phase decision to renounce our dependency on her – to dis-identify.

The denial of his basic softness and vulnerability which this renunciation involves will haunt man for the rest of his life – he is caught between the unfulfilled – and unfulfillable – regressive needs of childhood and the demands of adult masculinity. The paradox, as we shall see, is that one of the most compelling reasons why men cling to their masculinity is because they are so afraid of the impulse to merge with the mother, and that this fear is one of the major motives for their assuming masculinity in the first place. One of the major demands of masculinity is that one should not be a child or have the needs of a child, especially the dependency needs. The despair experienced as a result of this conflict between being a child and being a man will vary individually as a function of the extent of the 'real' nurturing and goodness of a man's childhood and the external pressures and stresses of his adult life. Under sufficient stress any man will regress, whereas some will regress under less and, indeed, rather ordinary stress.

There are clear differences between the male and the female in the way in which they reach sexual maturity. These derive largely from the demands which culture imposes on our children – particularly the demand for heterosexuality. Whereas, for the man, growing up involves identifying with the father and renouncing (dis-identifying from) the mother, for the woman it involves identifying with the mother and seeing the father/man as her potential mate and father of her children. The girl child has to change the object of her desire. We shall see later how this difference occurs. One of its obvious consequences is that the woman, in a sense, has to contain her own mother, whereas for the man the mother is always outside him. There can be little doubt that women, as a consequence of role-learning and the adoption of femininity, are much better able, in general, to care for themselves and others. Little girls are raised to be carers in adult life. This view – which has become the central principle of what has become known as feminist-object relations theory – was first promulgated in the UK by Orbach and Eichenbaum (1982). Their central recommendation for change in prevailing gender power structures was shared parenting of children (a view first put forward by Chodorow in 1978, and repeated in 1989). They believe that women's exclusive role in – and what they see as men's unconscious resistance to – parenting is the basis of men's power over women. Although it is widely credited with having problematized mother–daughter relationships as the source of women's 'compulsory caretaking', object-relations theory has also been criticized as reductionist and apolitical.

Although women are more vulnerable by virtue of their superior empathic capacities, which are also part of the female caring role, they are generally more resilient than men. I have no illusions that this is innate: women simply have no choice – this is what it means to be a woman. To those who doubt women's resilience or empathy, or ask 'If that's so why do so many more women than men get emotionally disturbed?', I can say only that a far smaller proportion of single women than married women get disturbed, and that women who stay single live far longer than married women; the evidence is very convincing that marriage makes women ill – the opposite statistics are true for men. Disraeli's advice that 'all women should marry and no man should' could not be less true or more chauvinistically self-serving. Some feminists have advised that men should carry a warning to the effect that 'This product can damage women's health!'

All this is not to say that women do not experience the same 'quiet desperation' as men. Indeed, it seems probable that their despair is greater still, given that the major demand made upon them is to give to others that which they so painfully experience being deprived of themselves – 'good' mothering. It is tragic to imagine a lonely, deprived child having to mother real children – and men who act like children – in ways which can enable them to grow up securely. This is clearly an impossible situation for both mother and child. It is in this conflict within the mother that the realistic basis for the infant's sadistic 'bad' mother fantasy may arise. The deprived and unhappy child within her will inevitably interfere with her capacity to provide 'realistic' good mothering, whatever the fantasy life of the infant she mothers. In any case, this infant would still develop a fantasy 'bad' mother. This conflict inevitably produces strong guilt feelings in women because it is impossible to live up to the learned expectations of being a perfect mother: the expectation of permanent and unconditional self-sacrifice and positive regard for her children. There is little doubt that men – through both personal and social pressures – provoke and use this guilt to maintain their subjugation. Adrienne Rich (1976) was the first to draw attention to women's oppression as mothers, and to men's appropriation of motherhood from women.

The public-work/private-home dichotomy has been the basis of a large body of feminist analysis during the last twenty years. This analysis took up what had been a central principle for structuralist sociologists: the universality of sexual asymmetry (Rosaldo and Lamphere, 1974). Even from a non-feminist structuralist perspective, it makes grim reading. This is a man's world. The public spaces belong to men. The world of work is predominantly for men. The private spaces are supposedly the preserve of women. The home is an icon of maternal care. It is the one place where women are the rulers, but only so long as they rule for men's benefit. Mothering – the quintessentially caring activity, as men would have it – is the essence of womanliness. Combined with most women's desire (socially structured or otherwise) to have children, it becomes a powerful weapon of sexual control for men (Chodorow, 1978).

These processes create enormous differences in the meaning and experience of falling in love for men and for women. For women this love undoubtedly contains several elements of the original symbiotic fantasy of the 'good' mother. It also contains a great deal of the more mature relationship with the 'good' father which develops out of the oedipal-phase decision to identify with the mother. (This is a slight digression from the main point of this chapter, but it will greatly strengthen my general point if I refer the reader to Freud, 1914, particularly pp. 88–9. It would be difficult to find a better-argued case for women's sexual and moral inferiority. Whatever Freud's route to this conclusion – and it was predetermined by his phallocentric definition of the problem – it simply drips with chauvinistic contempt, masquerading as faint praise, for women.) In any case, this decision to identify with Mother and submit to the power structure simply reinforces what seems to be the primary identification for all of us, but one which men have to renounce. Merging with the mother holds terrors for girls, but they are not the same terrors as men feel. For men, it would undermine the essential quality of our identity, our gender as males. The erect penis is a rock of stability to which most can turn in times of stress.

The desire to repeat, as it were, the original symbiotic experience is not in itself, however powerful, enough to explain the de-repression of the original princess 'imago'. It provides the motivation, but given that this was also present when the repression took place, there must be other factors which can undo the repression itself. Amongst these, certainly, are the fundamental biological differences between a post-pubescent male and an infant male: the hormonal activities, the eroticization of the genitals together with the – now psychically established – heterosexual desires to penetrate the female and impregnate her. These biological factors, however, also apply to animals and there is no reason to think that they feel the need to form lasting relationships in order to satisfy such purely sexual urges. The question here is how men structure, subjectivize, experience and adapt to social demands. It would be stretching credibility to believe that these demands - which, on the whole, disadvantage women - could have originated at the behest of women (Cucchiari, 1981).

What psychological factors are involved, then, in falling in love? The human need for completion is of primary importance. Quite simply, people do not like loose ends, and here we are talking about a loose end which influences the whole of one's life. The desire to repeat the - at best - initially disappointing situation is motivated by the wish to make it different this time, because we are aware that its unfinished quality is a major block to self-fulfilment and maturity. This may, of course, be only a partial awareness that does not amount to explicit knowledge - for most people it may be experienced simply as a desire to fill the existential hole left by the loss of the 'good world/mother' fantasy in its oceanic, blissful form: the loss of basic unity. The man's wish is to make the 'other' - woman - into self.

Unfortunately, it seems that most men operate, in this re-enactment, from the unconscious position that it will be different this time because the woman will play her role in the way he thinks it should have been played the first time round. She will not turn into the 'bad', rejecting and absent, indifferent mother who takes away her body full of good things, possibly to somebody else, and returns full of projected hostile - possibly homicidal - impulses towards the child. Nor will she have overriding needs of her own, including actual persecutory ones, which force him to cope with her 'otherness' before he feels ready - if he ever will. This time the infant/adult's 'falling in love' will succeed, where it first failed, in preventing the 'bad' mother's appearance.

This 'unconscious' blaming of the original mother and the refusal or inability - either because of fear for the self or lack of knowledge, or for other reasons - to see his own contribution and face up to the conflicts which he originally repressed is the source of many tragedies in the life of the male (see Chapter 5). The word 'blaming' is used in the passive sense here; obviously, at the time of the repression, notions such as responsibility have no meaning for the infant, and this is the case when the de-repression occurs. A crucial difference does exist in the adult's capacity for thinking and testing reality. This is of fundamental importance if he is ever to mitigate his fear and hatred of the feminine through the tolerance of the pain of his original loss, and his frustration of his wish to be absorbed by his mother.

By this time the young adult will also have been subjected to many years of education and indoctrination about the role of women and the relation between the sexes. He will have learned that normative masculine expectations of women support his own predisposition to have power and control over them. He will have learned by this time his culture's verbal language, which will be masculine. (See Spender, 1980; Shute, 1981: 'eliminating sexist language is necessary for eliminating sexism in any society'. The idea that language is itself a fundamental oppressive agent is not, however, undisputed - see Hintikka and Hintikka, 1983.) He will also have absorbed the multiple subliminal messages about women which are part of his normal culture. Spender's research demonstrated that it is normal for the teacher to ignore girls for long periods of time, but not normal for boys to be ignored; that boys call out from their seats and push each other; that girls are addressed collectively, while boys are addressed by name; that boys dominate the classroom by talking more loudly and roughly than soft-talking girls; and that boys talk for two-thirds of the time in mixed sex classrooms. Girls are an audience for boys. They learn to play a supportive role inside and outside the classroom.

Pat Mahony (1985) shows how girls are relatively invisible in classrooms, whether these are run by male or female teachers. She quotes Stanworth's (1983) research, which showed that for every four boys participating in classroom discussion, only one girl joined in. Boys asked twice as many questions as girls, and were praised three times as much by the teachers. In the classes researched, girls outnumbered boys! Teachers reported that boys are twice as likely to be model pupils. Interesting evidence shows that consciousness-raising by anti-sexism workshops for female teachers makes very little difference to such important interaction indices, even when the teacher makes a special effort to discriminate in favour of girls.

Is this simply indicative of the intractability of masculine dominance behaviour, or is it that female teachers act as males when it comes to transmitting sexist values and attitudes? Although the former is undoubtedly true, the latter also makes a contribution. To what extent is this due to the fact that women have been so indoctrinated to the supremacy of males that they now act as agents for the transmission of patriarchial attitudes and values? (See Chapter 7.)

The adult male does not begin this form of romantic attachment – falling in love – with the explicit notion that this time it will be different because he will redefine his expectations in the light of what is realistic with his partner. He rarely chooses to face the split in himself between 'good' and 'bad', and make explicit the pain and anguish, the fear and hatred, in a way which enables him to heal these divisions. Even given that such a process may take years of intermittent pain and anxiety, it seems to me that it is necessary if men wish to stop the compulsive repetition of failed relationships and be genuinely intimate with women. The alternative to self-awareness is inevitably that men will continue to act out repressed sadistic feelings towards the 'bad' mother. As we shall see when we look at male violence towards women, this is endemic and transcultural. Alternatively – or perhaps concurrently – a man can split by finding another woman and attempting to have two relationships at once. Research shows that domestic violence and infidelity are habitual for men. If you are asking which men I'm talking about, then you must be one of the only 20 to 30 per cent who, in recent studies of adultery, denied having extra-marital affairs, or the husband of one of the fortunate 60 per cent of women who denied ever being hit by their husbands – a gross overestimate according to feminist researchers who believe that physical and mental cruelty are men's stock in trade (Kelly, 1986, 1988b).

Another important psychological factor in the re-emergence of the 'good' mother fantasy is the basic human need to create. Love, however unrealistically based, is surely the most creative human activity – it is the basis of all creativity. It is a fundamental demonstration that one possesses more goodness than badness, and it would not be unjustified to describe all human activity as an attempt to create, discover or preserve goodness. The failure to create, either in love or in work, leads inevitably to the peril of anxiety, depression, and feelings of persecution.

Apart from the pleasure which the man feels at being in love – at the rediscovery of the 'good' mother – he is also engaged in the task of keeping his love intact, and as far as possible free from blemish. As we all know from more or less bitter experience, this can be a daunting task. Indeed, it seems to be impossible to preserve love in its purity and passion – even setting aside the simple effects of familiarity. For most men this struggle eventually becomes not so much one of preserving love as one of reining in one's active sadistic impulses towards one's partner. This is a task at which, all too often, men fail. The consequences of their failure are seen daily in the divorce and criminal courts and – to a larger, though less obvious, extent – in GPs' surgeries, where women receive regular prescriptions for tranquillizers and other drugs which help to keep them resigned, passive and uncomplaining (a practice much criticized in the recent anti-tranquillizer campaign which, for the first time, raised awareness of the dangers of 'mother's little helper'). The medicalization of woman's unhappiness is a much-commented-on aspect of men's control of women and their bodies. Bob Connell (1987) comments on the way in which women's resistance to domestic subordination became known as 'housewife's neurosis', thus 'depoliticising gender relations directly, while building a more mediated power-structure based on the authority of a masculine profession' (pp. 250–1).

THE FAILURE OF LOVE

Why is it so hard to preserve love? How does failure to achieve it become evident in relationships? What practical options are available to people in this predicament?

From an external point of view, the man's failure to preserve love and keep it free from the influence of his feelings towards the 'bad' mother arises not from the woman's failure to live up to his expectations, as men would have it, but from the contradictory and impossible nature of those expectations, which have been the stuff of fairy stories for as long as men have been telling them. One of the core stories concerns what I call the 'princess syndrome'. We all know how it goes: the frog, in one disguise or another, overcomes many obstacles, which represent his own ambivalence, to find the woman of his dreams and make himself complete – to fill the empty space left by the loss of the 'good' mother. The woman, or princess, is usually being held against her will by a witch, the 'bad' mother, or an evil king, the oedipal father, from whom she has to be rescued. The protagonist normally succeeds in rescuing her – he marries her and they live happily ever after. At least they say that they live happily ever after; it is impossible to tell, because the stories always end there – at the point where they have to get down to serious issues in their relationship, such as 'who does the washing-up?'

I have said that the man's failure to preserve his love depends on the impossible and contradictory nature of his demands and expectations of his 'beloved'. Why, one may ask first, does he make contradictory demands? Surely, if he wishes to preserve the princess he need only make demands appropriate to that wish, and his love would be preserved. The answer to this question is twofold. In the first place, no woman can actually cope with the demands made on a princess or a perfect/good mother – at the very least, she would need the capacity to read men's minds and anticipate their every want and need, often before the man himself is aware of them. Even if she were able and willing to do this, she would have to be willing to subordinate her sense of self totally to the man's needs and to exist solely for his gratification. Many women, perhaps even the majority, attempt to do this and feel extremely hurt, dismayed, confused and bewildered (sometimes crazy) at their eventual failure to satisfy as a fist strikes them yet again.

The second part of the answer lies in the man's character and psyche, but before looking more closely at this it will be helpful if I am more explicit about these demands. I do not pretend that the list below is by any means an exhaustive list – that alone would take up a whole volume; nor do I claim that it is original. In fact its contents are so widely known that they are almost a cliché. Not all men will readily identify with it in total, but I believe it represents the emotional background which men take into any loving relationship, however aware or unaware of it they may be. These demands constitute the core of the man's fantasy of the princess who will complete him and remove his existential loneliness at a stroke.

THE PRINCESS	*THE CONTRADICTION*
We want a mother who is a strong, independent woman.	We want a child who is totally dependent so that she can never abandon us.
We want a virgin with no sexual needs of her own.	We want a whore.
We want an intelligent woman with a mind of her own.	We want a woman who always defers to us and never bores us with her own opinions.
We want a woman to be beautiful and sexually exciting at all times.	We do not want her to be aware of her beauty or sexuality.
We want to be fed, watered, cleaned up after, etc.	We want a woman who can do all these things and look as if she has just left the beautician's.
We want a woman to bear our children.	We do not want a mother.
We want a woman who believes she'd die without us.	We don't want her to make us feel trapped or in any way responsible for her.
We want a woman who thinks we'll die without her . . .	. . . but who believes we could leave her at the drop of a hat.
We want a woman to meet our needs and be quite happy to be put away until we need her again.	. . . but not to make any demands, and never to assume that we need her, or be upset when we don't.

We want her to believe in committed relationships . . .	. . . and be quite happy that we don't commit ourselves to her.
We want a woman who can take being hated . . .	. . . but we hate her for her guilt-inducing masochism and feel contempt for it.
We want a woman who will love us whatever we do . . .	. . . but doesn't expect our love to be so unconditional.

We want a woman who wants to be possessed, and has no objections to being used in any way we see fit.

Before continuing with the answer to the question 'Why does the man make contradictory demands?' it is important to point out that the 'man as conscious adult' is in no way responsible for containing them. He is, however, responsible for acting them out in the face of all experience that they are unfulfillable, and that he causes suffering to his partners. He continues to make adult choices about this when he could choose alternative courses of action. He is not responsible for the choices he made as a child: the power structure offered him no other choice. I would not assert that every man's demands are the same; there are marked individual differences which derive from variations in personal history. That these contradictory demands can be profoundly abusive to women can be illustrated by a short case history which demonstrates how these demands are applied, and how self-deceiving men are as they apply them. This particular man was not a batterer; none the less, he had been seriously abusive for many years, simply by doing what many men do to their partners.

Paul

Paul is a very successful thirty-four-year-old professional man. He has been married to a woman ten years his senior for twelve years. Throughout the whole period of his marriage he had been conducting a chaste, idealized love affair with a business acquaintance, an older divorced woman. Two years before seeing me they had started a sexual relationship. This had broken up after two weeks because Paul could not cope with the intensity of his feelings. Since then, however, he had been unable to leave her alone, and continued to declare his love for her despite the fact that she had begun a new relationship. He told me tearfully that he believed something awful would happen to him if he did not see her every few days (it is not hard to guess what, given a dependency with this addictive intensity). He came to see me because of what he described as his obsession with her and the level of his guilt. He could hardly be in the same room with his wife without getting some quite alarming physical symptoms which, he had no doubt, were caused by guilt. He was completely at a loss to understand what all this guilt was about!

It emerged that at no time did he tell his wife about his affair, although she suspected it and confronted him; he lied to her, and told her she was imagining things. This was profoundly abusive. It makes a woman feel crazy – in fact, he was telling her she was crazy. He said that his wife treated him like a child, and he felt she was a mother to him. He then told me how he felt disgusted by her, and that he could not have sex with her because he felt – wrongly, he knew – that she was dirty. He talked of how, for the last five years, he had done almost everything alone. He always bought two tickets for theatre and concert outings, which she refused. Her account of this was that he always made her feel unwelcome; he ignored her, and was cold and unfriendly when they were out together. I asked if this was true, and he vehemently denied it. When I asked where she got that impression from, he became silent. 'Well, yea, I suppose it's right,' he said. 'I did give her that impression. I didn't want her with me.'

At this point Paul went on to tell me that ever since he met his wife he has felt that she was forcing him to be with her. He said he never wanted her, but stayed with her because she has two children from a failed marriage, and they were traumatized and needed a father. Also he is afraid that she would kill herself if he left her. (The childen had, in fact, grown up and left.) Now he hates her for what he describes as her dependency, and feels trapped by her. He has actually left her twice for a couple of days, but he was so afraid of what she might do that he has gone back. He said that at the beginning of the relationship he had been bowled over by her sexual desire for him. She wanted sex all the time, and he couldn't get enough. Now he is turned off by her sexual demands. He simply cannot take any more of her questioning him about his feelings and his intentions.

In fact she is a highly capable woman who managed to raise two children for many years without him, and is now saying that he should grow up and stay or go. His dependency, which he had always projected (as most men do) is now where it belongs – inside him – but he had transferred it to his ex-lover, where it was doomed to failure (of course it always is), but without the compensations offered by his wife. He wanted both worlds: that of the bachelor and that of the married man. Clearly, he has homicidal wishes towards his wife – mostly, as he put it, for 'getting in the way' of his satisfaction with his lover; and towards his ex-lover for betraying him with another man.

Paul began to acknowledge how he had treated his wife badly since their marriage, and how he could not understand why she puts up with it – she must lack self-respect. What did she want from him, he wondered? When I said that it was probably quite simple – that she wanted him to love and value her – he was able to acknowledge, with great distress, that that was the thing which frightened him most: 'I don't know how to love. I feel like a fraud.'

The root of these contradictions lies in man's fear of dependency and commitment, his lack of trust in femininity and his terror of his own vulnerability. They also rest on his desire to leave his mother and grow up in order to escape from these feelings, and his attendant fear that he is not mature enough to do so. He is caught between a need for security, which is based on his unfulfilled and unfulfillable infantile needs; a need for freedom from those needs; and an equally strong fear of either. The conflicts underlying these contradictions prevent the man being truly close to a woman because the impossible nature of his demands ensures that no woman can actually make the grade as far as he is concerned. Strange as it may seem, this outcome is also desirable for the man. Actually to get close would expose him to the risk of experiencing his original frustration and sadistic rage, or – even worse – the terror of the original loss of basic unity associated, through language, custom and sex roles, with the absent mother. These prospects are far more frightening than simply writing off his present partner as unsuitable.

In acting out such contradictions the man can be seen as oscillating, in his relations with women, between the expectations of a rather frantic, desperate infant wishing to be intimate with the 'good' mother and the expectations of an apparently independent, self-sufficient adult. If I say that men blow hot and cold, it will come as no surprise to women. I shall return in a moment to why men seem to be afraid of intimacy with women. My immediate concern is to examine the origins of the two positions between which the man oscillates.

THE POSITIVE OEDIPUS COMPLEX

Whatever one's views about the origins of the Oedipus complex – whether biological, psychosocial or a complex combination of the two – its influence in determining the course of the boy's gender identity – how he thinks and feels sexually in terms of whether he is masculine or feminine, and the implications of this – and his gender-role behaviour is profound. The consequences of its resolution are, however, unintended, whatever their many and far-reaching social and psychological implications. These consequences do not provide the motive for the resolution of the Oedipus complex. Of far more importance for the child are the immediate issues it helps him to resolve, and the the fact that it provides, however schematically, a model for resolving the same issues, and their symbolic derivatives for the rest of his adult life.

Lacan and Desire

What, then, are these immediate issues? The little boy, in common with the little girl, will have experienced a number of traumas in relation to the most important person in his life – his mother. In this context, a most apposite remark of Freud's merits a short digression so that we can examine its implications: 'We must reckon with the possibility that something in the nature of the sexual instinct itself is unfavourable to the realisation of complete satisfaction' (Freud, 1912, pp. 188–9). If one returns to Freud's original theories (see Lacan, 1977) as represented in *The Interpretation of Dreams* (Freud, 1900), which gave central importance to the concept of 'desire' – as in 'all dreams represent disguised wishes' – as distinct from the drive/instinct theory described in *Three Essays on the Theory of Sexuality* (Freud, 1905), one could substitute 'desire' for 'the sexual instinct' in this quotation. So what is desire? It has subsequently been pointed out that desire is a symbol of loss; that desire does not occur without the loss of its satisfaction: 'the only conceivable idea of the object, that of the object as the cause of desire . . . is . . . of that which is lacking' (Lacan, 1977, p. ix). Another way to express this is to say that you don't miss somebody who is with you – desire for them arises only when they go. More seriously – and this is surely the reason for 'the something in the nature of the sexual instinct [which] is incapable of satisfaction' – desire, ultimately, is a relation to primitive and infantile fantasy, not to reality.

Because of its relevance to understanding what I described above as the male encapsulated psychosis from which misogyny derives, I would like to take yet another brief digression and describe Lacan's understanding of Freud. In Lacanian terms, the object – at least, its absence – is seen as causing desire. The symbol 'mother' is the representation of the lost mother, with all the implied emotional chaos and aggression, and desire is always in excess of what is capable of satisfaction – we desire only what we cannot have. From this point of view, the boy child's entry into culture is predicated on multiple experiences of loss. Culture is made up of symbols, and symbols signify loss or absence in that they stand in representation of the thing which is missing. The physical maturation and cultivation of the child requires, as an essential precondition, the creation of desire. At all stages of his sexual development through the oral, anal, and phallic preoccupations, a central issue for the child is his relationship with his own 'desire' and the chaos and uncertainty that this represents. He feels incomplete – necessarily so, given that to feel complete would be the equivalent of 'no absences', no gaps represented by symbols which both deny and affirm them – no desire, no language, no relation, only basic unity with the primary object.

It is not surprising that the child should imagine that what he lacks is something or somebody 'out there' who could make him complete, given that the state of bliss which represents the absence of desire has been experienced in relation to an-other – the other who, he eventually learns, is structured as a mother who is 'in the gap where femininity falls' (Mitchell, 1986). Lacan (1977) has pointed out that the subsequent search for the 'other' is not only based on loss but guarantees its own failure. The aim of desire for the other is to be the sole object of the other's desire; with a little thought, however, we can see that if there is an 'other' out there, with the fantasized qualities, she herself will not require an 'other' – there is no 'other' for the 'other'. The fact remains that men try to construct femininity on the basis of this fantasy of the other, and in one way or another psychoanalysts have fallen into this trap. In strict Freudian terms there is no feminine or masculine, nor even bisexuality if this is taken to mean an equal attraction to men and women. This is a division which is constructed in language.

How do these considerations relate to the issues which may be resolved during the Oedipus complex, and in what way do they affect the male psyche to produce the contradictions we were considering above?

The means by which the boy resolves or otherwise leaves the Oedipus complex provide him with a template for his relationship with his desire which will function for the rest of his life. Whether the outcome is 'perverse' (as socially defined, this would mainly mean homosexual) or normal, it will persist into adulthood. Desire cannot be dissolved. The fantasy of an 'other' who will complete him is reawakened at puberty under the influence of his physical development. This will set in motion the final stages of the Oedipus complex, and determine whether he actually resolves it. Otherwise, his desire may find perverse outlets in the face of his anxieties about his incestuous desire for his mother and the consequent castration (ultimately a loss of desire itself in that it symbolizes fusion with the mother, or primary object) this involved.

From the perspective of the origins of misogyny, we must point out one further implication of the positive Oedipus complex. We have seen how the mother's initially 'perceived' – as opposed to actual – failure generates a split in the child's image of her, and how this forms the primitive roots of his misogyny, which has yet to be socially structured through language, in his oral-sadistic impulses. This receives reinforcement during the Oedipal period, where the split is elaborated to contain a male/female dimension. The child realizes not only that he cannot have his mother in the exclusive way he desires but that, in addition, she desires somebody else: Father. It could be said that every male child's first experience of love for a female person – as opposed to his early perceptions of Mother, who is neither male nor female – is an abject disappointment: the child always loses. Freud believed that this whole complex of feelings is not simply repressed, pushed out of consciousness, but actually dissolves – ceases to exist – in the 'normal' case. This belief, and the belief that the idealized, so-called genital character, who has no residues of his infantile dependency, can actually exist, seem to me to be wish-fulfilling fantasies of early psychoanalysts based on idealized expectations of the power of psychoanalysis, and on its essentially masculine nature. Early analysis expressed men's ultimate phantasy: that they can be free of their dependency on women.

Men never entirely trust women. Always in the background is the fantasy of a more virile man – the Father – whom their wife or partner would prefer, given half a chance. This residue of the oedipal father is present in every man, and provides one more reason for controlling and imprisoning woman – to prevent her from meeting him. It could be said, almost as an aside, that it is inevitable, when a man falls in love, that he should have the fantasy of the powerful other man who would be a more appropriate partner for his loved one. This is partly a wish-fulfilling fantasy in that it resolves the guilt caused by his incestuous possession of his mother in his unconscious – an inevitable consequence of falling in love. It may also be a way of making reparation to the woman, in fantasy, for his unconscious attacks on her.

DEPENDENCY AND SELF-SUFFICIENCY

We can now return to the question asked above: What is it in the male psyche which generates these contradictory demands? One set is accounted for by pointing to their source in the infant within the adult male and in his split-off, idealized perceptions of what he comes to regard as the 'good' mother.

Freud distinguished between two bases for choosing an object or a relationship. In the one he called narcissistic, a man chooses on the basis of similarity to himself. Essentially this is homosexual. The other sort of choice he called the anaclitic or 'leaning on' choice: a man chooses on the basis of a pattern of childhood dependency on someone unlike himself. This is the heterosexual object choice (Freud, 1914, p. 87n). Freud was at pains to point out that human beings are not sharply differentiated into two types according to their object choice; rather, that 'both kinds of object choice are open to each individual, though he may show a preference for one or the other' (p. 88). As I said above, this paper, 'On narcissism', is the one in which Freud can be seen at his most chauvinistic and sexist, and in which he states that healthy women are not really capable of a mature object choice. I do not want to pursue his argument here, but would recommend that the reader does so. It must be said that Freud – who was more able than some of his followers to attribute to the environment its true import for the development of the child – seemed utterly unable to appreciate the pressures put upon girls and women to be moulded to fit men's expectations and the fact that these pressures are supported by men's real power over women.

In general it is true to say that men expect women not only to service them in practical ways – feed them, look after them, clean for them – but also to be the source of what Freud called narcissistic supplies – to provide the affection, flattery, praise, and so on, which bolster a man's self-esteem. (For am amusing feminine account of the reality of this, see Spender and Kline, 1989). These are all normative expectations of women, and they are socially structured and reinforced.

Male object choice is literally a 'leaning on' type, and although

Freud did not mean it in this way, there is little doubt that it is women who are required to have the strength to provide the support. Men expect women to be the sole source of both the physical and psychological necessities for survival. This point must be emphasized. Men's expectations of women are based on what we experience as survival issues. The original experience of the loss of basic unity which has been described as the origin of desire, is so much more. It is also a life-threatening event once it is represented in the infant's psyche. The self may be socially constructed, but the organism is not; these are real physical anxieties connected with acute bodily discomfort. The unconscious fantasy is that if these expectations are not met, we will die. Of course this is a residue of our infantile experience with primary carers, usually mothers, and its connection with women is reinforced as we grow up in a world in which they spend most of their time servicing men. In fact this male fantasy about the consequences of woman's failure may not be quite so fantastic as it seems at first sight if one can believe the longevity statistics for unmarried as compared with married men quoted in the Preface.

This, then, is one source of the contradictory expectations we are addressing. They derive from the child's experience of having been kept alive by his idealized mother, who is full of life-giving, nourishing goodness. She is a mother who makes no demands: who unconditionally provides the essentials – and more – which the growing child requires to survive and thrive.

The opposing expectations are a product of the boy's resolution of his Oedipus complex. However partial this resolution, and whatever individual idiosyncrasies result from its many subtexts and unique environmental conditions, one of its consequences is the definition of women as a 'second sex' – inferior to men because they are castrated – of whom men are independent. Naturally enough, this definition is functional. It is required to enable the boy to resolve his dependency. How can one be dependent on an inadequate object? These expectations arise, therefore, from his unresolved infantile dependency on the one hand, and his fragile genital development on the other. The Oedipus complex is essentially a solution to the problem of how to deal with the unfulfillable desire for the mother which, in its most primitive form, entails total possession, a merging or fusing with her; and in its later form means giving her children.

From the infantile, dependent position the man will often go to quite desperate lengths to force the woman into being the princess. He may, for example, maintain his defensive – and clearly neurotic – idealization of her and choose to be depressed when evidence to the contrary emerges, rather than face his repressed feelings about the witch. Another solution is the one used by Paul: separating the loving from the hating feelings, and locating them in two different women. One of a man's greatest anxieties is that if he allows any cracks to appear in his perceptions, he will feel so much hatred that he will destroy the princess in the course of his attack on the witch – this anxiety will be in direct proportion to the relative balance of love and hate in his personality. These anxieties may be quite realistic. It is possible to treat somebody so badly that they will leave you – this would be a realistic destruction – or die; or to be so full of hatred for someone that it becomes impossible to recover one's love for them – a fantasy destruction. As we shall see in Chapter 8, many men make a more active choice: they attempt to destroy the bad object. I believe the evidence for this is not so much the recent research showing that 40 per cent of wives are subject to physical violence from their husbands (Andrews, 1987), as the rationalizations men use to explain their violence and the fact that many men, even after inflicting attacks of extreme viciousness, maintain that they are still in love with their victim.

Under certain circumstances – for example, with a highly adapted female partner – the repressed hatred of the witch can remain unconsciousness for a lifetime. This does not mean that it remains unexpressed. These sadistic feelings – for that is what they are – will find many outlets in the relationship without the man necessarily being aware of them. Most obviously, they will be expressed in the intensity with which he attempts to force his partner to live up to his demands – at least, those he is not too ashamed to make known. This will be clearly seen in the nature of his response to minor frustrations which he can rationalize as realistic – the quality of her cooking, her dress sense, her make-up, her political awareness, her physical attractions, her demands on him which mothers should not make. In effect he will attempt to control his partner. In most cases this attempt will be successful. Men's power over women is enshrined in law and custom which support their attempts to subjugate their partners to their will, up to and including physical assault. Although in many countries it is illegal to assault one's wife, the reality is that in practice it requires extraordinary circumstances for a man to be arrested and charged if he does so. Research has shown that the single greatest factor preventing crime is the likelihood of being caught and punished.

Many feminists maintain that women will submit to men's control and power because it is always underpinned by the threat of physical violence, and because women have no economic freedom which would allow them to leave a violent husband. My own work with hundreds of abusive men and their partners bears this out. It is time men began to listen to women's accounts of men's behaviour. It may be unpleasant and threatening, but it is becoming clear that men define women in terms which are most suited to their own needs. In most countries a wife is legally defined as a possession of her husband, and a man has the right to do as he wishes with his possessions.

The onset of falling in love begins with the true romantic – one might say delusional – phase in which every aspect of the partner's character and appearance is grossly overvalued. This period can last for years; its duration will be a function of the strength of the man's need to maintain the 'princess' fantasy. This will in turn depend on the extent of the threat posed by his internal witch. The more threatened the man is – because the more powerful the witch – the more desperate will be his manipulation of his partner and his perceptions to maintain the denial of his 'bad' feelings. At one extreme is the kind of man who goes from one relationship to another with a passion, the speed of whose development is matched only by the speed of its decline. Such a man cannot tolerate the risk of getting close – at the first sign of frustration of his fantasy, his feelings will die. This death of feelings is precipitated by nothing more complex than a knowledge of the 'other'. At the other extreme are men who completely avoid social relations with women because they simply cannot cope with the anxiety of any involvement which raises these intolerable feelings.

Of course these extremes, Don Juan and St Paul, represent a

minority of men. Although the issues are the same for all men, there are clearly quantitative differences for the great majority, who are sometimes promiscuous and sometimes withdrawn. How, then, do the majority of men deal with these conflicts? One imagines that what occurs in most relationships is that passionate love gives way, under the pressure of reality, to something approaching companionship and harmony. Indeed, as John Fowles showed (1981), Greek philosophers maintained that everybody has to choose between passion and harmony in their relationships, and that the two are mutually exclusive. A large minority, if the divorce rate is anything to go by, therefore settle for something rather more functional and goal-orientated. My own belief is that the majority of men are successful in establishing a high degree of control over their partners. Women file for most divorces, and the most freqently mentioned ground is cruelty. We have no way of knowing if this represents the most serious cases of abuse, or the most independent women. Shere Hite (1987) offers another possibility which accords more with my own experience: 98 per cent of the women in Hite's survey of 4,500 reported that they were profoundly dissatisfied with their relationships with men. The biggest problem was lack of emotional closeness. The women's most common complaint was: 'He doesn't listen'. All the men we work with at the Men's Centre have this same problem. They describe it in many ways: women 'go on', they 'nag', 'never stop talking', 'give it that' – accompanied by a gesture of fingers opening and closing next to the mouth – and so on. What it always boils down to is that they do not want to listen to their partners' concerns. Perhaps this makes some women give up, but it seems to make the partners of battering men increase their efforts to be taken seriously, and heard. Without exception these men are depressed in their relationships. Even though they may describe themselves as loving their partners, they do not want to share anything with them. I will return to this theme in Chapter 8.

If we take it – and I do not think this is unwarranted – that most people in Western cultures marry for love, and therefore that the 'princess' fantasy is in operation at the outset, a question emerges: what is the fate of this fantasy? There is evidence from people who remarry after divorce that they feel they make more realistic choices the second time around: this would indicate that to some extent the fantasy undergoes some modification during the period of mourning for the failure of the first marriage (Brannen and Collard, 1982). This would not be surprising in that the person is also, probably, mourning the original loss of the 'good' mother, and the mourning process involves coming to terms with hatred towards the lost 'object'.

For the declining majority who stay in the original relationship, the fate of the 'princess' fantasy must be different. Although in most cases there is some adaptation of it to accord with reality, my belief is that it is re-repressed, over time, in more or less its original form but leaving behind a memory that one's partner is more good than bad and a sufficient foundation for investing in building a harmonious relationship. Alternatively – and, apparently, in a large number of cases – the fantasy is transferred to other women who become objects of desire. To that extent the man will begin to experience his partner as an obstacle to his satisfaction (as Paul did). Recent research evidence is contradictory and indicates that fidelity may be as difficult for women as it is for men. There is evidence from the USA that 98.5 per cent of married people had stayed faithful during the year of a survey, 1990 (Lawson, 1990). This survey involved 1,400 people and contradicted earlier work. It has been suggested that the high level of fidelity represents a response to anxiety about AIDS, although most extant surveys, such as Shere Hite's (1981), which reports 70 per cent infidelity, do not focus on the last year, but on overall fidelity. No such large-scale work has been done in the UK.

A pro-feminist analysis such as this offers an alternative account of the fate of a man's 'princess' fantasy, whether or not he stays in a marriage. My understanding is that women perceive men as violent and abusive, and in the vast majority of cases they simply adapt to men's abuse. Where they are not victims of physical abuse, this is because they are submitting to men's control in the absence of real alternatives to staying in the relationship. Although there has been no research, the Women's Aid Federation in England (personal communication) believe there is as much abuse in second as in first marriages, and this is supported by my own experience in work with violent men. In fact the evidence is that men who are abusive in a first marriage are almost certain to be so in any subsequent ones.

This would tend to give the lie to any self-reporting by men that they make more realistic choices the second time around. It would point to the intractability of the underlying male fantasy, and the difficulty in finding any alternative to acting it out.

One of the more obvious consequences of any of these solutions is the reappearance of the 'existential' loneliness, alienation and emptiness which preceded the falling in love. This in itself need not be traumatic for the man, provided that there are other activities in his life which give him the opportunity to be creative and demonstrate that he is more good than bad. For most of us, work, although essential, is insufficient. In addition to the opportunity to make reparation, most people also need the nourishment of close relationships with others. Another consequence of the man's emotional withdrawal from his partner, and its substitution by controlling and dominating behaviour, is that the 'oceanic' union with the princess, which for most men is expressed and experienced only during sexual intercourse, becomes a source of fantasy with other women who are not yet 'spoiled' by his ambivalence. In this way he can act out the common 'chase and conquer' sexuality which aims more directly at achieving power and control over women. This is very much the basis of maleness, and it precludes real sexual intimacy with a woman because this would involve the release of the feminine and the arousal of feelings connected with castration.

A man's withdrawal of passionate feelings from his partner is not precipitated solely by his inability to cope with his anxiety and his hatred of the woman. It is also motivated by the guilt attendant on these feelings, and his desire to protect her from them. Paradoxically – and without his awareness – the woman will experience this withdrawal as hurtful. The man therefore succeeds in expressing, covertly, the very thing which his behaviour is designed to prevent expression of: his desire to punish his partner for her failure to live up to his expectations.

Given my belief that men do not innately need and cannot love women, it is clear that a large but declining number of men are meeting different needs in their relationships. Since it is not possible to gratify one's desire, perhaps it is sufficient to forestall abandonment by enforcing the dependency of women, and ensure continued servicing in the attempt to avoid the encapsulated psychosis. Not that I would in any way minimize the gratifications which female servicing provides for men. As Liz Kelly has pointed out (personal communication):

> I think it is precisely this . . . the loss of servicing . . . which men most fear if their power and control is threatened. The political explanation is sufficient. . . . men . . . get lots of goodies out of relationships with women – servicing of all descriptions, their self-esteem boosted and so on.

Up to a point, I agree. The challenge for me, however, is to develop a model 'which accounts for . . . how men's behaviour . . . is individually willed and socially constructed' (Schechter, 1982). Apart from the servicing, one has to point out the satisfaction of men's power needs and the gratification of sadistic impulses inherent in any male–female relationship, with its built-in imbalance of power. It is a moot point whether or not the satisfaction of these needs – for servicing, sadism or security – can be felt adequately to substitute for the more primary needs which are being denied.

A complete phenomenological description of the myths men hold about women would be endless. In confining myself to the most common, I hope I have been able to demonstrate that the oppression of women by men is based on men's clinging to infantile perceptions of women, which constitute part of the neurosis we call masculinity and are rarely pathological. Of course there are other reasons why men do not willingly relinquish their power over women, and these should not be overlooked. If it seems that they are overlooked here, it is simply because this is not a sociology textbook. The obvious loss of the social, economic and political advantages, with no apparent gain, would be enough in themselves, without all the complicating factors involving perceptions of their masculinity, to prevent men willingly bringing about their own downfall. It should be clear that these advantages are actually the result of the development of masculinity, and serve to reinforce it rather than being, in themselves, causative. This is the issue I shall address in the next chapter.

4 The Development of Gender Identity: The Fear and Hatred of the Feminine

Misogyny is a universal phenomenon. All women fall victim to it and all men, to a greater or lesser degree, inflict it on them. In a healthy world, misogyny would be regarded as an illness. I mentioned above but did not pursue – although I would not wish to minimize its significance – that misogyny is only one form of a deeper and wider phenomenon: the male hatred of the 'feminine'. I assume that by now it is clear that this hatred is only one side of the conflict of ambivalence. If we are to understand the nature of this hatred, we must consider what the 'feminine' means to men, apart from the obvious physical qualities which women possess.

For a man, the essential quality of femininity is its 'otherness'. This is the essence of the mystery of everything which is 'not me'. In regard to femininity it is also a mystery which men will never solve, because beyond a certain point in emotional development this 'otherness' is constituted from projected parts of the self. For an infant there is, for a while, truly an 'other' who completes him. The inseparable loss of and desire for this 'other' form the basis of personal growth and the core of men's fantasies about what constitutes femininity, on which the notion of femininity is socially constructed. It is doubtless true to say that most men believe that masculinity is transparent to women. It would be bewildering to most men to discover that they are as much a mystery to women as women are to them.

At this point, perhaps, a brief review of what has been said about the origins of misogyny or 'female-hating' will be useful. We have seen how the infant copes with the contradictory aspects of the environment, its benign and frustrating nature, by dividing the world (Mother) into good and bad. We have seen how, to some extent, all infants succeed, under the pressure of reality, in adapting to the real whole mother who represents both qualities and their derivatives. The core of the split into a frustrating homicidal witch and bountiful princess is, however, to a greater or lesser extent, repressed to the unconscious, where the infant struggles to keep the princess safe from the witch. This struggle will be the determining factor in the male's relationships with women for the rest of his life, and a major influence in determining his character, sexual and otherwise. Its outcome will be determined largely by the way his innate capacity for aggression and his sadism interact with environmental influences.

There has long been a debate about the nature of aggression and whether or not 'hatred' – certainly of the kind postulated here – is innate, or a perversion of aggression which arises from the frustration of other basic instincts. For most people this is not a sterile question. It has profound implications for educationalists and politicians and perhaps, in the long run, for the future of the human race, but by and large I do not think it is relevant here. Whether or not misogyny is innate may be beside the point. I believe that every man suffers from it (albeit sometimes to quite a minor degree amounting to no more than benign contempt for women), and that the social and psychological conditions which precipitate and reinforce it occur in every man's life. At the very least, I shall argue, the predisposition to it is innate and the social conditions are inevitable in that no woman – or primary carer – can be a 'perfect' mother from the infant's point of view; we all have to enter into society, and this requires a split between the organism and the self. In the circumstances, the Nature versus Nurture debate can be set aside without in the least influencing attempts to socially engineer desirable changes in men's behaviour. In any case, the documented abuse of women by men provides a sufficient agenda for social action, even if one despairs of any fundamental change in gender arrangements.

Fascinating as they are, I do not wish to do more than mention the complex changes and modifications which the unconscious 'good' and 'bad' mothers undergo during early childhood. The psychoanalytic literature clearly demonstrates the cognitive and emotional confusion that can arise, for a child, between objects, or even part-objects (we all possess a capacity for relating to bits of people as if they are separate from, or are, the whole), and their functions. Consider, for example, breasts, nipples, anuses and penises, mouths and vaginas and the functions of giving and taking, putting in and taking out. Add to this the products of these organs – faeces, milk, semen, urine, vomit and babies – together with the sexual confusion of male and female, and consider also that for the infant (as for the dreaming adult) all these objects, products and functions may be interchangeable and able, at different times, to represent one another. The permutations are complex in the extreme.

These embellishments of the basic split lie somewhere on the hinterland between the child's developing biology and psychology, and rather than pursuing these, I intend to look at the growing male's awareness of the role and status of women during this crucial period leading up to the full-blown Oedipus complex. Gordon Burns's book about Peter Sutcliffe, the 'Yorkshire Ripper', (Burns, 1986) illustrates this well.

In general, Burns documents the casual and chronic aggression and violence to which women in Sutcliffe's working-class culture were subjected, and the contempt with which they were regarded by men. This is a cultural norm, and it seemed to be accepted with resignation by the women, and expected of each other by the men. Male values are dominated by concepts relating to potency, and 'cissy' behaviour in men is abhorred. In this phallocentric male culture there is constant pressure to demonstrate one's masculinity, mainly by the conquest and maltreatment of women, who are largely regarded as 'objects' in the sexual politics of male relationships. One could speculate endlessly about the potential latent homosexuality in such a culture. Such speculation would undoubtedly lead one to believe that the idea of being a 'cissy' and the compulsive demonstrations of masculinity represent both a deep need for intimacy with other men and an equally deep and profound fear of being thought feminine or 'queer' if this need were not negotiated through a 'third term' – women. Attitudes to homosexuality in working-class culture are not nearly so liberated as one might wish. Unfortunately, it is still the norm to perceive and refer to homosexuals with contempt. One of Sutcliffe's biographers, Nicole Ward Jouve, has actually suggested that it was his failure to live up to the demands of masculinity and his fear of being thought 'cissy' which began the chain of events leading to his becoming a woman-murderer (Ward Jouve, 1986). She believes that the root cause of the killings was men's contempt for women and femininity.

Whether it is verbalized or not, this contempt for women can be clearly inferred from men's behaviour. One of a man's greatest failings – if not crimes – in the eyes of other men is that he does not exercise sufficient authority over his wife (Whitehead, 1976). This is also illustrated in Gordon Burns's book. He describes Sutcliffe's gentleness towards his wife, Sonya, and his brother's anger with her and contempt for Sutcliffe because he did not lay down the law. Women are second-class citizens both in the family system and outside, in the occupational, economic, academic, educational, artistic and political systems. In fact, wherever a child looks he is faced with explicit and implicit evidence of woman's secondary importance. The primacy of masculinity is axiomatic. (The UN World Report (*Women: A World Report*, 1985) shows clearly that this is not confined to Western society – it is perhaps even more apparent in developing nations.)

Although the child needs and wants his mother's love, he can see all around him that approval by men is what matters if he is to be a 'man'. As well as the implicit evidence of women's inferior status he is simultaneously bombarded, in industrialized cultures, by media images which portray women as they should be if they are to be acceptable in this male-dominated world – as sexual objects whose function is to stimulate male sexual interest, or as waitresses whose function is to serve. Women are rarely presented as prime actors who shape events. I well remember from my own childhood seeing, in a science textbook, a picture of a serious scientist at work in his lab; behind him, unnoticed and silent, apparently unaware that a picture was being taken, was a cleaner hard at work. The cleaner was a woman. On a more practical level,

I can also remember that during my childhood I only had to say, almost to the air, that I would like a cup of tea, and it would invariably appear. I was thirty years old before a partner told me that I had to stop believing in the toilet-roll and the toothpaste fairy!

Every day of their lives, boys are exposed to demonstrations of the minor role which women are forced to play (and made to believe is the only role they can play). We are exposed to the double standards of men who maintain reciprocal relations with each other, yet insist on and expect submission from women. We are given sex-role models which inform us that men are strong, don't show vulnerability or confusion, are never afraid, are not tender; their sexuality is split from their love, their mind from their body, their thinking from their feeling; they are never childlike, and so on. Even if the psychology of the child were not as important as it is, and if he were able to set aside his grief and rage about his 'deprivation' at his mother's hands, it is more than improbable that he would continue to see her without an overlay of contempt and denigration, or desire her without reservation.

I am not saying that these social pressures are entirely responsible for the boy's turning away from his mother. The social obstacles within the family as represented by the father, combined with the boy's growing awareness of the necessity of – and desire for – his father's approval, are enough to ensure that he will 'leave' Mother and turn to father as a model for masculinity and maturation. (I will turn later to what happens where there is no father. A minority of children now grow up in a nuclear family.) This will happen both because and in spite of the contempt and fear he feels for his father, arising from his rivalry with him. Freud himself was of the opinion that patriarchy was essentially a defence against the acting out of incestuous desires, in that the cornerstone of patriarchy is the definition of woman as property: the property of the father. Patriarchy is the ultimate achievement of the Oedipus complex in that it institutionalizes the primary family drama (Freud, 1913).

The social obstacles to the continuing desire for the mother are historically known as the 'incest taboos'. In *Father–Daughter Rape*, Elizabeth Ward (1984) makes a powerful case for regarding 'incest taboos' as the means by which the father, with the mother's help, can woo the boy into acceptance of 'male' role models. This involves rejecting Mother and taking on the values of the patriarchy to perpetuate the subjugation of women and the primacy of men. Woman as property is a cornerstone of this value system (G. Rubin, 1975).

Clearly, there are powerful social taboos against incest. It would not, however, be true to say that the only – or, indeed, the most important – taboos are social. It is quite clear that these social taboos have their counterpart in profound psychological inhibitions against incest. As we shall see, the social taboos are represented, in the family, by the father. Even without a specific injunction against incest, however, the psychological inhibitions will ensure that the Oedipus complex is resolved in a way that prevents the little boy from satisfying his incestuous wishes. Interestingly, it appears from all the evidence now emerging that the taboo is aimed mainly at preventing the little boy and the little girl from having Mother. The increasing evidence of sexual abuse of daughters indicates that it may function to reserve the right of sexual access to fathers. Although this follows logically from the analysis, it has only recently received empirical support. In the last few years I have looked forward to seeing men who have been raised in households without a father to see what differences, if any, there might be in their oedipal drama. My experience is interesting because it has produced a negligible number of 'deviant' outcomes.

In one case the man had attempted during his teens to have sex with his mother. He reported that he had begun kissing her while they were watching TV, and that while at first her resistance had been firm and gentle, it had ended in a wrestling match when he tried to caress her breasts. She had told him to stop and go to bed, which he did. The next day she had told him that while she understood his feelings, he would not be allowed to behave in that way with her again. Apart from continuing to masturbate with her as his fantasy he had obeyed this injunction. Ten years later, however, he had not given up the idea that she had enjoyed his attempted seduction (as he called it), or his desire to have sex with her. He still hoped it would be possible, and recounted subsequent incidents which, from his perspective, seemed to indicate that his mother was ambivalent about it. This was not his presenting problem. He had no desire to change the situation, although it was obviously (to me) the source of his presenting problem. In my experience this is a very unusual situation, although Nancy Friday (1980) quotes an analyst who says that it is not uncommon in his experience with men who are raised without fathers. In another case the boy had begun physically abusing his mother during his teens in a way that is directly comparable with that of men who abuse their adult partners. I have also worked with a man who was physically abusing his mother during his teens while his father was still in the household. His father had never been physically abusive, nor did he attempt to stop his son's behaviour. It was clear that the boy became the authority in the home. He had subsequently gone on to abuse his adult female partners.

What about the mother in these situations where there is no man around? Estela Welldon (1988) quotes one case where the mother actually carried on a sexual relationship with her son for some years, until he became an adult. Although she believes there are a great many more cases of mother–son abuse, it is impossible to believe that it could in any way match the scale of known abuse of daughters and young girls by men. Barnett, Corder and Jehu (1990) report a treatment programme for women sex offenders. The striking thing about these women – which the authors do not adequately address – is that they were all co-offenders with men, and all had a history of what the authors call marital discord. In my experience, marital discord usually means they were being battered and were probably unwilling participants in the abuse of their children, but the authors give us insufficient information to make an informed judgement.

All the other men who suffered from problems connected with the absent father (and 'absence' is a variable feast) presented with oedipal problems, but well within the limits of the normal complex, and often no different from those of men with fathers who were present. I agree with Jan Horsfall (1991) that positional identification is crucially important for boys, whether or not the father is present. In this respect, the boy will internalize the institutionalized power of the father rather than his personal power over the mother.

There is a sense, paradoxically, in which the absent father is more present than the present one. In addition, of course, we cannot discount the extent to which the mother transmits her own view of masculinity and maleness to her son. Inevitably there will be problematic areas of maleness for him, but these will be within oedipal limits.

In a sense the boy is 'pushed' from below by his fear of his desire for and consequent hatred of women (his ambivalence towards them), and pulled from above by his need for his father's acceptance and his fear of the consequences of his desire for his mother – castration by the father who 'owns' the mother. This provides him simultaneously with a sort of 'script' outline for his behaviour for the rest of his life, and the opportunity to express his hatred of women by adopting the more culturally accepted means used by his father and other male role models in society at large – seeing them as sexual objects, either in parts or whole (this is also a regression to his infantile perceptions) to be chased and conquered; denigrating their non-feminine capacities; denying equal opportunities to education, employment, and so on.

There is, of course, another side to this encouragement which the boy receives. Girls are actively discouraged from intellectual pursuits and encouraged, instead, to learn about being feminine – a definition provided wholly by men, albeit with the active participation of women (see Chapter 7).

An overriding factor in the boy's perceptions of women will be his social experience of them as caretakers – providers of nurture and comfort within the family. Outside the family he will be increasingly aware of the extension of this role of the woman as caretaker in society at large. If one looks at patterns of women's employment, one can see that the so-called service industries and the caring professions are dominated, at the lower end of the scale, by women: nursing, secretarial work, teaching, social work, day-care provision, shop work and so on. Interesting as this is, it has been more frequently remarked that all these occupations are consistently undervalued and underpaid. Women are not an adequate model for success in a male-dominated world.

A contradiction emerges: men are aware of their deep need for women, whatever modifications that need may undergo, and simultaneously discount women in every other respect: women are both venerated and despised. Given the nature of men's perceptions of each other (which we will examine below), it is not surprising that whatever their background they come to regard women as the only valuable source of emotional comfort, nourishment and security. It is extremely important to men that women should not regard themselves as fitted for men's tasks; this would be a direct threat to their value as mothers. To the extent that women become strong by developing capacities, interests and skills which define them as separate individuals, they effectively become the 'witch'. Apart from any difficulty a man might have in forgiving a woman for the abandonment this represents, there is the major problem that she may decide she is independent of men and actually abandon them by refusing the subjugated caretaking role which she has, historically, performed. In the event, such women are both secretly feared and overtly held in contempt by men. The imputation is forever present that they (independent women) have failed as women; they become 'castrators', 'bitches', 'ball-breakers' who are seen as wanting to become men. The veiled charge that they are lesbians, the ultimate failure of femininity in men's eyes, is never far away, and from a phallocentric perspective it is true that these women have actually failed to embrace fully the femininity imposed on them by men.

I described above the so-called positive Oedipus complex where the boy 'desires' his mother and fears and hates his father (see pp. 93–6). We saw how he resolves these conflicts through his 'castration complex', with the resultant denigration and contempt for 'castrated' women, and the ultimate distortion of his own 'desire'. In the context of looking at men's fear and hatred of the feminine in general, we must look at the Oedipus complex again from a different viewpoint – at what is called the 'negative' version. We shall fully understand how a man's relationship with the feminine side of himself evolves only when we have the complete picture. According to traditional Freudian theory, the resolution of the full Oedipus complex, around castration anxiety in boys and penis envy in girls, is what determines the individual's gender identity.

NON-ANALYTIC THEORIES OF GENDER IDENTITY

It should be clear at the outset that the psychoanalytic theory of gender identity is by no means the most widely accepted. There are at least six different ways of understanding how we all become boys or girls. I do not intend to give an exhaustive account of these different models here. It should come as no suprise that they are all, in one way or another, attempts to resolve the problem which has beset psychology since its beginnings: Which is more important, nature or nurture?

To my mind, it is only in the analytic model of identity formation that human passions have been accorded their true place in the unfolding drama which we call child development: 'in pursuit of rigour, some form of emasculation of man as an emotional animal has usually accompanied our traditional science of development . . . ' (Rosenberg and Sutton, 1972, p. 46). As I argue elsewhere in this book, however (see Chapter 7), Freud seemed overconfident in his belief that the Oedipus complex is smashed by 'the shock of threatened castration . . . ' (Freud, 1925b, pp. 248–58) or that it is 'abandoned, repressed, and in most normal cases, entirely destroyed . . . ' (Freud, 1932, p. 129). It may be that the Oedipus complex forces a partial resolution in favour of a particular option, but my everyday experience as a man and a clinician confirms that the struggle between what society would identify as the feminine and masculine aspects of himself continues (Erikson, 1950). Indeed, it is clear to me that society needs men to have unresolved Oedipus complexes; that we continue to live with the fear of the father (the Law). A truly free man would represent a real threat to social organization.

A central tenet of psychoanalytic theory is the notion of universal bisexuality. The essence of this is that whereas male and female may be biological givens – that it is anatomy which determines one's sex – masculinity or femininity, or gender identity, is not predetermined. Clearly, the environment plays a large part in the formation of sexual identity, though precisely how large is still open to some doubt. Thus one can read that 'although human masculinity and femininity may have biological roots, the greater part of gender identity is learned. It is thus differentiated from "sex", a term I arbitrarily reserve for biological attributes such as chromosomes, gonads and genitals' (Stoller, 1975, p. ix); and that:

> there is no single way to summarise the clash between those who place the greater emphasis on biological predisposition and those who counteractively emphasise learning and experience as the main factors contributing to sex role development. There is apparently a sufficient variety of abnormal cases at hand to support either position . . .
>
> Perhaps we may illustrate the problem by saying that if an animal's ratio of heredity to environment is 1: 1 in human beings the ratio is probably closer to 1: 10. Given this degree of flexibility in man, it is hard not to believe that the form of his sex role development will depend upon whether contemporary culture wishes to underemphasize the differences between genders or to overplay them. (Rosenberg and Sutton, 1972, p. 101)

With this in mind, Maccoby (1980) makes the pertinent observation that the similarities are greater than the differences between men and women: that men are as different from each other as they are from women, and that the same holds true for women. One is therefore entitled to ask precisely what it is that makes a man a man and a woman a woman, and whether there is anything other than childbearing capacities which is not ideologically imposed.

Money *et al.* (1957) present a long series of cases which demonstrate that even when an individual is assigned to the wrong sex, a core gender identity develops which is congruent with that assignment, provided nobody questions it. Beyond the age of about two and a half it becomes increasingly difficult, if not impossible, for people who are raised unequivocally to change gender identity. One study, however (Imperato, McGinley *et al.*, 1974), contradicts this earlier conclusion. Four boys of ten children in the Batista family, in the Dominican Republic, were born with normal female genitalia. At the age of twelve their vaginas healed over (sic), testicles descended, and they grew full-size penises. The Batistas were just one of twenty-three similarly affected families in their village, where thirty-seven children have undergone this change. They all shared a common ancestor from the mid-nineteenth century. All these children have taken on male roles, do men's jobs, and have married women despite the fact that they lived and thought of themselves as girls for the first ten years or so of their lives. The crucial lesson seems to be that they made the transition easily *because the culture was used to it and supported their new identity.*

This study provides strong support for a cultural, as opposed to biological, theory of gender identity formation. However, it contradicts Money *et al.*'s conclusion that this identity is inflexible. This conclusion seems to require modification to allow for a culture which acknowledges the existence of a third sex, one which can change at puberty. Imperato, McGinley *et al.*'s study is anticipated by Stoller (1968, pp. 29–38), who reports that children raised in neutral fashion because of their ambiguous genitals can fairly easily change sex – either because no strong gender has been established, or because they identify themselves as belonging to a third sex. Surgical sex change is not advisable where the patient has a strong gender identity which would be contradicted by such a change. Many studies confirm the essential correctness of Money *et al.*'s conclusion that gender identity is not amenable to change after about the age of two, when there is a firm assignment of gender and congruent child-rearing without parental confusion, regardless of the ambiguity of the infant's genitals. Children assume the gender identity and gender role consistent with the sex of rearing. Money is in no doubt about this:

> The hormones that bring about sexual maturation do not, according to all the evidence available, have any differential determining influences on the psychosexual, male-female direction and content of perceptual, memory, or dream imagery that may trigger or be associated with erotic arousal. On the contrary, there is strong chemical and presumptive evidence . . . that the libido hormone is the same for men and women and is androgen. Psychosexually, the androgenic function is limited to partial regulation of the intensity and frequency of sexual desire and arousal, but not the cognitional patterns of arousal. (Money, 1965, pp. 3–23)

None of this should be taken to mean that gender identity is independent of biology. It may simply mean that there are weak biological forces at work which are supported – or, in deviant cases, overwhelmed – by child-rearing practices and culture. Stoller

(1968) is firmly of the opinion that a child establishes what he calls a 'core gender identity' which is congruent with the sexual assignment at birth. This idea has many similarities with the psychologists' concept of pre-adaptive behaviour – the necessity to teach children attitudes and behaviours which prepare them to assume an adult sex role. Stoller maintains that infants develop a strong sense of whether they are boys or girls before the age of two and a half – that is, before they encounter the Oedipus complex. For him, this learning is non-conflictual. It derives not from oedipal conflicts, as Freud maintained, but from nurturing contact with the parents in an atmosphere of love. Stoller presents convincing evidence to support his thesis. As we shall see, this accords to some extent with the Kleinian view, although Melanie Klein believed that this knowledge of maleness and femaleness is innate rather than learned from interaction with the parents and physical awareness of the penis and vagina.

From my point of view, it is actually unimportant whether men are always men and women are always women in the sense in which we understand those terms at this moment in history. I believe it is inevitable that in the broader social system whatever is regarded as 'feminine' is – or will become – an excluded class, and this includes 'feminine' men. My argument is that men need an excluded other in order to define the male self. This exclusion is based on female secondary sex characteristics which are elaborated into a coherent ideology, without regard for whether there is any concordance between sex and gender role.

In the most extensive and authoritative study to date, Eleanor Maccoby and Carol Jacklin (1974) reviewed over 2,000 books on sex differences and concluded that although there are some differences between boys and girls, many of the most widely held gender-role stereotypes have little or no basis in fact, and such facts as there are have been systematically exaggerated. In spite of this, they acknowledge that these stereotypes are still deeply influential. This is a clear indication of the ideological basis of most of our perceptions of masculinity and femininity. This conclusion would hardly surprise feminists of the socialist school, but would be less palatable to the apocalyptics, who see a new dawn of separatism based on essential sexual differences, and in particular the innate superiority (essentially the maternal qualities and lack of aggression) of the female.

Of particular interest for apocalyptic (essentialist) feminists (and for psychoanalysis) is Maccoby and Jacklin's finding that in every culture where aggression is observed, boys are both physically and verbally more aggressive than girls. Quite how one interprets this finding is open to some doubt. There is clear evidence that parents, having had an unambiguous sex assignment for their unborn offspring, begin to sex-type them from the moment they leave the womb (Z. Rubin and McNeil, 1983) to such an extent that differences in aggressiveness can be observed within three weeks (Maccoby, 1980). Given that perhaps the most essential feature of sex-typing concerns the expectation of greater aggressive behaviour from boys than from girls, we should not be too surprised at these findings. Although Maccoby and Jacklin felt unable to draw any conclusion about post-adolescent males because of lack of data, we know that adult men are vastly more aggressive than adult women.

Before we look more closely at Freud's analytic theory of gender identity, we should examine what social learning theorists have to say. In essence, social learning theorists believe that gender identity is formed through imitation and reward – that is, the little boy copies other people he knows to be male, like himself. They approve of his behaviour; he perceives this approval as rewarding, and repeats the behaviour. This model has little to recommend it. There is scant evidence that young children imitate same-sex models more than opposite-sex models (Maccoby and Jacklin, 1974). One should, however, note Rubin and McNeil's findings concerning the sex-typing of neonates. Gender-role behaviour may be imprinted without the child's active participation. Interestingly (at least in the terms of this book), there is strong evidence that from about the age of six children do begin to imitate same-sex models, but this occurs *after* they have a fixed idea of their own gender identity. This would illustrate the importance of social learning for the child's developing concept of identity. As I pointed out above, however, as a theory of gender identity it presumes that which it attempts to explain. A theory of gender identity must account not only for the transmission of gender roles but also for their origins. Social learning theory cannot do this.

An overriding criticism of all non-psychoanalytic theories of gender identity formation is that none of them is able to gain access to the deep material which is the privilege of psychoanalysis or therapy. Casual self-reporting or behaviour observation will never enable a psychologist to understand the complex and conflicting dynamic psychological processes which are in constant activity within the human personality. Standard tests cannot measure them.

One's view of what ultimately decides the particular sexual identity and preferences of any individual will depend on one's theoretical framework – anthropological, biological, sociological, and so on. My framework is psychodynamic: gender identity is seen as a product of the conflicts evoked by the Oedipus complex. The way the Oedipus complex is resolved will determine how people identify themselves sexually. It is obvious from this simple diagram that the symbols which determine which side of this divide you line up on are shared by the whole world, and you have to make a choice:

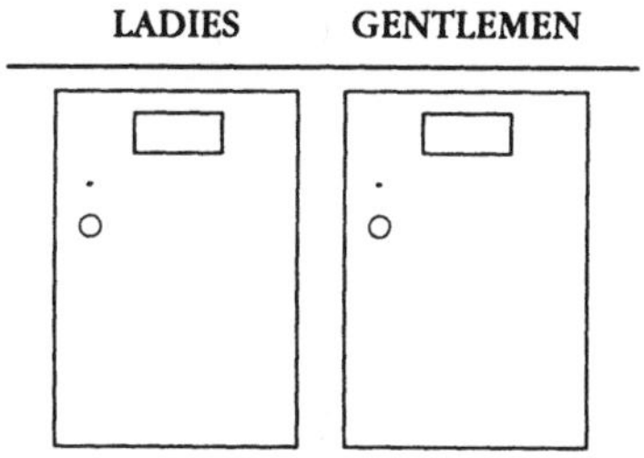

(Source: Lacan, 1957, p. 151)

It is quite possible to be in no doubt whatsoever about which door to enter, in the sense of knowing that one is possessed of male or female sexual anatomy yet, in an extreme case, to be possessed of a gender identity which is quite ambiguous as to masculinity or femininity. I might be in no doubt whatsoever that I am a man, yet quite confused about what this means except that I have a penis and am supposed to desire women.

In clinical practice, one rarely meets anyone who is unequivocally certain of his or her sexuality. Almost everyone, whether or not they know it at the outset of therapy, has unresolved and unintegrated opposite-sex potentialities and desires. These ambiguities constitute the psychological hangover from an incompletely resolved Oedipus complex. Even in these cases, however, I am inclined to agree with Stoller (1968) that the core gender identity is unambiguous in that the man or woman is in no doubt about their gender assignment. The unresolved elements in all of us (for example, an otherwise heterosexual man wondering what it would be like to suck, or be penetrated by, a man's penis, or his wish to have breasts; a woman's desire to have a penis, or her wish to suck another woman's breasts or vagina) undermine the certainty which theories other than psychoanalysis are inclined to ascribe to our perceptions of ourselves. I contend that these are not simply perverse fantasies but actually represent a basic fissure in the rigid gender types or sex role stereotypes into which individuals are squeezed by the outcome of the interaction between biology, psyche and culture. The causes are too numerous and the effects too varied to pursue here, but the 'negative complex' takes pride of place as a major source of failure to achieve the destiny for which society deems one to be anatomically appointed by the possession – or lack – of a penis.

THE NEGATIVE OEDIPUS COMPLEX

The negative Oedipus complex (Freud, 1923, pp. 28–40) is the homosexual element of the child's innate bisexuality which leads him or her to 'desire' the parent of the same sex and see the opposite-sex parent as a rival. Of course the intensity of the homosexual part of the constitution will vary from person to person – in some it will be the stronger aspect; in others hardly noticeable.

The boy's homosexuality will generate in him passive fantasies involving his father. Such fantasies, which involve being penetrated by his father or incorporating his father's penis, will raise terrifying anxieties about the possibility of losing his penis in the light of his reinterpretation of the knowledge that his mother does not have one. We have seen how he relinquishes his incestuous 'desire' for his mother, by identifying with his father, under the influence of his castration anxiety. Equally, it could be said that he generates castration anxiety in order to relinquish his impossible desire for her.

It is evident that the decision to identify with the father takes on an even more elegant quality when we realize how much more it does than provide a means of resolving the positive oedipal desire for the mother. By psychologically taking in the father, the boy is enabled to express his passive love for him without losing his penis or adopting a passive homosexual relationship with him. In Freud's words:

> At the dissolution of the Oedipus complex the four trends of which it consists will group themselves in such a way as to produce a father identification and a mother identification. The father identification will preserve the . . . relation to the mother which belonged to the positive complex and will at the same time replace the . . . relation to the father which belonged to the negative complex . . . the same will be true of the mother identification. The relative intensity of the two identifications will reflect the preponderance in him of one or the other of the two sexual dispositions. (Freud, 1923, p. 34)

The four trends of which Freud speaks are love and hate for the father and the mother. This means that if the homosexual disposition is the stronger, the child will have a more intense identification with the mother and will therefore adopt more 'feminine ways' of being; the reverse applies where heterosexuality is stronger. Here Freud also stresses the role played by the boy's love for his father in giving up his incestuous desire for his mother. His love for his father, his negative complex, coupled with his castration anxiety, gives him a stake in preserving his loved father by ceasing his homicidal jealous rivalry with him.

Little has changed in this formulation since Freud's time, although it is now believed that this process begins much earlier in infancy, and that it involves the infant identifying with parts of the father – for example, his penis – as opposed to the father as a whole person.

There are other factors at work in this process to which Freud did not draw attention. These have been highlighted in two books where the authors take a more psychological and sociological approach than Freudian biology adopts. Elizabeth Moberley (1987) draws the clear conclusion that the main reason for the boy's identifying with his mother and developing a homosexual outlook – a failure to develop an 'appropriate' masculine gender identity – is the father's failure to be a good object for him. In her opinion it is the father's failure to be a good father, and his providing the boy with a traumatic identification, which leads the boy to turn away from him towards his mother. The boy does not merely not identify with his father – he actually dis-identifies and detaches from him because it is too painful to continue the relationship. The external father, to all intents and purposes, might as well not exist. This enables the boy to seek a good father/male identification in later life through his homosexual choices. In Moberley's opinion, the boy has to do this in order to complete his development as a man – a development which failed because the real father was a bad one and did not provide the basis for the necessary identification. What is so difficult for the boy in this position is that his later choices will inevitably be affected by the internalized father from whom, as a man, he is still maintaining detachment.

In addition, it will be impossible for the adult homosexual to find the good father in another homosexual. What he is seeking is a good heterosexual father. As we know, one of the central fantasies of many homosexual men is that a heterosexual man will fall in love with them.

These conclusions are implicit in Morton Schatzman's review (1973) of Freud's famous Schreber case. Both Moberley and Schatzman clearly believe that social reality, the actual environment of the child and the qualities of the mother and father, is at least as influential in shaping the child's gender identity as his internal fantasy life. Moberley (1987, p. 96) says: 'authority problems *vis-à-vis* the same sex, whether involving defiance or hatred or competitiveness, may all be considered manifestations of a defensive detachment from the (same sex) needed love source'. She argues that healthy human growth and development require a satisfactory homosexual relationship. That is, each person needs the experience of loving and being loved by a parent of the same sex. Without this, same-sex relations will always be characterized by the dependency or aggression which expresses a fundamentally unresolved ambivalence due to the frustration of this need. She goes on to say that this need will persist in influencing the adult's behaviour – either by causing rigid, anti-intimacy defences to be instituted against it, or by causing the conflict between the need and the anger its frustration generates to be acted out in an oscillating or one-sided fashion. She believes that a successful homosexual relationship which has met the child's need for love from the same-sex parent is essential if he is eventually to enter his own sex and successfully relate to members of the opposite sex. To do this he must truly be 'other' than the opposite sex, and this can be achieved only if the child identifies with the same-sex parent in a relatively undefended and loving way.

In Moberley's view it is the father's failure to respond to this need in the child which is responsible for the child's future failure as an adult – either fully to become a man, or to relate successfully to women. You cannot become masculine if you do not identify with your father, and if you are not fully masculine, then women are not the fully feminine 'other' to you. She draws great support from Schatzman's book (1973), and there is no doubt that this account of the influence of the real environment is a powerful, persuasive and necessary corrective to Freud's psychobiological account of masculine development.

Psychologically, however, the situation is far from simple. A successful identification is very different from a loving, intimate relationship but, as Freud pointed out, the identification with the mother preserves the object relation with the father just as the identification with the father preserves the object relation with the mother. There can be no doubt that a successful identification with the father requires that the need for the father's love, which derives from the negative Oedipus complex, should be experienced by most little boys in the form of passive/feminine urges towards the father during the phallic phase. Most fathers of sons will recall the time when their little boy related to them in this way.

The boy's need to behave like this ceases with his identification with the father. This identification replaces the object relation which properly derives from the negative complex. Perhaps more important is the fact that this identification cannot take place until the boy begins to resolve his Oedipus complex after the onset of castration anxiety. The most loving father in the world will fail if the child brings to his feelings for him an intense amount of jealousy, hatred and fear left over from his earlier development. In this case, the environment will be defeated by the child's inner world. Whatever the relative balance of inner and outer, the outcome will be favourable only if the father is a good object for the boy. In other words, for this identification to take place the relationship must be felt as more loving than hating and fearing.

The relinquishment (not renunciation) of his passive homosexual feelings and his subsequent identification with his father is the essential building block in the boy's gender identity – or, at least, in enabling him to begin constructing a masculine sex-role identity consistent with his pre-adaptive behaviour. This becomes elaborated, and gender is established, with the addition of other constructs into the duality: passive/masochistic/feminine/castrated – active/sadistic/masculine/phallic. In case there is any doubt, let me spell out that these elaborations are by no means biologically based. They are ideologically constructed elaborations of a primitive sexual dimorphism which is entirely anatomical. According to anthropologists Rosenberg and Sutton (1972, pp. 75–6) this may become less and less necessary as society becomes more complex and requires greater role differentiation unrelated to basic biological or anatomical differences. Perhaps this accounts for the emergence of an actual ideology to justify women's oppression; it becomes stronger as sexual differentiation becomes less necessary.

It is clear from Freud's own account that he believed that male homosexuality results from an identification with the mother arising from a strong female disposition – that is, a biologically inherited factor. Not that either Moberley or Schatzman believes it to result entirely from environmental factors. Even in their scheme of things the child still has to be attracted to his father, or attempting to deal with a negative Oedipus complex. Freud's account is based entirely on a particular family arrangement – one which is common in our society, of a father, a mother, and unmarried sons and daughters. This arrangement, however, is far less universal than is generally believed. In fact, as I said earlier, the majority of people around the world do not grow up in a nuclear family. This fact is often used to undermine Freud's account of the development of gender identity. However, despite the wide variety of family structures, sexual differentiation is universal, and in the vast majority of cases women are the subordinated sex (D'Andrade, 1966, pp. 173–204).

This normative view of family life in psychoanalysis is reflected in its normative view of human sexuality. Psychoanalysis and psychiatry have long struggled with the notion of homosexuality as pathological. Connell (1987) and others argue that the medicalization of sexual ideology reflects the political role of psychiatry and psychoanalysis in controlling human behaviour by constructing 'a form of social authority and . . . control . . . which reaches beyond the business of treating physical diseases' (p. 250). The recent removal of homosexuality as a pathology from the American list of psychiatric disorders reflects a change in the balance of power and the end of a long-running conflict between the medical establishment and gay activists. It remains to be seen what the effect of the AIDS crisis will be. It is argued that the rise in the strength of the moral right in the USA, with the support of some powerful apocalyptic feminists like Catharine Mackinnon in the pornography censorship debate, which is also being joined in this country, could result in even greater oppression of homo and other 'deviant' sexualities. Actually, from a strict reading of Freud it makes as much sense to define heterosexuality as deviant (McDougall, 1990). Connell expresses his belief that 'the growth of medical authority highlights the extent to which the dynamic of sexual ideology is a struggle for hegemony. What is at issue is the power to set the terms on which questions of gender are understood . . . ' (1987, p. 251).

Regardless of the relative contributions of environment and biology or fantasy, most boys become sexually masculine and identify themselves clearly in this way. A fascinating study of gender identity formation in children who are raised by homosexual parents found that they developed a heterosexual gender identity and 'appropriate' sex-role behaviour. The proportion who identified themselves as homosexual was lower than for the population as a whole. What happens, in Freudian terms, to the majority of boys whose heterosexual disposition is stronger? (In case I have not already done so, I should make it clear that I do not believe in disposition. If it were necessary we could raise our children to make love to doorknobs and keyholes. Despite all the evidence to the contrary, Freud could not give up his attachment to biological disposition.) Freud makes it absolutely clear that when the boy resolves his negative (or inverted) Oedipus complex and renounces his desire to be his father's lover he is, in effect, doing away with the passive feminine side of himself. However – and this is the crucial point – what he is renouncing is not passivity itself, but passivity in relation to other men – not in relation to women.

I have lost count of the number of men who, confronted with their passivity – their refusal to share the basic servicing in their marriages, such as shopping, cooking, housecleaning, and do on – reply that when they were living alone they were able to do these things without difficulty. I believe this is true, and it is my own experience. It seems that we men not only do not eschew passivity in relation to women, but have a basic expectation of a right to be passive when we get into a relationship. Otherwise competent men can seem to become babies overnight when cohabitation begins. What is left, therefore, is a resolution which defines relations with other men on the basis of either aggression and competition or identification, and relations with women on the basis of passivity or contempt.

In relation to a woman the one alternative – passivity – will, as we have seen, generate attempts to force her into the 'good' mother role and complete the man by becoming his 'other' (this is my interpretation of Shere Hite's findings mentioned above); the other alternative – contempt – preserves the woman in the man's psyche as a denigrated, incomplete object. 'Desire' itself will ensure that this alternation between passivity and active aggressive contempt will continue in men's behaviour with women. Furthermore, it ensures that part of their own repressed femininity will be projected on to others who will be feared and rejected – for example, male homosexuals. Of course this is not the only destination for the man's femininity. If he is successful in coming to terms with his parents as a couple, he will also be able to identify successfully with the 'mother' in his wife. This is the ultimate level of sexual and emotional maturity to which a successful resolution of the Oedipus complex will lead. It represents the ascendancy of loving feelings, for both parents as individuals and as a couple, over hateful, destructive feelings derived from the original experiences at the hands of the 'witch'. Most men, however, do not seem to achieve this outcome.

CASTRATION ANXIETY: ON BECOMING MALE

So we can see that the 'castration complex', the fear of losing the penis, is the fundamental element in the male child's decision to relinquish his passive/feminine homosexual feelings towards his father. How does the penis come to have such psychological value? What does the psyche do in order to accord this geometrically insignificant (and comical, according to many of my female patients) piece of flesh such value? One can see from the universal importance of the phallus as a symbol, as well as from the extent of the child's fear of losing it – not to mention the horror this fantasy causes in grown men – that it is a man's most treasured possession.

It should be clear that this narcissistic valuation of the penis is finally established only when the genital Oedipus complex is reached. Until that moment the child will regard his mouth and his anus as the sources of greatest satisfaction. Whatever one's opinion of Freud's biological orientation, these are the fundamental facts of biological development. There is no disputing that the genital has to wait a while before it becomes more important than the mouth and anus as a source of sensual and erotic pleasure; even in adults these organs retain great capacity for the pleasures derived from infantile experience of sucking, biting, retaining, expelling, and so on.

The idea of the loss of the penis evokes the extremity of threat and terror equivalent, for most men, to death. It seems that some evidence of how it came to be so valued can be inferred from the symbolic and mythological status of the phallus – the logo of the patriarchy. I am sure I can safely assert that the essence of the phallus lies in its being in a state of erection. Only in this condition is it a symbol of potency, power and strength. The flaccid penis represents the absence of potency and procreative power.

Is it too great a leap to consider that the phallus itself is a symbol of massive denial of impotence and weakness – in effect, castration – which has already occurred before men discover the penis as a source of pleasure? The castration lies in their loss of the 'good' object/other which they were truly powerless to prevent and for which Mother eventually gets the blame – being, as she is, in the place where femininity is constructed as 'other' than male. The male child's subsequent discovery of her actual 'lack' of a penis and his own possession of one becomes both a symbol of revenge on her for, and at the same time a denial of, her castration of him. The crux of the phallus's symbolic power is that it derives from Mother's – woman's – lack of it. In so far as it forms the basis for a fantasy that he, rather than Mother, now possesses the means, he gains satisfaction, however inadequate, for his 'desire' to be the sole object of his mother's desire. The penis symbolizes what she so obviously lacks and, according to the child's way of thinking, must covet. In this way the phallus affirms that which it so strenuously denies.

The little boy's discovery of his mother's castration enables him to deny the 'loss' contained in his desire. It is not surprising that the thought of the loss of such a potent symbol should be viewed with horror, threatening, as it does, a descent into the chaos of 'desire' without hope of fulfilment – that is, exactly reproducing his earlier experience. It is equally unsurprising that the passive/castrated/feminine aspects of himself should ultimately come to be perceived with the same fear and contempt as the castrated mother/woman.

As the boy matures physically and intellectually, he will inevitably identify all those qualities which can be associated with this passive/active duality. The first and major one, which the Oedipus complex has resolved, is the question of what is feminine/castrated and what is masculine/phallic. One of the anxieties underpinning this process – that he will be castrated if he adopts a passive/feminine role in relation to his father – cannot be overstated, and it is this which will reinforce and add impetus to his male role-learning and the establishment of his gender identity. It will also provide the main bulwark of resistance to any changes in his relations with men, during his adulthood, in the form of homosexual anxiety. I will add that many grown men present for treatment with conflicting anxieties about being passive and assertive with other men – both these alternatives threaten castration.

In deciding, almost invariably, to identify with his father, the little boy relinquishes his mother, but not his need for a mother. After the decision to identify, he will spend many years being educated in male values which prepare him for his active role as predator, hunter, competitor, and the superior of women. During these so-called latency years he will receive many explicit and subliminal instructions about men and women both from his peer group and from the adults around him. Passivity, receptiveness, tenderness and emotionality will be defined as feminine traits. Although there are cross-cultural and subcultural differences, prescriptions – masquerading as definitions – of masculinity will be given to him which concern attitudes to being scared, confused, submissive or vulnerable, playing with dolls, running away, or showing feelings. Usually the injunction is 'don't'. In fact it would probably make very little difference if he were not told these things. To define feminine behaviour, he simply has to watch girls – his urge to differentiate, along with the little girl's identical need, will do the rest. This process is already well under way before the Oedipus complex makes an appearance. No doubt this is due to sex-typing by parents and masculine behaviour being encouraged. The child will know that such behaviour is important even if, as yet, he has no idea why. It is an answer for which the question has not yet been asked.

The little girl has the same need to make maleness 'other' as the little boy has to make femaleness 'other'. With a little help from his hormones and his biology – larger muscle groups for example – and under intense social and psychological pressures, he will devote his energy to those active pursuits for which he receives male approval. As I pointed out above, his need for intimacy with other men is repressed because of its castration implications. Instead, it is negotiated through competitive activities and, later, through the conquest of women. I have described social pressure as a 'pull from above'; similarly the psychological pressure constitutes a 'push from below'. One of the main outcomes of these combined pressures is the attempted exclusion from the masculine personality of any of the caring, tender qualities associated with the mother. From a Freudian point of view, this would vary according to both the strength of his innate homosexual disposition and his ambivalence towards the mother. The latter is dependent on the intensity of his latent, potential aggression and destructiveness in the face of what he constructs as the maternal failure symbolized by the internalized destructive 'witch' mother. This exclusion is not simply personal, as Jessica Benjamin (1990) makes clear. She believes not only that objectivity and rationality are the cornerstones of masculinity, but that this is reflected in the organization of culture, and reaches its zenith in the organization of the sciences, with their claim to objectivity, impersonality and gender neutrality.

It cannot be coincidence that the direction of the pull of social approval coincides with the direction of the push of psychological conflict. We saw above that Freud believed civilization (which I read as male civilization or patriarchy) to be the product of incest taboos, and that its main function is to prevent the boy from acting out his desire for his mother and his homicidal impulses towards his father (I am not convinced by this argument, as I will show later). Reducing this argument still further, one might say that the patriarchy is men's response to the inevitability of the experience of inadequate mothering (however this might be historically defined) and the development of the separate self.

To make this taboo effective is one of the main functions of patriarchal norms – to separate the boy from his mother. Whiting *et al.* (1958) found that severe initiation rites involving extreme degrees of pain or endurance, including some genital operations, prevailed in precisely those societies in which fathers were either psychologically or physically absent and the boy had spent all his formative years in exclusive proximity to his mother. These rites are essential to counter father rivalry, incestuous wishes and the boy's natural tendency to identify with his mother. Young boys have to learn the rules and roles of the dominant gender to enable them to enter into masculinity. Naturally, none of this is conscious in either the culture or the individual.

Sociobiologists would argue that this separation is the result of evolution in that it produces a system of sexual and role differentiation which reinforces a biological impetus and is species-effective. They would also argue that it increases the chances of species survival. However, Cucchiari (1981) maintains that it derives from the de-repression of awareness of primary sexual dimorphism (the denied knowledge that there are two sexes) and women's innate superiority as childbearers. He regards Freudian 'bisexuality' as representing pre-genital sexual organization – polymorphous, perverse, and decentralized. The individual development process which sees it become genital, localized and 'adult' through the Oedipus complex reproduces the process of development from the primal horde to a gender-differentiated society predicated on a symbolic order. The awareness of female power and the breakdown of a unitarian, sexually undifferentiated horde faced men with the problem of their own powerlessness. They were initially defined by what they were not: childbearers. The phallus as a signifier has its origins in this awareness of male powerlessness.

The basic rule the boy has to learn concerns gender differentiation. At its root is a denigration and devaluation of the life-giving – but emasculating – feminine principle. Feminine is unreliable. The chronic and universal discrimination against women, which keeps them infantilized and economically dependent, is, on the one hand, both a punishment for their supposed failure and a means for men to get what they can by way of redress. On the other hand, it is a guarantee that women will never again get the opportunity to be in such a powerful position in relation to men that the trauma could be repeated. As well as the potential rewards this form of redress offers (a female slave for every heterosexual man who is so minded) we must not ignore the penalty of failing to embrace masculinity: the loss of the approval of Father as Society.

It is a common male myth that men are strong. The injunction to be strong precludes, for example, feeling, or needing others, whether for intimacy or support. The fear of being thought weak, dependent, inadequate, 'cissy', and so on, enjoins men to hate those aspects of themselves which could be so described, and makes 'self-control' a highly prized male virtue. For men, the loss of control is the quintessential element of femininity. In keeping with the boy's decision to relinquish his passivity in relation to men, he will generalize this to include those aspects of himself which he comes to regard as feminine. These are as rigidly oppressed as are women in society.

The split between masculine and feminine which men institute is most easily observed, in non-Latin cultures, in the way in which men so firmly differentiate between thinking and feeling, often to such an extent that feelings are totally discounted. At its extreme this is a sort of computer mentality where logic is at a premium. It has long been recognized that the mind is unconsciously symbolic of the penis, and it is not surprising that its functioning is overvalued by men. In fact, the relationship between 'thinking' and gender – explicitly masculinity – has been the subject of searching feminist analysis. Perhaps more than most other disciplines, philosophy was able to endure longer in its claim to be sex-neutral by virtue of the level of abstraction of its phenomenal field of interest. The increasing influence of academic feminism, however, has led many feminist writers to draw attention to the historical connection between rationality and huMANity. As Ellen Dubois points out:

> the virtuous person, for Aristotle, is HE who develops practical wisdom, whose reason governs other faculties . . . the rational part is fit to rule over the irrational, and those members of society in whom the irrational soul dominates . . . children, slaves, and women. (Dubois *et al.*, 1987, p. 30)

> for women there is a dilemma which arises in the study of certain influential philosophers. A woman cannot, *qua* human being, appropriate their work, as it turns out in many ways to be a study of man. (ibid., quoting Garside)

RELATIONS BETWEEN MEN

One of the consequences of this generalized fear and hatred of the feminine is the straitjacket it imposes on relations between men. Given the immense limitations which male psychology imposes on genuine intimacy with women, one would have hoped to find some mitigation of existential loneliness in the possibility of intimacy between men. Instead, what does one find? Relations between us seem, whatever their external civilized appearances, to be dominated by ancient biological imperatives which would have more place in a group of hairy primates where males struggle for dominance and the right to inseminate all females. In other words, such relations seem to be dominated by mutual fear, aggression, violence and competitiveness. Who is more of a man? seems to be the question which dominates male relations. If I may paraphrase the psychoanalyst David Malan, 'It seems as if all relations between men initially involve a struggle over dominance and aggression. All men have to find a way to cope with it, and it is rarely resolved' (personal communication). Malan thinks that the best way for men to deal with these feelings – which he believes (mistakenly, in my opinion) to be biological in origin – is for them to made explicit in the relationship in a non-aggressive way.

This may enable men to use their competitiveness constructively – perhaps even enjoyably. Undoubtedly, it would be a step towards intimacy if such feelings could be shared rather than acted upon, although the anxiety this prospect arouses in men should not be underestimated. Apart from anxieties about open, unrestrained competitiveness leading to the destruction of one or the other – that is, unrestrained oedipal rivalry – the most prominent anxiety, which is never far from consciousness, is homosexual in nature. Most men have no model for intimate relationships with other men. The role-learning process stresses male, 'macho' behaviours of aggression and competitiveness – not values designed to promote mutual trust and intimacy.

Quite understandably, without a model for male intimacy there is the fear and insecurity of not knowing the physical boundaries – one of the main reasons why most private non-aggressive physical contact beween heterosexual men is of the back-slapping variety. At risk is the man's concept of self, and his image in other men's eyes. Being open about the 'weaker', feminine side of the self exposes one to the risk of being thought homosexual and also to the risk of actually experiencing homosexual feelings – maybe, but not necessarily genital – such as love for a man. Men have not ignored these issues. In fact, most theorizing about masculinity has been done by homosexual men, and it is they who have had the greatest influence on teaching about masculinity in feminist studies. Foucault (1979) in particular has had a profound influence on thinking about the construction of male sexuality. However, the writer who has had the greatest recent popular impact on men thinking about men is the poet Robert Bly, whose book *Iron John: A Book About Men* (1991), the so-called first handbook of 'masculism', was the top bestseller in the USA for over a year.

Bly's aim is to teach males how to be men by helping them to develop hidden qualities which he has identified. One particular quality, which has certainly received the most publicity, he names the 'wild man'; he defines this as the spirit of the primitive, unequivocally male ancestor which men must locate within themselves. The 'wild man' is not a primitive savage wedded to violence and domination, but he is capable of 'showing the sword'. His central qualities are strength and decisiveness. Bly, like many in the men's movement, is concerned with men's pain and suffering. The pain, as he sees it, is grief and hunger left over from the failed relationship with the physically and emotionally absent father. What men hunger for is physical closeness with an older man. Bly believes that this pain derives from growing up without a male role model, and his concern mirrors that expressed in academic psychology and psychotherapy about the impact of absent fathers on young boys' development. In a less academic but more accessible form, Bly expresses many of Moberley's preoccupations. Bly has developed a form of activity for men which greatly resembles many of the methods used in the 'growth movement' of the 1970s (symbolic initiation ceremonies, group hugging, reparenting, etc.) and is designed to help men to contact this source of male strength within themselves.

It is not surprising that Bly's work has come under attack from feminists who see it as a backlash against feminism: male dominance under a new disguise. Actually, it is not so new except in the labelling and marketing. In fairness to Bly, there is much in his analysis of men's predicament with which I agree. My own experience of men – that they feel impotent and insecure much of the time – is not so different from his. However, my understanding of its source and significance, and my prescription, are very remote from Bly's. His distinct aim is to empower men; my own belief is that men's power, both personal and institutional, is actually the source of, not the solution to, the problem.

For me, the question is: what alternative can be offered to men which relatively disempowers them but does so without psychologically castrating them? Unlike Bly, I do not believe this is possible without invoking their castration anxieties. He may be providing a positive emotional experience of male bonding, but ultimately this is self-defeating in so far as it is derived from the exclusion of women, his protests notwithstanding. I imagine that some of what men achieve on Iron Man intensives has long-term value, but I suspect it is at the expense of dealing with long-term anxieties and conflicts about homosexuality, violence and competition. Pre-genderless male bonding (a term derived from mother and baby studies) can hardly achieve real intimacy between identified males, unless by that term one means only penis possessors.

One should not minimize the deep and abiding anxiety, fear and/or contempt that most men feel towards male homosexuals. Changes in the law do not change attitudes, even though they may change gross, easily observed forms of discrimination. Public morality is still largely anti-homosexual, and regards homosexuality as an aberration and a perversion. The now notorious British Clause 28 is a good example of this morality. Notice how frequently one hears anxiety expressed about homosexual teachers in boys' schools, yet never the same anxiety about heterosexual teachers in girls' schools. The clear, unwritten, unspoken assumption is that homosexuals are more depraved, more sexually irresponsible, less trustworthy, than heterosexuals. Even allowing for the unlikely possibility that there may be a biological basis for such prejudice, there is also a clear existential account whose function is to buttress each person's concept of his sexuality. This subjective account of these attitudes is a product of the Oedipus complex, and it derives from the man's fear of his own femininity. This fear is a direct result of his castration anxiety which, although it has other origins, he comes ultimately to experience as the fear of losing his penis.

It seems to be a man's lot to live in constant fear of his father's disapproval. In adult life, this 'normal' paranoia extends to institutions and authorities, all of which symbolize the original role of the father with whom one identified, mainly out of the fear of castration and the inability to possess the mother. One wonders how many men experience the organizations in which they work as benign and holding rather than threatening. The latent rebellion against the father, with all its attendant risks, is an ever-present source of anxiety for men in their subordinate relations. Unfortunately, all too many institutions and authorities live up to this image of the 'castrating' father – not surprisingly, given that one of the important latent social functions of institutions is to uphold and further the patriarchal values from which male 'castration/impotence' anxiety is derived.

Men might appear to be as much victims of patriarchy (prisoners of gender) as women are and this, no doubt, is how a great many men would present themselves. Certainly it is true of some elements of the American men's movement, particularly the element influenced by the powerful re-evaluation counselling school (see Kreiner, 1991). Actually, I believe the notion of men as victims of gender is nonsense. In the final analysis, men have choices which are not available to women. It is true that women, if they are so inclined, can fight against an identifiable oppressor – men – whereas men can be described as self-oppressed. Clearly, as small boys males are not responsible for their choices. Grown men, however, continue to exercise these choices largely for the benefits they bring, not only in relation to women but also in relation to the fragile male sense of self. It adds insult to injury if men then suggest to women, in defence against the charge of misogyny, that these hidden costs make men as much the victim of oppression as the women whom they oppress. This is not to deny that men have great difficulties in relationships with both men and women, but the psychological root of these difficulties lies in the inability to be intimate with a free woman because of the unresolved childhood dependency issues arising from the relationship with the historically reconstructed 'bad' mother. These childlike, feminine aspects of men persist because they are afraid to face up to them. The prospect of intimacy with a strong, free woman is a fantasy in these circumstances – it cannot exist without mutuality and reciprocity. Additionally, men's denial of their feminine capacities imposes such limitations on their responses that genuine intimacy between them is virtually impossible.

I appreciate that I could be accused of describing all human relations as paranoid, at least in the non-pathological sense that people are generally suspicious and mistrustful of others. I believe this is true in so far as this 'paranoia' exists as a potential in all of us. Similarly misogyny, the pure hatred of women, exists as a potential which men both express and defend against in the control they exert over women to prevent the emergence of circumstances which would lead to the hatred becoming manifest. In the right circumstances, we are all a little paranoid. Another way of expressing this is to say that all human relations have to find strategies for avoiding the primitive fear and hatred which threaten to overwhelm the constructive urges which we all wish were the only ones we felt. Social rules for governing relations have evolved which allow for the expression of such feelings in culturally acceptable ways. For example, aggressive competition between men is encouraged, and winners are admired, in all fields of activity from sports to business management, but there are firm rules governing the lengths to which each participant may go. Sublimated and controlled aggression is the basis for much leisure activity, and institutions, from the smallest to the largest, have to evolve structures to prevent hostility and, more importantly, sexuality from becoming uncontrolled (although the extent of sexual harassment of women by men is beginning to be acknowledged as a serious problem in the USA and the UK).

It is not difficult to erect biological accounts of 'normal' male paranoia and misogyny in a form which indicates their interdependence. It also seems clear that if these are biological potentials, and they continue to have the same imperative value, particularly in relations between men, the future for the species looks grim. Perhaps one must take what little comfort there is from knowing that the greatest human characteristic is the capacity to learn beyond the demands of the immediate environment and biological inheritance.

It seems that if men are to alter their relationships with each other fundamentally they have much to overcome, following the early failure fully to heal the split between the 'witch and the princess'. It also seems that they will not be able to do this in isolation from their relationships with women; a change in one will necessitate a change in the other. What might such a change involve? Paradoxically, men must find ways of desexualizing their relationships with each other, in order to enable them to become more sexual. Repressed homosexual feelings and urges, and their associated anxieties, prevent men from being intimate, and from expressing a wider range of feelings with each other. We men need to find ways of de-genitalizing our relationships so that they can become more sexual in the widest sense of the word. A large part of the problem is the uncertainty about boundaries: feelings can so easily become touching; touching can so easily become caressing; and caressing can so easily become coupling. If we could learn to accept our homosexual impulses, and cease to see them as threatening, we would find that there is a world of difference between an impulse and acting it out – we may even discover that such feelings can be enjoyable. This does not represent an injunction not to act on these impulses. The crucial issue is the capacity for informed, uncoerced choice. This would involve major changes in men's perceptions of masculinity and femininity, and our attitudes to homosexuality. For this to be possible we must want to change the quality of our relations with men, and be motivated to increase our self-awareness markedly. What might that mean in this context?

In discussing the unconscious, Freud used an analogy to describe the way it operates and its relationship with the conscious mind. He said that living with the unconscious is rather like riding a wild horse: you hope to have the strength to steer it in the direction you wish to go, but if you fail you try to persuade yourself that in any case you wanted to go in the direction in which it is heading.

The Oedipus complex involves more than simply resolving conflicting feelings towards each parent separately – though as we have seen, this in itself is a daunting task. Perhaps more important for the male adult's peace of mind is his capacity to come to terms with his parents as a couple united in intercourse. The danger is that he may destroy them both internally with his jealousy and hatred. The task of finding a solution which does not deny him satisfaction of his desire or relinquishment of his objects is fraught with difficulty (Meltzer, 1973, p. 87). As we saw in our discussion of Moberley's work, a resolution which involves maintaining a good relationship with one of his objects only will leave him psychically impoverished in a number of predictable ways.

The achievement of the position of so-called 'genitality', which is completed during puberty, is generally thought to be the acme of man's development: he now has a psychology which is socially consistent with his anatomy, and with the existence of two-sex parents. Let us return to the question: what would be the consequences of an individual becoming aware of the means by which he arrived at this much-vaunted position – becoming aware of his-story? Assuming that it is possible for him to do so, the first consequence is that he would realize that his much-vaunted genitality is actually far less fixed than he would like to believe; it is a precarious achievement. Most men have to work very hard to hang on to it, challenged as it is by all manner of impulses which belong to other erogenous zones and earlier phases of development – the mouth and the anus, a fascination with tasting, smelling or looking, or enjoyment of fetishes (which most men enjoy to some extent), for example women's underwear or fantasies of, or actual pleasure in, causing humiliation or pain to a loved person. Although, as we have seen, men's aggressive and competitive feelings towards other men have multiple sources, I have seen many times how my male patient will use his anger in overdetermined ways, both expressively (of his penis envy; his jealousy about my possession of the mother, etc.) and defensively, against his love for me and all this implies. Whatever the social and biological advantages of heterosexual genitality, it seems that its main psychological function is to defend against the unfulfilled desire for Mother.

Terrifying anxieties are associated with this regressive need, because it is so full of the destructive impulses symbolised by the 'witch'. It matters little whether these impulses are the mother's or a projection of the child's – the social and psychological reality is that they are constructed around the concepts of femininity and motherhood; the 'witch' is gender-neutral. From the point of view of an aware adult who has already achieved a successful identification with his father, and now has ego resources which he did not possess when the original mistake was made, it may be possible to accept that he is not the man he thought he was, and that he may be rather more polymorphous and perverse than he has allowed for. Rigid genital masculinity is not necessary either for the preservation of the species or for individual well-being.

The choice is not between being a 'real man' and being a 'raving homosexual'. Neither is it necessary to 'act out' homosexual feelings in a sexual way, although awareness of them would probably do a great deal to improve relations between men and remove a burdensome set of unnecessary demands. Such a process must lead to a greater capacity for intimacy between men and, I think, between men and women, if only because of the loosening of the links between our concept of masculinity and feminine qualities and behaviour. It would also bring to consciousness the psychological roots of misogyny, although it will not weaken the strength of the feelings motivating it. This in turn must provide a wider range of options for men in all aspects of our lives. Without awareness there is no choice.

Whether or not men have the desire to alter the status quo is an altogether more thorny question. Increasingly one hears men speaking out about their dissatisfaction and unhappiness with normal male roles. These men are not only those who feel like gender victims and are part of what is known in the USA as the 'men's rights' movement (easily identified as a reaction to feminism), or those who assert that women are as oppressive and abusive as men. Although these may constitute the majority, there are others whose discontent is based on empathy with women's suffering at men's hands (which may well derive from a dominant identification with the mother and a failed relationship with the father), among whom I include myself. For example, there is the small and charmingly named MASS (Men Against Sexist Shit) in northern England. More seriously, there is the Campaign Against Pornography and Censorship which, although it has strong support from feminist women, is actively supported by many influential men. In the USA there is Men Against Pornography, founded by John Stoltenberg, and the Emerge collective against male violence to women in Boston. Also, despite many difficulties, both financial and political, men go on producing anti-sexist magazines such as *Achilles Heel* in the UK.

I would like to share an anecdote which illustrates the difference between the rights (men as victims) group and the 'empathic' group. A colleague attended a conference on working methods with abusive men. One workshop was entitled 'Denial and Collusion in Abusers' Groups'. For a long time the group concerned itself with issues about how men are raised to deny their loving feelings for women, and the pain this caused them, and how it could be confronted in groups. My colleague (who knows that this is a serious problem for men) became increasingly agitated, and could finally contain himself no longer. He interrupted to say that he thought the group was actually in denial at that point: that it was redefining the problem and denying the real issue, which is men's active abuse of women; and that there is so much of this to deal with in our abusers' programmes that we never have time to talk about denied love. His intervention evoked from the group a considerable hostility similar to the hostility such confrontations evoke in abusers' groups.

It may never be more than a minority who wish to change - just as feminist women may remain a minority. The important thing is that we should have the freedom to do so. In the workplace and corporate worlds, which are invariably male-dominated, the consequences of rampant masculinity are evident to anybody brought in from the outside, as I have often been, as a consultant on human relations. The exclusive emphasis on the task and the indifference shown to feelings and social processes, despite its apparent efficiency, can be enormously costly in lost time and production as people attempt to express their individuality using the task as a medium. Between men, in particular, ways of dealing with aggressive and competitive feelings can lead to painful emotional and financial costs as they try to avoid the 'one-down' passive/feminine/castrated position and act out the authority problems which Moberley (1987) describes. How relieving it is to be able to co-operate with other men, and for dominance/submission not to be the anxiety-provoking, sexually loaded issue it currently is. The failed identification with the father which leaves a residue in the need to prove one's masculinity, or the symbolic size of one's penis, is an area that is much debated within the men's movement as men struggle to find a model for masculinity which does not simply involve adopting 'feminine' qualities. Ironically, although Freud made much of female penis envy, it is my experience that men's envy of the penis can be debilitatingly severe.

The successes of the feminist movement might drive men to re-examine their relationships with each other. It seems that many American men, particularly those in cities, are threatened by the emergence of a strong, assertive woman amongst the professional urban middle classes. These men apparently feel castrated by this 'New Woman' and, frustrated in their attempts to be intimate with her, they are turning to other men for support and companionship. The emergent male liberation movement has a voice and is elaborating a theoretical base, which in the main is not psychoanalytic (Pleck, 1981), and a practice, as exemplified in the work of Robert Bly and Herb Goldberg (1976). It certainly does not seem that this 'New Woman' is becoming more feminine; these men feel that she is actually challenging for supremacy in a man's world with a man's weapons and wiles. Whatever one's feminist views – from the apocalyptic to the socialist radical or, indeed, none at all – I do not think that women can welcome this change with open arms.

5 The Don Juan Complex

We have looked at the processes and dynamics which underlie the formation of male gender identity and sex-role formation, and their connection with misogyny. Let us now examine how these underlying dynamics are expressed in men's relations with women. We can do this by taking an extreme example of something which seems to be common to a large majority of men: the inability to be faithful in a monogamous relationship, whether homo- or heterosexual (estimates vary between 60 and 90 per cent; see Lawson, 1990; Reibstein and Richards, 1991 for summaries of the data). Interestingly, the data also indicate that despite the AIDS crisis, more women are having extra-marital affairs than ever before. Men seem to possess of a sexuality which is founded not on intimacy or reciprocity but on the perception of woman as a prize, as an object to be chased and conquered.

The most famous cultural symbol of masculine chase and conquer, faithlessness and promiscuity is undoubtedly Don Juan. He is the eternal hero whose unrequited search for the perfect love leads eventually to Hell. Don Juan is a legendary Spanish nobleman whose fortunes have been the subject of over sixty poems, plays and operas by, amongst others, Mozart, Strauss, Molière, Shaw and Byron. The plight of Don Juan, like that of Oedipus, exercises a fascination for the male imagination which transcends time. Clearly, this is a hero with whom men can readily identify – if not in his behaviour, then with the conflicts which underlie it. I dare say, however, that few men would consciously identify with the more covert motives which, as a little thought shows, may be central to his search.

An obvious point about all the works concerning Don Juan is that they are predicated on the assumption that women desire nothing so much as to be the object of men's desire. It is probably not an overstatement to say that this is a fundamental difference between the sexes – women are constructed, by men, to be content to be the object of desire, whereas men are constructed to desire the object. From my argument in previous chapters it seems clear that this may be a seminal male defence against the basic unconscious male desire (as well as the source of his greatest fear): to be the sole object of his mother's desire. Leaving this aside for the time being, one might say that a woman's aim is to be loved, while a man's is to love. Freud hypothesized that this was one more example of the passive/active duality that characterizes male and female, such that female is passive/feminine/being loved, whereas male is active/masculine/loving.

Freud's view of the Don Juan complex, in which a man pursues and conquers many women, was that it represented an acting out of the boy's Oedipus wishes and anxieties – he desires the mother, but is overwhelmed by unconscious anxiety at the prospect of achieving his aim because of the threat of castration by the vengeful father (Freud, 1910). According to Freud, this is Don Juan's reason for leaving each conquest immediately it is achieved. There is some support for this view in the dénouement of the story, when Don Juan is taken to Hell by the ghost of an elderly man – the father of one of his conquests – whom he has killed, and who is clearly a representation of the father who prohibits the child's sexual activity. There is further overwhelming support for the oedipal interpretation in the fact that one of the greatest spurs to Don Juan's desire is the sight of a happy couple; he feels compelled to break it up by making the woman fall in love with him. This is clearly a compulsion to repeat the oedipal triangle. He desires nothing so much as a woman who is the object of another man's desire. This, however, is not a necessary condition of Don Juan's desire, although at times it seems to be sufficient. In any case, the actual presence or absence of a prohibiting father figure in each of his conquests has no real bearing on the issue of whether Don Juan is acting out his oedipal drama. The drama is internalized in every adult male. We all carry our fathers around in our heads in the form of our super-ego. He is just as much present now as he was when we were children. The father in the story is clearly meant to symbolize this, and one such character is sufficient to make the point.

Other authors have pointed out the unconscious homosexual content of Don Juan's behaviour, although this will not be pursued here. We have to see the merit and the innovative genius of Freud's interpretation of the oedipal drama in Don Juan, but it is also necessary to point out its limitations. The oedipal factor and the stress on Don Juan's castration complex are correct in so far as they go. The father in the story, who is undoubtedly the prohibiting oedipal father, is also the projecting screen for elements of the 'bad' mother. Throughout his life she has denied the child the gratification of his desires for her – from the initial oral one of fusing with her to the genital one of penetrating her and giving her a baby. Because of the intensity of these desires and the inevitable pain of their frustration – and let no one underestimate either – the child comes to experience her as harbouring homicidal wishes towards him. The earlier, oral conflicts are also a form of the oedipal drama. There are three terms: baby, 'good' mother and 'bad' mother. The parental imagos have not yet been sexually differentiated into Mother and Father as they will be in the Oedipus complex proper. This occurs under the sway of parental education, the introjection of sex-role stereotyping and the increasing eroticization of the genitals.

The projection of these prohibiting, destructive qualities on to the father (which actually has normative social value in that it leads to the Oedipus complex and to the acceptance of the Law – Mother is Father's property) leaves the boy free of his ambivalence towards the mother. In Don Juan's case, however, this clearly does not work for long – he is unable to sustain his idealization of his new conquest beyond the moment of her surrender. Once she yields, he loses all interest in her. As he explains to his servant Sganarelle in Molière's version:

> 'but once one succeeds, what else remains? What more can one wish for? All that delights one in passion is over and one can only sink into a

> tame and slumbrous affection – until a new love comes along to awaken desire and offer the charm of new conquests. There is no pleasure to compare with the conquest of beauty, and my ambition is to . . . go on for ever from conquest to conquest. I feel it is in me to love the whole world, and still wish for new worlds to conquer.' (Molière, 1665, Act I Scene 1 p. 203)

Woody Allen put it slightly differently when he said, 'So many women and so little time!'

A slightly different understanding of promiscuity is offered by my recollection of one male patient who expressed great anxiety about his seductive behaviour. Although he was searching for a partner, he reported that he was being completely indiscriminate in his choices, and all women were targets for him. This man had a complex and tragic history involving violent sexual abuse by his father, which has some relevance here, but the central issue I want to stress is that when he was not being seductive he felt completely empty and, as he put it, 'dangerously and terminally bored'. The danger refers to his history of acting self-destructively in this frame of mind, simply in order to experience some stimulation and get rid of the emptiness. In the past this had involved drugs, alcohol, gambling and food. Not unnaturally, he was acutely anxious when acting seductively.

It has already been mentioned that Freud, in his paper 'On the universal tendency to debasement in the sphere of love' (1912a), commented on the man's difficulty in combining his sensual and affectionate feelings in his relations with women. Most men can feel affection with one woman and not desire her, or desire her and not feel affection for her. His explanation was that the affectionate feelings are originally attached to the first object, Mother, and if these feelings become joined, in adulthood, to sensual feelings in relation to one person, then the man is threatened with the return of his infantile incestuous longings, with the attendant castration anxieties. This is why men repress their sexual desire for their wives, while retaining the affectionate feelings. In fact, most men are aware that when their sexual desires emerged with full force, at the beginning of puberty, these were initially directed towards their mother before being – usually very quickly – directed towards another person. It is clearly not representative of the population as a whole, yet in my seventeen years of practice as a clinician the majority of my male patients can recall that at the onset of puberty they would masturbate into their mother's underwear, and often dress in her clothes as part of a masturbatory ritual. These activities were always accompanied by acute anxiety of discovery by the father, and fantasies of terrible but unnameable punishment: castration anxiety. It is only at puberty that the sexual drive begins, however firmly, to reach its genital organization under the pressure of physical development. This usually involves reliving all the polymorphous impulses of infancy.

While I accept that such fears of the father as a rival, and the associated guilt, are important reasons for this separation of tender from sexual feelings, there are other, older and deeper motives for it which are not based on the oedipal triangle as experienced by the phallic child at around three to five years of age. Before we look at these, I must make it clear that the following re-emphasis is not in any way intended to minimize the importance of the Oedipus complex. I have already made it plain that I regret the increasing emphasis on the relationship with the mother in psychoanalysis and therapy. There are feelings and urges in the little boy during the oedipal stage of which he has no previous experience; these make for a discrete developmental conflict which is essential if the child is to reach psychological and sexual maturity and become a gendered subject. In addition, he has the capacity – which was not present at earlier stages – to see his parents as whole persons.

These older motives for separating tender from sensual feelings derive from the infant boy's early relationship with his mother and the breast. It should now be clear that by 'mother' I always mean the primary carer. This 'always' is not a social reality but a linguistic and psychological one – 'the place where femininity falls' (Mitchell, 1986) and where the child will eventually, in most cases, place the mother.

Don Juan's repetitive seduction and subsequent rejection of women, and his willingness to do or promise anything to achieve his ends, are almost psychopathic, in that he has no regard for the consequences of his behaviour and – at least consciously – is without guilt or remorse. It is clear that Don Juan has no love for women – nothing, at least, which would be recognized as mature love – indeed, that he is even unaware of women as physically or emotionally whole people. His feeling that he can love the whole world indicates the regressive, oceanic and narcissistic quality of what he calls his love. He is basically in a position of manic denial where he idealizes the qualities of the 'good' breast/mother/world and his union with it. He completely represses any feelings to the contrary, and the splitting upon which this is based. All the while, however, the world (the women whom he victimizes) is made to suffer from his unconscious intentions.

During its early years the story of Don Juan tended to stress the relationship between his outrageous sexual behaviour and his eventual punishment: in being sent to Hell. Later, this emphasis shifted somewhat: from the punishment of a villain to the assertion of the grandeur of a hero who had risen above the petty-mindedness of a repressive society. Essentially, the Don Juan story is a morality play. Its plot reflects its Spanish origins – a deeply Catholic culture which protects family honour and female virginity with the same vigour as it protects the cult of the Virgin and the Crucifixion. Psychoanalytically, the story contains a clear warning to men not to behave as Don Juan for fear that they, too, would suffer divine retribution, undoubtedly symbolizing castration by God the father.

Whatever the version, there is no doubt that audiences have responded powerfully to artists' fascination with the story of Don Juan. This fascination, like the fascination with all classic drama, must express some fundamental conflicts with which we can all identify. No doubt there is some comfort, for both men and women, in the standard version in which Don Juan gets his come-uppance. This reassurance is partially derived from the support the story provides for most people's repression of their own desires for promiscuity or infidelity; in the last analysis, this repression results from the Oedipus complex. It is not, however, this aspect of the story which will be examined here, despite the importance of the Oedipus complex in Don Juan's behaviour. Instead, I want to concentrate on the two-person relationship between Don Juan and the women he seduces because of what this tells us about male-female relationships and the man's particular difficulties in combining his tender and sexual feelings.

PROMISCUITY: DESIRE WITHOUT LOVE?

Given the chance, most men would probably behave with Don Juan's promiscuity if certain restraints were removed. Such a desire is certainly articulated by the vast majority of men with whom I have worked. There was no doubt a time in prehistory, after the emergence of sexual dimorphism, when the human male, and his progenitor, were under an imperative to inseminate as many females as they could or – more probably – desired to experience the pleasure of orgasm as often as possible. No doubt this impulse still exists, and is completely at odds with our present conception of an ordered society. The Oedipus complex prevents it by introducing the notion of the mother/female as the property of the father, and therefore unavailable to the child, forcing him to come to terms with the concept of the parental couple. The concept of women as property is central to the Oedipus complex (see G. Rubin, 1975).

In case this seems like a heterosexist argument, let me hasten to add that although there may have been a time when males inseminated as many females as possible under the influence of some form of periodicity, this was after the development of heterosexism – that is, after some form of gender differentiation and stratification had already occurred. There is no reason to believe that men are, innately, any more promiscuous than women. In fact, I am arguing here that men's sexuality is often not sexuality at all, but a form of defence against the more primitive feelings which threaten that sexuality in its essence – that is a man's gender identity. There is no doubt – Freud pointed it out many years ago – that when infants are exposed to painful feelings evoked by abandonment, separation or other forms of frustration, the discovery that they can give themselves pleasure is a life-saver. This pleasure takes the form of autoerotic, self-administered stimulation of the erogenous zones: the lips, the anus, and the penis or vagina. A great deal of what passes for sexual activity in males, as exemplified by Don Juan, is simply a form of masturbation.

It was commonly – and erroneously – believed that women give up masturbation after the discovery that they do not possess a penis, because it reminds them of their inferiority and humiliation. Men, on the other hand, continue to masturbate for the rest of their lives. It was Freud who first suggested women's abstinence for these reasons, but later research has shown that he was wrong (Masters and Johnson, 1961). Women continue to masturbate, but it is obviously difficult to obtain accurate comparative figures for male and female rates of masturbation. It seems to be a valid conclusion that the more difficulty a man or a woman has in resolving the traumas and conflicts which were associated with the original masturbation, the more difficult it will be to desist in adult life whenever those unconscious complexes are evoked. Equally, the frequency and intensity of the masturbation will be related to the severity of the trauma. Stoller (1975) has shown that the fantasies accompanying masturbation will, with careful analysis, reveal the nature of the original trauma, and how masturbation is designed to overcome it. Clinical practice confirms this observation.

A brief illustrative example may be useful here. A patient of mine, a man in his early thirties, had presented with severe difficulties in maintaining a relationship with a woman. He was clearly depressed, and it seemed as though this was a lifelong condition. It emerged that his mother had abandoned him at seven months, and that he compulsively masturbated. His treatment, predictably, revolved around his methods of dealing with breaks in his relationship with me. During the early years, and only during breaks, he was involved with prostitutes whom he paid to pretend to be his mother attempting to seduce him as her teenage son. She had to struggle with her desire, but ultimately these struggles had to fail, so that she could not refrain from seducing him. She failed because he was so desirable, and her desire for him was overwhelming. It was some years before he was able to contact the real grief about abandonment, his loneliness and the homicidal rage which this fantasy covered. Stoller's concept of the fantasy as a means of making triumph out of disaster could not be more clearly illustrated. His pleasure in masturbating was his way of denying the pain and rage of abandonment and loss, and his mother's indifference to him.

It is somewhat easier to obtain data about promiscuity, and there is little doubt that men are the more promiscuous sex (Hite, 1981). I think this reflects a very important aspect of women's development. It should be clear that it cannot be something innate in femaleness. Is it because, as feminists assert, woman's sexuality is controlled and shaped by men to preclude promiscuity so that a man will know his own children? The separation of sexuality from procreation, with the advent of birth control for women, has obscured a reality. It has always been women who have paid the price for promiscuity, their own or men's. This knowledge would, no doubt, have a restraining effect on female promiscuity, as would periods of pregnancy. Additionally – and more importantly – we cannot forget that women's whole view of their gender identity has precluded not just sexual freedom, but freedom as a sex.

Most people suffer from a conflict between the need for and fear of dependency. Dependency arises from the child's experience of the loss of his basic unity with his mother. Initially this will cause him to experience paralysing existential anxieties about falling apart or dying, which become what I think of as a primary encapsulated psychosis (Hopper, 1991). The absent object becomes persecuting when his pain and primary rage are projected into the returning object who, he realizes, is also the object who caused the pain of his initial loss. Not until he experiences separation will he feel dependent. Dependency, like desire, symbolizes loss. This is the origin of the conflict between the need for and fear of dependency, often experienced as the conflict between the need for security and the need for freedom. For most of us, certainly for men, this conflict seems insoluble because we attach security to the need for an intimate/dependent relationship with a woman (because that is where Mother is), and this is antithetical to what men regard as freedom. The sort of dependency sought for and fought against is infantile in origin rather than what might be regarded as mature attachment behaviour. When one's internal security is dependent on the presence of a real external person in this way, it is in fact impossible to be secure and independent because one is dependent on external circumstances. The fundamental difficulty is for the man to face up to his separateness from the object of his desire. True freedom, which stems from the attainment of individuality – the recognition of separateness, and the capacity for interdependence – is therefore unattainable, for both men and women, unless they give up the need for this infantile security.

In the distortions which occur in male development because of the inability to face separateness, freedom becomes a reactionary wish for freedom from dependency. Because of the reactionary nature of this wish and the way in which masculinity is defined, it becomes attached, as we shall see, to the atavistic freedom to be promiscuous. Men who find great difficulty in making or sticking to a vow of faithfulness, or even in making an honest commitment to it, have particular reasons for needing to reserve the option of promiscuity. They know there are going to be times when they will feel the need to be unfaithful, although they may not be aware of the reasons for this. As we shall see from Don Juan's behaviour, other things being equal, the origins of this need lie in the inability to preserve the goodness of the object.

LOVE WITHOUT DESIRE

Although men are afraid of commitment to an exclusive relationship, most of us will commit ourselves at some time in our lives, because of the mature need to bond and, perhaps, procreate. There are, however, other motives. Once the courtship period is over, we would also have to face the insecurity and loss involved in renouncing a relationship in which an attachment has formed. No doubt we have all heard the old saying 'all relationships get to a point where the partners have to get married or separate.' I have seen many times how this ends with men resenting their partners for – as they see it – 'taking away' their freedom to be promiscuous without guilt, and acting out their feelings in infidelities. Many of the men I work with will say, without guile, that they were trapped by their wives. It is not uncommon for a man to say that he was trapped by his wife's weakness and by his fear that she would do something stupid (?) if he abandoned her. These men have no awareness of how they use their partners as containers for their projected dependency: fears of abandonment, helplessness, loneliness and despair.

We are, all of us, born in a state of helplessness. Our dependency on the environment is total; self-sufficient survival is impossible. We are incapable of assertively manipulating the environment to satisfy our needs. Every individual's first experience of security or its lack is entirely a function of his or her relation with the environment – that is, Mother. To the extent that this relationship is experienced as 'not good enough', or is short of what is often called 'averagely expectable', the ground is laid for a potentially lifelong feeling of insecurity.

There is nothing unique about this. We all feel that to some extent we were not given as much as we needed in childhood. As the humanistic psychologists became fond of saying during the psychology revolution of the 1960s and 1970s, 'We're all lonely and afraid and unhappy'. Unlike them, however, I believe this is inevitable – not only because it is impossible for the mother to be perfect, but also because we are each born with the potential to feel the inevitable pain, frustration and aggression caused by the awareness of separateness. Add to that the fact that mothers will, for much of the time, be working at, or around, the limits of the child's tolerance for frustration (Winnicott, 1963b, p. 90), and the sad fact that we all have to learn to adapt to an external world, and the only surprising thing is that we don't all break down at some time. Of course, the extent of this adaptation, and the time at which the demands for us to adapt were made, will vary enormously. Whatever our individual differences, however, we have all suffered this blow to our narcissistic wish to be the centre of the world – that is, Mother's world.

Growing up is one narcissistic blow after another as we learn that other people exist and have needs of their own which do not include us. The split that arises between 'good' and 'bad' mother, which is the child's way of dealing with frustrating experiences – narcissistic wounds – enables him to cope with his own destructive feelings. Even if he is able to reconcile his contradictory images of his mother, there will still be a residue of unfulfilled needs for security and dependency. This reconciliation can occur only if he experiences his ambivalence, and the depression this entails. Apart from his grief at the loss of the ideal, 'good' mother, he will also have to come to terms with the fact that, through projection, the 'witch' is also a product of his own hatred of the mother who first abandoned and frustrated him. Such feelings are inevitable, because the bottomless well of desire makes frustration inevitable. As Winnicott pointed out (1963b, p. 86), even in favourable circumstances the child tends to note experiences which are frustrating or painful, not those which are satisfying. There is a natural tendency to remember the bad.

This depressive process is not, however, all loss. The integration of 'good' and 'bad' mother, and of one's own destructive feelings, give one the capacity to discriminate between good and bad. It also enables one to face the future with a sense of security in the knowledge that the 'good' mother may not be ideal but she is 'good enough', and one has not been able to destroy her: first in reality and secondly – and more importantly – as an internal object. One need never again be truly terrified of one's destructive impulses once the move has been made from fear and pain to love and pain in relation to one's internal and external mother.

As a result of these universal experiences, and the fact that we all have to struggle with the conflict between love and hate, we all have conflicts about dependency on another person. To some extent there is a residue of this infantile conflict, with all its primitive implications (cannibalism and oral sadism, anal sadism, etc.), in each of us. Don Juan – to return to the subject of this chapter – either has more than his fair share of unresolved infantile needs, or there is something in the nature of masculinity as it is constructed which makes it appear so. He defends against the feelings of existential loneliness, sadistic rage, frustration, and so on, and the depression and mental pain which would ensue if they broke through, by acting as if he has no particular attachment to anyone, and being outrageously promiscuous. In part he is reassuring himself, with each new conquest, that his mother is still alive inside him, and has not been destroyed by his hatred for her. He is also demonstrating to himself that his capacity for loving is intact, and has not similarly been destroyed. Every time he conquers a woman he is re-creating his mother: he is, in effect, bringing her back to life after destroying her internally with his greedy and destructive feelings. His conscious fear is of 'a tame and slumbrous affection', but his unconscious fear is of facing the full force of his ambivalence in relation to one person, and the terrifying truth that he is not capable of loving without also wanting to destroy.

In an interesting piece of research (Hanmer and Glueck, 1957) a number of convicted, fixated paedophiles were shown a picture of a semi-nude mature woman as part of a psychological test. The research was designed to test the hypothesis that men who are attracted to little girls are afraid of heterosexual contact. Whatever the methodological flaws in this research, it showed that these men did not come up with the sexual theme which might be offered by a 'normal' person. In general they came up with stories that the woman was sick, dying or dead. This is an intriguing finding in the light of my argument here. It has long been thought that men who are attracted to little girls are afraid of women (Storr, 1965). This research, although it is far from conclusive, indicates that women are dead or damaged for such men – reason enough for fear, one might think. Don Juan's internal object is damaged by his hatred of her but not, apparently, damaged beyond repair, as she seems to be for some of these offenders. Women are still good enough for him to experience his desire, however distorted, and in fantasy he heals a damaged woman with his penis – fucking a woman when she is unwell 'to make her better' is not uncommon. It may be that paedophiles harbour more intense feelings of hatred for and fear of women than normal men, and in fact this is supported by the constant finding that incest offenders are extremely authoritarian in their homes, even where the family is regarded as chaotic. (Glaser and Frosh [1984] make the distinction between authoritarian and chaotic families, but their examples make an unconvincing case for a strict division.) It is unlikely that all battering or abusive men are incest offenders – there are too many for this to be credible, even though it seems that intrafamilial sexual abuse may be occurring on a massive scale. However, about half the women in battered wives' refuges who have escaped from violent men report a suspicion that their husband assailants were sexually assaulting their daughters (reported in J. Herman, 1981). While this in no way undermines the political analysis of father–daughter rape (Ward, 1984), it offers support for the contention that men whose hatred of women is intense experience them as so damaged that they are unable to be intimate with them.

Like all defensive behaviour, Don Juan's betrays his unconscious feelings towards women in that he effectively 'kills' each woman by spurning her after conquering her. His unconscious anxiety and guilt about what he has done make it necessary for him to repeat his behaviour with another. He undoes the destruction of the last woman by re-creating the good object – the mother – through sexual desire. It must be said that, of course, he does experience his love as having some creative power for making good (reparation), and that he is expressing this with each new conquest. His tragedy is that his love is not sustainable because as soon as a woman becomes 'real' for him, after he has 'made' her, his destructive feelings begin to emerge and his passionate idealization breaks down. If his reparative urges were genuine, his compulsive promiscuity would cease. Once he had discovered that he had not killed his mother, and believed in his capacity for re-creating her, his promiscuity would have no point. What is it that renders his reparative behaviour – his conquests – so meaningless? He seems to be unable to learn from experience. I believe that his reparative urges arise not out of genuine guilt and concern for the object but out of concern for himself and his own destruction. He is unable to tolerate the pain of not being the object of his mother's desire, and of his sadistic, destructively envious feelings towards her. Reparation, to be successful, must have at its heart a true concern for the object and genuine guilt about the damage one is inflicting on it, both internally and externally. Without this, it is mere sentimentality.

All too often, the need for security is a need to have available a constant source of reassurance that one's destructive feelings have not taken effect. The fear is that one's hatred has destroyed the good breast/mother who is the root of all good feelings towards the world. This is the real source of unresolved infantile dependency needs. One's goodness is dependent on external evidence which, were it removed, could lead to one's worst fears – that one is bad and incapable of loving – being confirmed. Every time Don Juan leaves a woman, he also confirms to himself that he is not dependent on her, or on his mother. This dependency, which is so frightening for him, has at its root the same death wishes towards his mother as he experienced at her hands when he was made painfully aware of his unique vulnerability . . .

By acting out his conflicts, Don Juan manages to achieve quite a lot by way of compromise. His compulsive womanizing enables him to express his love for women and his hatred for them at the same time, although he is aware only of his love.

It is in the apparently unintended consequences of Don Juan's behaviour that we divine his hatred. He objectivizes women, makes them into 'things', and relates to them in an entirely utilitarian and self-centred way. This enables him to avoid facing his 'desire', and the pain this would involve. He deludes himself that he is achieving satisfaction, whereas each new conquest symbolizes his absolute lack of it. His promiscuity is the sexual equivalent of compulsive eating, and has the same desperate aim of denying its sadistic consequences – the envious destruction of that which it attempts to love and preserve. Don Juan is unable to face his inability to preserve the 'good' mother inside himself. We should not, however, be fooled into thinking that Don Juan is profoundly different from ourselves. The rising tide of divorces, and such other evidence as there is, suggest that infidelity is commonplace – even if not quite on the scale practised by Don Juan.

To return to the theme of the split between affection and sexuality: we can see its origins in this analysis of Don Juan. Primarily, he has no concern for the object of his desire, which is precisely the baby's relationship to the mother. His desire is simply to possess her. In a cannibalistic fashion he wishes to consume her so that she has no power to frustrate him, and precipitate his hatred and his fear of annihilation and death. It is not possible to possess an object in this way and still have it – you literally can't have your cake and eat it. It is a matter for debate whether Don Juan's cannibalistic desires are motivated more by love than by sadism.

Affection involves tender concern for the object and anxiety lest one's destructive impulses, whether loving or sadistic, should damage her. The splitting of one's affectionate from one's sexual feelings, therefore, has complex origins. At root it is an attempt to ensure that the object never becomes powerful enough to evoke our unresolved dependency and possessive needs by stimulating our desire, with all its naked force and fearful power. The man simply withdraws his desire in the face of its inevitable frustration.

The maxim 'You can't have your cake and eat it' does not cease to be true when the genital Oedipus complex, as opposed to its oral progenitor, develops. Even during the genital period, when the little boy wants to penetrate his mother and possess her with his penis, he knows that he cannot 'have' his mother and still keep her. If she becomes his lover, he will lose his mother. In summary, Don Juan is engaged in a search for the 'eternally good breast' or mother in the outside world. This search betokens anxiety about the threat of her imminent internal destruction as an internal object. Ideally, he would have had a mother who, he felt, could contain his destructive impulses and not be damaged by them (for example, by not withdrawing the breast when he was very angry), and/or he would not have been born with what he felt to be such destructive impulses and needs. The internal destruction of the 'good mother/breast' is similar to the destruction in depression, where one feels that there is no goodness anywhere in the world. Loss or abandonment is not worked through. The lost object becomes bad, rather than a source of both good and bad. The healthy working through of loss, as in the mourning process, requires the tolerance of ambivalence. This is the threat facing Don Juan: either the threat of depression – a combination of grief, hatred and guilt, and despair at the emptiness of the 'self' which betokens the destruction of the 'good mother' or primary object with whom the 'self' is identified – or, worse, the threat of disintegration and fragmentation in the face of the loss of the primary organizing principle of meaning, the good breast. His whole life is spent in a search for the good breast/mother who will not abandon him and cannot be destroyed by his hatred of her but can, as it were, absorb it and remain intact.

Marital infidelities are made of the same stuff. Although there may be many precipitating external causes, they are extremely complex psychodynamically. A common-sense explanation would be that an unhappy, frustrated husband seeks an affair, or is available for one, because he is unhappy. It may be that he also believes, because of the way he feels, that his marriage is over – or almost over. This explanation has much to recommend it. It is simple. It makes sense.

It avoids the necessity for thinking about personal responsibility, unconscious motivation and emotions.

A man in his early thirties consulted me because he was very unhappy in his marriage, which was sadomasochistic. Although the couple had started out well, apparently very lovingly, they now rarely exchanged anything other than insults and blows. Neither of them was capable of terminating the relationship. His wife expressly did not want to, and although he constantly said that he did, he was afraid to do so. He and his wife had always been faithful. They had a shared and articulated understanding that if either of them was unfaithful, the marriage would be over. He was convinced of this. About a year into his treatment, when he was temporarily living apart from his wife, he began a passionate - albeit short-lived - fling with a woman he described as 'perfect'. He was insistent that this was a way to end the marriage, and hoped that his wife would now agree to do so. She did not, and the emotional sadomasochism escalated. Since then he has struggled with his ambivalence and his - now conscious - need to punish his wife, and the satisfaction he derives from it. Almost without exception, he and his wife have been told by family and friends that the relationship is clearly over, and they should formally end it. This is an extreme situation. These people are bound together by neurotic needs and conflicts which will take some time to resolve. I introduce them here because of the clarity of the man's destructiveness in the relationship. He had undoubtedly initiated the sadomasochism after initially charming his wife into marriage. Both partners agree that this was so.

My understanding of infidelity differs from the common-sense one: it is that the unhappy husband who seeks an affair is in fear of his own destructive feelings towards his wife. He may even feel that he has killed her in that she is 'no good' any more - 'she doesn't understand me'. The very qualities for which he loved her and married her are now the ones for which he hates her. The primitive split between the good and the bad, the princess and the witch, has now been reversed from the idealized romantic love he first had for her. (The patient described above had split off his anger and hatred during the courtship, and had consciously hoped that his new partner would teach him how to love properly and be happy.) The new woman is now the idealized (and therefore unconsciously envied - *plus ça change*) container of those qualities, whereas the wife contains all the qualities of the witch. She is effectively dead inside him. He, of course, experiences that it is she who has changed and is now depleted. The truth - which he will fight so hard to deny - is that, other things being equal, it is he who has changed. The depletion is his in that it is the internal primary good object and his relationship with it which is threatened by his repressed destructive feelings. He is under imminent threat of depression if his rage should break through. As my patient shows, although he cannot see it, it already has. The amount of destruction which he expresses towards his wife by having an affair is obvious to any disinterested observer. Also (as we shall see in Chapter 8) real cruelty is commonplace in intimate relationships, and not confined, as is sometimes believed, to a minority of male psychopaths.

Another man exemplified these processess, in a different way, though very clearly. Although he was no Don Juan, he had begun an affair after fourteen years of marriage. This was no simple one-night stand. He fell passionately, obsessively in love with a woman he had known for ten years. The affair lasted only two weeks, although two years later, when he came to see me, he was still trying to deal with its consequences. His guilt was overwhelming and, indeed, had been the cause of his inability to continue the affair. He had conscious and very frightening fantasies that his wife would die, which not only expressed his fear about what he was doing to her unconsciously, but also, of course, contained a wish. His debilitating guilt arose from what he had already divined: that his affair represented a destructive attack on his wife, and was an expression of massive accumulated resentment. It became clear quite quickly that he had been living with this guilt since he had become self-conscious (his memory began when he was seventeen!), and that it had found a focus in his affair. He was profoundly disturbed by his infidelity. He had always been faithful in previous relationships; in fact he said that he 'had never been particularly sexually interested in women' even though his profession, in the arts, provided him with many opportunities for casual sex.

His mother had actually possessed many of the qualities of what I have defined as the 'witch'. Although she had been 'good enough' in terms of providing servicing to him and his authoritarian and domineering father, she was – rather unsurprisingly – cold, unyielding and unemotional. He could not remember ever being touched by her. One of his wife's greatest attractions had been her warmth and her enjoyment of physical contact – 'She couldn't get enough'. He now saw her as being like his mother, and had become disgusted with her sexuality. His greatest concern – indeed, his reason for seeing me – was the intensity of his anxiety that his wife would die if he separated from her, which he was adamant he wished to do. He described her as totally dependent on him – a perception which could not be sustained, and in fact represented his projected dependency and his unconscious infantile anxieties about his own viability and continuity as an individual. It is true that his wife was now very angry with him, and had been for some time. He had little difficulty in seeing that this anger was caused entirely by his constantly telling her, since soon after their wedding, that he was not sure if he loved her. He had encouraged her to service him and look after him, and now he complained constantly that she treated him like a child.

Such events do not occur by chance or by accident. There are always reasons why the repressed destructive feelings re-emerge. They have more to do, however, with the man's internal world than with the reality of his wife's behaviour, even where she may have changed considerably from the person he first met.

There is a further aspect of male behaviour in relation to women which, although it is not central to an understanding of Don Juan, is none the less very closely related in that it has its roots in the same anxieties about destructive impulses. It concerns the reaction of many men to the love of a woman. This can be a frightening experience, and the cause of a man's withdrawing his affection and becoming aloof. In fact, the apparent indifference to a woman's affection is very deeply rooted in unconscious anxieties.

Men often feel afraid of being loved because their original experience of it with their mother was that it meant they had to adapt to her need of them. The unconscious message which the mother gives the infant is: 'Don't be you. Be me. Please me.' This happens because the child has become a container for all the mother's own unmet infantile needs. The mother, in effect, treats the child as if he were part of her, not a person in his own right. He will quickly get the message that certain needs and feelings, which are central aspects of his developing self, are not acceptable if he is to go on receiving his mother's love. Essentially, this means that if he is to survive, he must not be himself. To a certain extent, this is a natural part of every child's experience. We all have to learn to adapt, and we grow up with a large part of our personality which we might call the adapted self. The extent to which this crowds out the development of a 'real self' will depend, among other things, on the extent of the mother's narcissism and the wound she causes the child by denying his real self any development. It will also depend on the child's reaction to this trauma in terms of how bad the narcissistic mother or 'witch' becomes in his internal world (the theme of maternal narcissism has been explored extensively by Benjamin, 1990 and Miller, 1980). The badness of this 'witch' is a product of the interaction between the child's innate aggression and the real mother's inadequacy. At one end of the scale, the child might actually develop a psychotic illness as a result. At the other, more benign end, it simply leads to 'normal' adaptation.

One consequence of this is that for the adult male 'I love you' may come to represent the most overwhelming demand for him not to be himself and, in addition, threaten him with the return of his repressed feelings about the bad 'witch' mother and his need for the good 'princess' mother. These feelings can be very frightening because they involve fantasies concerning the oral impulses to enter the mother's body in order to take it over and prevent the frustration and pain caused by the 'witch'. Such an impulse will entail the most aggressive and destructive feelings towards the mother, and create the fantasy of being savagely attacked and devoured by her: the most primitive of male nightmares. These unconscious impulses will be projected into the woman's love for him; she then contains the threat to devour him and take him over. Because of these primitive fantasies the male adult develops his characteristic indifference to a woman's love – an indifference which is supported with the resolution of the Oedipus complex and the adoption of a masculine gender identity predicated on women's inferiority and his contempt for them. This is a way of ensuring that he is not threatened by, nor does he threaten, the destruction of the internal 'good' mother. He must devalue his partner – 'She has nothing to offer me' – in order not to need anything from her and be aware of his own lack. Kleinian analytic theory maintains that this is a basic defence against envy, the universal and primary root of all destructiveness. Although I do not agree with this view of envy as innate, I believe it is a potent element in men's hatred of women. At its most extreme this is undoubtedly a psychotic way of relating, and it is to some extent a characteristic of all men's relations with women.

This brings me to a final point: I do not believe that men need or really love women in a genuinely altruistic and non-utilitarian way. I believe that men's desire is structured heterosexually during the Oedipus complex, and that this is not 'natural'. The structuring of desire around the female inevitably entails that it will evoke all the infantile feelings connected with the primary carer, who is universally designated female. To some degree these feelings are neither mature or altruistic for any man. The taboo of heterosexuality means that the escape from the male encapsulated psychosis is inevitably experienced as being through a relation with the female mother. This is not psychologically, biologically or socially necessary.

6 Pornography, Rape and Masturbation

Recent research indicates that one in six married women in the UK has been a victim of violent rape by her husband, and that in the USA as many as one in four women have been rape victims (London Rape Crisis Centre, 1984; Russell and Van Den Ven, 1976. World in Action, Granada TV, 1989). Of course it is difficult to obtain accurate figures about the incidence of rape. Estimates suggest that between 4 per cent and 40 per cent of rapes are reported. Only 15 per cent of recorded rapes go to trial, and of these only 1 per cent result in a rape conviction. This means that only one rapist in 250 to 2,500 is convicted (McNickle Rose and Randall, 1978). In one survey (quoted by Kelly, 1988b, p. 50) 41 per cent of a random sample of women reported experiencing rape or attempted rape. Diana Russell (1984) suggests that a woman has a 40 per cent chance of being raped in her lifetime. The Child Abuse Studies Unit at North London Polytechnic found in their 1990 survey of over one thousand schoolchildren that 59 per cent of girls under sixteen had experienced sexual assault (Kelly *et al.*, 1991).

The way in which sexual assault is defined will inevitably make a significant difference to the results of such surveys. If I use a normal male definition, I can say with certainty, as do many of the men I work with, that I have never sexually assaulted a woman. If, however, I give up my right to define sexual assault or aggression, I can think of five incidents in my life where I have effectively coerced a woman into sex simply by behaving as a normal male and interpreting resistance in a self-serving way. What this means for me personally is that I was raised to expect resistance from women, and that they want this resistance to be overcome.

I remember a client whose partner used to put embargoes on sex with him if he behaved in ways which upset her. These embargoes would last for weeks or months. He was very distressed by them, and evolved elaborate strategies for overcoming them. It became clear that even when there was no embargo she simply did not like being penetrated by him or probably, by any man. He used to get very angry with her and tell her she had a real problem in not enjoying sex. On one occasion he actually raped her. Although one may say she had a sexual problem, she did not see herself in this way. In this context, obviously the problem was his. He simply could not accept that any woman can not enjoy sex with men and, more importantly, has the right to be this way. He was determined to solve her problem, because he felt sorry for her for being deprived of the pleasure of being penetrated.

The statistics about rape reflect an abyss of appalling male violence towards women. However accurate they are, they tell a tale of abuse and private suffering which cannot be dismissed. The perception that rape is a marginal act carried out by perverts, or can be understood as the expression of psychopathology, is simply not sustainable in the face of statistics like these. Although it would not be true to say that psychoanalysis has ignored the problem of rape, it would be going too far to say that it has taken it seriously, either as a contributor to female pathology or as an element of the male psyche worthy of serious investigation. Lynne Segal (1987) argues that men are also victims of rape (although not on the same scale as women, and again, usually by men), and goes to some lengths to prove that the monolithic view of the capacity for rape as an essential element of masculinity propounded by writers such as Brownmiller (1976) is fundamentally mistaken and counterproductive. Socialist feminist motives for arguing in this way are clear: to counteract the growing dominance of the essentialist apocalyptic or revolutionary feminist viewpoint, so closely allied to the growth of the 'new right' which Lynne Segal and others see as a counsel of despair, ultimately damaging to the cause of women.

In some respects these arguments also apply to the issue of the sexual abuse of boys by their mothers. It is important to take into account the motives of those who suggest that it may be as serious a problem as the abuse of girls, but it must be acknowledged that however many studies there are of such abuse, there is simply no evidence that it is even close to being on the same scale. I do not want, however, to collude with therapeutic resistance to the awareness of this problem (Hunter, 1990). Groth and Russell (quoted in Finkelhor, 1986) found that just over half their sample of sex offenders had been sexually victimized, 25 per cent by a female. I think this finding should be taken as an expression of the offenders' 'vocabulary of motives' and their attempts to negotiate a non-deviant identity. I am struck by the findings of Mathews *et al.* (1989), who suggest that of the types of female sex offenders in their research, what they call the 'male-coerced' is the largest group. These are women who are forced by their male partners into sexual activity with their children, even though they may subsequently go on to victimize them without their male partners.

Some socialist and sociologist writers advance the view that it is not possible to talk about 'masculinity' because it is essentialist and monolithic. Bob Connell (1987) and Michael Roper and John Tosh (1991) advance the view that we can talk only about 'masculinities', because maleness has taken – and continues to take – many forms which are culturally and historically distinct. My own view concurs with that of Gini Whitehead (1991) who, in commenting on a similar argument advanced by Roper and Tosh, makes the point that

> the ample evidence of the ability of . . . masculinity . . . to adapt to changing cultural contexts, which forms the basis of . . . this book's . . . optimism . . . should serve as a warning against complacency rather than a basis for optimism. (p. 38)

I agree that the description of men, whether by male chauvinists or by apocalyptic feminists, is also prescriptive. Any contribution to a discourse cannot avoid contributing to the construction of the phenomenon it describes, no matter how much one attempts to get round this. My difference with the socialist feminist viewpoint is based on the significance of the fluid nature of masculinity. In some respects such a view is essentialist in its own right. This is, in any case, inevitable. Any category is essentialist in that it assumes the existence of an essential quality which allows placement within a category – for example, men and women. I have no quarrel with this. My unhappiness with the socialist feminist view is that it describes masculinity as if it existed independently of femininity, whereas my view is that the categories are 'essentially' interdependent, and that femininity will always be the excluded element of the masculine (rather than the other way round as Chodorow (1978) suggests). I think this allows for the fluidity of a construction of masculinity to suit any historical conditions, and an equivalent construction of femininity. At the present time one can find a wide range of differences in masculinities, both within and between cultures. Whatever the particular conception and form of gender arrangements, however, women are still subordinated and systematically abused. It is my conviction that the limits to gendered subjectivity are set not by material or historical conditions, but by the Oedipus complex.

Even though socialist feminists would argue that my view of masculinity is ahistorical and monolithic, I am not arguing that rape cannot be understood psychodynamically. In fact I believe it is very important to attempt such an understanding. One should not, however, be confused into thinking, therefore, that rape is exclusively a psychological rather than a social and political problem. In any case, it is important to understand that defining any problem as social rather than psychological is a way of allocating responsibility and directing the search for solutions. It does not in itself affect the nature of the problem; it simply enables those who define the problem as a social one to derive social policy implications. Of course, this works in reverse. Often, definitions of problems are rejected by the women's movement because of social policy implications which are antithetical to the needs of women – for example, a definition of male violence in marriage which locates its cause in failed interaction between the partners. This would imply a need for more resources for marital counselling, and for the wife to take a share of the responsibility for her predicament and her husband's violence.

Rejecting such constructions is not only justifiable but essential. Research is not value-free. One must be aware of the social policy implications in any way of understanding any problem. In this chapter I shall attempt to find a model of rape which integrates the psychological and social dimensions in a social psychology which accurately reflects the nature of rape and lays the responsibility where it belongs – on men. My purpose is to see how this political account of sexual relations and male dominance accords with a psychodynamic understanding of sexual violence and the relationship between desire and aggression. I shall explore the nature of the relationship between rape and pornography to see if, as essentialist feminists claim at the political level, they are seamlessly and inextricably linked in male psychology.

Although the academic and social scientific literature on rape is notable largely for its absence, theories about rape and pornography have been central to feminist thinking in the last two decades. It has become a central doctrine of dominant radical feminist thinking that rape is a political act, and a fundamental expression of the essence of men's relations with women. To give a brief – inevitably oversimplified – account of the radical feminist argument: sexual relationships can be reduced ultimately to concepts of power and property. Rape is seen as the basic expression of man's physical power over women (Brownmiller, 1976). It shows, transparently, men's capacity and willingness to use rape to force women to do their bidding. Although this model, the power model, is not without its weaknessess, it accounts for more of the phenomena of rape and sexual abuse than any other.

All forms of sexual abuse, including rape, are mainly inflicted by men on women. This long-established fact has often been obscured by apparently methodologically sound attempts, by systems theorists or academic family therapists, to explain why abuse occurs in certain kinds of family, or with certain kinds of mother, or with any other variable one cares to name. The simple reality that it is always men (or as near always as makes no difference) who are the abusers, and traditional models – psychoanalytic, family, marital or behavioural – will not address this gender issue. One might speculate endlessly about why it is not addressed. It may well be that it is simply too threatening to the established order – men's. So it is that one can read a major work by David Finkelhor (1986), one of the world's most respected researchers into familial abuse, which is mostly devoted to looking at the pathology of families, or victims, or mothers, or perpetrators, despite the acknowledgement of the male monopoly of abusiveness and its ubiquity, and despite his own excellent model of abuse, which states that for it to occur:

1 an offender must have the motivation to abuse;
2 he must overcome internal inhibitions against abusing; and
3 external obstacles against abusing; and
4 the child's resistance to being abused.

(These conditions are listed in order of priority.) This model is applicable to any form of abuse between males and females. What is so surprising – and Finkelhor acknowledges this – is that so much academic and scientific effort is spent in examining factors (3) and (4), the external obstacles and the child's resistance, rather than factors (1) and (2), which concern male responsibility.

This is not to say that feminists do not attempt to account for men's motivation. Mary Daly (1979) and Susan Brownmiller (1976), for example, share the essentialist assumption of female superiority, which evokes fear and hatred in men and mobilizes men's innate violence and aggression. Also, not all feminists – particularly socialist feminists – agree with this apocalyptic essentialist analysis of the relation between pornography and rape (Barry, 1982, pp. 77–92; Wilson, 1983). Elizabeth Wilson maintains that during the last twenty years there has been a 'convergence of feminist views about male violence and male sexuality towards seeing it as socially produced and legitimated rather than as a natural expression of male biology' (1983, p. 8). This is not quite true. Essentialists would agree that it is socially legitimated in patriarchal culture, but not that it is socially constructed. In fact, some feminists who would describe themselves as constructionists, like Dale Spender, see the process of construction as so overdetermined and inevitable that to all intents and purposes they are indistinguishable from 'real' essentialists like Mary Daly.

In the last ten years a raging debate has been taking place within feminism about the relationship between pornography and rape. In what has become known as the Dworkin–MacKinnon issue, feminists have had to make clear their stand on that most fundamental of civil rights issues, censorship. Andrea Dworkin, a leading feminist writer on pornography, and Catharine MacKinnon, a leading feminist lawyer, have managed to place before the legislators in Minneapolis a draft Bill to outlaw pornography, after persuading officials that there is a causative link between pornography and crimes of sexual violence (Everywoman 1988). The risk that such a bill would be used as a general right to censor has led to the formation of groups, both here and in the USA, such as Feminists Against Censorship (Rodgerson and Wilson, 1991). This complex debate embodies all the controversies which have so divided the feminist movement within the last decade. I shall refer to it below.

FEMINIST EXPLANATIONS

Judith Herman was the first (1981) to articulate the feminist consensus about the social legitimation of male violence as explicated in the power model. In *Child Sexual Abuse* (eds Driver and Droisen, 1989) Cathy Waldby and colleagues elaborate what they call the power theory as developed by feminist workers at Dympna House, a community-based incest centre in Sydney. Of particular interest here is that aspect of the theory which describes the real power men hold over women by virtue of gender. Political power, which they call structural power, is institutional power over others:

> . . . the power granted to individuals or classes of individuals by society. It is power accorded to one class of person over another, on the basis of certain factors such as gender, age, race, religion, intelligence, education, family status, political affiliation, income etc. Some examples of this are: the power of the rich over the poor, politicians over the unemployed, white over black, men over women . . . it gives the powerful the opportunity to exercise control over the lives of the powerless . . . is legitimised by society as a whole . . . and attempts at change by the powerless are thwarted by the very institutions which have power over them. (p. 102)

All men have this institutional power over women, and they also have the personal power to abuse this institutional power, whether over women or over children. This model dovetails neatly with the four-factor model (see above) outlined by Finkelhor. It provides a ground for that model by recognizing that all men have power over all women (and that all adults have power over all children), and therefore the potential to abuse that power in rape or child sexual abuse, but that there are individual differences in motivation - which are the focal concerns of the Finkelhor model. Waldby and her colleagues go further when they assert that men's misuse of their institutional power is legitimized by society.

In sum, this model makes it clear that rape would not be possible were it not for the belief - and the institutional support for it - that women are the property of men. They may be used, abused, ignored or discarded at whim. Rape is the logical outcome of a set of attitudes about and towards women which legitimize, in men's eyes, their oppression and abuse. Otherwise, such acts would not possible. Brownmiller and other apocalyptic feminists take the power model further: they see rape as a metaphor for the essential misogyny underpinning relationships between men and women. Rape and sexual violence are seen as the final link in a chain of progressively more subtle expressions of this fundamental notion of women as male property. 'Pornography is rape' has become a rallying cry for those who see little hope of changing masculinity or the inequality of power between men and women (Dworkin, 1981). Pornography actually uses women as sexual objects whose sole function is to titillate and gratify men. In simple terms: essentialist feminists argue that without pornography there would be no rape, because pornography is about men's power over women; remove the pornography, remove the power.

An extension of this argument is that pornography represents women as passive objects, responding to male sexual desire, not merely in fantasy but in actuality as the pornography is being produced. Peter Baker (1992) has made the point, as have many others, that pornography is the way most youths learn about female anatomy but also, more importantly, develop fantasies about female sexuality which 'set' earlier oedipal ideas about women. We learn from pornography that women are readily available, and are in a constant state of readiness for sex; that they spend a great deal of their life in a state of sexual arousal. This view is also expressed by Lynne Segal and Mary McIntosh (1992); 'Pornography caters to men's sexual fantasies of female availability and eagerness for sex in the context of societies which have proved unable to offer women protection from widespread sexual harassment, abuse and violence.' (p. 5)

The connection between socially structured aggressive male sexuality and male power over women lies in the construction of feminine sexuality, with women as objects over whom men have power, and to whom men have unrestricted access (Wilson, 1983). The definition of pornography used by Dworkin and MacKinnon in their draft Bill for the Minneapolis hearings (it was passed by the City Council in December 1983 and vetoed by the mayor, passed again in July 1984 and again vetoed), and later in the Bill which was passed by the Indianapolis City Council (approved by the mayor but later overruled by the State Supreme Court on the grounds that it infringed the First Amendment guaranteeing free speech) is fairly widespread and worth quoting, as it has become the basis of the CPC (Campaign Against Pornography and Censorship) and other UK campaigns:

> Pornography is the graphic, sexually explicit subordination of women through pictures or words, that also includes women dehumanized as sexual objects, things or commodities, enjoying pain or humiliation or rape, being tied up, cut up, mutilated, bruised or physically hurt, in postures of sexual submission or servility or display, reduced to body parts, penetrated by objects or animals, or presented in scenarios of degradation, injury, torture, shown as filthy or inferior, bleeding, bruised, or hurt in a context that makes these conditions sexual.

It is made clear that men, children or transsexuals can be substituted for women in this definition.

What can we say about pornography and its role in masculinity? There is overwhelming evidence of its role in the sexual education of young boys. As I said above, for most men it is the first source of information about the anatomical reality of women. I can vividly remember this from my own adolescence, as pornographic pictures of women were shared between my friends. I can also remember finding a pornographic magazine and hiding it in my bedroom with a mixture of excitement, fear and shame. I had the acute sense that this represented a slur on my mother. As I grew up I became increasingly familiar with porn and the range of images which were available, and the storylines which were sometimes integral to the pictures, but more often seen as a separate source of arousal. The images and stories in soft porn are always the same, and they communicated very important messages to me about my masculinity, and more importantly, about feminine sexuality. The women were always available; this was illustrated with pictures of gaping vaginas and anuses of such graphic quality as to deserve inclusion in a gynaecology lesson. Pornographic pictures and stories depict women as offering unconditional physical intimacy and closeness without any of the mess associated with relationships. Women are presented as being only sexual beings: one-dimensional objects. They are presented as not only being in a state of constant readiness for sex – as 'always wanting it'; they are also presented as being desperate for and obsessed with sex. Porn is full of stories of men innocently going about their business – cleaning windows, or delivering the post – and coming across women masturbating or opening doors in a state of nudity and then effectively raping the men or responding without reservation to their advances.

Of course this reinforces another myth, but this time one about male sexuality: that we men want 'it' all the time, and if we don't, there's something wrong with our masculinity. I have no doubt that pornography contributed to future distortions in my relationships with women, although I do not believe it was causative. It certainly corroborated everything I had already learned about the relative positions of men and women and added new and, in retrospect, disturbing and false messages about women's sexuality as well as reinforcing what I already suspected was my own. In my masturbatory fantasies using pornography I was always in charge, doing what I wanted to the woman and being loved for it – indeed, being encouraged to reach greater heights of perversity or aggression. I should add that this has never been my real experience of sexual intimacy which, apart from being wonderful, can also be confusing, emotionally painful and scary. There is an enormous gap between the illusory power I felt in using pornography, the control I exercised over women, and the reality of sexuality. In pornography, men and women do not make love. There is no tenderness or emotional closeness: sex is something that men do to women – almost like work, and always successfully. This message is explicit in most pornography. Sex is a performance, with the woman as a willing sexual slave. For many men, this performance and the wielding of sexual power over women is the most important source of validation for their male self-esteem, even when it is gained through masturbation. As Peter Baker puts it (1992) 'Needless to say . . . in pornography . . . the men do a good job and the women are always satisfied.'

In their pamphlet *Pornography and Feminism: The Case Against Censorship*, Rodgerson and Wilson (1991) insist that the essentialists (Dworkin is named) have got it wrong in implying or asserting that pornography causes male sexual violence against women, and that

> all men are potential rapists waiting to be activated by pornography . . . she has the problem upside down. Pornography may mirror the sexism of society but did not create it. Pornography as we know it – mass produced, for a mass audience – is a recent invention. Women's oppression, unfortunately, came long before porn. (p. 38)

The essentialist case has attracted a lot of support from the moral right both in the UK and in the USA, where MacKinnon, in particular, is actively involved with prominent moralists and puritans. Socialist feminists are united in their efforts to resist the dominance of this view of the inherent badness of masculinity. In a direct echo of Lynne Segal's (1987) plea for more imagination and less despair from feminists, Rodgerson and Wilson draw a contrast between:

> today's campaigns against pornography and the many sided activism of the seventies. Then the aim was to build women's confidence, to increase our independence and autonomy, to transform society. This was a challenge to traditional patriarchal right wing morality, not a capitulation to it. Today, by contrast, the anti-pornography campaigns rely on the idea of women as victims; not much confidence building there. They offer no new ideas, since, whatever they allege to the contrary, their view of pornography is identical to that of traditional conservatism. They offer no remedies save more censorship at the margins of the mass media, leaving untouched and uncriticized the much more pervasive daily diet of sexist, but not explicitly sexual,

> images . . . giving . . . respectability to the moral right and fundamentalist lobby. (1991, p. 39)

Rodgerson and Wilson are worried that such campaigns as the CPC, which is opposed to censorship but wants MacKinnon-style legislation introduced in the UK to replace the present obscenity laws, would lead to wholesale use of such legislation to censor any sexually explicit material, and would lead to rabid sexual repression. It could place in the hands of the state a powerful means of controlling any sexuality which puritans or moralists believed to be deviant or unacceptable. In addition, they make the less palatable point that there has been an explosion of pornographic material produced by and for women (I think this is an exaggeration when one considers the amount of porn available for men), which would fall under the influence of such legislation – in particular lesbian erotic literature such as *Quim* and *Serious Pleasure*, and films such as *Desert Hearts*. They argue that 'the production and consumption of such pornography can be erotic acts, and we have the right to participate in these acts' (1991, p. 74). These and similar arguments are also prominent in the excellent collection of essays *Sex Exposed* (eds Segal and McIntosh, 1992).

Although I wish it were possible to legislate against pornography, particularly where it involves the depiction of violence, or real violence, against women, I agree that it cannot be done without also risking the misuse of such legislation by placing in the hands of a moral minority a powerful tool for sexual repression. Although I disagree with much of the socialist feminist analysis of violence, I agree wholeheartedly with Feminists Against Censorship (Rodgerson and Wilson, 1991) that what is required is education, persuasion and information, and concerted efforts to end public and private violence, unequal pay and lack of opportunities for girls and women.

As a political analysis, the power model places more emphasis on the social context of pornography as consumerism than on its relation to male desire and the intractability of men's power. Dworkin, in her testimony to the Minneapolis hearing, reported the dimension of the problem in the USA: 'pornography is part of the traffic in women. In this country it is a seven billion dollar industry . . . we are dealing with an endemic and systematic dominance of men over women' (Everywoman, p. 11). She is making the point that pornography is not simply symbolic of women's oppression, but is actually oppressive of enormous numbers of women. She is clearly aware that many of these women make the choice to take part in such acts, but mainly from necessity, and usually after being abused as children (this point is well established; see J. Herman, 1981). As we shall see, however, the political and dynamic analyses are not necessarily contradictory.

Feminist writers such as Rich (1980), Dworkin (1981), and Kittay (1984) have made a significant contribution to our understanding of the connections between images of sexuality, heterosexuality, and sex and violence, and how these reflect and strengthen the ideology of masculinity and legitimate the objectification and degradation of women. Their argument seems flawed, however, in that although none of these authors would *explicitly* argue that pornography is causative – they see it as legitimating or reinforcing male power – they speak with one voice in believing that its removal would be successful in diminishing male violence. If pornography was *effectively* banned, it would herald a fundamental change in patriarchal – male – beliefs, attitudes and behaviour.

Many – some would say the vast majority of – women might feel offended by the radical, revolutionary, apocalyptic feminist accounts of their relations with men (Segal and McIntosh [1992], say that they are 'astonishingly offensive and discouraging'). Essentialist feminists would reply that these women are the product of deep, extensive and complex conditioning, and are unaware of the extent of their own oppression. This may seem patronizing in the extreme. Actually, any feminist view is extreme to anybody who never questions their assumptions about their sexuality. The problem for radical feminism of this essentialist sort, however, is that it can seem to find little, if any, value in heterosexuality. Do we not assume that even if heterosexuality is socially constructed, the vast majority of practitioners find it sufficiently gratifying to wish to continue practising (perhaps we hope to get it right one day)? Or do we consider that the limits to subjectivity, and hence to sexuality, are so rigidly structured, however fragile and conflicted our preferences might be, that we are simply unable to consider radical alternatives to failure?

At this point I want to make a few anticipatory remarks about the relation between heterosexuality and violence. Emerson and Rebecca Dobash, who are among the foremost researchers into marital violence (1980), locate the causes in the patriarchy as a political system, and an ideology: sexism. They argue that this is reproduced in the system of marriage, which enshrines the rights of men and the subjugation of women. A serious flaw in their otherwise brilliant and moving account of this serious social problem is that a great deal of violence – from battering to rape – takes place outside the institution of marriage, in both dating and cohabiting relationships. To my mind, the Dobashes fail to give due weight to the determining influence of masculinity. It is masculinity which is at the root of violence, not the institution of marriage.

Considerations such as this led feminist thinkers such as Nancy Chodorow (1978) and Michèle Barrett (1980) to concentrate their attention on heterosexuality and its transmission, as compulsory heterosexuality (Rich, 1980), through culture – in particular the family, with its underpinning of ideas such as romantic love, motherhood, monogamy, and so on. These feminists have no truck with the collusion theories which see women as having an investment in their own oppression. They – and I – see this 'collusion' as being based on the necessities imposed by the gross power imbalances between the sexes. It is the collusion of the hostage with the captor rather than a *folie à deux*. It is very easy to forget that collusion requires equal power. Without it, apparent collusion is actually the acquiescence of the relatively powerless.

It is very difficult to disagree with the radical feminist analysis of rape. Although some writers (Herman, 1981; Wyre, 1988a), including myself – and, presumably, all rapists – believe that rape can be a sexual act for the perpetrator, rape is always an expression of extreme violence against women. I have never been in any doubt that my own rape fantasies are an admixture of sex and aggression. The corollary to this argument is that this violence is latent in all male–female relationships. It is seen as the underpinning of the property rights men assume over women, and as the ultimate guarantee of male supremacy (Brownmiller, 1976). Although this analysis seems extreme, any doubts are resolved, for me, by the indisputable evidence that 40 percent of men use actual violence against their female partners and see this as normal and appropriate, and that one in six women in the UK report having been violently raped by their husbands. One could say, with some justification, that 40 per cent does not indicate universality, either latent or explicit. This is a crucial issue – it goes to the heart of my understanding of the connections between control, violence and male sexuality. I will address it more fully in this chapter, and in Chapter 8.

I think the emphasis in some radical feminist thinking about male sexuality and violence on the primary causative nature of social and cultural factors is a weakness in that it fails to account for individual will. In America there is an interesting – albeit rather depressing – challenge to the separatist conclusions of feminist essentialism. It comes from what might be called the 'new feminine right' – Phyllis Schlafly (1977) is the most prominent example. Schlafly went on to lead the opposition to the Equal Rights Amendment, a potentially epoch-making law which would effectively have outlawed sex discrimination across the USA. Her opposition was based on the threat of feminism to what she – and apparently the majority of women – saw as traditional values which upheld the family way of life and included women's right to be cared for and supported by men. She and her supporters believe that one of the consequences of feminism is that it encourages men to abandon their wives and children. Apparently many women were persuaded by the anti-ERA group that the increasing divorce rate was largely a result of feminism. This group believes that men are innately irresponsible and will jump at the opportunity to lead lives of unbridled and irresponsible adolescent sexuality. As they see it, women's only power to prevent this is the strength of the marriage ties, to which they see the ERA as a threat.

As we have seen, cultural theories presume what they are trying to explain. Any attempt to account for gender must not assume its existence. It is crucially important, of course, to analyse how gender and heterosexuality are socially reproduced, but it is equally important to understand how social pressures are subjectivized in the individual psyche, and to develop a model which accounts for individual will and social construction. The social reproduction of gender tells us little about its origins. A failure to develop a true social psychology may be a recipe for despair when social engineering does not fulfil its promise. Social factors define and circumscribe behaviour, but these factors are also influenced by – and eventually expressed through and by – the individual. I have said that it simply makes no sense to think of culture as originating anywhere except in the individual psyche. I believe there is no alternative way of thinking about individual behaviour which can rival the wisdom or depth of psychoanalysis, particularly its metapsychology, despite its damning and woeful neglect of social, cultural and political frameworks of analysis and its total ignorance of power relations. However, many influential feminists are as guilty of neglecting the inner world as many analysts are of neglecting the outer. Psychoanalytic experience can make a major contribution to our understanding of the processes which lead to rape – a thought which many feminists (mainly of the revolutionary or essentialist school) reject because of the undoubted phallocentric nature of Freudian and post-Freudian analytic thinking. That is, they see it as an expression of that which it purports only to describe: male power.

RAPE

The definition of rape will vary according to the context in which it is placed, and who is defining it. A central point to make here is that, universally, rape is an act which is defined by men. Men see rape as a sexual act, and this betrays their confusion of aggression and sexuality. The point cannot be overemphasized that for women, rape is an act of violence. There *is* little doubt that for men, rape is – at least consciously – a sexual act. That it is largely motivated by hatred and sadism is obvious to a third party. For the man it is an act of forced possession in which the sadism is largely denied even when, as is often the case, it includes overtly brutal behaviour.

None the less, the legal definition of rape is fairly clear. It is equally clear that feminists would greatly extend the range of acts which are defined as rape. There is not much doubt that from a moral point of view, an extended definition would seem to meet the needs of natural justice. Although rape is easily identified as a sexual act carried out by one person on another against that persons' will or without their informed consent, by and large it does not include such acts in the context of marriage. In fact, physical and sexual abuse in marriage is rarely considered illegal and, where it is, it is seldom acted upon by law enforcement agencies. Despite the many statements to the contrary there is clear evidence, in the way such incidents are treated, that police and other agencies regard a wife as a possession of her husband, and that marriage is a sacrosanct institution beyond interference by the state (Dobash and Dobash, 1978; Klein, 1979). The October 1991 UK court ruling in which a husband was sent to jail for raping his wife, from whom he was separated, is a major step towards the goals of feminist groups such as Women Against Rape, but it will do little for those women who are raped by husbands with whom they are still cohabiting so long as there is no financial protection for wives who leave violent husbands. Wives will be prevented from bringing a case by lack of resources (Hall, 1985). These institutional values and attitudes towards the victims of marital violence are not a stone's throw away from those which apply to the relationship between master and slave. Naturally, most institutions are run by men.

Perhaps more extraordinarily, it is not unusual in rape trials for the defence to claim that the woman brought it upon herself 'by her behaviour'. Often this might mean no more than that she looked attractive or was on the street alone. It is also a commonplace male myth that any woman who is raped was 'asking for it' and – bizarrely – secretly enjoyed it. The extraordinary underlying message is that women ask for it simply by being women. It is not unusual for the victim in a rape case to be treated as if she were the defendant, and for her prior sexual behaviour to be regarded as a suitable matter for cross-examination and as evidence for the defence. These double standards were evident in the Kennedy rape trial in the USA, where the victim's sexual history was picked over with relish by the defence lawyer, but the court was not allowed to know that the defendant had a history of complaints of sexual assault against him. It is common knowledge that any known prostitute who makes a complaint of rape will probably be advised that the case is not worth pursuing because the courts will not convict a man who rapes a prostitute. Rape is regarded as a hazard of her profession, and she is seen as fair game. A large proportion of the women in rape cases report that the appearance in court was a more distressing experience than the actual rape.

One should not underestimate the intense violence involved in rape. In every case there is always the threat, whether explicit or not, of murder or mutilation. Without this threat, rape would not be possible. Whether or not the rapist is aware of it, he is acting out the most intense feelings of rage and hatred towards women in the context of his sexual desire. One is tempted to add that it would not be possible for him to do this if he were not physically stronger. However, more is involved than physical strength. Many women are stronger than many men, and only 0.1 per cent of charges of sexual abuse are made against women. While the man's ability to overpower the woman physically is important, it is obviously more an enabling than a causative factor in rape.

That rape is an expression of extreme violence and rage with women is self-evident. How far might one say this of pornography? From one feminist point of view (the radical revolutionary) there is little to choose: pornography is rape, rape is violence, therefore pornography is violence. This syllogism is obviously false; there is no *prima facie* link between rape and pornography. It is far easier to make the connection, at least from a pro-feminist perspective, in political than in psychological terms. The link lies in the culture which provides the seeding ground for pornography and sees women as sexual objects to be exploited for male use. Psychodynamically, as we shall see, it is possible to connect the objectification and fragmentation of women, as seen in pornography, with feelings of extreme violence and sadism as well as regressive infantile experiences. Tellingly, there is overwhelming evidence that stranger rape is hardly ever random or spontaneous. It is usually well planned in advance (contrary to popular belief, this is also true of child sexual abuse, whether or not the child is known to the perpetrator). Great care is often taken in choosing a victim, fantasizing about the act, and devising precautions to avoid capture. There is evidence that stranger rape, like marital rape and violence, is not an isolated event in a rapist's life, but simply one act in a complex and repetitive process or cycle. Pornography may play a part in this cycle as the rapist builds up to committing the crime (for a more detailed description of this, see Wyre, 1988a).

Much pornography is essentially soft, and is used in private for masturbatory purposes. Soft porn, however, is only the publicly visible face of this massive industry. Hard-core pornography, which is more hidden, always involves the actual – not simply the depiction of – degradation and abuse of women. It often involves real mutilation and death. Superficially, soft pornography seems to hurt no one. Of course, this in no way contradicts the feminist analysis of the exploitation of the women involved in pornography, or the evidence that they are usually victims of prior abuse, as children (Herman, 1981; James and Meyerling, 1979; Kelly, 1988; Wyre, 1988b). Equally, we have no way of knowing how pornography is used by the many men who engage in unreported incestuous rape or in sexual abuse of their wives, as they force them to act out the fantasies they see in magazines or videos. We need more research in treatment programmes for identified offenders.

The reality is that pornography cannot be decontextualized. It is condoned and encouraged by patriarchial culture, and reflects the underlying ideology of sexism by perpetrating the idea that women's bodies and sexual parts are commodities. Masturbation utilizing pornography reinforces a man's view of women as passive, responsive, available objects. Unlike victims of rape, however, victims of pornography are, perhaps, less clearly identifiable. They are the unfortunate women whose bodies are used in this way, and the millions of other women who are being abused by men, and suffer from having femininity defined and represented in this schizoid fashion. I think this is a weakness in the socialist feminist case made by Segal and McIntosh (1992) or Rodgerson and Wilson (1991). They argue – rightly – that many women in the soft-porn industry are sex workers by choice. They assert that these workers would say that far from doing them harm, prostitution or pornography provides them with a degree of autonomy and freedom that is not available to most women. True as this may be, it simply fails to take into account the possible consequences for the partners of the millions of ordinary men who use pornography.

I have personally spoken with hundreds of women whose husbands used pornography, bringing it into the home without their consent. The vast majority of these women feel deeply betrayed, outraged and humiliated – not only by the presence of the pornography itself but also by the many coercive attempts men make to get them to act it out. Later in this chapter I shall attempt to make a more direct and ultimately personal link between sexual violence and pornography. This will be easier when the violence and rage in rape are more clearly understood.

Before attempting to account for the rage and violence which are involved in – indeed underlie – rape, it is important to correct any impression that the explanation offered is, in any way, an excuse or apologia. The argument offered here – that all men are potential rapists – could be seen, without justification, as diminishing individual responsibility on the grounds that it is shared by all. Equally, if it seems that men are being portrayed as essentially evil – or, more precisely, that masculinity is portrayed as evil, and femininity as innocent and good – this is a false impression.

Whatever the deep, primitive processes which motivate the man in an act of rape – both the extreme, aberrant, serial kind and the, equally perverse, but more socially syntonic marital kind – it is quite clear that the male myths of women's secret rape fantasies, and secret enjoyment of rape, are based to a large extent on what men interpret, in women's behaviour, as their complicity. This is not to say, however, that women are complicit in being raped, or that their so-called complicity is based on anything other than the mass psychology of terror. Women who are raped are innocent victims.

Most men live with the assumption, both conscious and unconscious, that female sexuality is masochistic; this in itself provides justification for the conscious 'provocation/collusion' fantasies and myths. As I hope Chapter 7 will make clear, this unconscious male assumption of female sexual masochism mirrors certain fundamental facts about female sexual development and – more importantly, to me – social reality. Perhaps more significantly, it reflects men's awareness of their own sadistic and punitive impulses towards women, and the comfort derived from imagining that these are mirrored by female masochism. It is no justification, however, for a persecutor to assert that his victim derives satisfaction (there is never any pleasure in rape) from suffering, even where the persecution is mild, let alone where it is life-threatening. In this context, Stoller (1975) believes that people seek out humiliating situations which they fear because they give the illusion that they are in control, and this provides a reassuring defence against their terrifying helplessness – the masochistic illusion of pleasure from pain. Nevertheless, I hardly need to point out that although it may be true that many women's most arousing sexual fantasies may involve being dominated and even raped (Friday, 1977; Segal, 1986, pp. 98–100), there is a world of difference between this and actually being or wanting to be raped. Anyone who believes that rape is an enjoyable experience for the victim is either perverse or wilfully ignorant of the truth.

Stoller's analysis implies the theory, analysed by Finkelhor, that many rapists and sex abusers have themselves been the victims of sexual abuse during childhood. Finkelhor, (1986, p. 127) quotes some studies in support of this view, and points out that these must be questioned – not just because perpetrators are only too keen to present themselves as victims (Scully and Marolla [1984] refer to this as 'the vocabulary of motive that rapists use to excuse and justify their behaviour and negotiate a non-deviant identity') and therefore not responsible – 'It's not me it's my childhood' – but, damningly, because this would not explain why, given the fact that almost every abused child is female, there aren't many more female sexual abusers. Estela Welldon (1988) believes there may be many more than we currently suspect, but the helping professions cannot see this because it is so antithetical to the notion and ideology of motherhood. The validity of her belief remains to be tested although Finkelhor is doubtful. 'There is no reason implicit in the theory why girls should not master their trauma through an identification with the abuser just as boys do,' he comments, remarking on the near-male monopoly of abusiveness (p. 127) and the understanding that it derives from identification. The facts are plainly against an interpretation of a rapist's motivation as deriving solely from his experience of the pain of being a victim and defending against it by identifying with his aggressor. Given that all children have to face the pain of separation and loss, we would expect women to be as abusive as men – unless there are other factors at work which produce different responses in men and women.

Over and over again, in the accounts of women who have been raped, one reads that they were afraid that if they put up any resistance to their attacker they would be physically wounded, even murdered. Often the rapist will interpret the absence of resistance as evidence of complicity, even encouragement. On the face of it, this is quite astonishing. The act of rape is inconceivably violent, whether or not there is actual tissue damage. How can a man perform such a gross act of destructive possession, without, apparently being remotely aware of the 'real' significance of such violence? How can he delude himself that the woman's passivity represents enjoyment rather than her fear of being killed – a fear which is realistic, and based on his threat to escalate his violence?

Studies show that men tend to blame women for rape. One series of studies (Malamuth and Donnerstein, 1984) showed that 57 per cent of male students, after being shown pornography depicting women enjoying rape, might rape if there was no risk of apprehension. Although research into pornography is confusingly contradictory, to say the least, this work also shows that students exposed to films of rape are desensitized and have more callous attitudes to women afterwards, and that normal healthy males become aroused by scenes of rape. This rather gives the lie to the concept of 'deviant sexual arousal' as a motive for actual rape, and illustrates a clear connection between dominance, aggression and male sexual desire. As we shall see, the arousal of rapists is neither deviant or perverse. Liz Kelly (1988b) records that rapists are, in fact, the group of sexual offenders least likely to be seen as abnormal by researchers, even though much of the work which has been done with convicted offenders is devoted to constructing personality profiles of rapists. She quotes research by Rabkin (1979), who found fifty subtypes of rapist in the literature! This is clearly not a fruitful line of research if its outcome is a subprofile for each rapist. It simply illustrates that what all rapists have in common is that they are male, and that rape is linked with men's traditional attitudes to and belief systems about women.

Is rape a simple biological release, born of sexual frustration, or is it a more complex act, with profound psychological links with many forms and types of male behaviour towards women? As we shall see, sexual rape is indeed a complex and overdetermined expression of normal male attitudes to women. Although it may provoke horror and outrage in some men - based largely on the knowledge that one holds the very attitudes and beliefs about women which make rape feasible - it is simply, without minimizing its terrifying nature for women, a visible, easily defined and extreme example of the way men express their misogyny in all aspects of their lives - economic, political, relational or sexual. As a feminist patient of mine once remarked, 'Women get screwed whether they like it or not, without their consent, and against their will.'

Sexual activity is massively overdetermined. Perhaps it would be more accurate to say that seeking sexual gratification is overdetermined. All men - and women, too - are familiar with the swift pang of unfulfillable desire which arises in contexts where any action would be entirely inappropriate. Freud himself mentioned train travel as one of the situations where such desire commonly occurs. One American study reported that men have sexual thoughts, on average, once every eight seconds. This is not an altogether undesirable state of affairs from the point of view of the species. Provided that it is confined, as it is in the vast majority of cases, to enjoyment of the desire, a second look and a sigh of regret, most women are not offended by - and in fact might even enjoy - such encounters.

Not infrequently in the groups I conduct with abusive men, someone will raise the issue of looking at women. It is a difficult issue to examine critically, because it goes to the heart of normal attraction processes between men and women. When men are asked to examine this behaviour, they are extremely resistant. Almost without exception they become confused and vehemently assert that it is a 'natural' behaviour to look at beautiful women. The invitation to think about it is perceived as threatening. The range and variety of behaviours which looking (usually it is intrusive leering) involves are both disquieting and, occasionally comical. Some men will go for long periods without being aware of females. Others are, at times, under what seems like a compulsion to leer at every woman they see, and feel quite unable to stop. The fear of getting caught is commonly expressed in these discussions. One man described how he wears dark glasses so that he can look with impunity. In the men with whom I work – and I believe they are typical – this compulsion, often quite frenzied (I will say more about it below in connection with pornography), is prevalent. One man described, with great humour, how he was involved in a shunt crash with six cars because all the drivers were looking at a beautiful woman. We hear appalling and derogatory descriptions (for example, fat cows) of women who do not attract this attention because they do not fit the stereotype of female beauty.

The men we work with believe, without exception, that women like to be looked at in this way. It is clear to me that the impulse to look is stronger when these men are actually with their partners, and that it must be understood in the context of the relationship. The aspect of it which concerns me here, however, was articulated by a man who opined that he 'could not understand how the men in the city offices he visited could work around all those young women who were wearing hardly any clothes'. Surprisingly, after some urging and patient waiting, he began to talk about a time when he had employed a beautiful young woman in his office, and how his male employees were always coming in on false pretexts simply to look at her. He himself had no desire for her at all. He was asked if his lack of desire might have something to do with knowing her, and he said that this was true – that he had got to know her as a person. All the other men in the group identified with this and were able to begin articulating the differences between objectifying women, splitting them into bits (tits, arse, legs, etc.), and getting to know them.

This objectification is the crucial process here, turning women into things or collections of things. For men, women are sexual objects at these times, not people. Objectification is a profoundly complex yet normal activity for men. It involves denuding women of any individuality and complexity, any internal world, any capacities except those connected with sexuality. Although this may seem to the man to be a loving or creative act, it actually involves enormous hostility and aggression towards women, and in fact this is often quite conscious in the sexual fantasies which accompany the leering. Looking or leering is itself a hostile act, because it is a forcible intrusion into the woman. Men like to retain control of how women define men's behaviour, and in this case they will insist that looking is not aggressive or intrusive (despite frequently going to some lengths to avoid being discovered doing it); that women are really gratified by it, and do not define it as sexual aggression.

Betsy Stanko (1985) writes that women often do not define these acts as sexually violent, because 'women's experiences of male violence are filtered through an understanding of men's behaviour which is characterised as either typical or aberrant . . . Women who feel violated by typical male behaviour have no way of specifying how or why typical male behaviour feels like aberrant male behaviour' (p. 10). Liz Kelly's (1988a) continuum of sexual violence is designed to show how 'typical' and 'aberrant' (p. 75) behaviours shade into one another, and what concerns me here is the move from 'normal' impulses and their social control through the escalation to rape. Let me make it clear that control in this context is not meant to imply that men are innately sexually ravenous beasts. It may be that a great many of us do have to control or inhibit these impulses, but this sort of sexual desire, which is about dominance, power, control and conquest rather than relationship, is the consequence, I believe, of the psychic and social construction of masculinity; it is not innate.

A Psychoanalytic Explanation

There can be no doubt that sexual frustration plays a very large part in the complex motivation of rapists, but one must not simply accept this at face value. Nicholas Groth and Ben Birnbaum's (1979) study *Men Who Rape* showed that the vast majority of abusers had access to other, normal, sources of sexual gratification, although Wyre (1988a) concludes that what he calls 'anger rapists' are responding to rejection by 'normal' sources. The study most quoted by feminists is Manachim Amir's (1971) – of 1,292 convicted rapists. His conclusions are not dissimilar to Groth's and Birnbaum's: that they are psychiatrically normal, and are not deprived of normal sexual outlets (they have girlfriends). Amir's sample contained a large proportion of working class and black men and he concluded that social factors were predominantly causative of rape. His conclusions have been criticized on the grounds that his sample exacerbated classist and racist bias, because the vast majority of convicted rapists are likely to be working class and black. The majority of rapes are not reported (75 per cent of women reporting sexual assault to the London Rape Crisis Centre between 1976 and 1980 did not inform the police: Tempkin, 1987), and the majority of rapists are never caught or sentenced.

Sexual frustration implies the absence of sexual gratification – that a sexually frustrated person is simply one who is not in a relationship which affords the opportunity for gratification. As any reflecting person will be aware, however, sexual gratification has little to do with one's lack of sexual activity. It seems to depend on largely non-physical factors, mostly the degree of alienation from desire (as a relation with fantasy), the quality and nature of the fantasies involved, and the extent of the intimacy experienced during the sexual act. These conditions for a man's experiencing sexual satisfaction depend ultimately on his relationship with his partner. This, in turn, will depend on his emotional maturity and the extent to which he has been able to come to terms with his partner in other aspects of their life together.

Rapists clearly feel frustration at a very deep emotional level, whether or not this is intensified by actual physical deprivation. Wyre (1988b) presents evidence that many of them masturbate several times a day and have a high level of sexual arousal. This must be understood in the context of what we know about male sexuality and compulsive masturbation. In *The Psychoanalytic Theory of Neurosis* (written in 1946, and still the standard introduction to psychoanalysis), Fenichel says:

> Since the attempted satisfaction never can be achieved the patients [who, although it is not made explicit, are always men] try masturbation again and again . . . and . . . masturbation can become the uniform response to any kind of stimulus . . . (p. 191)
>
> excessive masturbation represents an attempt to find a genital discharge for nongenital tensions, which cannot succeed. (p. 245)

Finally, in describing excessive and obsessive compulsive masturbation as an 'addiction without drugs', he says:

> the lack of satisfaction increases the striving for satisfaction . . . and . . . the protection of the Gods, which would make a relaxing satisfaction possible, may be sought with the same *aggressive fury* [my italics] by masturbating. (p. 384)

There is no evidence that deprivation is an essential factor in the history of most men who rape – quite the contrary, when one considers that the vast majority of rapes are by husbands on their wives. It is far too easy to be sidetracked in our view of rape by the Peter Sutcliffes of this world. The reality is that a woman is infinitely more likely to be raped in her own home between Friday and Sunday nights than as she walks alone down a darkened street.

Obviously, men who rape have an intense need which they cannot satisfy in the normal way; they therefore feel that they will have to take satisfaction from a woman by force. Equally obviously, they experience this need physically, specifically sexually. The unconscious situation is rather more complex. In fact, the acts which many rape victims are coerced into performing show that their assailant's need is more than simply sexual.

The rapist experiences his relations with women as ultimately frustrating; he feels constantly let down by them; more, he believes that women, representing the internal 'bad' mother, deliberately engineer his frustration and anger, and derive sadistic satisfaction from his loneliness, suffering and frustration. To put it simply: he feels a victim of a persecuting, sadistic witch whom he is psychologically powerless to fight. He perceives sexual relations – correctly, in my view – as essentially sadomasochistic, and unconsciously he is the victim. He lacks the resources and the motivation (after all, he thinks, don't all men feel the same about women?) to seek any insight which would enable him to undo this faulty perception, and it becomes a self-fulfilling prophecy. He has all the impulses of a child faced with the fantasized 'bad' mother – he fears and hates her, and longs for the benign security and intimacy of the 'good' mother – with all the physical strength of a grown man, yet none of the impulse control which comes with maturity and self-knowledge. He yearns for the satisfaction of the 'good' mother, yet he is dominated by the 'bad' mother. Additionally, of course, the 'bad' mother still retains the infinitely desirable characteristics of the 'good' mother. She has the breasts, the skin, the smell, and so on, and is still extremely arousing. The rapist's sexual frustration is not of a genital kind; it is much more to do with regressive needs of a pre-genital nature which he has learned to sexualize, and which are not all creative.

However much the rapist might represent it as purely sexual, it is self-evident, as I have said, that rape is a violent act, and that one of its main motivations is to enact violence. Every rapist has a need to express violence towards women. If his frustration were purely sexual, a whole range of options is available to him for satisfying it, which do not involve violence. Whether or not tissue damage to the victim is involved, sadism is a major motivation of all rapists. Perhaps it would not be going too far to say that one of the unconscious goals of the rapist is the annihilation of the object.

So the rapist yearns for the satisfaction of the 'good' mother, yet is dominated by the 'bad' mother. There is a fusion of his desire to bond with the good and attack the bad. The sadistic act of rape is unconsciously a reversal of the position as he has experienced it previously, unconsciously – from his masochistic, and ultimately paranoid, suffering at the hands of the bad witch, to his vengeful sadistic punishment of the sexually masochistic woman. Transparently, therefore, rape is also an act of retaliation against the arousing 'bad' mother. Rape, unconsciously, is both a 'taking from' and a 'putting into' the woman. What is taken is the possession of the split-off 'good'-mother body, which is full of good things. The physical possession is real, but much more important for him, consciously, is the fantasy possession – the union with the 'good' mother which provides him with the intimacy that is lacking in his life. It is the 'bad' mother he is attacking so that he can, as it were, move her out of the way of the 'good' mother with whom he wants to fuse, as well as punishing her for her arousing qualities. Obviously, a massive projection of the 'bad' is involved.

Let me illustrate this projection. For two or three weeks, Arthur, a client in a group for abusive men, had been describing his wife, to whom he was seriously abusive (this always includes sexual abuse). It dawned on me – rather slowly, I confess – that I was experiencing the most violent feelings and impulses towards this woman (not, I must admit, an entirely strange experience to me in my own relationships). I found myself thinking that if I lived with her I would be at least as abusive as my client. I shared this thought with the group, and with some relief they all confessed that they were having the same guilt-laden feelings. I invited the group to describe their perceptions of Arthur's partner. The adjectives which this elicited described the most appallingly frightening and vicious woman who really should not be out of jail or hospital. This was a great shock to Arthur, who began to cry and tell the group how much he loved her, and that she was not like that at all. It gradually dawned on him that he constantly struggled against this internal witch whom the group had described, and that it was she whom he was abusing. Slowly, the other group members began to share the confidence that they each had a similar internal partner towards whom they had those same feelings, and who was not even remotely like the real woman they loved or cared about. They all admitted that they were terrified of this internal woman, and wanted to destroy her. My purpose in reporting this is not to discuss how to work with this issue but simply to illustrate how men carry around this internal object, and that we are rarely aware of it.

How does the man committing rape enjoy it? There seem to be only two possibilities. The first is that he is aware of the violence of his act and the power and control he is exercising over his victim, and enjoys it. Indeed, this is his motivation: the arousal of his sadism and the sadomasochistic role reversal. This is reinforced by the freedom for perversity and the pleasures of orgasm. The second is that he is not aware of his violence, in which case he is carrying out the most massive denial of reality, and splitting off parts of himself in order to delude himself that he is simply enjoying the 'good' mother. It seems unlikely that the man could be aware of doing both, or he would stop. I think it is here that we come close to the myth of the woman who 'wanted to be raped and enjoyed it'. By splitting himself into good and bad, he simultaneously recovers, in fantasy, the bond with the 'good' mother. He expresses his sadistic, hateful feelings for the 'bad' mother (described above in the story of Arthur) by violently penetrating her and acting out his sadistic conception of the primal scene, reversing the sadomasochistic roles. He believes that the 'bad' mother is sexually masochistic and enjoys the punishment which violent penetration inflicts, otherwise how could she, as the abandoning, persecuting witch, have allowed herself to have been penetrated by his father?

Freud and many subsequent researchers have shown that the child sees the act of parental intercourse as sadomasochistic, and experiences it as a persecution in that his beloved mother has betrayed and abandoned him. This evokes his early paranoid anxiety in relation to the 'witch' mother, and his homicidal impulses related to these anxieties. These feelings contribute to his interpretation of the parents' sexual intercourse. The noise and behaviour involved seem violent to him, because of his projections of his hatred. Moreover, the intercourse stimulates in him overwhelming excitement, for which there is no genital outlet, and he feel this as a threat to his fragile psyche. The threat is compounded by the many contradictory impulses aroused in him by his bisexuality. To different degrees, he wants to make love to and kill both his mother and his father during the primal scene. Another source of the sadomasochistic primal-scene fantasy is the child's knowledge of his mother's lack of a penis. To him, at this fragile stage in his development, this is an actual 'absence'. He concludes that his mother has lost her penis during the act of intercourse, and that intercourse involves his father doing something violent to his mother's genitals which results in the loss of her penis.

There are levels of violence in rape which go beyond any required to make the woman do the rapist's bidding. I want to make it clear that I do not accept that violence is instrumental to rape: it is expressive and gratifying to the rapist, an end in itself, a component of the rapist's sexuality. The instrumental nature of violence is also propounded by some clinicians who work with men who batter women. This is a very useful concept in work with abusive men, but it is a limited truth. As one man said to me after he had virtually destroyed his home to frighten his wife into not being angry with him, 'I've never felt so powerful. I thought I could do anything, even walk through walls!' I believe it is important for us men to acknowledge and understand the pleasure we get from violence (including emotional abuse), in particular the power and control it affords, if we are ever to abjure it.

The differences in the type and level of violence in rape may be significant to understanding a particular individual's level of perversity and the extent of his psychosexual regression to infantile ways of thinking and feeling, but it must first be acknowledged that it is integral to his sexual desire and his way of relating to women. These remarks certainly apply to stranger rapists. They are also applicable to family rapists in so far as the rape involves violence rather than coercion. This, however, is a matter of degree. Coercion cannot be divorced from its context. That context is the intimate connection between dominance, aggression, violence and heterosexuality. Understanding the regressive and perverse processes of the rapist in no way diminishes his individual responsibility, even though it may account for the way his desire is structured so that women become his victims. Nor does it account for the adult beliefs about and attitudes to women which seamlessly connect this desire with his behaviour, and define women as appropriate victims.

This explanation of the rapist's motivation seems to accord with the feminist model I outlined briefly above. Rape is simply a vivid and extreme example of men's behaviour in all aspects of their relations with women. This particularly vile crime occurs when attempts to deal with the 'bad' mother – by preventing her from gaining control of herself and, by becoming separate, him, either in the world or in his psyche – break down in a man who has no other resources for dealing with his feelings. He has learned that a real man would not put up with such treatment from a woman, and it is a slur on his masculinity if he fails to correct the situation by objectifying her, bringing her under control and asserting a man's natural right to access to a woman's body: a right which he did not question at the beginning of life, as an omnipotent infant; a right which was reinforced as he grew into manhood.

In rape, it is obvious that woman is regarded as an object to be used or abused according to the man's conscience – or lack of it. In this sense rape is a visible and obvious expression of men's perceptions of women: that they are 'an object of exchange between men'. Woman's status as 'object of exchange' derives from the whole system of kinship and symbolism which is represented by the Oedipus complex. Paradoxically, woman achieves (if that is the right word) this status by virtue of her power in both the male and female imagination. Precisely because the 'mother', as she has been constructed, is so powerful as the first, and perhaps only, love object for all children, it is necessary for social relations to be organized so that this emotional bond can be broken. This is achieved, for boys, with the realization of Father's presence and the prohibition that his presence represents – Mummy belongs to Daddy: she is Daddy's property.

In cultural terms the Oedipus complex describes the requirement for the child to learn the norms which bind society, of which the most fundamental are those concerned with ownership and the property rights and penalties which ownership bestows. Jessica Benjamin's (1990) synthesis of these norms is hard to better, and is worth summarizing. Basing her argument on the sociologist Weber, she says that rationality is in fact a male rationality. It appears to be gender neutral, to have no subject. Yet its logic dovetails with the Oedipal denial of woman's subjectivity which reduces the other to object. Rationalization defines the process in which abstract, calculable and depersonalized modes of interaction replace those founded on personal relationships, authority and beliefs. The idea of rationalization elevates means to the status of ends; it forms a bridge between intellectual history and the history of social and economic relationships. It describes the essence of modern social practice and thought. It is a *gendered* discourse and forms the basis of male domination (pp. 185–8, author's emphasis).

Although she writes as a psychoanalyst, Benjamin is drawing on the history of feminist scholarship. Her conclusion is that the world is a masculine place in which the feminine is excluded and marginalized, by the gendered rationality of social organization and 'the subjugation of woman by man which is the psychosocial core of unfettered individuality', and a consequence of the Oedipus complex (p. 189). One consequence of the 'woman/mother as property' which lies at the core of the Oedipus complex is that mother–son incest is far more rare, and implicitly less acceptable, than father–daughter incest. This follows from the subject status of males (sons) and the object status of women (mothers). It is a well-established fact that by far the majority of father–daughter incest – a strange word that implies mutuality and a relationship rather than gender-based sexual abuse – cases never see the light of day.

Traditionally, in known incest or child abuse cases, there has been a preference amongst professionals for keeping the family together. Many cases do not get beyond intervention by social work agencies and into the criminal justice system (CIBA, 1988). The implicit assumption is that in a real sense, the family structure has not already been shattered by the father's sexual intercourse with his daughter; that this is somehow within the acceptable, albeit questionable, limits of family life. Furthermore, the emphasis on 'collusive mothers' who fail to protect their daughters absolves the man of responsibility as effectively as the idea of a seductive daughter. There are many cases in the literature where it is explicitly stated that the mother drove the father to incest because she was working too hard, or not hard enough, or refused him sexual access, or otherwise failed in her role as homemaker, housekeeper, lover, mother and cook (CIBA, 1988; Driver and Droisen, 1989; J. Herman, 1981).

The assumption that the father has the right to this sort of servicing from a woman, his wife, and that if she fails him he has the right to expect it from the nearest available female, is endemic. Again, such cases are full of references to role reversal in so-called 'dysfunctional incestuous families'. This refers to the frequent finding that before the paternal abuse – 'rape of his daughter' (Ward, 1984) – the daughter had taken over the mother's role and duties because of some maternal inadequacy. The idea that the father should take over the parenting duties, the protection and care, in a situation where the mother is unable to – probably because of depression resulting from his abuse of her – is simply never considered. Rather than mothers and daughters being offered therapy as a first option, priority should be given to consciousness-raising classes which teach them how they are both survivors of abuse. Ideally, therapy should combine both. The perpetrator should be punished and offered concurrent treatment or re-education. Treatment of perpetrators should not be seen as an alternative to punishment. The preservation of the family should not be a primary goal of intervention.

I do not wish to convey the impression that the objectification of women occurs only as the result of the allocation of property rights for which the Oedipus complex stands as a metaphor. There is ample evidence that young infants objectify their mothers, or primary carers, in extremely primitive ways. The objectification and fragmentation of women into breasts, buttocks and legs, for example, predates any awareness of them as objects of exchange between men. During puberty – when sexual desire is at its height and the Oedipus complex is being resolved (mostly) into heterosexuality – the boy is surrounded by part-object representations of women which fit neatly into his early primitive ones. These cultural influences are deliberately structured by men to orientate our desire, and they shape, express and reinforce the primitive, more biologically determined relationship with the primary carer. Even if the primary carer is a man, it seems inevitable that with the cultural shaping of heterosexual desire, men will attach their desire to women. These early methods of dealing with trauma and conflict – splitting, projection, denial, sadomasochism, and so on – will exert their influence in times of stress (when a man fails to get his own way with a woman, or she fails to live up to his expectations), whether these originate in the outer or inner world. The dehumanization of women, which I encounter all too often in my work with men who are violent towards their female partners, makes them suitable 'objects' for all forms of abuse. Their dehumanization and objectification are necessary conditions for the violence.

It is overwhelmingly clear to me that the conditions which make this possible are extant in the social and cultural representations of women, and the teaching of masculinity. It is equally clear, however, that these conditions are not the source of men's abuse, or of their capacity for dehumanizing women. I vividly remember one violent man with whom we had been working for some months. He was a 'typical' batterer. He was not disturbed; like many, he was highly educated, in a good profession, loved his children, and so on. We had patiently and painstakingly unpicked each of the triggers which set off his cycle of violence. It became clear that this process could go on for ever. With the undoing of one trigger, another would always appear. Finally he recognized the endlessness of this process. He was asked, given what he had discovered, what he now thought caused his violence. After a long and painful silence, in which he seemed slunk in depression, he said, so silently that it was hard to hear, 'I hate her'.

Some feminists (e.g. Ward, 1984) think – with some justification, I believe – that psychoanalysis offers implicit support to the values and attitudes which make rape possible. Psychoanalysis is a complex discourse, and although it certainly has monolithic structural and intellectual qualities, one must be careful about any generalization, especially such a damning one. There is no doubt, however, that from a feminist perspective, any reading of Freud's paper 'On narcissism' (1914) would support Ward's case. There is also Jeffrey Masson's book *The Assault on Truth* (1984), in which he began a crusade against Freud and psychoanalysis which he continued in his later work, *Against Therapy* (1989). In *The Assault on Truth*, Masson engages in polemic around a long-standing debate within psychoanalysis about the status of 'real' and 'fantasy' (see Scott, 1988, for a summary of this debate). As Joel Kovel, an independent New York analyst, puts it:

> Masson's crusade is a fairly straightforward one. It is that Freud, through a defect in moral courage, betrayed his own most revolutionary discovery, the seduction theory of hysteria; and that in so doing he set psychoanalysis on the path to its own sterility . . . betraying [and, I would add, blaming] the child victims of seduction and the cause of women as well . . . he did so by . . . moving to the position that neuroses were essentially caused by fantasies. (1985, p. 114–15)

Masson's work, unlike Ward's, is rooted within the analytic establishment. Before the publication of his book he was at its heart not only as an analyst but as the future guardian of the Freud Archives, who was given permission by Anna Freud to examine the documents in Freud's Hampstead home. It was there, in Freud's correspondence, that he uncovered what he believed to be irrefutable proof of what he regarded as Freud's moral cowardice, the disclosure of which would permanently undermine the practice of psychoanalysis. Joel Kovel points out that Masson's work and his belief in its revolutionary impact are not so unique – only the most flamboyant entry into the budding tradition of casting doubt on the pieties about Freud. The status of the 'real event' has been a central theme of the work of another notable defecting analyst, Alice Miller, who, in a series of books (1979, 1980, 1981, 1987) has written about the real destructive effects of parental abuse of power on children, and urged a return to the early, pre-analytic Freud of 'catharsis theory' and dammed-up real reactions to external trauma. Her work, however, is much more respectful of the analytic tradition and, unlike Masson, she does not accuse analysts themselves of bad faith.

Masson asserts – as Ward and others, including psychoanalysts, had asserted before – that Freud actually suppressed what he knew to be the truth about the scale of infant sexual abuse because he was afraid of public reaction. Ann Scott, however, asserts the contrary. She is critical of Masson's scholarship and his 'muddled thought'(1988, p. 90), and points out that Freud's discovery of infantile sexuality brought him into greater difficulty professionally than his seduction theory. She adds that, in any case, 'analysts have been more sure than Freud was himself of the destructive effects of sexual abuse' (p. 97), and that she had found little evidence in the analytic journals to support Masson's view that analysts show a calculated indifference to the issue. Joel Kovel is not so sure. Like Scott, he is critical of Masson. He comments: '*The Assault on Truth* . . . is as vain, shallow and bombastic as one would expect. But there is more to it than that. Serious questions and real scholarship lie buried beneath layers of trash. For all that he works to deserve it Masson cannot be ignored' (1985, p. 114). Kovel himself cannot be ignored, and his view of the serious questions of real scholarship in Masson's work is worthy of attention, even if one agrees with Scott's well-substantiated charge that Masson's book is permeated with 'confusions of logic, mistakes of fact [and] caricatures of others' positions' (1988, p. 90).

Kovel's ironic, scholarly yet well-grounded intellect is sufficiently iconoclastic to see the real meat in the Massonic sandwich in a way which the Masson of *The Assault on Truth* is not. However, Masson seems to have learned his lesson well if one is to judge by the central theme of his later work. *Against Therapy* (1989) is entirely given over to examining the power relations between psychoanalyst and patient. Kovel's reading of Masson sees exactly this. As he expresses it:

> a special complication arises for the workers in the vineyards of the unconscious . . . actually a double complication. Being technocratic, analysis is forced to adhere, as a matter of social survival, to a discourse structured . . . to be antithetical to desire i.e. opposed to its naming; and being bourgeois . . . is forced to adhere, as a matter of economic survival to prevailing systems of authority and class partiality i.e. domination . . . psychoanalysis both exposes patriarchal relations and reinforces . . . them . . . it becomes more patriarchal and authoritarian in its cultism and more backward than the rest of technocratic society. In this contradiction may lie some of the roots of . . . its peculiar difficulties with women as well as . . . its well known intellectual stagnation. (ibid., pp. 122–3)

It is striking that so little could stir up so much. This could only be a function of the cultism and mystification which are the hallmarks of psychoanalysis as a profession. Scott points out that Masson's approach leaves out the possibility that Freud could make an error of judgement without this compromising the whole fabric of psychoanalytic thought. I hardly think this is Masson's fault when generations of analytic trainees are confronted with the consequences of doing so – such as those faced by Masson himself. Kovel suggests that he may have offered himself up as a victim, but he acknowledges that this is, in any case, essential. Masson's fate was predictable and he should have foreseen it, but it ill becomes analysis to blame the victim yet again.

With the growing impact of feminist thinking and the challenge to professional hegemony, this issue is not likely to go away, and the stakes are high. Is it real seduction or the oedipal working over that produces neurosis? If it is the real event, psychoanalysis is a sham, because what must be addressed is the real power of fathers, and their abuse of this power. Like Ann Scott, I believe that even if Masson's central charge is substantial – and there are grounds for believing so – this would not of itself lead to the dissolution of psychoanalysis. Apart from the complexity of analysis – which, as Scott rightly claims, Masson ignores – there is no doubt that the internal reworking of real trauma actually occurs, and that there is no linear connection between trauma and the development of a neurosis. Uncovering this highly subjective connection in a personal narrative is the very heart of psychoanalysis, and it is crucial to understanding desire and sexual fantasy.

Masson's work has faced fierce criticism and, in fact, led to his expulsion from the analytic movement. It has provoked enormous public controversy, and even a legal battle between Masson and another author, Janet Malcolm (Malcolm, 1983). Given the heat generated by this debate, it is worth looking at the facts of child sexual abuse. There is a growing body of evidence that a very large percentage – the estimates vary widely, from 5 per cent to 60 per cent (Finkelhor, 1986) – of children are actually sexually abused, and clearly, Freud was wrong in minimizing this. This unpleasant reality is now impinging on psychoanalytic consciousness, despite the odium heaped on Masson when he published his conclusions (CIBA, 1984, p. xviii). Was Freud simply naive (a charge which is impossible to sustain), did he deliberately suppress his evidence, or has the incidence of child sexual abuse increased since his day? We may never know.

In her book *Father-Daughter Rape*, Elizabeth Ward (1984) provides a contextual analysis of rape. In her view:

> father–daughter rape was the foundation stone of the interrelated theories about sexuality which Freud developed . . . he moved from an awareness of father–daughter rape (the seduction theory) to create an entire superstructure of metaphysical [*sic*] concepts in order to protect himself (the fathers) from having to face the truth about the rape of girl children by the Fathers. The distortion which Freud made of his initial discovery of father–daughter rape was conceived within the framework of male supremacy and ultimately functioned to reinforce rape ideology. As such, Freudianism permeates every form of therapy in the western world. Freud is by no means alone as a theorist who viewed the world through male supremacist spectacles, thereby causing untold suffering to women and girl children – but his name, and the term Freudianism, still stand as the signpost and place name of a way of thinking, of practising therapy, which demands thorough analytical criticism and debunking for the sake of all raped women . . . The popularisation of Freudianism functions as subliminal 'psycho-scientific' ideology, reinforcing male desire to believe that women want to be raped. Freudianism holds that girl children unconsciously desire intercourse with the Father: thus we have the sexualisation of girl children as the

> reason for their being raped by the Father. By this and several other means, Freud managed to blame the victim.' (p. 183)

Kovel (1985) acknowledges that Freudianism reinforces male supremacist phallocentric ideologies. I doubt that he or any other analyst would agree with Ward that they also reinforce or encourage rape ideologies which lead to victim-blaming in cases of woman abuse. It must be admitted, however, that this is true of many analytically derived explanations of men's abuse of women and children. All systems of therapy which are based on Freudianism – and most are – will invariably assume that each person is to some degree responsible for their own predicament, and has an unconscious investment in maintaining it. The emphasis on inner reality to the exclusion of the outer realities of male power means that women are doubly victimized.

There is no doubt that the Freudian theory of the development of femininity must be total revised to take account of male supremacy and the raising of girl children to be passive and seductive heterosexual adults who are subordinated to men. It would not be true, however, to imply that this has never been problematic to the analytic community. The debate has raged, sometimes bitterly, since the first women trained as analysts – Ward does acknowledge this. In particular, Karen Horney (1926, but see also 1924, 1933) confronted the Freudian view of women as seen through men's eyes. She posited that male depreciation (Freud's 'normal contempt') of women arose from male envy of women's reproductive capacities, and that female masochism is actually enforced passivity. Today's feminists would add that this enforced passivity is underpinned by violence or threats of violence.

As we shall see in Chapter 7 my position is close to Horney's. However, Freud's understanding of masculinity has stood the test of time, and while we must see his theory of femininity as severely limited by his failure to take male power and violence into account, we must appreciate that he was attempting to understand how gender differentiation and identity came about. Contrary to Ward's thinking, he was not trying to develop an ideology which would reinforce rape ideology. Even though there are probably no analysts or therapists who would agree with this, it is undoubtedly implicit in most models derived from analytic theory, and is explicit in some. Such a development has certainly occurred, but it is risible to believe that this was Freud's conscious intention. His rejection of the seduction theory of hysteria was conditioned by his disbelief that so much abuse was possible ('It was hardly credible that perverted acts against children were so general': Freud, 1954, letter 21 September 1897). Is this so hard to understand in a man living in the nineteenth century, when so many well-intentioned men and women have the same difficulty in the late twentieth?

In the face of the intense critical analysis of Freud's theory of the Oedipus complex, particularly the female version, it is not credible that it could have survived for almost a century only because of the male hegemony within psychoanalysis. There is also little doubt that the Freudian theory has some core validity in the way it describes what men do to little girls and women. The female Oedipus complex (see Chapter 7) is the result of men's construction of femininity out of their own lack. It is predicated on male power and violence and *serves* to reinforce 'male supremacy . . . and rape ideology' (Ward, 1984). I should add – for the sake of completeness, if not clarity – that the internal 'witch' and 'princess', the basis of the male construction of femaleness, are fantasies. They are erected by the child to account for his desire and his division from himself. They establish the basis of the woman/feminine as a fetish, as other than male, with whom the man can establish a mythical unity. Woman becomes all that man is 'not' (rather than man becoming all that is not woman), and needs if he is to complete himself. This is what is meant by the statement that there is no such thing as femininity, only masculinity.

Freud's findings are unpalatable – and wrong about women – but he was a passionate investigator, as concerned as today's feminists to unearth the mystery of phallic dominance.

Although many daughters might disagree, Ward asserts – and I agree – that there is no qualitative difference between the father who commits incest with his daughter and the father who doesn't. The differences are quantitative with respect to such matters as the intensity of desire, degree of guilt, strength of impulse controls, and so on. For example, Finkelhor (1986) describes how many researchers hold to the theory that sexual abuse of stepdaughters by their stepfathers is so common because these men have not had the chance to raise these children and de-eroticize them through the everyday experience of contact since infancy. This is actually a rather astounding admission; it clearly implies that all girl children are sexual objects to men if they are not their daughters! This is a very uncomfortable truth, not only for men but for professionals working with abusers. It sheds light on why so much professional energy is devoted to keeping the family together (see CIBA, 1984). In this way, professionals do not have to ask the difficult questions about the family's role in constructing female sexuality, and question its moral and functional base.

As we have seen, women and girl children are regarded as possessions of men the world over, and men have different ways of exercising their power over them – at the extreme, this is expressed through rape. It is essential that rapists are not defined as insane or otherwise seen as outside a frame of reference which makes their behaviour explicable. This does not mean that rapists cannot be differentiated from non-rapists in a meaningful way. It is a vitally important distinction, both morally and legally, that most men do not physically rape women despite the fact that most men benefit from the activities of rapists. These benefits stem from the restrictions the threat and fear of rape impose on women's freedoms – of speech, movement, dress and behaviour. Susan Brownmiller has defined rape as an act of terrorism by which 'all men keep all women in a state of fear' (1975, p. 34). It was Brownmiller who 'gave rape its history', but it was Susan Griffin who set the terms for future feminist debate about rape in her ground-breaking article (Griffin, 1971): 'I have never been free of the fear of rape . . . I never asked why men raped; I simply thought it one of the mysteries of human nature' (p. 26). The apocalyptic feminist slogan 'All men are potential rapists' derives from the understanding which subsequently developed of the construction of male sexuality around the eroticizing of dominance. As Sheila Jeffreys explains it:

> The slogan simply means that if male sexuality is constructed in such a way that men associate sex with aggression then every man is capable of rape. The slogan means that women are not in a position to know

> whether the men they meet are likely to rape or not . . . some men may feel entirely innocent but it is not possible for women to treat them differently. To a woman in a train carriage or on a street every man is a potential rapist. The judicial system expects her to act on that assumption and will hold her responsible for her own victimisation if she treats a man who subsequently rapes her with ordinary human politeness. (1990, p. 241)

Given this perspective on rape, one might ask how it is that all men do not develop into rapists. We all share the same infantile traumas in relation to our mothers, and we all end up connecting sexuality with dominance and aggression. According to Freudian theory, it is because the resolution of the boy's Oedipus complex not only imposes prohibitions through the establishment of an agency of control (conscience, or the super-ego) but also allows for the expression of misogyny through the institutionalized oppression of women, and dominance of men, upon which heterosexuality and society are based. It is rather ironic that Freud's description of the female Oedipus complex led him inexorably to the idea that women do not develop a super-ego or conscience as strong as a man's. From all the available evidence, it would seem either that the reverse is true or that a great many men fail miserably in the attempt to identify with the father.

Actually, this is an illusion. The identification with the father, whether as a patriarchal authority or as a real person, is obvious in men's abuse of women, which all little boys will have observed. The conclusion that men can expect to be in authority over and to receive servicing from women is inescapable. From a woman's point of view, it would seem that a man's failure or success makes little difference. If he fails he may become a batterer, a child sexual abuser or a rapist. If he succeeds he becomes a partriarchal authority who regards women as less than human and expects submission and obedience from them, whether or not this expectation is out of awareness, or unconscious. If she embraces her femininity, the woman will submit and obey. If she does not, he has the right to chastise her. Where's the difference? It seems that the male super-ego is predicated on the notion that the man will behave in a civilized fashion so long as women are conforming to his expectations and demands – being what women are supposed to be: princesses. The male super-ego contains permissions to batter and sexually abuse if the woman fails – becomes a witch. In this way his behaviour becomes her responsibility.

Given the construction of male sexual desire, without the super-ego the pleasure-seeking id would make all men rapists. From this perspective, rapists and users of pornography are inadequate personalities who have not succeeded in resolving their Oedipus complex and whose sexuality has not coalesced into that rather fragile, genitally dominated position which we call masculine maturity. It is rather ironic that the trauma of the genital Oedipus complex, which leads to the setting up of the major intrapsychic agency of social and emotional control – thereby preventing most men from acting out their many socially unacceptable impulses, including the impulse to rape (and we should remember that 57 per cent of men say there is a likelihood they would probably rape if they could be sure of not being apprehended) also reaffirms the ideological basis underpinning rape – women as the property of men; as castrated/passive/masochistic objects of contempt. The earlier emotional basis of misogyny is structured, institutionalized and reified by the oedipal resolution when the boy child accepts the Law – Mother belongs to Father – and, reluctantly or otherwise, his masculinity. The male super-ego contains and affirms the ideology of abuse.

THE USE OF PORNOGRAPHY

How does this way of understanding a rapist's behaviour – in terms of his internal relations with 'princess' and 'witch' – help us to understand the role of pornography in our phallocentric culture? One of the first and most obvious points is that we live in a world in which women are presented as sexual objects and playthings for men: where women's naked bodies and images of bodies are used as an inducement to purchase all manner of products, from drain-cleaners to motorcars. An essential, implicit element of pornography is that men have power over women. This is inherent not only in the use of women for pornography, as MacKinnon and Dworkin have shown, but also in the use of these images in men's masturbatory fantasies. We are surrounded by images of naked and semi-naked women whose purpose is to stimulate arousal. Women have always been, and will continue to be, objects of men's desire, and that may be all to the good (I have no doubt that it is). These images, however, express much more. They aim to exploit this fact for other ends, and I believe that in doing so they reinforce the processes which underlie rape. There is no evidence that pornography causes rape, but there is a lot of evidence about its use by rapists. There can be little doubt that it makes rape easier to contemplate because of the deep structure of meanings it conveys about the role and status of women in society, and their significance for men and male culture.

The standard definition of pornography is 'the explicit presentation of material which aims to stimulate erotic, not aesthetic feelings. Any literature containing this is pornographic' (*OED*). Such a definition, of course, is widely open to question without being merely sophist. Is it necessary, for example, that this material is produced with the intention of stimulating sexual feelings, or is the fact that it does so sufficient for it to be defined as pornographic? Actually, it is impossible to decide. Such arguments have provided – and will no doubt continue to provide – lawyers with employment for a very long time. It seems clear, however, that whatever the arguments about whether a particular image is pornographic, we live in a pornographic culture with respect to images of women.

I do not intend to discuss the true nature of pornography. My main concerns are, first, to examine what the user of literature or publications (including films) broadly defined as pornographic is doing both consciously and unconsciously; secondly, to understand what the nature of pornographic publications tells us about the relations between men and women; and thirdly, to examine the link between rape and pornography.

What can be said with certainty, and without recourse to analytic concepts, about men who use pornography? The most obvious fact is that they seek sexual stimulation through external material in isolation. This material is an impersonal object between their desire and themselves. Whether or not it is objectively pornographic, it is the means to an end: arousal and ejaculation by masturbation. Setting aside, for the moment, the emotional after-effects, usually guilt, shame and depression, what does the man achieve by his behaviour, and why does he indulge in it rather than seeking more gratifying sources of satisfaction? Is it necessary to distinguish between infrequent users of pornography and those for whom it is the major source of sexual satisfaction? I think not. In common with my other observations about male sexuality, I believe that the differences between them are quantitative rather than qualitative. All men, other things being equal, are either users or potential users of pornography. This is not to say that there are not many men to whom it is morally repugnant and who would not dream of indulging such impulses. This aside, what is of interest is that the vast majority of men masturbate, and that there is a clear connection between masturbation and pornography.

MASTURBATION

To understand pornography, we must first appreciate the role of masturbation in male sexuality. One of the difficulties in writing about masturbation is that it is almost identical to writing about sexuality itself. Freud said that the subject of masturbation is inexhaustible (1912, p. 254), although, surprisingly, he never wrote a long paper about it. As one renowned analyst remarked, 'the conflicts around masturbation are in essence the conflicts around sexuality' (A. Reich, 1956). Masturbation is one of the most frequently referenced topics in the Index volume of the *Standard Edition* of Freud's works, taking up almost a whole page, although each entry is a passing comment rather than a lengthy examination. I do not intend to document his findings fully here, or to reference every comment. Instead, I want to try to relate masturbation to pornography. Although Freud does not refer to pornography, it existed in his time, albeit not as a multi-billion-dollar industry.

It is common knowledge that in the nineteenth century it was established medical opinion that masturbation was a form of illness and could cause all manner of physical and moral degradation. Catalogues depicted and sold metal and leather devices designed to prevent children from masturbating (Rogers, 1989). Such moral and religious values masquerading as scientifically proven fact are no longer seriously held in twentieth-century medical or psychiatric circles.

Freud was of the opinion that all masturbation is infantile, and involves an emotional and psychological regression to childhood sexuality and fantasy (1912, p. 251). While I accept this, it is equally true that masturbation is an integral part of adult sexuality, however regressive this may be. It was Freud who pointed out the integrating function of the genitals in the genital drive: without genital ejaculation and orgasm, there is no possibility of sexual satisfaction. Pre-genital sexuality has no means of direct discharge unless it becomes subordinated to genital sexuality; there are no oral or anal orgasms. Most adult, genital sexuality, however, contains elements of these earlier interests.

The genital drive – that is, the urge to penetrate with the penis as the ultimate source of sexual satisfaction – is an exceptionally fragile organization, and although other and earlier sexual drives become subordinated to it in the sense that they seek orgasm, this subordination is related to ends only, and is no guarantee that the means are less important. ('There is no genital drive. It can go and get f... [. . .] on the side of the Other', Lacan quoted in Mitchell and Rose, eds 1982, p. 35.) It is important to recognize male sexuality as it is rather than erect an idealized conception of the genital character (W. Reich, 1933). The genital character, who has fully resolved his infantile Oedipus complex, is a virile, dominant, forceful masculine entity in comparison with whom all men will feel inadequate. It should be clear by now that any idea of normative or normal sexuality is imaginary. The object of analytic inquiry is to explain and understand the acquisition of sexual identity, and to liberate 'desire' through the articulation of unconscious infantile sexual fantasy.

Masturbation can obviously be an occasional healthy safety valve in circumstances where there is no immediate prospect of a sexual relationship. On the whole, however, it is a regressive outcome of a very complex psychological process – more an indication of emotional alienation than of physical isolation. This alienation is not only from the 'other' but also from the self. Masturbation is generally performed alone, and is a source of guilt to most men. They do not normally discuss it with their friends, and even with a psychotherapist it tends to be a difficult issue to raise. At first sight it is odd that a seemingly innocent act of self-gratification could be a source of such guilt and shame – unless it is less innocent than it seems. The only way to find anything approaching a satisfactory explanation for these feelings of guilt and shame is to look at the unconscious fantasies which lie behind the conscious ones leading to masturbation.

Essentially, masturbation is an attempt to avoid the experience of anxiety. This anxiety can have many specific sources, and can reflect fixations at any stage of sexual development. In stressing the defensive quality of masturbation I do not want to imply that it does not also have an expressive function which indicates something rather more positive about the human character – the preference for experiencing good feelings rather than bad ones, and the temporary defeat of Thanatos or primitive aggression by Eros. At its root, it is the experience of desire which we seek in masturbating, and desire is only a relation with fantasy. Other things being equal, however, masturbation is symptomatic of disturbance. Generally speaking, although the person may experience sexual frustration, this is rarely what lies behind the impulse to masturbate.

Masturbation is self-stimulation and gratification. It is the equivalent, psychologically, of thumb-sucking. Children resort to these autoerotic acts when there is no available external source of satisfaction. At its simplest, it is a way of giving comfort to oneself. (This is not meant to imply that it occurs only in the absence of the loved and needed object, although this is a major motivation.) As such, it is inevitably associated with pain and loss. As any parent will know, children will perform autoerotic acts even in their presence. Apart from the control over satisfaction, rather than having to rely on the external object, as well as the satisfaction which it provides for the child, it can clearly signal the existence of conflicts with the primary, satisfying object – Mother.

My concern is to understand those circumstances where masturbation is the chosen means of satisfying desire – in the broadest sense, where the desire is not necessarily sexual – and where there are other means of satisfying it. In general terms, it is taken that the most obvious way for a man to satisfy desire is in a relationship with a real person. Generally speaking, for men, this is a woman. Given that this is usually not an impossible expectation, in that a very large proportion of the human world seems to spend a great deal of time looking for the other-sexed proportion, why should a man choose to express his desire in isolated and isolating self-gratification – which, in any case, usually increases frustration because it is so physically unsatisfactory – rather than in a relationship? One answer to this lies in the fact that the loneliness of masturbation is an expression of the problem, rather than a symptom.

The origin of loneliness lies in the failure to be intimate. We fail because of inhibitions in our capacity to love. Any person whose capacity for loving is impaired is, to that extent, incapable of feeling loved. While I acknowledge that there are many potential causes of the inhibition or failure of the capacity to love, my contention is that the primary cause relates to the fear of 'desire' and surrender to the rage and sadness towards the lost object (the 'princess') who provoked that desire and whom we learn to blame for its failure. There is a constant conflict between desire on the one hand, which pushes towards the 'other' and the loss of self, and the ego – the 'I' – on the other hand, whose function is to preserve itself in the face of its imminent destruction by desire.

Masturbation and the Internal Object

I pointed out above that one consequence of desire is that the infant evolves the templates of two views of his mother/world – which are later structured, during development, into a good 'princess' whom he loves and wishes to incorporate by eating, and a bad 'witch' whom he fears and hates, and wishes to destroy. The consequent conflict this establishes in his relation to all objects – the conflict of ambivalence – is repressed, and one of the functions of the 'I' is to ensure that it stays repressed. Repressed conflicts, however, do not die – they find means of expression which the 'I' does not notice; for example, the husband who is angry with his wife, and in order to protect her – prompted by guilt, or concern, or both – withdraws; this withdrawal hurts her, and therefore has a destructive effect even if he does not consciously intend it. Whatever defences are set up to cope with this ambivalence, they all involve the institutionalization of the failure or inhibition of the capacity for intimacy. They become what are commonly known as character traits.

One may, on the face it, be leading a full and meaningful life, yet for all of us, to some extent, a sense of anxious, guilty loneliness is an ever-present source of pain. The acquisition of language guarantees this. Even those who have been fortunate enough to come to terms with ambivalence will still have experienced the irreversible loss of the idealized, omnipotent 'princess' and the oceanic bliss of being loved by her – cause enough for grief in the healthiest individual. For the great majority of us this ambivalence is never permanently resolved – it is a lifelong struggle of greater or lesser intensity which involves both victories and defeats, regressions and advances. Freud recognized this in 'On the universal tendency to debasement in the sphere of love' (1912), although he locates his explanation in the later period of the Oedipus complex rather than, as I do, its oral-phase precursors. The events of everyday life are processed through this unconscious ambivalence, with unforeseen and unintended consequences. Most people's conscious mental life and activity are motivated by constructive aims and feelings; generally speaking, it is the destructive impulses which undergo repression – or at least, those impulses which are experienced as destructive. As a result, much of our conscious activity is evaluated by unconscious parts of us which are hostile to our conscious aims. In this way, occasions of intimacy, pleasure or achievement – the only worthwhile life events – can be spoiled or devalued by our unconscious, repressed, destructive impulses.

At worst, the result of these processes is the felt destruction of the 'good' by the 'bad', both inside and outside oneself. The individual is unable to make up for the emptiness he feels, which results from the original ambivalence towards the mother/world, because he relates to external sources of 'good' in the same ambivalent way and with the same spoiling consequences – quite literally, nothing is good enough to withstand his destructive attacks and emerge unscathed or undamaged. In the extreme case – not so rare as one would like – quite serious emotional disturbances can result: schizoid states where all the badness is felt to be outside, and depressive states where it is felt to be inside. These extremes have their 'normal' counterparts which, although they are not pathological, can be extremely troublesome for the sufferer. In essence the individual has disturbed relationships with his internalized objects or the mental representatives of past and present people in his life, such that these are not experienced as nourishing or sustaining and may even be threatening and dangerous. While I am not suggesting that women do not suffer from similar dilemmas, I am suggesting that such disturbed internalized relationships are the core around which masculinity is structured and against which it is intended to defend us. Females, on the other hand, usually make a primary identification, based on love, with the feminine mother (this throws up interesting questions about why mental illness is overwhelmingly a female malady, and I am inclined to share the view that woman are 'not mad but angry').

To the extent that men's internal relationships are disturbed - and this will be true in so far as our external relationships are disturbed, and vice versa - we will have to struggle with feelings of loneliness and alienation. It is because of our ambivalence that we can rarely experience wanting anything wholeheartedly - either because it is already spoiled, or because we are afraid of our capacity for spoiling and cannot face another disappointment: a vicious circle.

There is, unfortunately, a fundamental truth in the depressive way of seeing the world in that there is no external object, whether it be a lover or great wealth, which is capable of making up for the originally perceived failure and its consequences. This failure is a necessary condition for maturation and entry into the social world. We have to look to ourselves for salvation and attempt to come to terms with that failure by finding the means to forgive - easier said than done. The world and the people in it have a dynamic of their own, which means that none of us can control events to our own satisfaction. We cannot prevent failure or disappointment; indeed, the most serious disappointment of all is that there is a world out there which is entirely separate from our needs and feelings, and has its own needs and feelings that do not concern us. This so-called narcissistic wound can be profoundly deep. Desire arises at the moment when we become aware of our separateness and is a profound acknowledgement of it, as well as an attempt to deny it.

The reality of the object of our ambivalence is for all of us, at times, too much to cope with. Withdrawal of desire in its sexual form, or acute awareness of our ambivalence – in the sense that we are spoiling the person, or turning her bad internally – can lead to anxiety about an imminent state of depression. The anxiety is that we will psychologically empty the world, both internally and externally, of 'good enough' objects, and be left with the resulting acute sense of emptiness, loneliness, despair and frustration. One can only speculate about the amount of rage required to do this in the extreme. In such circumstances it seems that one can experience desire – in the form of sexual excitement – only for a fantasy as opposed to a real, or personally known, object. One can control the objects of fantasy; at least for a short time there is little danger of being disappointed by them in one's search for 'oneness' with the object, or in becoming the object of their desire.

I once had the opportunity to treat a man who was obsessed with pornography in what seemed to me to be a unique way. Since his teens, when he had drawn a naked woman in a school book, he had collected pornography until he literally possessed a library of it. It was catalogued, indexed and cross-indexed as thoroughly as any public library. This man would masturbate many times a day as well as making frequent visits to prostitutes, massage parlours and peepshows. Much of his life was absorbed with this passion. Not unnaturally, he was unable to maintain a sexual relationship with a woman. When he first met a woman to whom he was attracted he would be able to complete intercourse satisfactorily. His interest in pornography would decline, but not disappear. After a few months he would be unable to desire his partner and would resume his full-time sexual fantasy life with his collection. He eventually discovered that he masturbated and collected when he was anxious or depressed. With hard-won insight, and some encouragement, he managed to reduce his interest and destroy his collection. He was still masturbating twice a day.

Eventually, details emerged of his hidden feelings towards his partner, and his day-to-day behaviour. (All too often, as analysts and therapists, we pay too little attention to detail in search of the broader picture. Who said what to whom, and in what way, and where, are essential to curative and therapeutic understanding.) It became clear that he was passive in relation to household chores, expecting her to do all the servicing. If she failed, he would become withdrawn and uncommunicative. He would then stop desiring her and turn to pornography and masturbation, often attempting to involve her in his fantasies. He saw that the crucial element of his masturbatory fantasies was that their objects were entirely within his control. He also reported that during masturbation was the only time he felt good. In the course of his therapy he became increasingly angry and - worryingly for me - overtly violent with her, and began to understand that the pornography was a form of covert attack. As he integrated and understood his rage and anger his masturbation reduced and he became extremely anxious and depressed. Finally, he became aware of the massive guilt arising from his attacks on his wife.

This case history illustrates two fundamental aspects of masturbation. First the importance of experiencing one's desire as a creative force for good, without the hatred and failure normally associated with it. In a way one is demonstrating to oneself that one is more good than bad, more creative than destructive. This involves a substantial splitting of one's knowledge of the real world, at least so long as the fantasy - of the perfect object - is needed. Orgasm, however, usually leads to the awareness that the fantasy object is flawed - if only by virtue of the fact that she is not available. In spite of this, the reassurance that one is capable of 'desiring' will provide some relief from the anxiety that there is nothing 'good' in oneself or the world.

Secondly, the fantasy object is a denial of the one quality possessed by real objects: self-determination. She is totally within a man's control. She is omnipresent. We have power over her in a way which is not possible in reality and which mitigates against her becoming the 'witch' and evoking our destructive rage. Patients are likely to masturbate at times when they feel abandoned or let down by an important object. The meaning and content of the patient's fantasy, the structuring of his desire, can provide important information for his therapy, but understanding his motives for masturbating is as important.

I must emphasize that whatever else masturbation means, it also expresses the person's belief that a 'good-enough' real object is not available. This non-availability is more often than not a reflection not of the real world but of his inability to perceive anyone as 'good enough' – anyone who will not stimulate his repressed hostility and destructiveness by being separate from him.

Although it is difficult to obtain precise figures, it is clear that many men use pornography as an aid to masturbation. The provision of books and other 'sex aids' is an international, multi-billion dollar business. This expresses, among other things, the relative barrenness of men's inner worlds. There is nobody 'good enough' to use as an object of fantasy, and external sources of stimulation are needed to enable the man to experience desire through sexual excitement, whether or not his frustration is specifically sexual, when he is so cut off from his emotionality. It is a sad expression of his alienation from the 'object' world of sexual relations and his need to find somebody 'good' outside.

One consequence of the use of pornography is that the eyes and the thinking processes become intensely over-energized. Whereas in sexual relations all the senses are involved to varying degrees, and the whole body becomes intensely energized – which is why orgasm is satisfying – in masturbation it is mainly the genitals and the eyes which are involved – this is one reason why orgasm is unsatisfactory. Looking, therefore, is or becomes of the greatest significance in the use of pornography – far more so than in 'normal' sexual activity.

Looking is a deeply complex psychological process. To some extent this complexity is mirrored in the commercial aspects of pornography as a consumer product. After all, one might ask, why is it necessary continually to produce new sexual images, or at least old images with constantly changing bodies? A cursory examination of the items for sale in any newsagent's will testify to the limited range of images, and the pornographers' paucity of imagination. Why isn't one pornographic book or film as good as any other? The clear answer to these questions is that pornography, as a consumer product, has the psychological equivalence of a tea bag – once it has been used for the purpose for which it was produced, it is of little further value. I have treated many men who report that after using pornography they feel compelled to throw it away as quickly as possible.

Unless one assumes that the audience for pornographic images is constantly changing, one must conclude that people are buying it in the way they buy other consumables, like tea bags or newspapers. Clearly, however, pornographic images are not really like tea bags; it might be more accurate to liken them to pictures of tea bags. Generally speaking, looking at something does not change its material nature in the same way as hot water chemically alters tea. Looking at newspapers does change them: what was unknown becomes known; what was outside the self is now inside the self, or has been discarded, or filed for future reference, as a matter of choice. We should examine the fact that pornography is altered psychologically, so that it assumes the status of a tea bag or an old newspaper, to see whether this metamorphosis is of a different nature from that involving other consumables.

Looking at pornography is a consuming process, like eating, but the devouring is a psychological act with emotional as opposed to physical waste products. It differs from other forms of consumption in that whereas they leave one with more than one began with, pornography, on the face of it, leaves one with less. No doubt the man does not intend it to be so at the outset, when the pornographic image or object is regarded as good, as food is when we are hungry. This requires a denial of the reality of its unsatisfactory qualities which, if they were acknowledged, would render it incapable, even in fantasy, of assuaging desire. After all, if one is hungry it is impossible to be satisfied with reading cook books or menus. It is clear that all pornography involves the use of idealization to enable the man to fulfil his desire. The image, which he has to place between himself and his desire – in order to stimulate his desire, from which he is alienated – has to be idealized if he is to avoid his overpowering rage and thereby preserve the 'goodness' of the image for as long as is necessary.

Only when the defensive idealization breaks down will he be aware of his split-off feelings. Whether or not he becomes aware of his rage, he will be aware of other feelings which are residues of it. The previously 'good' image is now 'bad', and has to be expelled; hence the need of men to throw away the pornographic material – the man becomes as alienated from the mental representation of the pornographic image as he is from real objects; this is the alienation which led to his initial need to masturbate. In much written pornography, the rage which lies behind it (Masud Khan, 1979, pp. 219–26), and prevents the individual from being connected with his desire, is minimally disguised in the material itself, or made very explicit – as in *The Story of O.*, *Justine*, and so on. It is notable that nobody ever gets permanently hurt or damaged in these stories, no matter what practices they submit – or are made to submit – to. This connection between rage and pornography is the reason why relationships in pornography do not deserve the name. It is impossible to relate pornographically and to integrate our tenderness, affection and sexuality – the mature intimacy for which we all strive. All masturbatory fantasies contain sadistic impulses towards the object of fantasy. The control and manipulation of the object of fantasy, making her submit to all manner of – possibly perverse – activities, is, of course sadistic. In addition – and perhaps more importantly – the object is dehumanized. She is not seen as a person with feelings or wants of her own, except in so far as she expresses the man's desire to be the object of her desire. She exists simply to please the man. She becomes a thing on whom he vents his vengefulness for both her earlier failure and her later betrayal with his father.

These conflicts were clearly observable in one patient, an artist in his thirties. He was a highly cultured person, and in many aspects of his life his tastes were refined. However, he was very passive. He was unmarried and 'complained' of bisexuality. He was particularly ashamed of his collection of child pornography. It quickly became apparent that he used this collection most around the times of breaks in his treatment. Our eventual understanding of this was a significant factor in his quite organically losing interest in both little boys and girls, and in pornography. The point of interest here, however, is his relationship with this collection.

After he had used it to masturbate, he would be overcome with guilt and shame. He would want to throw away the books and magazines, but he was unable to in case he was caught 'in the act'. Instead he would hide them from himself in inaccessible places in his home, and be persecuted by fantasies that the police would come to arrest him and find them. Naturally he often tried to have himself arrested by playing elaborate games with prostitutes and policemen. For days after hiding his collection he was afraid of it. It became a literal persecutor. He was afraid that if he looked at it he would be damaged in some indefinable way, and would go to quite elaborate lengths to avoid being in contact with it. After a while these feelings would subside and he would feel free to use it for masturbation. These paranoid anxieties give substance to the notion of the actively persecuting 'witch'. The pornographic 'princess' had become the devouring persecutor by a process of projection. His realization of the denial involved in masturbation came only after orgasm, and represented the failure of his attempt to eroticize his desire. The rage and destructiveness towards the lost, abandoning object who was persecuting him by her absence then surfaced and was projected on to the pornography, which was felt to be vengeful and damaging.

This patient, who was also highly perverse and polymorphous in many other areas of his life, had this in common with all other men: he would feel the deepest guilt and shame after masturbation. Let us leave aside, for the moment, the fact that his persecutory anxiety was perhaps more than normally manifest. These depressive feelings which commonly follow masturbation are not entirely due to the repressed destructive feelings which are indirectly expressed during it.

The unconscious fantasies which lie behind masturbation are incestuous in nature. Masturbation remains problematic in psychotherapy until the original object of the fantasies, the mother, is uncovered. The regressive return to infantile methods of gratification brings with it the anxieties associated with infantile sexuality. The image which lies behind the pornographic image is the shadow image of the mother as she was seen by the child. As we have observed, the wish to have sex with the mother gives rise to anxieties about the loss of the penis – the fear of castration by the vengeful father. To illustrate the tenacity of these infantile anxieties, it is remarkable how many men still hold to the theory that masturbation will cause blindness or damage one's capacities in some other way, the damage being symbolic of castration. My patient still had these magical beliefs. Before long it became apparent that I was the policeman who would take him away. A dream pithily expressed this fear of me. I broke into his house, dressed as a policeman, and 'took away his tools'!

Despite the regressive nature of masturbation, it cannot be denied that it is also an attempt to heal the split between the 'good' and 'bad' mother images whose existence actually makes masturbation neccessary. In *Men in Love*, Nancy Friday (1980) makes it clear that she believes masturbation represents the defeat of hate by love. I believe, however, that it is a skirmish signalling the existence of hostilities rather a sign of ensuing peace. There is no doubt that masturbation expresses what it is intended to deny: that the internal good object is damaged or dead. Masturbation is an attempt to breathe life back into the object and the self by experiencing desire for it. Afterwards, all one has left is the dead or damaged object, who is further depleted – and perhaps even made dangerous – by the attack the masturbation represents. This danger is compounded by the castration anxieties which will inevitably follow the fantasy possession of the mother.

Before leaving this subject, I will say a little about the relationship between concern for the 'other' as expressed through tenderness, compassion, and so on, and sexuality. There can be no doubt that a truly intimate relationship, even allowing for no-holds-barred erotic behaviour, is characterized by the presence of concern for and awareness of the other. Such involvement represents a high degree of emotional maturity and integrity and the ability to surrender this integrity, secure in the knowledge of regaining it, and in the trust of the other. Most men are incapable of such relating, for the reasons I give in this book, yet they are sufficiently aware of their shortcomings to find them a continual source of guilt and frustration. Masturbation, with or without pornography, allows for the expression of uninhibited concern-free sexuality: one does not have to feel concern or tenderness for a pornographic image. Equally, often a man is capable of feeling tenderness only when he masturbates because his ambivalence prevents him from feeling it in a real relationship. This is the point of pornography: it is adaptable, in a way that real people are not, to the fantasies of its consumer.

What can we now say about the connection between rape and pornography? If such a connection can be demonstrated, apart from the connection seen through feminist political analysis, it can be only in the similarities between the internal representation of the object held by the rapist and the man who masturbates. Of course it is nonsense to imply a seamless connection in the unfortunate way that many feminists do. There are clear differences between pornography/masturbation and rape, just as there are between men who rape and men who don't. This, however, does not rule out the existence of a qualitative connection in men's minds.

This connection is in the internal representation of woman as object, as thing, not human. The split-off sadistic part of the man's psyche contains this representation of woman from his earliest experiences of separation. As we have seen, she is both infinitely frustrating and desirable, and is assumed to want to cause men pain. Through a series of transformations during the child's development of a masculine gender identity, these roles are reversed. The man's sadism becomes characterological, though it is masked as the more acceptable male contempt for woman, and his masochism becomes the property of woman or femininity. This psychological representation is expressed through pornography. Pornography is both culture's – men's – expression of the male unconscious and an explicit statement about the status of woman. She does not exist in her own right; but simply as a vehicle through which men attempt both to experience and to deny their desire. Pornographic woman is a fetishistic object. She stands in for people who do not possess penises, those whom we men define as women and whom we need in order to define ourselves as men. She represents woman as possession; as dominated and controlled. This includes those types of pornographic imagery which are sadomasochistic and represent women as powerful and dominating. Masturbation is, above all, a denial of loss, and an attempt to triumph over it and over the lost object. One might say that, in part, masculinity is the triumphant – and in extreme cases sadistic – sexualization of loss.

There is another connection, therefore, between pornography and rape. This connection is indirect in so far as it is in the similarity between the frames of mind of men who are masturbating or raping. Both are struggling with loss and – to greater or lesser degrees of consciousness – vengeful, sadistic feelings towards the object. Obviously masturbation entails some transformation of sadistic feelings in that fantasies involving pornography do no immediate damage to a real person (apart from the damage already inflicted on real women involved in the production of the pornography; the damage which will be inflicted on more women in order to get them to make more which men will buy, and the damage inflicted on all women as they are reduced to sexual-object status in the eyes of pornographers and men who use it) and are often not explicitly sadistic. The sadism is expressed through the fantasy control of the object, and in making her a dehumanized puppet whose existence is determined solely by the satisfaction of male sexual desire. The sadistic need to triumph or retaliate is far less intense in masturbation than in rape.

Some feminists (Dworkin, 1981) assert that the existence of pornography and the explicit representations of women it involves give men permission to rape. This is difficult to prove or refute. It is either self-evident or nonsensical. To me it is self-evident that it gives some men this permission. However, it is not pornography which is responsible for rape, but the definitions of male and female from which pornography derives. Pornography is not art: it does not push back the frontiers of perception. It is a mirror of prevailing conditions; it not only reflects but also reinforces and reconstructs those conditions.

7 Female Masochism

MASOCHISM DEFINED

It is often stated, explicitly or otherwise, particularly by practitioners using a systems model in working with female victims of crime, or with couples facing marital difficulties, that women collude with men (or culture/society) in maintaining their oppression and subjugation (see, for example, Benjamin, 1990; Temperley, 1985). This view that victims contribute to their suffering is widely established in popular and scientific mythology. Often, it is asserted that there is a psychological basis for this collusion in the character trait, shared by all women, of masochism. The explanation is that women actually encourage men to subjugate them because they enjoy both submitting to the powerful male and the suffering, whether chronic or acute, which this entails.

In this chapter I take a close look at masochism in an attempt to understand just why and how it has come to be linked so exclusively with femininity, and what it means to derive pleasure or enjoyment from pain and suffering. If there is such an exclusive link between masochism and femininity, does this provide any justification for the assertion that women collude with their oppression by men? I shall examine how it became so powerfully established that it is seen as motivating and underpinning this assumed female collusion.

Masochism is not a 'thing' – it is a psychological construct, and my use of the word is not intended to convey any moral or pejorative judgement, although this is not true of its everyday usage, including, frequently, its use by psychoanalysts. It is variously defined as a sexual perversion in which the subject derives pleasure from having pain inflicted on him- or herself, or as the character trait of bringing ill-treatment, humiliation and suffering on oneself. As far as the latter is concerned, given the statistics in the Preface, it would seem that there is a *prima facie* case for female masochism.

In classical psychoanalytic theory the notion of masochism has caused a great deal of agonized thinking, because it seems to be a direct contradiction of Freud's 'pleasure principle', which states that behaviour is governed by the desire to seek pleasure and avoid pain (Freud, 1920; 1923, p. 159). There is also a tendency – for reasons which will become clear – to link, or confuse, submissiveness with masochism and dominance with sadism. One surprising fact which might complicate the debate is that the group of people who can be described as sexual masochists – those who require pain in order to experience sexual arousal and relief – is composed mainly of men (Havelock Ellis, 1937, p. 178). There is no doubt that masochism is seen as feminine as opposed to masculine, when these are used as psychological rather than biological constructs.

The conflation of the anatomical constructs of male and female and the psychological constructs of masculine and feminine has been responsible for much confusion in debates concerning the general application of psychoanalytic findings to 'normal' life. Because of this conflation, Freud has been accused of biological determinism, and his now infamous statement 'Anatomy is destiny' (Freud, 1910, p. 189) is often quoted – entirely out of the context in which it makes sense – to justify the charge. Before I discuss feminine masochism and its relation to anatomical femaleness, let us look more closely at the issue this charge pinpoints as we examine the traditional Freudian account of feminine development, then attempt to understand and reconstruct it using the model employed so far.

FREUD'S ACCOUNT OF FEMALE DEVELOPMENT

Throughout his life, Freud hoped to find natural scientific bases for his psychoanalytic discoveries, but equally he realized that biology and psychology are not interchangeable. Although to some extent his initial biological orientation left an ineradicable mark on his theory, he very early abandoned any formal attempts to develop a psychobiological theory (without actually abandoning the hope of it). Rather, he determined that the 'true' aim of psychoanalysis was to explain how the biological person becomes an individual. Psychoanalysis became the study of how we become men and women, and how each of us subjectivizes this process. When Freud said 'Anatomy is destiny' he meant that the male/female dichotomy, which is largely present at birth (because the presence or absence of a penis is the basis on which we construct individuality, and this is the only discernible difference between infants), prescribes and fixes an individual's place in society. All other things being equal, the first act of a doctor or midwife after a birth is to sex the baby, usually by checking to see if it has a penis.

In a sense the person is born into an identity. The infant does not know this identity, or its place in the social system – it literally has to become his or her self. This self will be largely determined by or constructed around the anatomical distinction between the sexes, the possession or non-possession of a penis. Freud 'discovered' that each individual encounters, on the way to becoming a self, a number of apparently universal psychological traumas and conflicts, the resolution of which provides identity. At the risk of being tautological, one could say that the universal psyche (the unconscious) has provided these traumas in order to help the person become a self or subject. The psyche which emerges from these traumas is, for most people, culturally consistent with their anatomy. Penis possessors grow up to be men and psychologically masculine; and non-penis possessors grow up to be women and psychologically feminine. So Freud's assertion that anatomy is destiny refers to such a complex interaction of language – boy/girl/son/daughter/brother/sister – which is culture, with biology and unconscious mental processes, that there seems to be little individual freedom of choice.

Freud did not, however, imply that masculine and feminine were preordained – simply that they seemed, historically, to be inevitable. His concern was to describe what it meant, and how it came about, that one was masculine or feminine. I have already argued that he got it fundamentally wrong as far as femininity is concerned, and that he shed far more light on what it means to be masculine than he did on what it means to be feminine. In spite of this he realized that the development of boys and girls is far from psychologically symmetrical.

The Pre-Oedipal Period

Freud struggled throughout his life with the 'problem' of femininity – the problem, as he saw it, being to determine whether there is anything which could be described as essentially feminine as opposed to masculine, or to what extent the distinctions are entirely cultural. He went to great pains on many occasions to stress that the passive/female versus active/male duality refers only to the aims of the drives of men and women, not to the drives themselves, which are always, by definition, active. For example, the female sexual drive aims at being penetrated, which he considered passive, whereas the desire to be penetrated and the behaviour leading to penetration he considered active.

It is necessary to recapitulate on Freud's account and draw out the significant differences between what happens to little boys and little girls that makes them into men and women. Freud saw sexual development up to the Oedipus complex as necessitating the child's negotiation of a number of phases. These phases are differentiated by the part of the body with which the child is most concerned during his growth. Roughly, they follow the child's preoccupation with, first, her mouth; second, her anus; and finally, her genitals. These phases are known as oral, anal and phallic.

Anality

Freud attached great importance to the influence of the anal phase on the development of sadism and masochism. At this time (two to three years of age) both boys and girls are preoccupied with the anus as a major source of pleasure and anxiety, and their sexual theories about the origins of babies – with which all children are preoccupied – concern reproduction by and through the anus. The child also experiences great anxiety connected with her conflicts concerning the retention and giving up of her faeces to her mother. The struggle for mastery of the self and the world is encapsulated in the faeces. Accordingly, whether or not to give them up can mobilize the child's ambivalent feelings of love and hate for the mother. The faeces can be seen as a gift to her or as an attack on her, and both expulsion and retention can express loving or hating. It is at this stage that defecation comes to symbolize giving and withholding. This phase is of great importance in psychological development because it is the first time the child begins to struggle with the notion of a relationship with a whole object who is outside the self. The faeces, inside the body, come to be identified with the object, so that evacuation can be felt as its destruction, and retention with control and possession of it. These so-called anal-sadistic feelings will later play a large part in the child's adoption of femininity. They are a source of much anxiety and guilt because of their hostile, destructive nature, which will be mobilized during the Oedipus complex.

Metaphorically, anality and anal conflicts encapsulate a major dilemma for all children – in particular, issues about whether to adapt to or resist parental control. This problem is related to the parents' demand that the child make an effort to use the toilet rather than simply evacuating waste products at will. Control of self and resistance to control by others are major preoccupations for all children at this time. The intensity of this struggle will vary as a function of the parents' need to control the child and the child's unresolved sadistic feelings. Freud believed that the anal phase mobilized a major and universal human conflict concerning activity and passivity. He saw a biological component in this conflict in that the 'active' instinct to master is mobilized by the attempt to control the musculature of the anus, while the 'passive' instinct to renounce control is mobilized by the experience of the faeces passing through the anal mucous membrane. There is such inevitability in the conflation in the child's mind of the conflicts concerning activity/passivity and control with unresolved sadistic feelings that a dichotomy emerges between controlling–activity–mastery–sadism and being controlled–passivity–helplessness–masochism. We will return to the significance of this for the little girl.

Bisexuality and the Oedipus Complex

One of the most important discoveries of depth psychology is that there is no innate gender identity which is fixed and parallel to anatomy. Even given that the world over, people with penises will enter a door marked 'gentlemen', any psychotherapist can confirm, from daily experience, that the sense of sexual identity is very troublesome, confused and uncertain, regardless of how fixed it may seem to the person's conscious mind. There is, as one would expect, disagreement about the reasons for this lack of sexual certainty – specifically whether it is a primary uncertainty (innate), as Freud concluded, or secondary (derived from experience), as other, post-Freudian, schools of thought would have it.

In the earlier part of his career Freud made the seemingly natural assumption that heterosexuality is innate, and that the positive Oedipus complex was the determining factor in each person's acquisition of their natural sexual identity. The little boy or girl simply grew into what was natural at the appropriate time. Very soon, however, clinical experience cast doubt on this simple model, and the important *Three Essays* (1905) seemed to consign 'natural heterosexuality' to psychoanalytic history. In spite of some uncertainty, from this point Freud continued to affirm the centrality of innate bisexuality in his theory of human functioning. It is clarifying to view this use of the word bisexuality as a shorthand for the universal undifferentiated sexuality which is found in children, often referred to as polymorphous perversity. It means that children seem to desire both parents in a pre-genital sexual way (Meltzer, 1973) – not bisexuality, but sexuality without gender.

During this pre-genital period – and before the sexual drive is, apparently, organized into a relatively coherent, gendered and socially syntonic genital function – the child has no knowledge of how babies are produced. In Freudian theory the child assumes that reproduction is something to do with those aspects of his own body which at that time are giving him pleasure. These areas of the body, which Freud called the erogenous zones, are primarily the mouth and the anus. Before the genital period proper the genital area does assume primacy, but not as adults know it. During this so-called phallic phase the child derives pleasure from his penis but is unaware of the full extent of its functioning. Thus at various times the infant's theories about conception can concern eating, defecating or genital penetration. He does not conceive of penetration of the vagina; at this point he is unaware of its existence. At this stage, children, both boys and girls, hold to the view that everybody has a penis. As we shall see, it is this belief which has caused the greatest dissent from Freud. Some groups – in particular the followers of Melanie Klein – hold that this view of the child's is secondary and defensive rather than reflecting primary ignorance of the vagina.

In this world of undifferentiated sexuality the child can occupy different positions of desire with respect to the parents. From an adult observer's perspective, there are active and passive hetero-sexual and homosexual desires at work. Sexual satisfaction is not derived from a predetermined object (I take it for granted that satisfaction is object- – that is, person- – related); desire has to be structured. In fact, there are always residual elements of this in adult sexual life.

Freud's understanding of sexuality, based on the original simplicity and naivety of his assumption of innate heterosexuality and the positive Oedipus complex, was significantly improved with the discovery of the 'negative' elements. His final formulation of the full Oedipus complex seems a better representation of most people's experience of the drama of sexual life. Although the Oedipus complex is seen as the crucial event shaping the child's gender identification – actually, identity itself: there is no self, or identity, without a division between the sexes – there are major differences, between boys and girls, in its precise part in this process, and in the outcome of the complex itself. In an important respect the Oedipus complex functions identically for boys and girls in that it introduces a third term – the father – into the mother–child relationship.

The Phallic Phase: the universal penis and female castration

So the task facing boys and girls in developing a gender identity is significantly different. To develop a gender identity consistent with the social construction of their anatomy, boys do not have to change the object of their desire – woman – but simply renounce some of its aims. Neither do they have to change the primary erogenous zone – the penis. Not only do girls have to change their aims – to be penetrated rather than to penetrate – and the object of their desire from Mother/woman to Father/man, they also have to change the erogenous zone from the clitoris/penis to the vagina. These differences arise because all children share their first love object – the mother – and because the erogenous zone which dominates their sexual activity at the most intense point of the Oedipus complex is the genitals.

At this stage, all Freudian theorists agree that all children believe they have a penis. Girls believe their clitoris is a little penis; they have to find a way not only of switching their desire from women to men but also of switching their desire from the phallic, masculine clitoris to the vagina (Freud, 1905). This involves renouncing the desire to penetrate in favour of the desire to be penetrated. We should remember that passive/active are cultural constructs, but there is little doubt that the girl's renunciation of her desire to penetrate – giving up her penis – involves embracing passivity. The renunciation of sexually passive aims in boys has its counterpart in the necessity for girls to renounce their sexually active aims.

Freud described the girl's task during the oedipal process as one of moving from masculinity to femininity, in that at its conclusion, she has to embrace her 'anatomically destined' womanhood and leave behind her phallic masculinity, with all its component wishes to conquer, penetrate and possess: in other words, her active-sadistic-masterful-aggressive impulses.

The path to femininity is strewn with difficulties which have no parallel in the boy's development. This follows from the evident fact that whatever the girl's awareness of her condition, and regardless of whether her 'masculine' clitoral sexuality is primary – as Freud believed – or secondary – as many Freudians and post-Freudian culture theorists believe (Horney, 1926, 1933; Jones, 1933; M. Klein, 1921–45), the girl does not possess a penis. While there is no denying the clinical evidence for the existence of castration anxiety in the boy, its existence and function for girls are more problematic. How can one develop anxiety about losing something one has never had? At the very least, castration anxiety must be a very different experience for the girl. While Freud recognized this, he was compelled to envisage castration anxiety for little girls as pivotally important for their assumption of a feminine identity – an identity which he saw as being primarily based on the need to have babies. The crucial difference is that whereas in the boy castration anxiety leads to the dissolution of the Oedipus complex, in the little girl it leads to its formation.

Interesting as it would be to trace the history of Freud's ideas on the female castration complex, we must confine ourselves here to an examination of his final thinking (Freud, 1932). We have seen that the boy fears castration by his father; this fear reinforces the prohibition of his continued incestuous desire for his mother. The father, therefore, acts as a third element in the son/mother couple, and is responsible for the boy's entry into culture and masculinity. The girl, however, discovers that she does not possess a penis and regards this as a wrong which she has suffered at her mother's hands, one which she may attempt to deny, compensate for or remedy.

During the phase in which the castration complex arises, around the ages of three to five (the phallic phase), children believe in sexual phallic monism – that is, everybody has a penis. Male and female do not exist. The antithesis is between having a penis and being castrated. This is a founding principle of Freudian psychoanalysis. Without universal phallic monism, the castration complex could not exist in women. Of course it is still valid to posit it as a secondary, defensive phenomenon erected to avoid painful feelings – in fact many analysts have. For them (Chasseguet-Smirgel, 1976; Horney, 1924, 1926, 1933; M. Klein, 1921–45) the child has an intuitive sense of the existence of the vagina, and she turns to the fantasy of the clitoral penis – the phallic phase – as a defence against the pain of the early frustration of the wish to have a penis in order to satisfy her mother. This wish is perfectly understandable in itself. What could be more natural than that this profound love should take physical form? Freud saw the female penis as primary, as not deriving from anything else, and throughout his life he continued – unsurprisingly – to deny the existence of vaginal sensations in little girls: such sensations would undermine his theory of infantile sexual phallic monism. We now know that he was wrong about this, just as he was wrong about the loss of sensation in the mature clitoris. Nevertheless, his theory survives.

For girls, in Freudian theory, the emergence of gender awareness usually results from necessity rather than choice. They are driven to the vagina only when they discover the inadequacy of what they had assumed was their penis. The little girl, like the boy, has centred her existence on her relationship with her mother. As she grows and develops, all her feeling, thinking and urging occur in relation to her mother. Naturally, she does not question whether it is correct to feel this way. She is in love in a way, and with an intensity, which will never occur again in her life. From this point of view, the idea that she should want to do everything imaginable in this relationship is entirely understandable – including giving her mother a baby, or having a baby by her mother – whether this involves oral, anal or other sensations and activities. During this early, pre-phallic phase the child is not having genital sensations – or, at least, sensations which can be organized into a meaningful gestalt. At this stage of her growth it would be no more correct to say she believes that everybody has a penis than to say she believes that nobody does. The genital area does not yet exist for her to organize in this way.

Critics of the Freudian theory ask what the little girl does with her everyday experiences of seeing her father's penis and her mother's lack of one. This criticism is valid, whether it is directed at those who hold to the idea of innate vaginal awareness which is denied in favour of the fantasy phallus, or to those, like Freud, who hold to universal primary phallic monism. How, they ask, could the child arrive at a theory that everybody has a penis when her pre-phallic existence may be full of naked evidence that there are two sexes? The answer is that until the child's own genital area is awakened, when it begins to be a source of masturbatory pleasure, such observations have no significance. They constitute an answer for which there is, as yet, no equivalent question.

The child may deny acknowledgement of her vagina for as long as she possibly can – hardly surprising, given that to acknowledge its existence is painful for her. It involves her relinquishing, at a time when she is unwilling, the most important object in her life – Mother – and her deepest desires in relation to that object. During the phallic phase the stage is set for the girl's move from the pre-oedipal masculine attachment for the mother to the Oedipus complex. The day dawns when she can no longer deny the 'inadequacy' of her sexual apparatus compared with that of her father, her brothers or her male playmates, in relation to its capacity to satisfy Mother. Furthermore, she begins to realize that the mother whom she has coveted, of whom she desired to take possession, is equally inadequate. This discovery brings with it a resurgence of all her hostility towards her mother (similar to the boy's, and rooted in identical experiences of separation and frustration), whom she now has further cause to blame for not providing her with the thing she values most: a penis.

A crucial difference in the fortunes of this hostility is that whereas the boy initially splits it off and directs it towards his father, before resolving his Oedipus complex, the girl directs it towards the mother. She feels that her mother is responsible for this failure, as she was for all the other, earlier, ones, and her recognition that she does not possess a penis dashes for ever her hopes of possessing the mother, or becoming the object of the mother's desire. In something akin to the sour grapes syndrome, she turns away from the resulting grief and depression into a search for a 'good' object in order to make life worth living. All things being equal, she will finally choose her father and begin to idealize him in precisely the way she once idealized her mother. The mother then becomes the recipient of the projections of all the qualities of the 'witch'.

The Link Between the Anal and Phallic Phases: The Special Female Factor

During the phallic phase the dilemmas about activity and passivity evoked during toilet training, the anal phase, have particular relevance for the child's struggles with her emerging genitality. Throughout the whole of life, but particularly in childhood, this is a major axis of meaning: at some point everybody wishes to do to others what they have previously had done to them – what they have experienced passively as objects of another's activity. This duality is never entirely resolved, and remains a major source of conflict. This conflict is rather more intense for girls than for boys. For a girl it involves renouncing her sexually active (culturally masculine) wishes for her mother so that she can discover and develop socially acceptable, passive feminine wishes for her father. The crucial question is how she achieves this mighty leap from desiring Mother to desiring men.

The turning away from the mother cannot simply be the consequence of all the earlier disappointments the child experienced with her – not enough milk, too-early weaning, the birth of siblings, and so on (in a nutshell, the emergence of desire). If it were, then we should also expect boys to turn for ever away from women and heterosexuality. There must be another factor involved for a girl which is not present for a boy: the discovery that she does not possess a penis, as well as the recognition that her mother is similarly lacking. For this reason her long-developed hostility gets the upper hand, and women (femininity) 'are debased in value for girls just as they are for boys, and later perhaps for men' (Freud, 1933, p. 127).

Now the problem becomes more complicated. If the girl debases femininity – or the people without penises, including herself – the move to embrace her socially prescribed destiny is further impeded. According to Freud, this shift is initially accomplished by the girl's hoping to get the penis from Father in order to use it with Mother. She then substitutes for this wish – which, she realizes, is equally doomed to disappointment – the wish to have a baby by her father. This wish for a baby is the symbolic equivalent of the wish for a penis; it is the beginning of the female Oedipus complex. Of course this substitution is not easily achieved: the adjustment to reality involves substantial pain. The girl is helped to make these changes partly by the fact that in renouncing her phallic active wishes and behaviour when she realizes she does not have a penis, she makes room for her passive impulses to emerge and dominate her sexual life. The castration complex and penis envy push her into her positive Oedipus complex where she will, by and large, remain for the rest of her life, with the wish for a baby taking over from her wish for a penis.

Her contempt for women is never entirely overcome. It is repressed beneath her secondary wish for a baby which, in her unconscious, is the penis she has always longed for. This account of the assumption of a feminine gender identity raises many questions which cannot be taken up here, but it does go a long way towards explaining why the vast majority of women submit to and appear to collude with their own oppression, in that it emphasizes the relinquishing of active in favour of passive aims – the acceptance of self as object rather than, as with men, self as subject. Dinnerstein (1976) and Benjamin (1990) have elaborated the consequences of this split for the future of humankind. Their grim analyses should be compulsory reading for all male politicians.

Freud's Account of Masochistic Development

What, then, can be found in this account of female infantile sexuality to justify the psychoanalysts' – and men's – attribution of masochism to women? Before addressing this question, I must provide a context by restating the major theme of this book: that the trauma of the birth of the subject, the self, in the separation from the primary object leads to the development of a psychosis which is encapsulated by primitive internalized sadomasochistic objects. I believe this psychosis is the origin of male misogyny. The question which concerns me here is its fate in the female.

Sadomasochism can be described as a derivation of the human impulse to master and control. This impulse, an essentially admirable one, is innately connected with the duality between passive and active wishes – between doing as a subject and being done to as an object. Freud and his followers were – and still are – unsure of the process by which the instinct or desire for mastery metamorphoses into taking pleasure from giving or receiving pain. To account for the paradox of pain as pleasure, Freud was led to theorize a death instinct of which masochism is a direct, and sadism a secondary, expression. I shall consider the issue of how pain can be gratifying later; for the moment, let us examine how the instinct to master can become sadomasochism.

In the early years of development, every child experiences a greater or lesser degree of pain and suffering at the hands of what he or she perceives as the 'bad' mother. The child is virtually helpless and probably, initially, her only source of mastery of her environment is the pain or pleasure she is able to inflict on her mother. How many of us can ignore the pitiful wailing of a distressed child? Childhood is a painful and frustrating experience, and for many the struggle between the 'good' and 'bad' mother is an all-too-equal one which leaves in its wake a fundamental doubt about the existence of the 'good'. I have described the difficulty we have, both as children and as adults, in coping with our helplessness and powerlessness in this situation.

During the period when the parents are demanding that the child exercise some control over his or her bowels, the child discovers not only that she or he can gain satisfaction from the act of mastery, but also that there are erotic pleasures associated with the retention and expulsion of faeces. The instinct for mastery becomes fused with the sadistic rage associated with earlier impotence; when this is combined with anal-erotic pleasure, the issue of control becomes a preoccupation with domination and sadism. This harks back to the earlier period when the sexual impulse – in the broadest sense, the impulse to life (libido) – was fused with aggressive impulses. The retention and expulsion of infantile rage becomes actualized in the child's faeces, which are identified with the object of the rage; refusal to 'perform', or uncontrolled evacuation (elimination), being a direct expression of hurt, rage and impotence, as well as the guilt and the fear of rejection they arouse.

Sadism derives from the child's capacity to identify with the objects whom she experiences as her persecutors – a process known as identification with the aggressor. Her earlier encounters with the 'witch' – who, in favourable cases, is largely a product of her own projected destructiveness – and the subsequent internalization of her provide the basis for sadism. She becomes identified with this powerful internal persecutor and is no longer the helpless, impotent victim of early infantile existence. As a result, her internal world is also changed: she is now capable of doing to herself what she previously experienced the 'witch' as doing to her. She is also able to do the same to 'real' people in the 'real' world. Sadism, therefore, is a perversion of the child's devastating experiences with the divided mother. The question of whether these are real or imagined experiences is irrelevant to the child, although the adequacy or otherwise of the mother is clearly crucial in determining the demonic intensity of the 'witch's' perversity. However weak or powerful she is, her existence is as inevitable as the opposition of night and day. The duality of sadomasochism is now established in the child's psyche.

The earlier experiences of helplessness and impotence in the face of the all-powerful mother, both 'good' and 'bad', are the basis of masochism and masochistic fantasies. The pain of masochism is life-affirming. The underlying annihilation and discontinuity (the encapsulated psychosis) would be far more terrifying. The pleasure of masochism – not simply the physical kind, but also the far more prevalent moral, or emotional, kind such as feelings of rejection, hurt or inadequacy with which most people struggle most of the time, which seem unrelated to any external stimulus – is in the unconscious reassurance that the more terrifying fate – annihilation by the demonic witch – has been avoided, and that there is an all-powerful person 'out there' who presumably could, if the child were able to work out how, make everything better. Jessica Benjamin (1990) observes that this is one of the benefits women derive from their status as female 'object' to the male 'subject', and that in submitting to male power, woman keeps alive her internal mother with whom she has so strongly identified: 'his assertion of subjectivity and difference is like a breath of the inaccessible outdoors. He embodies activity and difference for her' (p. 79).

The experience of the masochism of 'self as object' is universal. Given that this experience is common to boys and girls, however, we are no nearer to understanding what it is that, supposedly, becomes essentially feminine about masochism. To understand this we must trace the course taken by masochism from the point of view of its links with the active/passive duality and its resolution during the Oedipus complex. This duality does not refer to the amount of aggression with which aims are pursued. In the child's mind, however, a conflation occurs in which what could be described as femininity becomes equated with passivity, while masculinity becomes equated with activity, and the factor of aggression is the primary distinction.

The choice seems to be between being the hunter or the hunted, proactive or reactive, subject or object. Whichever position is chosen, whether it is the anatomically destined one or a – socially defined – perverse one, the other position is always being hidden or repressed, and it is always gender-differentiated. Hence all men have a feminine side against which they will struggle, and women have a masculine side which they too will struggle to repress. The motives for the repression, however, are markedly different for men and for women. So the options are the same for boys and girls. The crucial question is why girls choose (I do not use this verb in an active sense; I do not believe girls have a real choice) the one and boys the other: object–passive–masochistic–feminine–castrated versus subject–active–sadistic–masculine–phallic.

It is insufficient, in the context of the female child's 'choice' of the 'masochistic position' (becoming feminine), to assert that female strivings, with all their seemingly frightening, masochistic implications – having babies, being penetrated (Chasseguet-Smirgel, 1976) – simply emerge as a natural development at the appropriate age. This would be the same as asserting 'innate natural sexuality' and arguing that gender differentiation is of no more significance than whether one is right- or left-handed. Even if this were so – and clearly, there is an anatomical component – the female child would still have to make sense of these changes and find a way of accounting for the move from the mother to the father, the hypothesized change from clitoris to vagina, and the change from activity to passivity. She would also have to extend this further to justify – or, at least, prepare the ground for generalizing – her passivity. This generalization undoubtedly occurs: it does not simply contribute to, but is seen as the essence of, womanhood.

The significance of lack

The significantly different factor in the girl's experience, compared with the boy's, is her discovery of her 'absent' penis and the sadistic fantasies this stimulates and reawakens in relation to the mother.

To reiterate: it must become obvious to the girl child that the only person who is going to give her the penis she longs for to satisfy her mother is her father. This further intensifies her negative feelings towards her mother, who not only failed to give her a penis, but is now a rival for both her father's affection and his penis. This wish for the father's penis is essentially a masculine one in that it is intended to make up for the inadequacy of the clitoris – the girl is still dominated by her phallic strivings. I believe it is important to unpick the symbolism of this wish. Although it clearly takes the precise form of wanting a penis, it actually represents desire or wanting itself, regardless of the object of desire. At this stage of development children are well aware that there is an external world to which the father belongs, in which he is an agent. More than anything the child sees the father – now idealised – as the way into this world (Benjamin, 1990, pp. 102–3). The penis represents this, and it is no mere fantasy. The wish is the beginning of the female Oedipus complex, where the mother is the third element in the triangle and is the girl's hated rival. Despite the intensity of her sadistic feelings for her, the girl realises that she cannot displace her and take her father's penis.

The penis symbolizes potency, power, completeness, creativity and independence: constructive opposites of the essence of the child's earlier relationship with the mother. Yet for her, as for the boy, the penis/phallus is a paradoxical affirmation of the psychic reality which it is erected to deny – her impotence. Unlike the boy, however, the girl does not have the choice of maintaining the denial, at least consciously – she does not have a penis. I do not doubt that the phallic fantasy exists and persists unconsciously in some women; I have worked with many women who dream of having a penis, and it is striking how often this dream appears during difficult times with men who are maltreating them.

In Freudian theory the determining factor in the decision to make the masochistic move is the girl's sadistic feelings towards her mother. If the active wish to have the father's penis is to become the passive wish to have a baby, the girl has to identify herself with (become like) the hated mother. Clearly, this is impossible unless she can find a way of dealing with the destructive feelings which would inhibit such an identification. A solution to these destructive urges is also necessary for other reasons. Her wish to have the father's penis is also a sadistic wish in that she initially wants to take it from him, partially to supplant him in her mother's affections by having the capacity to be the object of her desire, which requires a penis. In fact, the girl must repress these sadistic wishes which threaten the 'good' object status of her father. In addition to the intense guilt which they cause her in relation to him, they are a source of depressive anxiety about turning him 'bad' which would leave her without a 'good' object to love.

The repression of these sadistic feelings inevitably affects those other aspects of the girl which contain similar sadistic elements; in particular, it opens the way for a return of the passive, masochistic attitudes which were prevalent at an earlier stage of development and which, combined with the identification with the now 'castrated' mother, will lead to the transformation of the 'wish for a penis' into the 'wish for a baby'. The maternal identification leads the girl to emphasize her passive/receptive instincts which she sees her mother acting out in her relationship with the father (Benjamin, 1990, pp. 85–131 gives a full and excellent account of this process). This is reinforced by her anxiety that all aggressive, sadistic feelings engender the risk that the repression will break down.

Sadism and masochism are, in a sense, extreme developments of the passive/active duality. They arise out of our experience of ourselves as 'objects' in our infantile relations with our mother. The pain and rage which result from this experience are, in my opinion, the roots of masochism. As children gain more mobility and capacity for mastery of the environment, they are able to express more of the active, 'self as subject' side of themselves – this too is gendered, in that these qualities are seen as being associated with the active, exciting father who has access to the public world. In this context that means sadism, and treating others as objects. When the girl renounces her passivity in favour of the idea that her clitoris is a penis, she is embracing the sadistic side of herself. With the realization that her clitoris/penis is a dead end, she renounces her aggression in favour of her passivity. This final move, which is the acceptance of her femininity, is a 'masochistic' one in that it involves coming to terms with the potentially terrifying and painful experiences of castration and birth, and the reacceptance of the passive/masochistic self as object which was earlier repudiated in favour of her 'phallic' myth.

This account of the development of female sexuality and the 'masochistic move' is clearly an incomplete explanation of how women come to accept their subjugated role in culture today, but it is a full enough account, for our purposes, of the development of a psyche consistent with female anatomy. The female child's guilt about her wish to take her mother's place with her father is often generalized and displaced to all forms of achievement, so that women become inhibited about any activity which could, either symbolically or realistically, be interpreted as surpassing the mother. They are aided in these inhibitions by the association of all forms of achievement with aggression and control, which would also stimulate guilt in relation to the sadistic wish for Father's penis.

Although masochism is - or more accurately, becomes - an essentially feminine characteristic, it is also, because of our innate bisexuality, an imminent fate for all men. Masochism is not female - it is feminine. Women choose it at the expense of their sadistic, aggressive drives, which will always be a source of anxiety. One cannot overemphasize that a 'feminine masochism' (of an essentially moral nature) does not refer to a characteristic, innate and exclusive, of women - merely a seemingly inevitable one for them.

A CRITIQUE OF FREUDIANISM

This account leaves many questions unanswered. Perhaps I should offer my own general opinion of it before I take up some of the detailed issues. I believe - and my clinical experience confirms this - that the outline of the female Oedipus complex quite accurately describes how little girls develop their gender identity. I am convinced, however, that it entirely ignores the power dimension in gender relations, and that this is the crucial factor which determines the Oedipus outcome for the little girl. In brief, the little girl's awareness of the male's privileged position in society - as she sees it in the beginning, this means in relation to

Mother – leads inevitably to penis envy and the wish to possess a penis of her own. This, however, is predicated on already existing heterosexual relations in which women are subordinated and males, including little boys, are superior. There are no positive images or definitions of femininity which do not accord with men's definitions of the female role. Women are defined in terms of their relations with men – mother is father's object of desire. It is a testimony to the power of men that their control of sexuality has gone fundamentally unchallenged. Some feminists would argue that the Oedipus complex is a figment of a patriarchal imagination, devised to justify men's right to dominate and oppress women by asserting the complementary nature of the innate passivity and submissiveness of women with men's 'natural' dominance.

The Freudian account leaves a lot to be desired if it presumes to represent a value-free and fundamental truth. As many feminists have pointed out, Freud's theory is actually the most powerful intellectual underpinning of male dominance and female submission. Some (see Ward, 1984) would go further, and insist that this was by design – that Freud was actually, knowingly rationalizing and justifying male privilege and supremacy. Although this is a difficult case to sustain, it is patently true that his writings are shot through with the most outrageous sexism. His paper 'On Narcissism: an introduction' (1914) is rightly regarded as one of his most important works. As I have said, however, it does not take a close reading to reveal its thinly disguised denigration of women. After explaining why women are not inherently capable of real object love because of their narcissism, he says: 'it is only themselves that . . . good looking women . . . love with as much intensity as the man's love for them' (p. 89). He goes on to compare women with children, great criminals and humorists! We should not think, however, that this great man lacked awareness. Indeed, on the same page he attempts to forestall the attack he must have known would come: 'it is not out of place to give an assurance that this description . . . is not due to any tendentious desire on my part to depreciate women . . . tendentiousness is quite alien to me'. There is more in the same vein but I can only urge the reader to go to the original.

Female Passivity? The Unlearning of Aggression and the Acceptance of Control

What, then, are the implications of Freud's failure, in his account of female development, to allow for the power inequality between men and women? More important, perhaps, than his failure to address men's motives for it, his account fails even to acknowledge that women and female children are the victims not only of systematic control but also of systematic abuse by men in the interests of asserting and maintaining their dominance and superiority. Important as this legacy has been for generations of women who may have been angered by his blind spot, my opinion is that he cannot be reproached for it. My experience with late-twentieth-century men is that it is profoundly difficult for them to acknowledge their need to dominate women, or indeed the fact that they do so. These elisions in Freud's account, however, call into question the origins of female passivity, female masochism and phallic monism in a manner which goes beyond psychodynamics and into sexual politics.

There is no doubting men's motivation for defining femininity as passive, or attempting to discover whether feminine aims are passive. Although from one feminist point of view the argument is spurious – men have the power, and the end result, whether or not men choose to exercise that power (women as a secondary sex) will remain the same – for men, the debate has a purpose. If it can be proved that women are innately passive, this provides the perfect rationale for their power base. Any angry woman who questions it can readily be marginalized as a female failure. If women's aims are innately passive, then there is a clear explanation for their 'collusion' with their present subordinated role and lowly status in the world. They would not be interested in activity or agency in the world for its own sake, in any form – the pursuit of wealth, or power, or sexual freedom. Being done to would always be more satisfying than doing, being desired more than desiring, being possessed more than possessing, and so on. This is not mere sophistry. Apart from our obvious stranglehold on all real power, there are powerful voices being raised against feminist attempts to deconstruct and reconstrue gender relations – not all of them male. Roger Scruton, an Oxford don and once a darling of the Conservative right in Great Britain, has even suggested that feminism was a plot hatched by men in order to break men's debilitating heterosexual allegiance and not interfere with men's pursuit of power. Like many writers: 'he repeats the dominant discourse surrounding male sexuality . . . that it is an overpowering instinct "which with force and might demands fulfillment" and which women "should work to quieten and constrain" ' (L. Segal, 1990, pp. 208).

Important issues are at stake. Clearly, the whole complex of constructs which we use for defining and understanding sexuality is man-made, and apart from the aims of feminine genital sexual drives – which are self-evidently, in terms of this construction, receptive/passive – the constructs active/passive refer entirely to male-valued activities. In other words, they simply reflect patriarchal dominance and its phallocentricity. In this way, the notion of the feminine as the 'secondary sex', as a sort of shadow of masculinity, is reinforced. In 'Freud and female sexuality', Janine Chasseguet-Smirgel (1976) summarises Freud's understanding of women:

> as . . . therefore a series of lacks: the lack of a vagina, lack of a penis, lack of a specific sexuality, lack of an adequate erotic object, and finally the lacks which are implied by her being devoid of any intrinsic feminine qualities which she could cathect directly and by her being forced to give up the clitoris. (p. 275)

The implications of this accurate summary are devastating for women. What it actually means is that they are little more than failed men. Female sexuality is defined entirely by reference to women's relation to the (absent) penis. It is relatively easy for analysts to demonstrate that women are unconsciously preoccupied by conflicts about the penis, in particular envy of it. Every attempt by a female patient to protest the inequalities in the power relation between men and women, express anger about women's maltreatment, complain about men's obvious social status, or, at its simplest, anger with men, can be interpreted as penis envy. This interpretative set is made all the more unassailable when the analyst is a man, and the power inequalities are made more extreme than they might otherwise be because of the distortions introduced by the transference.

The Freudian view simply ignores sexual politics. Freud saw the way society was organized, with men in charge and women subordinated, simply assumed that this was the natural way of things, and set about explaining why.

Passivity

Leaving aside the pressures on women to act passively, in accordance with men's expectations and under the threat of abuse for failure to conform, it seems nonsensical to assert that the aims of female drives are innately passive. If we take it as read that active/passive is a social construction, girl babies are as intense in their feeding as boys. They do not simply lie there and expect the breast to be put in their mouth; they are active in seeking and extracting milk from it. At this stage there are no differences between male and female infants which deserve to be called sexual differences. Later, after the separation between sexual and self-preservation instincts has occurred, and femininity is established, the female sexual drive is undoubtedly passive in its aims, but only in terms of the social criteria used to delineate this quality. I cannot recall how many times female patients have described to me the occasions when they have been inhibited from acting on what they feel to be dangerous sexual impulses simply because they are afraid of other people's disapproval.

In my experience, women are as sexually active as men. The 'masochistic move' will always be inherently unsatisfying for the vast majority of them. There is nothing natural about it, and the repressed will always strive for expression. The identification with the father, which has to be denied and repressed in order to make the masochistic move, cannot lose its excitement and its attraction; men do not want to face this simple truth. I have worked with a large number of men who are anxious and occasionally terrified of sexually active (aggressive) women. Men are afraid of women who are clear about their own sexual pleasure, and make sexual demands. It has always been obvious to me that this is anxiety about not being in control. More often than not, when these men can articulate their anxiety they will describe it as feeling as if they are being devoured by the woman. Frequently, they are aware that they are afraid the woman is going to steal their penis. Even though the end result of sex is penetration of the woman, receiving the penis is no more innately passive than taking food into the mouth. Women are not supposed to be active when they are being penetrated – it simply isn't feminine.

Freud's account of femininity has hardly been spared attack from inside and outside psychoanalysis (Deutsch, 1924, 1930; Lampl-de-Groot, 1928). Ruth Mack Brunswick's paper (1940) is very important; and Juliet Mitchell says 'the mother is where femininity has landed' (1986, p. 397). These attacks, however, are recognized as increasingly irrelevant by some (MacLeod and Saraga, 1988, p. 29), who acknowledge the real contribution psychoanalysis can make in helping the victims of child sexual abuse in particular, and that analysis has not minimized its seriousness (see Goldstein, Freud and Solnit, 1979). This point is also well made by Ann Scott (1988) in her account of this debate. She disagrees, however, with many feminist attempts to take control of the construction of such events by renaming them; for example, Ward's (1984) 'father–daughter rape' instead of incest.

It requires little thought to conjure up an alternative, feminist explanation of woman's renunciation of activity, sexual and otherwise, even one that acknowledges the absence of a penis (Miles, 1988). Given that women are battered by men when they begin to assert themselves and act independently, or simply in ways which men do not like, in a relationship (see Chapter 8), it is probably just as well that girls learn early what behaviour is regarded as appropriate by their masters. Couple this with the worldwide economic oppression of women, their dependence on men and their primary responsibility for children, and it is not hard to understand why they should 'collude' with their abuse and renounce any activity which their male partners take exception to or define as inappropriate. (Appropriate in this context simply means non-threatening to a man's control, or his expectations of women.) This precludes women developing sexual preferences which are not to men's liking, or priorities which interfere with their primary function: to devote themselves to male satisfaction.

This adds an essential dimension to the psychodynamic explanation. It points to the boundary between social pressures and the psychological developments required of an anatomically female child in order to find men desirable, as opposed to women; the point of gender identity in which femininity is defined as passive, castrated and masochistic.

A short case history will illustrate many of these issues. A young man came to me after attacking his wife when she confronted him – not for the first time – with her desire to have children. The attack itself was not serious, although he had attacked her in similar ways many times, and – unusually – did not deny that he had a strong desire to hurt her. He exercised self-control on this occasion, as on others, and left the house before inflicting serious physical damage. She herself reported that being hit was better than his usual emotional abuse and depression, which drove her crazy. After some months of working together, this man had reached a point where he could define much of his behaviour with his wife as emotionally abusive. He is the son of an alcoholic father and, consequently, a seriously depressed mother who turned to him for emotional support in her husband's absence. He had decided that his role in life was to make his mother happy – actually an impossible task. His wife, in fact, was a very happy person when he met her, although she had become chronically withdrawn and depressed as a result of his treatment of her. Her happiness had been one of the main attractions for him: he believed that she might be able to teach him how to enjoy life.

One day he recalled an incident which, he thought, said everything about his marriage, and made him feel deeply ashamed and guilty. It concerned an occasion, just after they married, when he met his wife at the airport after a short trip. In the car on the journey home she was bubbling with happiness at seeing him again, and was particularly keen that he should admire the way she was dressed. She had managed to pick up some beautiful clothes for a knockdown price, and was wearing them especially for the reunion. My client recalled that he simply could not share her happiness; this deepened the depression he had felt before picking her up. He thought the clothes were beautiful, yet he heard himself saying that he did not like them. Her mood was destroyed and she was plunged into misery as he systematically set about undermining her joy. He told me that his wife enjoyed sex with him and, in the beginning, would request that they make love. Whenever she did this he was unable to comply, and their sexual life soon ceased. It was some time before he could begin to articulate his envy of his partner's capacity for happiness, and of her secure childhood. During the twelve years of their marriage she was reduced to a withdrawn, antisocial and chronically anxious person, whilst his career, in a profession which they shared, progressed quite spectacularly. It became clear to him that he needed her to be unhappy so that he could feel happy. He went on to recall how he had systematically lied to her during their courtship. He had always felt tense with her because of the effort involved in pretending to be happy, when, in his own words, 'I never was'.

There is a great deal about this man's history and complex psychology which I cannot share, and although he exemplifies many of the dilemmas experienced by modern men in relation to women, that is not why I tell his story. I use it to illustrate the obvious: he became successful; she failed. The more passive she became, the more active he became. As she fell into depression, she doubled her efforts to be a good wife. She ceased to be a sexual person because she knew her sexuality upset her husband. She thought the problems in their marriage resulted from her own failure, and suffered deeply from guilt and shame. In spite of a good relationship with her family she kept the problem which dominated her life from them after her one attempt to talk about it aroused disbelief and shock.

On the face of it this woman, whom I met many times, contradicts much of what I have said about female development. Before her marriage she was happy, active, successful, independent and assertive. She described herself as knowing who she was and what she wanted. In a sense this was true, but as she told me, 'It all really meant nothing to me. Even though I was having a good time, I was just waiting for the right man to come along. On my own I was no one. I didn't bother with men until I met (my client). I knew immediately he was the man for me. As soon as I set eyes on him I knew we'd get married.' All this sounds somewhat improbable, rather like a penny romance. However, it is fairly typical of what little girls are led to aspire to and want as adults. There are few other choices.

MASOCHISM: A FEMALE CHOICE?

Given that the Freudian account describes how little girls learn to adjust to a male-dominated world and how this is subjectivized, to what extent is it therefore justifiable to assert that women's apparent collusion with their own oppression derives from their masochism? Is it even justifiable to assert that most women experience themselves as the victims of oppression? Probably not. This would hardly be surprising. Women the world over are raised to be unprotesting and compliant. Increasingly, however, feminist-inspired research is showing interesting results when women are asked the right questions (Hanmer and Maynard, 1987). If, for example, women are asked whether they feel oppressed, they will probably answer no; if they are asked whether they have ever had sex with their husbands or partners when they did not want to, 63 per cent answer yes. A survey for the British television programme 'World in Action' in December 1989 indicated that 14 per cent of married women reported that they had been violently raped by their husbands.

Although Freud warned explicitly against reducing sexual difference to the factor of aggression, it is quite clear that the way in which little girls metabolize their aggression, at the behest of men, is the most important single factor determining their gender behaviour. The conflation of passive/masochistic with female and active/sadistic with male, through the connecting concept of castrated/phallic, ensures that women learn to expect suffering at the hands of men, and believe that this is the way of the world. Women's impotence, however, is not the result of castration, it is a social reality; intrinsically, they possess the greatest power of all, the power to bear children, but even this is subject to control by men. Childbirth has become medicalized at the insistence of the male-dominated medical profession. The vast majority of pregnant women have their babies in hospital, and are defined as patients. It was the feminist analysis of the connection between the medical profession and its colonization of women's bodies that led to the setting up of Well Women's clinics and women-staffed pregnancy centres all round the world as women reclaimed their bodies.

The little girl is surrounded by the evidence of women's secondary status – a status which will be all the more obvious to her as she grows and discovers its emotional and physical reality. The growing girl's phallic myth, apart from its essential psychological significance, can be seen as a natural expression of protest against her inheritance, as a female, of institutionalized powerlessness and the loss which heterosexuality represents for her. Penis envy is grounded in social reality, not simply in the little boy's ability to pee further or, in theory, satisfy the mother in a way which is impossible for the girl. It must be recognized, however, that if this concept did not exist, some other metaphor would be required to explain the masochistic move which betokens her assumption of femininity and her entry, as object, into the male-dominated symbolic order.

The vast majority of girls make the passive 'choice' because they do not really have a choice. They can deny their lack and retain their homosexuality, or they can cling to the hope that one day they might have a penis and begin to adopt masculine characteristics. An essential point here is that Freud and his followers consistently pathologize a girl's failure(!) to internalize patriarchal norms and values – essentially heterosexuality and female passivity – as represented in the positive Oedipus complex. The psychoanalytic account of gender differentiation – indeed, analysis itself – works, given the social constructs mother–female; father–male. What might be seen as a girl's natural protest against the gross inequalities between men and women, and the subordination (oppression) of the female, is seen instead as symptomatic of neurotic failure. Self-empowerment thus becomes self-enfeeblement. This is why I believe that where possible, consciousness-raising should be an essential precondition of psychotherapy for women. It probably goes without saying that this represents a real threat to capitalism in that it could seriously undermine women's commitment to heterosexuality and the family – the underpinnings of economic order.

The word 'choice' is stressed in the account of the girl's move to the masochistic position to emphasize that this is an unconscious decision. Psychologically, as we have seen, the child really has no choice, given that she can never, in a heterosexual world, satisfy her own desire to be the object of her mother's desire. Nor can she retain the mother as the object of her own desire. It will be many years, however, before her sexuality, her gender identity, will become conventionally heterosexual. During those years, she will be struggling to internalize the meaning of becoming female, and to come to terms with her growing awareness of the social and political consequences of being different - for example, during periods of adolescent homosexual longing.

As to whether the Oedipus complex describes the way in which the child subjectivizes her development, or actually constructs it, it makes little difference. Although the Oedipus complex actually does both, under present social arrangements - the worldwide dominance of men and the subjugation of women - little girls' anatomy is their destiny, because men have made it so.

MEN AND THE SOCIALIZATION OF GIRLS

We must clarify and examine men's role in rearing children, particularly daughters, and how this contributes to - indeed, underpins - the girl's assumption of her destiny through to the masochistic move.

I have already mentioned Freud's difficulties with his early seduction theory of hysteria. He could not believe that so many little girls were being sexually abused by their fathers. We now know that he was wrong. However, along with Ward (1984), I would rename his seduction theory a rape theory. It involves the abuse of gender power and adult authority with little girls.

Although, for obvious reasons, exact figures are hard to come by, some researchers estimate that as many as one in ten to one in three girls have been incestuously abused (Baker and Duncan, 1986; Kinsey *et al.*, 1948, 1953; Nash and West, 1985). Some feminists think these figures underestimate the true scale of female child sexual abuse, and point to the indequacies in the research methodologies of these surveys (MacLeod and Saraga, 1988).

These statistics fail to take into account the widespread sexualization of physical contact between fathers and daughters. At its most elementary, this will involve no more than the sexually differentiated behaviour which fathers act out with boys and girls, and the encouragement of reciprocity by the use of reward and punishment. At its extreme, in what seems to be a large minority of cases, it will involve explicit sexual abuse. The consequence of this abuse, apart from the man's immediate gratification, is that the girl infant is educated into adopting the primary attributes which men define as feminine – chiefly her sexual passivity and accessibility to men. She becomes possessed: literally Daddy's little girl. She learns that if she is to be loved she must become an erotic plaything, and devote herself to enhancing men's self-esteem.

The fact that psychoanalysis can repeatedly demonstrate the existence of girls' sexual fantasies about their fathers should in no way distract us from these fundamental truths. The vast majority of little girls, like their mothers before them, are victims of abuse. The fundamental abuse is the introjection of a male-defined femininity. This abuse may be emotional and psychological only, but for many people it also includes sexually abusive physical impingement, and it is irrelevant that this may also accord with one of the infant girl's polymorphous sexual fantasies. Let us not forget that she has similar fantasies, probably much more intense and primitive, towards her primary carer (Mother), and that in spite of this men have a virtual monopoly of child and adult sexual abuse. Little girls cannot satisfy Mother (even metaphorically) because men say so, and because Mother's sexuality has been similarly constructed and defined by men.

The Freudian account of feminine development provides a justification for the oppression and subjugation of women by not even remotely addressing the fundamental power relations on which the development of femininity is predicated and without which it simply could not subsist in its present form. Psychoanalysis is a male institution. One of its consequences, even if this is unintentional, is that it reinforces heterosexuality and the subordination of femininity without which man might be excluded from matriarchal society (Thomas, 1907, quoted in Miles, 1988). The masochistic/passive/castrated female is essential for male dominance. Men have control of the public domain of reality definition. We have no way of knowing what a woman might be if she were not defined from a position of lack. Woman is constructed according to men's definition of what is appropriate – not only consciously but also unconsciously, in the structure of male language. The designation 'female' is, at root, oppressive because of the conflation of anatomical femaleness with social and psychological femininity as defined by men, and the well-documented actual oppression of women. Masochism is an oppressive term used by men to justify their continued oppression of women. It is socially constructed; furthermore, the behaviour and attitudes it describes are the only option left to little girls. There is no evidence that women enjoy their subordination. Those who are willing to listen to women's accounts of their existence find quite the contrary.

Psychoanalysis is phallocentric – even in those post-Freudian models which are preoccupied with the primary relation with the mother. Actually, I believe this phallocentricity is appropriate for analytic work with men. My critique concerns its application to women. There are ways of deconstructing female sexuality and conducting therapy with women which do not involve these demeaning implications. What is required, particularly of male therapists and analysts, is that we should begin to discuss with colleagues the nature of our interventions with both women and men. I know that as a male therapist I am different with women and with men. My attitudinal set is different, and it frames the way I perceive the phenomena with which I am confronted.

Let me illustrate. I used to interrupt women more than I did men. I would have some interventions which were only for women – I would never call a man a martyr (I would not call a woman one now, but there was a time . . .). I would frequently accuse a woman of being sexually seductive; the only male patients I accused of this were gay ones. A friend of mine, a highly talented artist, was recently given an interpretation (I would prefer to say accusation) by her – very eminent – analyst that she wanted to be raped because she wore attractive clothes – sometimes short skirts – and probably because she is very beautiful. Would he have said the same to a man?

I have no way of knowing, but I think not. I was unconsciously orientated towards helping women to become more happily heterosexual. I would never have considered that it might be constructive to help a woman to reorientate her sexuality. This also applied to men, but less so.

Not that the kind of criticism to which feminism has subjected analysis has gone unobserved. There are signs that Freud's original radicalism is returning to modern analytic thought, and that sexual identity is once again becoming the problematic terrain which he identified. Ultimately, I would hope that if the critique is taken seriously, psychoanalysis and other models which derive from it will no longer be social guardians, rooting out deviant identity and adjusting it to the demands of oedipal normality. This will mean that the family and heterosexuality will not be the criteria, latent or otherwise, against which to measure mental health. It raises questions about the political role of analysis and therapy. I believe one of our central tasks should be to subject extant social structures to critical deconstruction – not only politically, but also in their implications for our patients' psychological development. The increasing bureaucratization of analytic or therapeutic training is unlikely to help this process. Bureaucracy is 'opposed to desire, i.e. its naming' (Kovel, 1985). The radical anti-psychiatric movement which began in the 1970s had much the same objectives, although it lacked many of the deconstructive techniques which feminists have subsequently developed.

For women, social reality does not change. The penis is all-important; one is defined according to one's relation to it. This has become, for most women, a psychological reality also. What men have called female masochism might be an appropriate description of the girl's apparent decision to assume a feminine role if, in fact, there was really a choice to be made, but this is a myth. Sexism, as a linguistic, social, economic, psychological and political system of oppression, is intended to deny any such choice. The fact that the masochistic move 'seems' to be adapted to the need for procreation, and is consistent with anatomy, is neither here nor there. If sexual division is necessary – and this is not a sustainable belief – it can be for this alone. Only a simple anatomical distinction is required. Femininity, sex roles and female subordination are for the convenience of men. The organization of culture around the primacy of the penis provides a sharp focus for masculinity and the assurance against a collapse into the chaos surrounding the origins of desire.

Can there be much doubt that a great many women feel a deep sense of inadequacy? For that matter – though for different reasons – so do men. A significant difference is that men have available a simple defence against it: the erect penis. Female inadequacy, and the concomitant penis envy, is a reality. My work with men who are violent towards women, and who are struggling to come to terms with their controlling behaviour, reinforces my conviction that men have an investment in engendering deep feelings of inadequacy in women, and that women who refuse to submit expose themselves to the most severe forms of chastisement to force them to adapt to men's expectations. In childhood, this inadequacy – which has its psychological origins in the inability to satisfy Mother, and therefore possess her – has its social origins in the oppression of women, and so long as primary care is defined as the special province of women, it inevitably becomes focused on the lack of a penis. Psychoanalysis has probably contributed more than any other discourse to the maintenance and construction of motherhood and mothering as special feminine roles. In many of the major social work training institutes, this is still the case.

William Gillespie (1975), in a brief discussion of female narcissism, which is generally regarded as more extreme than its male equivalent (see Freud, 1914), links it with women's 'complaints about being a woman'. He quotes a paper by Béla Grunberger, who points out that this complaint may derive from every mother's ambivalent feelings towards a baby girl, which the girl interprets as being caused by her own inadequacy. Gillespie stresses Chasseguet-Smirgel's view of the importance of the little girl's lack of a penis in helping her to cope with the omnipotent mother. The essential phallocentricity of psychoanalysis, and its reflection of social reality, could not be more evident. The mother will inevitably see her girl children as secondary and inadequate because boy children are more valued. She introjects this reality as a psychological fact, and passes it on to her little daughters – not only through her patterns of interaction with them but also through their learning of language, in which woman is always defined from a position of lack (no-thing). Men, with the co-operation of complaisant women, are instrumental in raising girl children to feel inadequate, and to introject the notion that only by giving birth to sons – a substitute penis – and attachment to a man can they feel complete.

In 'The Stockholm syndrome', Dee Graham, Edna Rawlings and Nelly Rimini (1988) draw attention to battered women's apparent inability to leave a relationship in which they are being abused. They compare this with the psychological effects suffered by survivors of terror. They point out the dependency a hostage develops on their torturer or terrorizer even to the point where they may begin to espouse the terrorist's values. This identification with the aggressor – which they call the 'Stockholm syndrome' – is a survival mechanism in extreme situations of life-threatening intensity. The parallels with battered women are evident. Could it be that this syndrome applies to all women, not just those who are being battered? Might it not describe the lot of women and little girls the world over – the fact that they are all raised into a world in which they must introject male definitions of reality for fear of the painful consequences of refusal or defiance, and that the girl's disavowal of her active, aggressive impulses, to which the masochistic move can be traced, derives from her internalizing male injunctions about female aggression? Russell Dobash, a sociologist who has specialized in male violence to women, says (1990) that men who batter do so because they have learned that this is a way of dealing with conflict (as we shall see, I believe that it is a way of avoiding conflict), and that those who do not batter have failed to learn as well as others. If we apply the paradigm of the Stockholm syndrome, it might be more accurate to regard these men as being freed from the necessity of battering or abusing, because they are living with women who do not need to be battered or abused in order to be controlled.

The mother may well be where femininity has landed, but is it simply provocative to assert that it did not fall, but men placed it there quite deliberately and are determined to fight – with malice aforethought if necessary – to keep it in its place? The obscurity of femininity, that 'dark continent', both reflects and is symptomatic of unconscious male intent rather than feminine opacity.

I will now look at an area in heterosexual relations where men's belief that masochism is an essential trait in all women could not be be more evident: male abuse of women. That this is a common belief, one that could not more accurately or fully reflect attitudes to women, is evident from the most often repeated statement about women who are subject to violence from their male partners: 'They must like it, or why would they put up with it?' Examining male violence to women will enable us better to apppreciate the underlying politics and psychology of battering and male power, and to understand how little girls are tamed and feminized. It will also illustrate how commonplace, rather than deviant, are the means and uses of mens's oppression of women.

8 Men Who Batter

If it is not safe to let oneself be dominated, then it is not possible to be fully feminine.
(Anthony Storr on women, in *Human Aggression*)

Another black eye and a few broken ribs are, of course, just the thing to make a woman feel deliciously feminine.
Elizabeth Wilson on Anthony Storr,
in *What Is To Be Done About Violence Towards Women?*

Any account of the difficulties in relations between men and women would not be satisfactory if we failed to look at the actual violence which seems to play such a central part in so many of these relationships. Indeed it would probably not be an overstatement to say that violence is the underpinning rather than simply a central part of heterosexual relationships. A survey of over 1,000 women in the British Isles carried out for the Granada TV programme 'World in Action' (August 1989) elicited the information that one-third of all married women had been the victims of violence from their husbands, and 14 per cent had been violently raped by them. A survey by the Australian Office of The Status of Women revealed that 23 per cent of men believe that it is justifiable for a man to shove, kick or hit his female partner if she does not obey him, wastes money, fails to keep the house clean, refuses to sleep with him or admits to sleeping with another man (quoted in Horsfall, 1991). As mentioned earlier, research on over one thousand children by Child Abuse Studies Unit at North London

Polytechnic (Kelly *et al.*, 1991) concluded that almost 60 per cent of the girls up to the age of sixteen had been sexually abused by males. Sexual abuse in this context is defined as unwelcome, intrusive sexual contact. Along with Liz Kelly and other feminists, I define this sort of contact as violent. It is physical impingement predicated on the use or threat of force.

Violence represents the visible and unnacceptable face of male power over women. According to some feminist writers, violence is a demonstration of the ultimate failure of that power. Elizabeth Wilson (1983), for example, argues that violence represents the collapse of the patriarchy and the failure of patriarchal authority. Jan Horsfall states that violence is the 'ultimate resource available to all husbands who wish to wield power over their wives' (1991, p. 16). She seems to support Wilson when she asserts that battering is an indication that patriarchal relations and their practices 'are under duress either from outside and/or inside the family'. She continues, however: 'if both men and women were well adapted to the patriarchal structures, men would have no need to exercise their superior physical power'. She seems to be saying here that battering is a failure in adaptation and, by implication, mainly by women. To some extent, this mirrors my experience: that women are more likely to be battered when they fail to live up to the man's expectations of appropriate wifely, motherly, or womanly behaviour.

There is some *prima facie* evidence to support Wilson's thesis. When men attack women, they are feeling threatened by feelings of impotence, weakness and victimization. It is difficult to conclude from this, however, that battering represents the collapse of men's authority, simply because the man feels that his authority is being challenged or threatened to such an extent that he believes it is necessary to reimpose it and remind his victim of the power differential. In fact, my experience indicates that whenever a man's authority – which usually means getting what he wants at that moment – is challenged by his female partner he will feel threatened by impotence and helplessness if he fails to exercise his dominance. His abuse or violence will help him to avoid this threat, but to say that this is his motive, as many analytic thinkers do, is to miss the point entirely. In this chapter I intend to elaborate why violence is more expressive than defensive.

The violence represents the assertion of men's authority in a way which they believe is acceptable and carries little risk. It is clear that Wilson wishes – and one must sympathize with her – that it represented the collapse of patriarchal authority. In my work with men who are violent towards women – batterers – incidents of real violence which involve physical contact and attack seem to be triggered by a breakdown or collapse of control, but 'seem' is the operative word. I say 'attack' rather than fighting, because fighting is interactional, and interaction is not what battering is about. In my experience it is not possible for a man and a woman to fight, except in the most unlikely circumstances. In any case, 'to fight' is an interactional verb, which implies recripocal activity; this is rarely the case when men abuse women.

Lynne Segal (1990) argues in much the same vein as Wilson. For both these writers, as socialist feminists, the perception of male violence as the central element of heterosexual relationships is monolithic and ahistorical. They do not accept the argument of what Segal calls the American cultural feminists (those of an essentialist, apocalyptic persuasion like Mary Daly, Andrea Dworkin or Susan Brownmiller) and others, like Catharine MacKinnon, who – as she rightly says – sound more and more as if they believe in essential, biological, sexual differences, however much they espouse the theory that gender is a social construction. Segal and Wilson make the point that not all men are violent towards women, and that it is insulting to women who are in relationships with non-violent men to assert that they are brainwashed by men into accepting male definitions of appropriate behaviour. They argue that it is important to understand what makes men violent at some times but not at others, and why some men are never violent. Westergaard and Resler offer a simple explanation:

> In any society, the patterns of people's lives . . . take the forms which they do . . . in large part because certain social mechanisms . . . are taken for granted . . . The favoured group enjoys effective power even when its members take no active steps to exercise power. They do not need to do so . . . simply because things work their way in any case. (quoted in Horsfall, 1991)

The way they work, in any case, is determined by the differential distribution of power based on gender, which is called patriarchy.

Some feminists (Hart, 1988; Kelly, 1986) suggest that there is a continuum of male violence, and that gynocide is seamlessly connected to wolf whistles. Although I do not agree with the use made of this continuum by some apocalyptic feminists, particularly the call to censor pornography, it has a special importance in work with violent men, as I will make clear.

I believe that male violence is a sign not of the collapse of the patriarchy but of a particular patriarch's feeling that he has lost, or is in danger of losing, control over his partner. The violence is an attempt to maintain or re-establish that control, and it is predicated on the belief that it is appropriate and right for a man to control a woman. Violence is about power; it is the attempt to assert control over another. The ubiquitous violence and other forms of abuse which men inflict on women succeed in this. They maintain the superior position of men both in general and in particular.

In addition, rather than representing patriarchal collapse, it seems to other feminists that men's violence against women simply makes extant what every woman knows to be true. Stanko (1985) goes further:

> The brutal rape, the sexually harassing comments, the slap on the face, the grab on the street - all forms of men's threatening intimidating and violent behaviour - are reminders to women of their vulnerability to men. Try as they might, women are unable to predict when a threatening or intimidating form of male behaviour will escalate to violence. *As a result women are continually on guard to the possibility of men's violence.* (emphasis added)

For her, women's behaviour is predicated on the assumption that any man can turn violent at any moment.

This may seem an outrageous statement, although Stanko makes a convincing case. As a man, however, it is not my place - or, indeed, my right - to contradict. Only a woman can say what is threatening for a woman. For far too long men have assumed this prerogative - the very essence of power - the right to define another's reality. What is certain is that the 'victimology' which has so coloured our view of women's position in society is based on and reinforces patriarchal assumptions about women – that is, men's assumptions and definitions of femaleness. Women have never been allowed to define their own experience of femaleness and have internalized men's definitions of them to the point where, for example, female victims of male abuse, whether sexual, violent, or simply discriminatory, feel ashamed and guilty. It is not uncommon for rape victims to agonize about what they did to make a man behave in that way. Horsfall (1991) and many other writers have argued that forms of behaviour which seem normal and unthreatening are so defined by men, not by women's experience of them. A clear example of this is that rape continues to be defined as a sexual crime – that is, in terms of the man's behaviour to the woman – whereas for the woman involved it is never anything other than a crime of violence. It is predicated on violence, violently acted, and with the threat of more violence for non-cooperation. The deep confusion between sex, power and aggression may be shared by women, but it is, in the main, only men who act out their confusion in this way.

The title of this chapter, 'Men Who Batter', is intended to surprise. The phrase 'domestic violence', commonly used to describe such family situations, clearly implies a dynamic between the partners which assumes that they are, in some way, equally responsible for what is happening. This is simply not true. 'Domestic violence' seems to be an attempt actually to hide the fact that it is men who beat women, and that battering is a gender-based crime. As Wilson (1983) points out, it also implies that there is a particular sort of 'problem family' which can be isolated and compared with all other 'normal' families, in which violence of this sort does not occur, and happiness and peace reign because power is equally shared. Stanko again goes further when she says that the identification of some men as aberrant as opposed to normal blinds us to the truth: that male violence is central to any understanding of male–female relationships. She insists that the wife-batterer is no different from any other kind of man. I can only add that this is supported by my direct experience of intensive counselling with over two hundred batterers.

The orthodoxy – which, I believe, is offensive to women, as well as badly mistaken – that violence in relationships is a shared responsibility is widely established. 'It takes two to tango' is simply the benign expression of a set of beliefs about 'domestic violence' which were more directly expressed by the notorious (he insists, misunderstood) Judge Pickles in 1990 when he asked a wife accusing her husband of battery: 'How do I know you didn't deserve it?' Apart from judicial attitudes, which are overwhelmingly male, there is the virtual clinical hegemony of Freudian-derived thinking which insists on the victim's contribution to her own abuse. The notion of the masochistic woman refuses to lie down. In many publications, like Jeanne Deschner's (1984), or Jean Renvoize's better-known work (1978), there are no clear-cut victims or perpetrators, only couples in need of help. Often, one need only read the cover in order to know the content, for example, 'Characteristics of abusive couples' (Rosenbaum and O'Leary, 1981).

Male violence against women is high on the list of most commonly recorded crimes of violence (see Preface). This is even more astounding when we take into account some estimates that it is also the most unreported and under-recorded crime of violence. One study estimates that it may be unrecorded by as much as 270 times: in other words, only one in 270 crimes of domestic violence – wife-battering – is reported to the authorities. I do not want to go into the sociological analyses of how these reported incidences are dealt with by police and other statutory authorities. Suffice it to say that there is overwhelming evidence that the attitudes which produce such crime are as prevalent in these authorities as they are in the public at large (Dobash and Dobash, 1980; Leghorn, 1976). To feminists it is rather like asking the criminal both to judge and sentence himself.

It is a commonly held view that male violence towards women is one part of the so-called 'cycle of deprivation' – that men who batter are actually victims of battering themselves, and that it passes on from generation to generation like a hot potato. Renvoize is the writer who has done most to popularize this view, although the evidence for it is not conclusive. There is some evidence (Gayford, 1975) that a high proportion of batterers, probably about half, were themselves battered or witnessed battering when they were children. Gayford's information, however, was taken from a hundred victims. Our research at the Men's Centre shows that the majority of the men who have contacted us were not subjected to such abuse as children, nor did they witness abuse by their fathers on their mothers. Although it is impossible to check, those men who were victims as children often have brothers who were also victims, but have not become batterers. Of course, this raises important questions about where our clients learn this behaviour, and the beliefs and attitudes which support and enable it.

These considerations also raise interesting questions for those involved in attempts to change male behaviour. Such questions go to the heart of the boundary between politics and pathology. For instance, if one defines battering as a pathology, then this clearly suggests treatment for a sickness: men who batter are abnormal, and need help. While this would undoubtedly rope in a great many men who are reported to the authorities for such behaviour, it would do nothing – if research into women's experience is to be believed – about the fundamental problem: that we live in a male-dominated world where gender is the major determinant of meaning, and women's position is founded on male power – institutionally embedded, culturally legitimated and reproduced, and maintained by abusive behaviour, including threats of violence and actual violence.

I have said elsewhere in this book that in a sane society misogyny would be defined as a sickness. To my knowledge, there is not one society where this is the case, although in most societies battering is, *de jure*, defined as a crime. However, apart from the – well-documented (see S. Edwards, 1981, 1984, 1985) – inefficacy of the police and judiciary in enforcing the law in battering cases, there is little doubt that in almost every country the helping professions use models for understanding male violence which support or collude with this inefficacy. Although there are only four intervention programmes for work with batterers in the UK, there are over two hundred in the USA, and they have developed a number of different models of intervention with batterers. According to Straus, Gelles and Steinmetz (1980) they can be roughly divided into those which stress intrapsychic causation, those which emphasize sociopsychological causation, and those orientated to a sociocultural level of analysis. Those models which collude explicitly are the sociopsychological, usually called systems theories, in which all actors in a system are assumed to be equal players (marital therapy is similar) and causation is understood as circular or interactive rather than linear. In other words, the woman is contributing to her own maltreatment by behaving in ways which upset her husband. The 'couple' have an investment in continuing with the violence, and the interaction between them is producing it. David Adams (1988) analyses five different clinical approaches to the treatment of batterers, and recognizes that most programmes use a variety of techniques drawn from different approaches even where one model is dominant.

No model of intervention with abusers need be – or actually is in practice – exclusive. Most programmes have a number of explicit goals: to increase self-esteem; to teach appropriate expression of feelings; to change behaviour; to teach new skills or anger management; to restructure attitudes or beliefs, rigid sex-role expectations, and so on. These goals can be easily derived from the level of analysis of the causes of the violence – whether it is seen as being within the individual, the relationship or the culture. Those programmes which emphasize the sociocultural causes and locate men's abuse in the context of the social acceptance of violence, the use of violence to control women, men's power over women, and women's subordination, are in the minority in the USA. They focus on the decisive, instrumental nature of male violence. In the UK, it is too early to say which view will prevail in the specialist centres which are established, but the issue is already generating heated debate as the orthodox, consensual views are challenged (Baker, 1991; Jukes, 1991; Pepinster, 1991).

I want to examine a non-consensual model of battering – what might be called a pro-feminist model. We will see how this way of understanding male violence can be used, in a treatment or educational setting, to confront a man with his responsibility for his behaviour. In Chapter 7 I outlined what it entails to accept a pro-feminist position in understanding men's violent behaviour. In my own work, the Stockholm syndrome concept forms the basis of this understanding, and this implies a clear strategy of educational or clinical intervention to help men to overcome their violence. I shall examine, in a more specific way, the idea of a continuum of control and violence in heterosexual relations, and attempt to contextualize violence within that continuum. Finally I will compare in some detail the understanding derived from a pro-feminist model with the more traditional research findings.

SOME CASE HISTORIES

I will begin with some illustrative practical examples, which will be as short as possible. They are intended to illustrate the central thesis of this book: that men hate women, that male violence is expressive of this hatred, and that this violence is simply the most extreme of the methods used by men to maintain women in a state of submission and helpless subordination; that men do this in order to prevent woman from becoming the bad and abandoning object who would evoke the man's sadistic and misogynistic feelings; that this is achieved by controlling women's thoughts, feelings and behaviour so that they remain within the boundaries defined by men as acceptable.

It is not possible to do justice to the richness or poverty of a life in a few short notes. I have tried to stick to the most relevant data for my purposes, despite the risk of distortion of the individual involved and the complexity of our work together. Obviously, I have made some changes to protect the anonymity of these men, whom I will call Jim, Alan and Winston.

Jim

Jim is a successful property developer. He has been married for fifteen years, and has two children aged five and seven. He was referred by a marriage guidance counsellor to whom he had gone for help. He had initially defined his problem as his wife, but I assumed that he had been referred on because he was violent towards her. The problem, as he saw it, was that she was an alcoholic and would stay up, often all night, drinking herself into insensibility, only to collapse into bed the next morning when it was time for the children to go to school and Jim to go to work. If he confronted her with her drinking, she would become abusive and even physically violent. She refused to recognize that she had a drinking problem: this could provoke violent rows when he would batter her unconscious for her neglect of the children, or her drinking. She had made many visits to hospital casualty departments after a battering. She would often not know what day or time it was and would, for example, try to get the children dressed for school at ten o'clock on a Sunday morning. They would often go out in the morning without food. As I listened to Jim, it was impossible not to feel sympathy for his plight. How, I found myself asking, could he stay with such an awful person? He unhesitatingly replied that he loved her and realized that she was sick, that there was 'something not quite right in her head'. 'So you think she's crazy?' I asked. 'Yes, I do,' he replied,'or at least, there's something not quite right with her.' 'Is that why you hit her?' 'Yes and no.' 'I hit her to make her stop.'

Alan

Alan is a middle manager in a large public company. He lives with his fiancée of two years' standing. He referred himself because he has begun to be very violent with her. In the last such episode he dislocated her shoulder by swinging her around, and bruised her face badly with his fists. As a result he spent a day in jail and was released only when his fiancée withdrew the charges of grievous bodily harm. He was charged with a breach of the peace and bound over for six months. Asked what happened, he told me how she 'had been going on at me for days' about when they might get married. She 'just kept on nagging at me and would not shut up'. Finally, he had had enough and just hit her to shut her up. This was the same scenario for all the violent attacks he had made on her: they were all a response to her nagging. She became a harridan, and she was 'very bad'. He just had to stop her. 'So you hit her because she's bad and you have to stop her from being bad?' I asked. 'I suppose so,' he said. 'I would do anything to stop her nagging. I suppose I do it to control her so that she won't nag me. She's so unreasonable!' 'Who defines what's reasonable in your relationship?' Alan smiled. 'I do,' he said, with a huge grin.

Winston

Winston is a highly skilled electronics engineer. He was about to appear in court on a charge of grievous bodily harm against his live-in girlfriend. He had hit her with a bottle and broken her leg during an argument about why he was late home from work. It was clear that he was going to use his consultation as grounds to appeal to the court to mitigate his sentence, and maybe the charge too. It impresses magistrates if the accused has made efforts to seek help before they appear. It shows evidence of good intent, and is no reason for refusing a request for help. His partner had always 'nagged' him about his fidelity. She was constantly accusing him of being involved with other women. He denied that there were any grounds for this 'insecurity' (his definition). She had been abandoned by her father when she was quite small and he thought this was why she was so insecure. 'Is that why you broke her leg?' I asked, 'Because her father abandoned her when she was small?' He laughed at this, but it was obvious that the remark struck home. 'No, I think she's paranoid. Her jealousy is paranoid.' 'So you hit her because she's crazy?'

ANY Man

This man is actually a composite of many who attend programmes at the Centre. He may seem to have no place in this chapter, in so far as his behaviour does not always involve physical violence. It is my belief, however, that in many ways he can be most seriously abusive without ever physically damaging his partner. His particular fascination for me is that he illustrates what I believe to be a primary source of unhappiness for women: that intimacy problems (problems with being close to people) are actually gendered. In the family and marital therapy literature there is a much-debated couple commonly known as the pursuer wife and the distancer husband – she chases; he backs away. In the more benign cases it is as if they are connected by a twenty-foot pole, and she is always moving forward. In more serious cases, backing away is not so passive; it can involve physical or emotional cruelty to drive her off. Often the connection is very clear - for example, the man who became extremely abusive to his partner every day after making love. We work with many distancer husbands who seem to embody this male problem about being intimate with women. On the face of it, it may seem that this is genuinely a systemic problem. The difficulty with this understanding is that we end up defining the woman's need for intimacy, which is the essence of trained femininity, as pathological. In fact men tend to withdraw from any relationship once it begins to become involved and difficult.

Without exception, men who experience this difficulty say they feel overwhelmed by the woman's need for closeness - a need which they define as neurotic in a variety of ways. Actually, this represents a truth about masculinity. We learn early on that men should not have a need for intimacy; that in a man it represents weakness, vulnerability and neurosis - all the qualities of femininity. The problem is that this learning contradicts a basic need in all human beings. Men who come to us with a problem of abusive behaviour deriving from this common pattern in male-female relationships are frequently very unhappy - not because of their abuse, although this may also contribute, but because they are very lonely. They are incapable of mitigating this in any way, and depressed about their inability to be intimate without being in total control of the emotional distance. They want to be intimate when they want it, not when their partner does. Clearly, this is impossible. A person who is controlled by another is not a subject, and one cannot be intimate with an object. However, it is possible to fuck with one if one can get and retain control.

One of the difficulties with this, as I have already made clear (as did Simone de Beauvoir, 1949 and Jessica Benjamin, 1990, amongst others) is that woman is object to man's subject, and this is her primary experience. In effect, if it is impossible to be intimate with an object, it means that men can never be intimate with a woman. This is why sexuality is so important to men: it is the only way left for us to have the experience of intimacy. Consequently, control of female sexuality is of paramount importance.

Of course the distancer has no experience of being in control;

he experiences only the anxiety of being overwhelmed, or wanting to abuse in order to drive away. He is not capable at first of seeing that withholding his affection or attention is controlling and abusive. It renders his victim (if she hangs around, and she usually does because he has begun the relationship – hooked her, in fact, by being very charming, attentive and affectionate) extremely dependent and powerless. This difficulty represents one of the few times when I believe men are victims of gender and conditioning in so far as we are dealing with fears of intimacy rather than abusiveness. As I have already made clear, men in relationships which are formally intimate, like marriage or cohabitation, will have evoked all their primitive conflicts about the 'princess'/'witch', the conflict of ambivalence or love and hate. This conflict will cause depression. It is my observation, with clients and male friends alike, that relationships with women cause them to feel depressed. Being alone, however, makes them even more depressed.

A woman living with such a man has a profoundly difficult problem. She has experienced his affection and love at the outset of the courtship, and is utterly bewildered at the course of events. She believes – with reason – that he loves her, and cannot understand why he is now so distant and disapproving of everything about her. Woman's experience of this has been well documented by Sandra Horley (1991). She is really in a double bind. If she pushes towards him, he pulls away or abuses her more actively. If she withdraws, she resigns herself to not getting the intimacy and support she longs for. It feels as if she cannot win. And this is precisely how the man is structuring the situation: as a competitive win/lose battle for control. She finds this bewildering; he can experience loss of control as terrifying. Traditionally, marital therapists have focused on the woman's pursuing behaviour, suggesting to her, for example, that she might consider giving her husband more space. This is even more confusing to the woman, because it has the effect of pathologizing her need to be intimate.

It is obvious to me that marital therapy is contra-indicated in this situation. The source of the problem is the man's anxiety. I can readily acknowledge that he is unlikely to attend for any form of treatment if he is seen as being to blame for the marital difficulties, but is blaming the woman for the sake of preserving the relationship a better strategy? I am afraid I have no simple answer to this dilemma. One must take the bull by the horns and confront the basic institution: the marriage and its viability. If the man is unwilling to seek help for his anxieties (not by any means a simple or guaranteed option), my own preference is to inform the woman of my understanding of the situation and ask her if she is prepared to continue with his game, and the confusion and pain it causes her. If the man is not given an incentive, he will not deal with the issue. Even if he attends for marital or joint sessions, his motivation is usually to get the therapist to pathologize his wife's behaviour and stop her 'giving him a hard time' – to cease being unhappy with him. Of course he feels aggrieved, because his expectation had been that if he provided, she would be happy – after all, that's what all women want, isn't it? Her unhappiness is a continual source of confusion, resentment and guilt for him. His preoccupation with and training for the public world does not fit him for the requirements of the private world of nurturance and intimacy. The man feels that he is keeping his end of the 'bargain', while his partner stubbornly refuses to see how much effort this takes.

Even though the gender base of this source of marital conflict is clear in clinical practice, and is readily derived from theory, marital therapists have not fully taken this into consideration and devised appropriate clinical strategies which do not further disadvantage women. The real challenge is how to present these to the man without driving him away, particularly when men are so resistant to attending for marital or family sessions. If marital therapy is to be the treatment of choice, the two guidelines must be: first, not to pathologize the woman's behaviour; secondly, to confront the man with his responsibility in a way which enables him to see the potential benefits of facing up to it. At the moment my favoured strategy is to get the man to the point where he can accept the offer of individual counselling.

I recall one couple where these dynamics could not have been more transparent. The man was in the habit of actually leaving the home for days at a time when his tension at being 'pursued' was at such a level that he might physically attack his partner. This situation had prevailed for some years. Contrary to systemic understanding, it was clear that his partner found this behaviour very disturbing and depressing. Of course her unhappiness and anger gave him a further reason for withdrawing, as it was difficult for him to cope with any strong expression of emotion from a woman, especially anger. Her behaviour intensified his guilt, fear of and anger with her; it is clear that at these times she seemed to him to be a threatening witch. After a couple of sessions, I put to them my understanding of what was happening. I had earlier confronted his constant attempts, in the sessions, to define her need for intimacy as crazy and infantile. He seemed relieved that at last they had an explanation with which they could both agree, and that his anxiety had been recognized. Although he understood that he was being told he had a broken wing, it gave him comfort to be told that half the world suffered the same disability.

A Stranger

I never saw this man in person. The following details were given to me by a colleague who had a number of telephone conversations with him. I am including them to enable the reader to compare a traditionalist understanding of battering with a pro-feminist one. The man first called because he said he had a real problem with violence towards women. It emerged during this conversation that he was on the run from the police and a charge of grievous bodily harm. It transpired that he had broken his wife's back during an attack. He was obviously very anxious about what to do. My colleague advised him to give himself up to the police and phone again after he had been charged. The man refused to do this. He was advised to think it over. About a week later he rang with further information. It seemed that he had been referred to a male psychotherapist who had apparently listened with sympathy to his tale of his wife's behaviour. She would not do any housework, refused to shop or cook or look after herself properly, and was generally unpleasant to him. She spent much of her time in bed watching television. He had made her sound impossible to live with, according to my colleague, but in our experience this is par for the course. It is very easy for the inexperienced therapist to be taken in, and collude with the batterer's perceptions of his partner. In any case, the therapist had apparently advised him that his wife was crazy. In his opinion she had provoked the attack by failing to live up to her proper role as a wife. He advised that the man should give himself up and said that he, the therapist, would appear on his behalf and testify to this effect. Now of course, there is no way of knowing how much of this is true. Batterers are, to say the least, economical with the truth. My colleague could say only that the man sounded very convincing. I ask the reader to bear this tale in mind when other men are being discussed.

Some of my remarks to these men might seem a little sarcastic to the type of clinically informed reader who has been raised on a diet of unconditional positive regard (not the only kind, I might add) and thinks that this is the only way people will be encouraged to change. This may or may not be true. It seems to involve discounting behaviour change as not really genuine because it comes not from the inside out but from the outside in. It involves an element of self-control and cognitive change, without regard for the affective change usually regarded as the *sine qua non* of authentic growth. None the less, a change in behaviour will often lead to a significant change in attitude and feelings.

Medium- to long-term research on the work of non-violence programmes such as the one from which these cases are taken shows clearly that they can have a high rate of success – up to three in four – in helping men to stop their violence (Edelson and Syers, 1989). This compares very favourably with the alternatives – open-ended analytic group treatment, relationship therapy or individual psychotherapy and analysis. Data for some of these other intervention strategies are hard to come by. Other models – in particular couples therapy and open-ended analytic groups – have been shown to be ineffective for the very good reason that they imply either that the man's violence originates from some deeply buried trauma – this, of course, is partly true, but that is not the point – or that it is the woman's fault – which is not even remotely or partly true – and fail to confront him with his responsibility for his behaviour.

I recall a man who was seriously battering his wife, at times when she was holding their young baby. He was referred to us by a marital therapist to whom they had self-referred at the woman's instigation. The referral arose mostly from the counsellor's anxiety about the child. It emerged from my consultation with him that he started to batter his wife after he discovered that she had sex with another man. I should mention that although they were married and had a child, he still lived with his parents while his wife lived in the joint marital home. He was 'not ready to take responsibility', as he put it. Naturally the situation was more complex than he appreciated. The salient point, however, is that it emerged that he had been seriously abusing his wife physically before her affair, but did not define his behaviour as abusive. It became clear that the affair had provided him with the justification he needed to begin attempts to control her movements by using violence without guilt. The point I want to make here concerns his behaviour towards the counsellor who had referred him to me. I had advised her that his wife's depression was probably caused by his abuse – the constant jealous interrogations, accusations, name-calling and physical violence – and that if he was able to stop this, she would probably get well. The counsellor agreed with my assessment, but we both thought the wife should be offered counselling to deal with the trauma which had been inflicted on her. I subsequently heard from this counsellor that my client had been phoning and complaining in an abusive way about her neglect of his wife. When I asked him why he did this he replied that he simply wanted what was best for her. The irony of this cannot escape the reader. He failed to see (actually denied) that he was responsible for his wife's situation, and that if he had been more genuinely concerned for her welfare he would never have abused her in the first place.

Any model which allows a battering man to evade responsibility for his violence will not succeed in helping him to stop. The extent of a batterer's denial, minimizing, projection and splitting, his capacity for self-deception, is quite something to see in an otherwise healthy man. It is not uncommon for a man to say during an initial consultation that he pushed his wife. Later, under persistent questioning, it will emerge that she happened to be at the top of the stairs at the time. Then, he will insist that he had not meant her to be so badly injured. When he begins to accept that maybe he had meant this, he will vehemently protest that she deserved it for the way she treated him. If these men presented in the same way with any other problem, any competent therapist or psychiatrist would have little hesitation in diagnosing a disturbed personality.

Let us look at what was subsequently learned about each of these men.

Jim

Jim had been battering his wife since before they were married. It emerged that she really did have a serious drinking problem, but it is not unknown for battered women to develop such a problem as an escape from years of chronic and terrifying abuse. She had not had a drinking problem before they were married. When Jim had not been systematically beating her, he had been systematically cruel to her verbally. He had humiliated and undermined her to the point where it became impossible for her to function. She suffered from the Battered Woman's Syndrome, a clinically definable set of behaviours resulting from chronic abuse. The woman will be passive, confused, emotionally labile and cognitively disordered. Her grip on reality is weak. Jim was now using his wife's symptoms of the previous years of trauma as a justification for his continuing abuse and violence. It was true that she was disturbed, but he had driven her to it. A simple cure for the worst of her disturbance would be a judicial separation with injunctions against harassment.

Alan

It emerged that Alan was very ambivalent about marriage. He admitted that he had serious doubts about the relationship, but was afraid to share these with his fiancée in case she left him. I do not want to pursue his obvious difficulties with unresolved dependency, but to focus on his understanding of his fiancée's behaviour. He defined her as nagging. He was in no doubt that she was 'a nag'. It took very little to get him to appreciate that what he defined as her nagging was in fact an attempt to get him to listen to very deep anxieties about the direction in which the relationship was heading

(Dobash and Dobash, 1980, define nagging as what women do when the man has decided that the conversation is over). She was nearing the limits of childbearing age, and wanted some reassurance about his intentions. He was unable to respond to her because she confronted him with feelings over which he had no control, and made him very anxious. This enraged him. His lack of responsiveness to her insecurities was actually the catalyst for her insistence on discussing them – a response to the abuse which his economy with the truth represented in their relationship. Not to put too fine a point on it, he consistently lied to her so that he could have his cake and eat it too.

In terms of control issues and sexism, he believed, in common with most men, that he had the right to determine what was talked about and when, and in what terms. Most men assume the right to determine the discourse and its frame of reference. It is evident from the Preface that this is something boys and girls learn from their earliest days at home, and it is reinforced by external authority figures including, surprisingly, women schoolteachers. This is not an attempt to single out teachers; it is only too apparent to any growing child that women are represented as objects to be moulded and defined by men.

It soon became clear that Alan felt that his fiancée nagged him almost constantly about everything. What it boiled down to was that he simply could not bear to listen to her concerns about anything, and experienced as nagging her insistence on being treated with respect and equality. For her, this involved having some control over what was talked about and when. Of course he then felt that she was out of control. His response to feeling that he could not control her 'nagging' was to use violence. For a while this had the intended effect. When her anxieties about the relationship exceeded her anxieties about his violence she would raise these issues, and the cycle would begin again. Clearly we could, if we wished, speculate about her wish to be attached to a violent man. This is irrelevant to his behaviour. The important point is that when men define women's behaviour, it is a device to make them invisible. A woman is not a person with real concerns, 'she is a nag and my violence is justified'. She becomes a thing.

Winston

As batterings go, this is a fairly simple case. Winston enjoyed his wife's jealousy. He went out of his way to provoke it. He would make arrangements and not keep to them. He would go out at all hours without telling her where he was going. He insisted to me that he was being faithful and, irrelevant as it is, I believed him. What was important was his enjoyment of her possessiveness and her insecurity, and the power this gave him over her. Obviously, Winston has some fairly serious personality problems which need not concern us here. The point of interest is how he used her symptoms of his emotional abuse of her as a justification for battering her and eventually breaking her leg with the bottle. As with every other man we have worked with, it emerged that the battering was simply the high point of his abuse of Sandra. He had been systematically cruel and emotionally abusive to her for years before he was forced to approach us. He controlled all the major decisions in the relationship. He retained sole access to the bank account despite the fact that she was working too. She did the shopping and the cooking and the cleaning. He hated her thinking that they were a couple because he began to feel that he was trapped, and that she believed she had power over him. It enraged him that a woman thought she had power over him. He felt that her insecurity was a strategy for tying him down. Her jealousy was a sign that she felt she had some proprietorial rights of ownership and control. His violence was a way of re-establishing the rightful pecking order.

One can almost hear the dissenting voices. This is unfair to men? It takes two to provoke an argument? There's always two sides to a story? And the women's is writ large on the casualty admission card! Height? 5ft 4in. Weight? 8st. 5lb. Reason for Admission? I was having a fight with my boyfriend, and he broke my leg. How big is your boyfriend? 6ft 2in. How much does he weigh? 13st. 8lb!

This is not a joke. I have yet to come across a single case where a man does something to a woman which could be called battering as the result of a fight. What men do to women is bully, browbeat, abuse and attack.

This perception is a real challenge to men's way of defining relationships and women's behaviour. It is also a challenge to consensual ways of defining what happens in relationships. Models such as 'mutual projective identifications', in which it is assumed that two people in a relationship behave in ways that will ensure that the other acts out the undesirable or unacceptable parts of themselves, have no place in this way of seeing things. This is not to say that mutual projective identifications do not occur but that they have no place in a man's decision to be violent except as a more sophisticated justification. There is no seamless connection between a projective identification and a clenched fist in a vulnerable face, except from the male point of view. I have no doubt that male violence is an attempt to control women. It is clear from my work with violent and abusive men, however, that they use massive projections in their abusive behaviour: they project all their own sadistic impulses into the woman. This enables them to see the woman as threatening and persecuting – in short, sadistic – and their own violence as a response to her attacks. Apart from the real benefits the man's abusiveness brings in the form of servicing, unchallenged authority, and control, the projection of his own badness also relieves him of the necessity of facing his guilt for his destructiveness. Unfortunately, this is a process which will forever prevent his emotional growth, as well as driving his partner crazy.

Before continuing this discussion, I want to introduce a man who was a patient of mine in long-term psychotherapy, because I learned a great deal from him about the underlying dynamics of abusive behaviour in general, although he was not at the time – and never had been – a physical abuser. I also believe we can learn a great deal from him about why it is so difficult for men and women to find stable relationships today – that his story embodies many of the difficulties which lead to the breakdown of relationships and provide the subjective motive for violent abuse.

Christopher

When we first met, Christopher was thirty-five, and a successful author. He presented with multiple problems. He was unable to sustain a relationship with a woman. He became anxious, depressed and emotionally withdrawn in a relationship, and described himself as terrified of women he had lived with. He also had substantial problems with work, and was prone to attacks of severe depression when asked to commit himself to projects. He had difficulty in finishing things. He came to me after his third long-term (five-year) relationship had broken down. What follows is actually an interim report: he is still in therapy after many years.

Christopher is the middle child of three children. His father was very abusive to his mother, and Christopher witnessed this on many occasions. He was also brutally beaten by his father. One incident to which he frequently referred was one in which he was beaten by his father for not fighting another boy at school because he was afraid. He was also beaten for crying when he was being beaten. He had felt extremely sorry for his mother, who had frequently used him as an outlet for her distress at her husband's brutality. She told Christopher how much she hated her husband and wanted to kill him. She had actually tried to leave him on many occasions, but was unable to find any financial support or alternative housing, and was forced to return. Christopher remembered that he decided his main aim in life was to make his mother happy and never, as she instructed him many times, 'to be like his father'. He also decided that he could not be happy so long as his mother was unhappy. In spite of these memories he also remembered that until about the age of four or five he had loved his father very much, and was proud of his strength and masculinity. His father frequently boasted of his fights with other men, his strength, and his masculine prowess with women.

Christopher had remained faithful to his promises. He had not become like his father in what he defined as the important respect, violence, and as his mother is still alive and unhappy, he was unable to be happy. Also, true to his promise, he duly transferred on to all his female partners the desire to make them happy above all else. This consisted mainly of doing his utmost to give them what they wanted, and never saying no. He was completely incapable of setting boundaries with women unless he behaved in a rigid, cold, heartless and cruel way – actually just like his father whenever his mother had the courage to make any of her needs known to him.

He usually acted like this when he was overwhelmed by his partner's needs and felt that he would be destroyed by her (this, of course, involved massive projection of his own unacknowledged neediness) and that he simply could not do enough to make her happy, as these latest demands demonstrated. Naturally, when he did this he suffered enormous guilt and would attempt compulsively to repair the damage this behaviour caused. He would become transparent to his partner, effectively experiencing himself as nonexistent, so that he had no needs of his own and was entirely devoted to giving her what she wanted. Not unnaturally, he accumulated massive resentment about both the guilt and the compulsive giving, which he experienced as depleting. In spite of himself he unconsciously experienced any of a woman's needs, or especially demands, as indicating her unhappiness, and he felt guilty that all his efforts to make his mother happy had clearly failed. Again he also felt resentful that he had, as he put it 'broken his balls' to make her happy, and nothing was good enough.

It became clear to him – and, fortunately, caused us both to laugh when he expressed it – that 'a happy woman is one who has no needs and makes no demands'. I commented that such a woman sounded like a dead one. In fact he actually could not tolerate being in an intimate relationship with a woman. It emerged that simply being in her presence was sufficient to evoke his rage, guilt and defensive compulsiveness. He was than able to begin unravelling his rage with his mother for demanding so much of him as a child that he become transparent and devoted his life to making her happy (which in any case was impossible by this time – her husband had so damaged her that martyrdom was her only option), and also with his father for not protecting him from the demands she made on him. It also provided one key to the overwhelming – at times suicidal – guilt which dominated his relationships. His depressions began to be less serious as he unravelled this complex of feelings and saw how every time his partner had a want or need, he actually wanted to kill her.

Obviously Christopher is much more complex than this simple account can convey. I believe, however, that even so, one can divine some of the difficulties men experience in relationships with women, which lead them to feel abusive. I actually believe that he represents a distinct subtype of the men I work with: I think of this as the helpful abuser. At the other extreme is what I think of as the oedipal abuser, who is much more like Christopher's father and, from what I can gather, his grandfather. (I do not want to imply that this case represents an explanation for abusive behaviour. I am completely convinced that the cycle of abuse is not a necessary or a sufficient condition. Christopher himself is an example of an exception to this theory.) I have no doubt that, like Christopher, his father felt like a victim of his mother, particularly of her secondary, symptomatic martyrdom. From Christopher's description of him, however, it sounds as though he was much more into the stereoypical oedipal resolution of masculinity, which involves overt control and domination, contempt for women, and ill-disguised pleasure in sadism. This is very different from Christopher's covert and quite omnipotent control of his partner, and his identification with the mother he wanted for himself.

What generalizations can we make from this information about Christopher?

The first is that he embodies many of the feelings of the abusive men I work with – whether helpful, oedipal or any other kind: in particular, that women just go on making demands, and will not be satisfied with what they are being given. Also, that many of these men feel quite destructive, often homicidal rage towards their partners when demands are made, and equally suicidal guilt about the rage. They also feel that their own needs are not being met. This was certainly true of Christopher because his only real need in a relationship was, as he put it, 'to be left alone'. In the circumstances, this was all he could want of his mother, as she was incapable of giving him the nurturing he needed, and the relationship was perverse in that he was her support. He was not aware of wanting anything else from a relationship with a woman, except that she should be happy which, in any case, meant 'Leave me alone'. Actually, this desire to be 'left alone' is so frequently articulated by abusive men that it is something of a joke in our programmes. It is apparent that what they find intolerable is to have demands made on them. What many men really want is to treat women like objects or utilities, to be taken out of the cupboard when required for sex or food, or comfort, and put back after use. Despite his initial denial, this was also true of Christopher, who got quite a lot from his relationships which he did not value or actively spoiled afterwards – again, a common complaint of women about the men they live with, who accuse them of always putting their own needs first.

There is something of Christopher in all the abusers with whom I have worked: that they seem unable to take anything from women except the basic provision of physical servicing. Although I have made clear my conviction that abusers do not suffer from any form of psychopathology, the men with whom I work labour under extreme difficulties in forming intimate relationships, or feeling close to anyone. This common observation has led many researchers and clinicians to conclude that abusers are suffering from a form of personality disorder, a condition which is often characterized by this limitation. This notion has had such an important influence on work with abusers, as well as the popular imagination, that it is worth spending a little time examining it.

PERSONALITY DISORDER

Personality disorder is a complex diagnosis. As Bolton and Bolton observe (1988):

> The diagnosis . . . has always been problematic. Many personality disordered persons have no major complaint about themselves. The usual reason for seeking clinical attention is the effect that their behaviour has had on others. As a result, some fear this label is more a judgement than a diagnosis . . . ' (pp. 63 f.)

They define ten different diagnoses of personality disorder. In reading these, one is reminded of the search for a rapist personality in which almost every rapist ends up inhabiting his own diagnostic category.

The descriptions of personality disorder cover almost every type of difficulty experienced by abusers and, as the Boltons observe, their range goes some way towards explaining why:

> family violence practitioners struggle to describe why so many perpetrators were not crazy, but were also not normal. The anger, unhappiness and rigidity that are part of these disorders are a frequent presence in clinical reports on the adults in a violent family. (p. 73)

My own experience of violent male abusers supports this assertion – in particular abusers' rigidity must be not only described but explained: I will do this shortly. However, most – indeed the vast majority – of my clients do not act out in any situation except in the home on their female partners and children. This is the singular failure of any attempt to account for male abusiveness in pathological terms: it does not account for the fact of the exclusive choice of the female as victim. There is little doubt in my mind that this is the major source of the motivation for producing a victim syndrome, usually derived from the concept of female masochism, which has generated such anger from women's groups. I would add that I work with many men who are not violent abusers, and they often exhibit the violent abusers' anger, unhappiness and rigidity. They also voice many of the same complaints about relationships with women.

There are much stronger grounds for the Boltons' support for affective disorder as a major contributory factor in male violence and abuse. Many of the men I work with seem to be depressed and, in fact, to have a history of depression. In the majority, however, this is in evidence only in their relationship with their victims, leading me to believe that it might be symptomatic rather than causative of their abusiveness. Not surprisingly, the majority of their female victims suffer from depression – or 'learned helplessness' (Walker, 1978, 1979) – as a result of the experience that their life is totally controlled by their abuser. In so far as affective disorder is concerned, we are still left with the problem inherent in any pathological explanation: accounting for why it is almost invariably women who are the victims.

Rigidity

The best way I can describe the way this manifests itself in abusive men is in the frequency with which they get into a position with their partners where they say 'I don't care', but usually express it more primitively. In this frame of mind they are able to be as cold, cruel and hard as they wish, with no thought or anxiety about the consequences. It allows them to behave in a remorseless way towards someone whom in other circumstances they will say they love. 'I don't care' is generally thought of as the sociopathic position. In my experience it represents the last defence of the person who cares too much, and simply cannot tolerate the pain and anxiety of doing so. Most abusive men cannot tolerate being in a state of need, particularly need of women. Not surprisingly, they often have to cope with severe envy, which is also intolerable to them and against which they institute all manner of defences: spoiling (sour grapes), contempt, arrogance, scorn, boasting, self-sufficiency and, lastly, rigidity in their use.

This amounts to a complete refusal to acknowledge any vulnerability whatsoever. Anything can be included in the definition of vulnerability – guilt, culpability, compromise, uncertainty, sadness, fear. It also includes the absolute refusal to acknowledge the existence of the other person as an independent, thinking, feeling entity. Definitions of their own and others' behaviour are not open to question or debate. The truth is known, reality is clear, guilt is located (in you!), reasonableness and rationality are obvious. Thoughts are repetitive and circular. Speech is accusative and interrogative, telling but never asking, except to trap. The rigidity is also physical. Muscles are hard, gestures are stiff and threatening, backs are straight, fingers point, hands chop, necks are stiff, tones are tight, harsh and clipped, teeth and jaws are clenched, eyes stare. All in all, the man feels pretty powerful at this time. This feeling increases as he sees his victim's fear. One important source of this rigidity is that the man is often aware that he wants to attack his partner physically and is struggling at the same time with the desire to do so. The problem is that his desire to punish her and his fear of being dominated and damaged are too strong to enable him to stop before acting out.

Confronting the rigidity of abusers is crucial. Often, as with much of their behaviour, they are surprised when they first become aware of it – the first step to loosening it. It is an ever-present feature of abuse, and fortunately it is acted out in the immediacy of their contact with us, unlike their violence. This provides many opportunities for constructive intervention. A distinct change of behaviour is noticeable, with the loosening in rigidity which marks a watershed in treatment. The desire to punish, to inflict suffering, is the key issue to be addressed in achieving this.

Remorse and Guilt

The key to reaching this watershed is genuine remorse for the suffering inflicted, both intentionally and unintentionally, actually and in fantasy, on his victim and passive participants such as children. Men often confront me with the charge that all we do is try to make men feel guilty, and this is self-defeating. If that were true, it would indeed be almost pointless. I say almost because I am not convinced that guilt is an entirely negative emotion. The social contract is based on guilt. As I explained in earlier chapters, guilt is the foundation stone of remorse, and I do not believe that men will cease to abuse unless they can be helped to experience genuine remorse.

It is important to distinguish between genuine remorse and phoney guilt and remorse, which is an attempt to negotiate a non-deviant identity as someone who is capable of feeling guilt, and is therefore not character or personality disordered. It is also a defence against real guilt, which many abusers suppress and which exercises its power unconsciously – it is the source, I believe, of the rapidity with which batterers escalate from a perception of threat to the experience of crisis, rigidity and abuse. During the 'hearts and flowers' stage immediately after an attack, many abusers will apologize and promise never to abuse again. This promise may be experienced as sincere at the moment it is given, but it is actually an attempt to revise history, and does not lead to change. Genuine guilt and remorse are based on a real appreciation and empathy with the victim's suffering, and a desire to preserve the good object. It does not fade with the victim's acceptance of the apology and the promise, but is sustained and worked through. Even if abusers were not abusing, the unconscious source of guilt would still be active in the sadistic attacks inflicted on the internalized primary object.

It is fair to ask whether pro-feminism is not simply replacing one form of chauvinism, the male, with another, the female. When it comes to defining women's reality, the answer cannot be other than yes – and perhaps not a moment too soon. The point is that there is no such thing as a value-neutral position on such a vitally important issue. As I said above, all models imply that responsibility can be apportioned in some way. For example, the masochistic woman is simply a later version of the seductive (and therefore abusable) little girl. It is only to be expected that we men will wriggle and squirm and cry 'foul' at female chauvinism. This is particularly to be expected from men in positions of social power and authority in institutions other than marriage where their power derives solely from their gender.

Not that the cry of 'foul' emanates only from powerful men. A constantly surprising fact is the number of women who are vocally opposed to feminist thinking. One often wonders if it is possible for a woman to be sexist. It seems that women often take up what would certainly be seen as sexist positions and attitudes if they were espoused by a man. It is not unusual, however, for victims of oppression to identify with the aggressor, particularly if doing so bestows privileges otherwise denied. Any oppression of women by women which results from this identification is dynamically and politically distinct from the primary oppression to which they and their victims are subjected.

Those in the caring professions who so vociferously assert that feminist thinking is biased and unscientific do so from the position that there is a kind of thinking which is not. The thinking they usually have in mind is male thinking (Chesler, 1972; Strouse, 1974).

I Do It Because She's Crazy

You may have noticed that the idea of the woman's badness or craziness occurs in the case histories I have presented. There is little or no doubt that when a man batters or emotionally abuses a woman, he is in the grip of a belief system about her which defines her as crazy. The particular sort of craziness may vary from man to man, and the behaviour he uses to justify this assessment will differ also. What all abusive men have in common is the belief in female craziness and mental incompetence. Popular culture and stereotypes of women reinforce and further these perceptions. It is well known that women are illogical, cannot string two consistent thoughts together, are generally incompetent, irresponsible, unreliable and altogether not to be trusted. In brief, they suffer from a generalized mental handicap which is nothing short of total disability. I am in no doubt that as a man's perceptions of his partner's craziness escalate – the more witchlike she becomes – so does the severity of his violence. Of course, this perception is entirely delusional, and as he articulates his perceptions of her (fucking whore, bitch, slut, cunt, etc.) in emotional abuse and she denies his accusations, she seems more and more to be what he is describing. The man perceives her as crazy purely as a result of his projections on to her; this perception is correlated with the degree of her determination to act as an independent person outside his control and, primarily, with the intensity of his determination to prevent her. Not that her denial of his accusations is essential. Even if she acknowledges that she is a very bad person and is sorry for treating him so badly, she will be attacked in any case.

In other words, her craziness is that she does not do as he wants when he wants it in the way that he wants. He does not question this perception because he knows that at some level it is socially syntonic, and that in any case he has a right to determine and control everything she says and does. She is as crazy as the intensity of his rage with her. Precisely what determines the level of his rage is open to question. It is probably a function of many different factors, including: his perceptions of the strength of her determination to be independent of him; his fear of the consequences if he fails to get her back under control; his perception – unconscious or otherwise – of the severity of the failure of his primary caretaker, and the intensity of his feeling that she is a destructive witch who wishes him dead, and the unresolved sadistic impulses with which this has left him.

Of course, one of the fundamental anxieties with which abusive men struggle concerns survival. The original failure and its consequent sadistic impulses are indelibly associated with pain and vulnerability. Helplessness and vulnerability in men are inextricably linked with sadistic impulses. The primary vulnerability is, of course, death or, more probably, fear of annihilation. As we have seen, the separated and abandoning object, who is completely beyond one's control, is experienced as being full of destructive wishes towards one – hence the intensity of the pain and dread of abandonment. This is evoked by every attempt – or perception by a man of an attempt – by his partner to free herself from his control. His perceptions may be entirely irrational to an impartial observer. His behaviour, however, is not; his abusiveness and violence are goal directed behaviours dedicated to re-establishing his control and her fear of independence.

MEN'S SUFFERING

Some programmes for abusive men recognize this link between vulnerability and violence. However, they take it to an illogical extreme. Because these men feel like victims, they aim to put them in touch with their fear and pain, and with the life-threatening anxieties they experience before inflicting a battering. This approach is fundamentally flawed: it presents the man as a victim. Now, it is true, of course, that he is a victim: we are all victims. We are all lonely, sad and unhappy to differing degrees. It goes with the territory.

The flaw has a number of sources. The first is in the assumption that the man is the woman's victim, whether in the present or in the distant past of his childhood: the assumption that the threat is – or was – a real and external one (as Alice Miller, for example, maintains). It should be clear by now that I do not believe this is true in most cases. Even where it is based on actual maltreatment by the mother, I would maintain that this in itself derives from the construction of femininity and mothering in accord with men's needs and against women's best interests (Jukes, 1991). None the less, it seems to me that even if we were to broaden the definition of child abuse – and one could undoubtedly make a case for this (as Alice Miller does) – the threat I am referring to here is an internal one stemming from the infant's reactions to experienced deprivation and frustration.

I sometimes find myself in a similar position to Freud in his dilemma about the reality of female child sexual abuse. The number of men with whom I work who report memories of violent abuse by their fathers, even though they are not a majority, is quite alarming. In many cases this is, without doubt, a real memory. In the majority it is not verifiable. In my opinion these men probably experienced violence from their fathers, although on nowhere near the scale remembered, and the memory is strengthened by the boy's projected aggression. In addition, the fear of the father is reinforced by the awareness of his violent potential, which prevents the boy from being close to him and from appreciating his loving and caring qualities. I believe the boy actually cuts himself off from his father. The real threat is to the integrity of his internal world and his internal objects from his own destructive, cannibalistic and sadistic impulses. It is also a threat to his external world in that he may lose a servile, submissive and unprotesting slave with whom he can have his own way. In my work with abusers, it is this latter threat and the expectations which underpin it which we attempt to destructure.

The second source is in the nature of the emphasis on the man's suffering as the cause of his violence. We all suffer. Passively or actively, we all abuse women. We all oppress women. We are violent not because we hurt but because being hurt has become perverted into a desire to inflict pain. No matter how this is interpreted or justified with sophisticated psychological theories – Freud (1905) explained it very well – this is the basic fact. Emphasizing a man's suffering before he takes responsibility for his violence and his sadism may even profoundly reinforce his capacity for denying and justifying his violence, and seeing women as persecuting evil witches who have to be controlled or, failing that, destroyed. Contacting and staying with the hurt may be all well and good, even essential, at a later stage in the process, but only after the need for revenge and gratification of the sadistic impulses has been worked through at a cognitive and behavioural level, and after the man has given up his sexist expectations. Unexpressed sadism will always interfere with or stop the expression of love and concern. In any case, the hurt and sadness, apart from being results of the abandonment which he interprets from his victim's failure to give him what he wants (the failure to live up to his expectations), is very probably expressive of his unconscious grief and guilt about his badness. The hurt may be the result of the pain he is causing rather than the pain caused to him.

PSYCHOLOGY AND CULTURE IN MALE VIOLENCE

At a number of points in this book I have felt a need to apologize. This is one such point. It concerns an issue which has been raised before: the assertion by some feminists that men are controlling and abusive of women because they have been educated to believe that women are there to service them and meet their needs, and that they are entitled to do anything necessary to ensure this: the 'I want what I want when I want it' syndrome. Without doubt, this is true, just as it is true – and the evidence supports this – that even men who are not actually, actively abusive benefit from institutionalized male dominance and power. My need to apologize is related to the assertion that this is more than simply the result of education and culturation. It seems obvious that in order for men to behave in this way, and to have developed a culture which allows, condones and even encourages it, there must be some psychological origins of the wish to do so. Socialist feminists cannot be right in their assertion that it originated in culture itself. This reifies the concept of culture. It provides culture with a mind and motivations independent of those individuals and groups which contribute to it. Actually, it takes little thought to conclude that the 'I want what I want when I want it' mentality is a failure of individual male development on a worldwide scale which has become a foundation stone of culture and the institutionalized oppression of women.

This book asserts that misogyny is universal, and that it has its roots in male sadism. Experience shows that it is possible to mitigate and even eradicate an individual's sadism and misogyny through intensive analytic or therapeutic work, but this is clearly impossible on any large scale because the resolution of such sadism is an arduous, expensive and time-consuming task even in favourable cases. Programmes which attempt to deal with it in any other way (such as the one I work in) have set themselves a mammoth undertaking: to stop the violent and abusive behaviour which derives from this sadism; to do so against the background knowledge that it may take many years of individual attention to achieve this in psychotherapy; to achieve this goal in a time-limited context which does not pretend to touch these deeper levels of functioning but focuses instead on the cognitive aspects, the learned and conscious expectations, attitudes, thoughts, feelings and beliefs about men and women which accompany a batterer's behaviour.

Such work with violent men demonstrates what many feminists have been saying for many years: that male violence does not exist in a vacuum. The isolated physical attacks - for they are often isolated - (some men may be physically violent only once in every two years; some only once in the course of a long marriage) - cannot be divorced from their context. This context is invariably one where abusiveness is ongoing, multifaceted and relentless. From a pro-feminist perspective, abusive behaviour is any act which makes a woman do something she does not want to do (Adams, 1988, p. 191). The physical attacks are often more like punctuation marks in an abusive landscape. If they are isolated, they conceal a long history of oppression which takes many forms. In our work we use the idea of a continuum of abuse derived from the work with women who have sought safety in refuges, which I will present later. We actually give this continuum to men during our first contact with them.

Of course it must be said that abusiveness and oppression vary widely in intensity between different men. There may be many reasons for this, but I vividly recall suggesting to a women's refuge worker one psychodynamic hypothesis to the effect that differences in individual men's abusiveness may be correlated with their emotional development and resolution of successive nuclear conflicts connected with orality, anality and genitality. The general tone of this was that intensity and frequency of attacks might be related to the man's stage of emotional fixation, and the extent to which he had failed to resolve his fundamental ambivalence. Her reply was unforgettable.

'Maybe it's much simpler than that. Perhaps', she said, 'they only do as much as they need to get their own way.'

It seems evident that there are enormous individual differences in battering and abusive behaviour. To suggest that it might be worthwhile understanding the source of these differences need in no way detract – or distract us – from our main objective: to stop the violence. Nor does the recognition of individual differences in any way weaken or undermine a feminist political analysis of male violence: that it is an expression of male power and domination of women, founded on sexism. A number of male beliefs are central to sexism; for example:

> they are entitled to nurture from a woman; that women should serve and obey them; that it is their prerogative to chastise their wives; that they are superior to women; and that women's subservience to men is part of the natural order. Men are allowed to control women and are generally permitted to use almost any means short of homicide to do so. These beliefs and practices are components of . . . sexism . . . The family structure in a sexist society reinforces men's control over women. Men are assigned the ultimate authority in the family. Nothing inherent in the male gender renders men the appropriate wielders of power. Rather, this 'legitimate authority' is given to men based on the system of beliefs and values that supports men's control over women – sexism. (Hart, 1988, p. 5)

My argument is explicitly supportive of this feminist analysis of sexism. For the moment, however, let us pursue a line of thought which seems contradictory. It stems from my practical experience of working with men who are extremely abusive towards women, to the point of committing criminal offences such as grievous bodily harm and rape.

I have often observed that the sexism model, although it works well as a paradigm, sometimes has to be stretched beyond credible limits to account for particular incidents of violence, incidents which do not follow disobedience by the victim or in which it is impossible to perceive how she might have frustrated her attacker's expectations. In fact, one discovers in these cases that there is a long-running and strategic frustration which is a continual source of resentment for these men, but they are unable to articulate it ('I don't feel loved, cared for, appreciated by her'). I have met men who acknowledge that they are abusive and struggle against it with a will, but none the less inflict violence on their partners. Seemingly, they do so without providing themselves with any justification: they just want to do it, and don't know why.

In fact, many men acknowledge without difficulty after the event that their justifications are utterly without foundation. I am not simply describing the sort of reframing of violence which occurs with many men during the aftermath of a violent attack – known as the 'hearts and flowers stage' – but men who say they feel no remorse, yet could in no way be diagnosed as psychopathic. It is clear that these attacks and the perceptions on which they are based – 'She's crazy' – are generated entirely internally, and that these men are simply looking for an excuse to be violent. Once one begins to analyse the process of escalation, it is easy to see how the man is preparing the ground for a battering. In order to do this he has to be convinced that he is dealing with a crazy person. This perception of her badness excludes any other qualities she may possess. She becomes an object, and a crazy one at that. The perceptions and the behaviour feed on each other until the man reaches flash point. Escalating non-physical abusiveness evokes behaviour from her which he uses to intensify his perception of her as out of control and bad, which leads to a further escalation of abuse. As far as the man is concerned, the vicious circle can be broken only by violence (Jukes, 1988).

This gets us back to my central thesis: that the crazy, abandoning object is ever present, and is largely a function of the man's own sadistic urges. These urges can be evoked by any frustration in the real world – an argument with the boss, a traffic jam, a car breakdown, imagined slights from others. The fact is that in the encapsulated psychosis formed by the birth of the self, nothing is good enough to replace what has been lost. I do not believe that in attempting to understand the individual dynamics of battering, one is necessarily undermining the pro-feminist analysis of men's power. This echoes Jessica Benjamin's analysis (1990) of feminist objections to any attempt to analyse what she believes is women's complicity in men's abusive behaviour. Like Jane Temperley (1985) she believes that women are complicit. Although there are similarities, however, I do not believe it is the same. I am not arguing that women are complicit. Nor am I arguing – and this is the basis of feminist objections – that male abuse of women is a pathology. I am simply asserting what seems obvious to me: that although men may act in concert as a gender, they also have individual motivations and histories which produce individual differences. Even re-education requires us to understand the way in which new information will be received and processed. In fact, we must address that process and try to make it explicit in our attempts to prevent men from being abusive.

Not unnaturally, many men – the majority? – will vehemently deny that the above description is in any way representative of their perceptions or behaviour towards, and expectations of, women. This includes those who present themselves for help in anti-abuse programmes. You may not find this so strange if you think that disclosed abusers are not representative of men as a whole, that they are qualitatively different from men who do not violently abuse.

I realize that research evidence such as I have presented about the scale of violent abuse seems to support the contention that not all men are abusers and that we are dealing with an aberration, a form of deviant behaviour. Even if 40 percent of men are violent, that is still a minority, albeit a significant one. I believe it is crucial to present persuasive argument that this is not true. It weakens my argument substantially if I cannot demonstrate to the reader that all men are abusive. Clearly, it hinges on what is defined as abusive, and I provide a detailed account of that in the continuum below. The majority of men will respond in the way I have indicated because they insist on the right to define what is and is not abusive behaviour. As I have already argued, this is one of the privileges of masculinity. In work with abusers we use the definition of women who are experts on male abusiveness – survivors of it. If the reader is not convinced of the justice of this, it will be impossible to persuade him or her. Here is a selective catalogue of what survivors define as the continuum of abusive male behaviour. The reader can judge for him- or herself.

Physical abuse

Slap, punch, grab, kick, choke, push, restrain, pull hair, pinch, bite, rape, use force, threats or coercion to obtain sex or indulge in sexual practices which she does not want.

Use of weapons, throwing things, keeping weapons around which frighten her.

Abuse of furniture, pets, destroying her possessions, tearing or spoiling her clothing.

Intimidation – standing in the doorway during arguments, angry or threatening gestures, use of your size to intimidate, standing over her, driving recklessly, uninvited touching, covering her mouth to stop her talking.

Threats of violence, verbal or non-verbal, direct or indirect, self-inflicted injury – for example, hitting your head on walls or threatening suicide.

Harassment – for example, uninvited visits or calls, following her, checking up on her, not leaving when asked.

Psychological and emotional abuse

Isolation, preventing or making it hard for her to see or talk to friends, relatives and others. Making derogatory comments about her friends.

Yelling, swearing, being coarse, raising your voice, using angry expressions or gestures, embarrassing her.

Criticism, namecalling, swearing, mocking, putdowns, ridicule, accusations, blaming, humiliating. Angrily waking her up from sleep.

Pressure tactics – pushing her to make decisions or hurry up, walking in front of her, using guilt, sulking, threats of withholding financial support, manipulating the children.

Interrupting, changing the subject, not listening or responding, picking up the newspaper when she wants to talk, twisting her words, topic-stringing.

Economic harassment – getting angry with her about 'where the money goes', not allowing access to money, the car or other resources, sabotaging her attempts to work, believing you are the provider and thinking that she could not survive without you, saying that the money you earn is yours.

Claiming the truth, being the authority. Claiming the right to define what is logical, rational, reasonable or fair in the relationship. Calling her stupid or otherwise defining her behaviour as illogical, unreasonable, irrational, etc. Logic-chopping, lying, withholding information about your activities, infidelity.

Using pornography, including home videos, against her wishes.

Not helping with childcare or housework, saying that you have already done a day's work. Not keeping to agreements. Abusing your power over the children, either emotionally or physically.

Feeling stressed and tense, and using this to get into a frame of mind where you blame her for everything which goes wrong: things you can't find, mess, etc. This is usually a prelude to a violent attack.

Emotional withholding - not expressing your feelings or giving support, thinking your problems are more important than hers, not giving attention or compliments, not respecting her feelings, rights or opinions. Not initiating conversation about the relationship, but expecting that your partner will do it all. Sulking.

Not taking care of yourself and refusing to learn basic life skills, cooking, etc. Abusing drugs, alcohol, not eating properly, not making friends and seeking help and support from them. Believing you have the right to define appropriate wifely and motherly behaviour, and not offering your expectations to negotiation. Criticizing her motherly qualities or performance. Accusing her of neglecting the children or using threats of taking them away, etc.

Telling her that if she doesn't like it she knows what she can do - pack, leave, etc. Not acknowledging that the relationship is important to you, telling her that you don't need her or love her, etc.

This checklist is not exhaustive.* Men will often be able to identify other forms of abuse which are peculiar to them.

Might I just add that although it is unlikely that any man cannot identify at least one of these behaviours which he has not inflicted

* This checklist is freely adapted from the one in use at the Emerge counselling programme in Boston, Mass. with the permission of its author David Adams.

on his partner, whether past or present, it is important that he understands how this checklist can be used to diagnose how abusive he is and why he acts in particular ways. Invariably any man can identify many forms of behaviour on this list which he uses frequently, whether or not he also resorts to physical abuse. Each of our clients is given this list. To begin with we ask him to go through it during the assessment interview so that we can determine the scale of his abuse. A supplementary issue is how frequently he uses each type of behaviour. This information forms the basis of his contract with the Centre and the group to which he is assigned.

We begin by asking him to keep a diary of his contact with his victim/partner. This is an important task, because it is a way for him to become familiar with what constitutes abusive and controlling behaviour. Every day he is expected to go through the list and review his contact with her to determine whether he has acted in a controlling or abusive fashion. Many men say that it is a waste of time because they are abusive very infrequently. We usually counter this by reminding them that they have a long history of abusiveness, as do all our clients, and that if there is nothing for that particular day, they should think about the past. This, however, is usually unnecessary once we include in the daily diary-keeping those occasions when a client has wanted to act abusively but refrained.

If he has difficulty in recognizing that he has acted abusively, we ask him to begin making a list of every time he feels resentful or angry with his partner, whether or not he is aware of expressing it. Surprisingly, this is very difficult for most men to do, and they usually begin by asserting that they never feel resentful. I am not suggesting that all resentment or anger is evidence of abusive impulses, although this is usually true of abusers. It is also true that physical abusers are unaware of alternative ways of dealing with these feelings besides acting them out. Reality-checking them and testing them is one of the real values of a group. This information also helps us to begin modifying the man's expectations of his partner, and helping him to assess them more realistically. The micropsychological process which leads to abusive attacks begins with accumulated and suppressed resentment about a woman not doing what the man expects and wants her to do.

THE CONTINUUM OF MALE POWER

At every level of society men are in positions of privilege and power over women independently of class, race, colour, occupational status, income, size, intelligence or any other criterion. It is not necessary for a man to exercise this power by being abusive or violent towards women. As we saw in Chapter 7, women are schooled in how to relate to male power from the moment of birth. They know that being successful with a man – and hence as a woman – entails learning 'appropriate' submissiveness and the capacity to 'reflect them at twice their natural size' (Spender and Kline, 1988). All men benefit from sexism, whether or not they are actively abusive. Even those whose abusiveness gets no further than the automatic belief in sexism, which is a necessary condition of masculinity, benefit directly from other men's violence:

> The existence of . . . rape and battering . . . against women means that all women must restrict their lives (what they wear, what they say, where they walk or work). This means that regardless of whether all men rape or batter, all men economically and socially benefit from these acts since they give us greater access to jobs, positions of influence and mobility. Rape and battering also create the need for male protection from 'bad' men . . . they serve to keep the entire population of women in line. (Adams, 1982, p. 2)

The reader will appreciate that this is an expression of the beliefs of those who subscribe to a fairly revolutionary or apocalyptic version of the origins of men's dominance. It is virtually identical to Dworkin's (1981) belief about the function of rape in maintaining their dominance. Interestingly, David Adams, who is one of the best-known and most successful workers with abusive men, explicitly expounds a constructionist position (1988). This illustrates the difficulty, which I share, of not slipping into essentialist thinking even when one clearly believes in the social construction of gender.

Any man reading this who questions whether women are so oppressed may try a simple experiment. Start paying attention to all the ways in which women are put down or men put women down, either implicitly or explicitly. Look at the sex-role stereotyping in newspapers and magazines, or on television, whether in advertisements or soap operas. Listen to all those little jokes about women which imply their incompetence and men's superiority. The first thing you will discover is that this is a full-time occupation – they come so fast and often that there is hardly time to register them. Sexism, the assumption of male superiority over women, is endemic. The interesting part of this experiment is when you attempt to attack this pervasive sexism. Try some gentle confrontation with friends. Question their control of the family's only car, or the fact that only they can decide to spend money without consultation, or who decides what to watch on TV, who makes the tea, quietens the children, has a room of their own, decides where to spend the family holiday, and so on. You will soon discover that you have few friends left. At best, you will be accused of being humourless or boring. At worst, you will be threatened. Your confrontation will generate enormous hostility. Your membership of the male club depends on accepting male power over women – which, according to club rules, is your 'natural' male birthright – and its corollary, the assumption of female inferiority. If you decide to attempt to relinquish that power – it is almost impossible actually to relinquish it – you will have to make new friends.

This brings us back to a crucial element of male violence mentioned earlier: it occurs in a context. It is not a series of isolated acts, whether on the street, in the random rape of strangers, or in the home against a partner. This context is sexism, and it permeates all levels of society, whether institutional or personal. As Brownmiller expressed it: 'all men keep all women in a state of fear'(1976, p. 15).

Many feminist academics (for example, Kelly, 1988a) have begun to revise the traditional views of male violence – that it is aberrant or deviant – by placing it in a context defined by the concept of a continuum of controls used by men over women, of which violence is the most extreme. The concept of a continuum has been used to connect rape to heterosexual sex, and it is worth digressing to examine this issue in some detail. Although it is a contentious notion, it is beginning to gain ground as feminists increasingly question the 'natural' origins of heterosexuality. If heterosexuality is imposed by men on women – as is being increasingly argued, particularly by lesbian separatists – then it becomes easy to link 'normal' heterosexual sex with violent rape (Gilbert and Webster, 1982; Jeffreys, 1990; Williams and Holmes, 1981). Kelly (1988a) has gone furthest in operationalizing the concept. However, she resists creating a hierarchy of abuse because it is impossible to make judgements about what is more serious (p. 49). She illustrates this with McNeill's findings, published in the same collection, that what women fear most when they are 'flashed' at (when a man exposes his penis) is death.

The concept of a continuum generates controversy among feminists. In fact, according to Lynne Segal it was the connection of 'normal' sexuality with rape and violence which:

> produced that final and fundamental rift between feminists at the end of the 1970s and which shattered any potential unity about the nature, direction and goal of feminism. Opposing attitudes to heterosexuality and to the significance of male violence blew apart the women's movement of the seventies. (1987, p. 65)

It was this identification of sexuality as the primary social sphere of male power which, according to Segal, gave the revolutionary, cultural feminists a focus around which to rebuild a sense of sisterhood, by enabling the identification of a single, concrete enemy, 'HIM, over there!'(p. 66) and the 'identification of all women as victims of all men'(p. 70). She thinks this was disastrous for feminism, and for heterosexual, socialist feminism in particular.

However, revolutionary, apocalyptic feminism gained the ascendant in the 1980s. Sheila Jeffreys (1990, p. 289 ff.), for example, questions why some feminists, especially socialist feminists like Segal, are so resistant to politicizing heterosexuality. She concludes that the liberal view, which urges combating the ways in which free expression of sexual preference is restricted, is actually a covert attempt to remove any threat to the system of heterosexuality, which she has no doubt, is the basic institution of oppression:

> From heterosexuality flow all other forms of oppression. Heterosexuality is the cornerstone on which men have grounded the norm, located the source and the standard for defining all relationships . . . the concept of difference . . . rests on a value system

> where one is superior and the other inferior, one dominant, one dominated. (p. 297)

Strong stuff, but in my opinion irrefutable. The question remains: what do we do about it? I will come back to this in my Conclusions.

To return to where we began: the notion of a continuum of male violence and abuse which connects rape with heterosexual sex. I reproduce one such continuum produced by David Adams and Barbara Hart of the Emerge Men's Violence Counselling Project in Boston, USA. Although this does not explicitly mention heterosexuality, it is an unavoidable conclusion from the inclusion of sex roles – the operational expression of heterosexuality.

Violence

- Rape
- Battering
- Sexual Harassment
- Homicide
- Pornography

Subliminal cues to

Covert controls

- Anger
- Emotional Withholding
- Conversational Politics
- Body Space and Politics
- Sex Roles
- Pornography

Are reinforced by

Institutional controls

- Male Monopoly of Policy-Making Institutions
  Business – Government
- Male Control of Reality-Defining Institutions
  History – Science – Art
  Religion – Psychology – Medicine

It is obvious at first glance that this continuum is decidedly pro-feminist. All forms of male violence towards women are very firmly placed in the context of universal sexism and men's power over women. Obviously one could extend this list as one wants, particularly to account for culturally specific forms of oppression and violence such as clitoridectomy in the Middle East, foot-binding in China, scarification in certain African tribes or bride-burning in India. As I said above, models such as this are not only invaluable in working with violent men, they are also indispensable in female consciousness-raising. But such a continuum gives no indication as to why men want to be this way; why they (we) want to control women.

We have seen that the radical socialist feminist understanding of the causes of sexism, the universal oppression of women, lays the blame firmly on cultural reproduction and transmission. For them it is a highly complex and variable phenomenon, expressed and maintained in a complex interweaving of material, cultural, economic, psychological and historical conditions. For socialists it is the study of changes or cracks in the structure of male dominance which offers grounds for optimism that things may be altered by political activism. They do not maintain that it will be easy, even though the idea that sexuality is taught and sustained in observable ways renders it at least amenable to a change which would be impossible if it were simply obeying a biological imperative.

Even socialist optimism, however, seems to be difficult to maintain – and not just because the tide in feminist thinking is running against it. As I said above, even Lynne Segal seems at times to express doubts about whether her optimism is misplaced in the face of the transhistorical dominance of men. Unfortunately, many feminists, working from such continuums and with the notion of socially constructed gender, discovered that raising consciousness, although indispensable, simply did not produce the liberation it promised because it did not restructure heterosexual desire. As a result, many turned to psychoanalysis in an attempt to unearth the unconscious content of femininity and the nature of desire. This book is not primarily concerned with the female unconscious, but as we saw in Chapter 7, it is seen from within psychoanalysis as being structured by the Oedipus complex, which enshrines men in positions of authority and dominance and women in the complementary space. This continuum gives no indication as to why men want to be this way – why they (we) want to control women. I hope my argument goes some way towards rectifying this elision.

INTERVENING TO STOP THE VIOLENCE

It seems apposite to say a little about the pro-feminist perspective on the treatment and re-education of men who are sexually and physically violent towards women. Of course any model of intervention implies where the responsibility for the violence should be located – in the couple (systems theory or family therapy), the woman or the man (pro-feminism, psychoanalysis or therapy) or extra-personal factors (stress, diet, modern living, etc.). It is not impossible to adopt a pro-feminist position in relation to battering, and to recognize simultaneously that there may be psychodynamic processes in men which, while accessible to feminist psychoanalysis, are not accessible to feminist political analysis. The difficulty is to develop an integrated social psychology which does not minimize men's responsibility for their behaviour (It's because of the way they were treated as children; They're insecure, etc.) or blame their mothers, or present battering as a sickness and not a psychosocial, political and criminal problem which requires wide-ranging social policy strategies involving government intervention.

I cannot go into great detail about treatment or re-education of violent men; this would require a separate volume. However, I would like to say something about the broad guidelines which we adopt in work with them.

Conflict Phobia

One of the most interesting facts about men who batter – or, indeed, are exclusively emotionally or verbally abusive – is that, without exception, they are conflict-phobic in their relationships. This may seem rather bizarre. Actually, it is quite consistent with their abusiveness. Violence and abuse are techniques men use in order to avoid facing the uncomfortable reality that their partner is a separate person with needs and thoughts and feelings of her own. In my work a great deal of time is spent teaching men to deal with conflict. Inevitably, this is more difficult than it sounds.

Denial

The primary aim of these men is to deny that any conflict exists, for all the reasons detailed in this book. Denial is the main way of doing this. Once they learn that their partner is a separate person – no easy matter – and can live with this knowledge, we attempt to teach them rudimentary interactive skills, such as listening and asking questions, in order to allow their partner her own existence and to enable them to elicit and understand the nature of her separateness. The ability to tolerate differences is hugely lacking in abusive men, and to some extent in all men. Difference is usually interpreted in terms of right – me – and wrong – her. We use a four-stage model of denial in work with abusers. Each man's progress through the programme is based on breaking down his denial at each level. Briefly, these levels of denial are:

1 Total denial

This is the 'I am not violent' position. I have worked with men who say that they woke up and their partners were covered with bruises, and they did not remember causing them. This is usually associated with alchohol abuse. It is difficult to differentiate total denial from mendacity, and research on this is urgently needed.

2 Denial of responsibility

Here the man acknowledges that he is violent, but uses some form of excuse to shift responsibility for it to someone or something else. It covers the 'vocabulary of motive' discussed above, which is about negotiating an acceptable identity. The most common is that he was drunk: It's not me, it's the alchohol (why don't drunken women attack men?). The other is justification or provocation – this is the

'She's crazy' position, and his violence is negotiable: 'If she changed, I would stop being violent'. We make it clear that nothing his partner does justifies his violence. We take a determined moral stand and inquire, for example, how he would feel if he was hit every time he disagreed with her. Loss of control is also quite a common excuse, but as I pointed out above this is the only situation where his control of his rage is faulty. He will often talk about how his boss provokes rage in him, but he never hits his boss. Naturally, a firm moral stand is not enough in itself. He must discover the need to control his partner which his violence expresses, and examine the origins of this need. Insecurity, low self-esteem and an unhappy childhood are also given as excuses; these are all variations on the theme of sickness.

3 Denial of frequency, intensity and severity (minimization)

The man acknowledges that he is violent and that he is responsible for his violence, but lies about its full extent. This is an attempt to bolster his faltering self-esteem and negotiate a non-deviant identity. Twice a week becomes once a month; his violence is isolated from all his other abusiveness and controlling behaviour, particularly his emotional and psychological abuse. A real battering which lasted all night becomes a couple of quick slaps and a push.

4 Denial of consequences

The man refuses to see that his behaviour has any significant effects on his partner or his children, and his relationships with them. He does not want to see that she is always afraid of him, and particularly so if he is being nice to her. He refuses to see that she is losing her capacity to think for herself, and he uses her symptoms of his prior abuse as justification for further abusive behaviour. He denies that it is disturbing to his children. He insists that his wife loves him, and that this is obvious from the fact that she never says no to sex. He shows no understanding of what it must be like to be afraid of the one person you are supposed to feel safe with if you are a woman, or how it might feel to live in constant fear of physical violence.

ANGER AS ABUSE

There is much discussion of anger. Most men do not realize that anger with women usually arises because they are not behaving in ways which men define as appropriate. The anger is actually a technique of control and a form of abuse, not a cause of it. Signs of anger are letting the woman know that she is overstepping the boundaries of acceptable behaviour – acceptable to men, that is. As a result of this way of understanding anger, we do not stress anger management in work with abusers. Although this is a necessary first step simply to stop the most serious violent abuse, it is important to get men to examine the origins of their anger. It is not difficult for most to learn that it arises out of failed expectations, and that these are usually sexist and chauvinistic. The abuse is aimed at getting the woman to live up to these – often impossible – expectations. Our aim is to switch the man's attention to his expectations and motivate him to change them. The basis of this motivation is the surprising intensity of his dependency on and need for his partner, despite his extreme abuse of her. It should come as no surprise that abusers are almost incapable of containing ambivalence.

A great deal of attention is paid to the man's explanation for his abusiveness. Most often, he will say that he is not in control when he attacks his partner. This is very easy to contradict. Using sophisticated role-plays of actual incidents, we can show him that at every stage of the process leading up to his attack, he was making decisions which were going to result in violence or other abuse. He will learn that even when he was physically attacking her, he was making decisions about how to hit, where to hit, how hard, and so on. These decisions are accessible to awareness, and it is very painful for a man to realize that he was completely in control at the time of the attack, and that he makes a strategic decision about how much violence to use and when to stop. Actually, he has a choice. He can go on believing that he loses control and is therefore in some way crazy, or he can accept that he is in control and is responsible for his behaviour and begin to experience the guilt, remorse and empathy with his victim which must precede a decision to change. Inevitably, depression accompanies this process if it is effective.

It is very instructive to question batterers about their general level of anger, resentment or rage when they are at work or otherwise out of the home. Although most describe themselves as placid and quiet, in line with their conflict phobia, they will readily acknowledge that their level of arousal is very high. Why, then, do they not attack people outside the home? We know that batterers are generally less socially violent than the male population as a whole. Clearly their violence is not associated with the poor impulse control beloved of psychiatrists. How is it that it is always women who get attacked? Batterers become very confused when they are confronted with these simple contradictions in their own behaviour.

TRUST

It is made clear to all the men who come into an abusers' programme that trust is an issue in our work with them. It is not possible to trust a batterer (Jukes, 1990a, 1993). I realize that this must sound appalling, but experience of trusting men in abuse programmes has taught me a painful lesson: not that batterers cannot be trusted at all, but that it is impossible to know which can be trusted and when. I have had some experiences of trusting what men in groups were telling me about positive changes in their ongoing behaviour with their victim, only to discover later that during this time they were inflicting systematic physical violence on her. It took a while to realize that trust is the one currency that batterers abuse in relationships. They constantly re-establish it with their partners after inflicting a battering, only to abuse it later. We now monitor with the victim where it seems safe to do so, and she is the judge of this. If she is in any doubt about the consequences of taking part in a monitoring scheme, we do not pursue it. Our programmes are aimed at decreasing, not increasing, the risks to women. We also advise her to involve the police, and to press charges if she has not already done so. The evidence is that this, combined with re-education, is the most effective strategy, and we support the application of the law to battering (Jukes, 1990b).

The Non-Consensual Basis

This rather sketchy outline of the nature of work with abusive men – and we believe that most men would benefit from such a programme – might convey some of the flavour of the processes involved. I said that I intended to describe a non-consensual model for such work, and I hope I have gone some way towards this. It is easy to describe precisely what is non-consensual about this model. Most professionals involved in marital or family work use a variety of systems theory as the basis for intervening. The systems theorists' position is that families or marriages behave like other systems – for example a central heating system where the behaviour of the air temperature informs the thermostat whether to turn the boiler on or off, up or down. The elements in the system interact with each other, and causation is circular. In a family or a marriage this would mean that whatever the presenting problem, each person in the system would have a part to play in creating and maintaining it. The man's behaviour – let us call it A – causes the woman to behave in a fashion – let us call this B – which induces the man to do A. Any arguments about who started it – which, of course, are common currency in arguments in a relationship – are irrelevant to a systems theorist, since the objective is to change the total system rather than judge who is in the right or the wrong – a quagmire in which couples can often be stuck. From this point of view it makes little difference what is induced to change, since any change in any aspect of the system will induce change in the other contributing elements.

As should be clear from the examples quoted from my work with abusive men, I take the attitude that causation is linear, that the man is totally responsible for his abusiveness, that his partner's behaviour is a product of his abusiveness, and nothing she does can justify his violence or abuse. Of course women as well as men can behave in ways which provoke violent feelings and impulses in others, but the decision to be violent is expressly the responsibility of the abuser, regardless of the degree of provocation. Although the woman may well have problems which contribute to difficulties in the relationship, these pale into insignificance where there is ongoing abuse and the threat of violence. This inequality in the power relationship is the basic problem with which I work. I see this as the starting point of the system, and it is a real and worldwide social inequality. One could never compare the violent or provocative behaviour of a battered wife with that of her male abuser. Once the man has given up his abusiveness, there may be scope for some joint work of a marital or systemic kind if the woman wants it, and if she is free from fear. There is little doubt that from a feminist perspective men's violence and abusiveness, in all their manifestations, form the coercive underpinning of the development of a femininity which is adapted to men's needs. This includes the reproduction of mothering practices and social and psychological theories which define, and therefore control, female sex-role behaviour. Inevitably, appropriate role behaviour is precisely what is required to maintain the prevailing power structure: male dominance and female subordination.

Conclusions

Though pedantry denies, it's plain the bible means,
That Solomon grew wise whilst talking to his Queens.

(W.B. Yeats)

I should like to start by confessing to a certain amount of anticipatory anxiety at reaching these conclusions. It does not concern the reader's judgement of my efforts to address this fundamental problem – that is now out of my hands – but, rather, the direction in which the text has led me, so to speak, by the nose.

I began by hoping that I could make clear the psychological factors which underpin the universal oppression of women by men. It is for the reader to judge whether this has been achieved. Apart from the depressing collection of facts in the Preface, this oppression has been assumed, and the text has been devoted to understanding its origins and persistence rather than any attempt to persuade men that we do indeed oppress women.

I made it clear at the outset that this was to be, as far as possible, a psychological rather than a political, economic, biological or anthropological account. Not that this in any way removes the dilemma which faces anyone in the human sciences who attempts to explain the causes of behaviour. The most fundamental – and oversimplified – conflict in these disciplines is between those who stress the effects of nature and those who stress nurture. Is it biology or environment which shapes human behaviour? I hope I have steered a path between these alternatives by stressing the interaction between anatomy and culture, with the individual and group psyche acting as mediator. Nevertheless, it remains possible to support either of these stark alternatives.

One of the major difficulties of the task I set myself – to account for the oppression of women, by men, in psychodynamic terms – is that one realizes very quickly that this oppression is based entirely on gender. This seems to be stating the obvious, but the implications are profound: any explanation of this oppression must not assume that which it attempts to explain – that is, sexual differentiation. The fundamental weakness of the theory of the Oedipus complex is that it does precisely that: it assumes the existence of men and women. Any explanation, therefore, must pre-date the Oedipus complex; it must account for how sexual differentiation came about. This is, so to speak, the bottom line.

The psychological origins of misogyny, and the ultimate structuring of the original experience, are relatively clear. I have postulated that the origin of the 'self' leads to the development of an encapsulated psychosis with a psychic skin of primitive sadomasochistic objects, and hence to the eroticization of dominance – heterosexuality. The processes by which misogyny is perpetuated, both socially and psychologically, are also clear. Placing Mother in the gap where femininity falls seems to guarantee that it will continue indefinitely. This placing of Mother seems immutable, given men's constant need to reassure themselves about their potency in the face of the demonically sadistic 'witch' mother of the primitive psyche and the even more terrifying prospect of the inevitable no-self which accompanies no sex/gender. A true deconstruction of mothering would involve nothing less than the destruction of gender. Even a utopian revolution in childcare arrangements will not alter this so long as men define all sexuality and women remain the essential object of male desire. I apologize for the apparent reification, but I am convinced that the main aim of patriarchy – of men – and its ideology, sexism, is not the induction of little boys into manhood (although this is fundamental) but the separation of little girls from their mothers in order that they might be available to men. Only if this is successful will men continue to feel that the gap is fillable. Here I agree with those feminists who argue that heterosexism is the fundamental incest taboo (see Ortner and Whitehead, 1981): the injunction that forbids homosexuality.

I must confess the obvious: the explanation so far, however effective an explication of misogyny, fails this acid test of accounting for gender origins. All that we are enabled to do is hypothesize a pre-symbolic time when gender did not exist, and posit that this is what infants recapitulate during their movement to the Oedipus complex. There must have been a time when humankind was unitarian: an Eden-like period of non-differentiation destroyed when Adam bit into the fruit of the tree of knowledge – differentiated sexuality – and was cast out of his unitarian paradise. The primal gap between the unitarian and differentiated self is the one into which femininity has 'fallen', and into which men have ultimately placed Mother. The loss of the breast, at least in psychoanalysis, has become a metaphor for this differentiation. This 'gap' is an essential condition of personhood. It is not fanciful to believe that it is made flesh by the division of the sexes. In the male psyche, woman lies on the other side of the gap, tantalizingly within reach yet utterly unreachable.

The pressing awareness of the confusion surrounding the connection between anatomy and childbirth – a conundrum experienced by every little human being to this day – would have gone hand in hand with some social restructuring and symbolization along gender lines. This must have been a late consequence of the development of some form of symbolic order if one considers the enormous leap required in the capacity for conceptual and abstract thinking in order to connect intercourse with childbirth. In her admirable book *The Women's History of the World* (1988) Rosalind Miles addresses the issue of male dominance; she describes the move from magical to symbolic thinking – and hence men's awareness of cause and effect – about the origins of babies. She asserts that before this move women were the dominant gender, and that this dominance derived from their procreative capacities. It would be hard to better her description of the use men made of the awareness of their role in procreation (phallus in wonderland!) in order to achieve dominance. Her description of female dominance, however, fails the acid test: it presumes what we actually need to explain. What about the time before this hypothesized female dominance – the time when there was no means of knowing – or, more accurately, no incentive to know – that only certain members of the species, not yet designated female, could bear offspring?

Having offered a psychology of masculinity which accounts for men's motives in oppressing and brutalizing women, we are left with the issue which bedevils feminists and other academics of every description: how did it come about that men, rather than women, achieved this position of dominance? It seems that we may be left with a rather banal explanation: ultimately, men's power is founded on an innate anatomical dimorphism which bestows on them greater physical strength and psychological vulnerability, and on women long periods of physical vulnerability. This capacity for dominating women is not, however, as I said much earlier, enough to explain men's dominance. It had to be combined with motives for doing so. This occurred alongside the development of the symbolic order and gender differentiation – the motivation derives from blaming women for the loss of basic unity. The female parallel for this encapsulation has to be suppressed and educated out of little girls so that they might become women. I believe that this provides a sufficient explanation for women's enforced submission.

The subsequent psychological and social elaboration of innate anatomical/sexual dimorphism to its present-day extent far exceeds any requirements the preservation of the species might impose. It is this excess, sexism, and the extreme lengths to which men go in assuring their superiority over – and continued control of – women which I have attempted to address.

It seems that there is no way of actually knowing what, if anything, 'a woman wants' (Benjamin, [1990] asks: 'does a woman want?'). What a woman wants is always what is socially structured. Effectively, given men's control of social structures, women become what men want them to become and want what men want them to want. The idea that there is a true and innate femininity which would express true wants is – like masculinity – a product of the male imagination, perennially unhappy with the femininity it has produced, which falls so far short of the ideal 'other' whom we imagine could complete us.

It is a truism to point out that sexuality is defined by men. The basis of the social structure is the desire of all children to be the sole object of their mother's desire, and to fuse with her. Culture intervenes in this relationship to ensure that the mother–baby bond is broken and to weaken the power of the mother/woman. The paradox is that the sole object of the mother's desire – if she has learned her lessons well – is the unattainable phallus, for which she substitutes the father. Her desire for the phallus is probably a secondary formation which arises out of her failure to fuse with the mother. This is socially structured; little girls have to be separated from their mothers for men's sakes. She adapts to the alternative which is provided for her. This alternative reflects and reinforces the power of men. Boys eventually settle for having a penis and girls for having a baby, as both a substitute for and a defence against this basic desire. The phallus is a false symbol which derives its power from men's fear of impotence and helplessness.

The power of men – ultimately the power of the Father – is that they represent the Law: authority, rationality, reason, logic. These derive from the basic Law of the father's possession of the mother: he is both symbol and upholder of the Law. The continuation of culture (men's culture, heterosexuality) is presented as necessary for the continuation and preservation of the species and as requiring the upholding of the Law. If we men were able and knew how to back off, and allow little girls the space to grow in the public sphere rather than the private, which has been their only domain, who knows what might emerge? Of course this is an impossibility. The deconstructionists, like the socialist feminists, assume that because things are constructed, they can simply be reconstructed. This is ultimately a belief system. It is a wish-fulfilling fantasy. Language and culture are products of the human – largely masculine – mind. The Oedipus complex sets the parameters within which human subjectivity is structured. In fact, it does more: it sets the limits of thought and language about sexuality. The unconscious is structured by language and culture, whatever its innate qualities. We have no way of knowing what, if any, innate qualities there may be, because there is no knowing without language.

I am inclined to think that sexual dimorphism and gender identity were constructed by men to account for the fundamental experience of impairment, incompletion and loss (Moberley,

1987). The female lies, in the male imagination, on the other side of the gap between the incomplete self and the complete pre-self. The universal experience of the loss of paradise, infantile narcissism or whatever, led men to construct femininity as we know it, and with it the hope that this loss could be assuaged and even completely negated. Male and female seem to be psychological derivatives of – and metaphors for – the biological separation of the child from its mother and the individual from the horde. As a consequence, women go on being the victims of the anger and rage which derive from the unfulfillable expectation of satisfied desire.

The statistics in the Preface show that men are prepared to go to extremes to enforce the oedipal Law. Normal contempt for women shades into a misogyny which borders on the gynicidal. The liberation issues which face the vast majority of the world's women are rather more urgent than those which face the Western feminist. Although they are qualitatively the same, they are life-threatening on a scale unimagined in the West. These problems cannot be divorced from the problems of poverty in the developing world, and racism in the predominantly white developed world, but the fact remains that in the struggle for resources, women and girls suffer more often and most tragically.

Psychoanalysis cannot contribute to the relief of these problems. Although it can do much to clarify our understanding and even free many well-off individuals from the yoke of sexism, it is impotent in the face of a political inertia which is profoundly and deeply rooted in the individual and collective unconscious.

One cannot pretend to have any prescription for the wider problem. It may be that there is no solution to men's oppression of women apart from social evolution. My own thinking on this issue is still developing. All I can offer is a statement of my present position as I wrestle with the confusion which arises. Other things being equal, I do not believe men will ever give up power over women. This does not preclude action on a wide variey of fronts designed *de facto* to render women more equal, and to widen the range of choices open to them for combating men's abusive enforcement of their power. In fact I think this represents the limits of the possible.

One does not have to deny, as some feminists do, the gains of feminism over the last twenty years in order to assert that it may be impossible to change fundamentally the unequal distribution of power between men and women. We can – and should – applaud and, indeed, work for changes which stop men's abuse of their power over women. The enforcement of the law against battering, or charging men with rape in marriage and giving women the idea that they have a right to expect justice – these are not small things. They represent a threat to the most vile and damaging ways in which men abuse, and assert, their power over women. In themselves they represent major changes to the limits of male behaviour. Men's power over women, however, does not consist of abusive behaviour or maltreatment. A fundamental change in the distribution of power requires changes in all our most fundamental institutions, not simply preventing men from abuse.

I think it is clear that I have no great faith in the value of social engineering as a means of changing men's power over women. Unlike socialist feminists (see L. Segal, 1990) I do not believe that gender arises only from culture, or the structure and organization of institutions. These certainly reflect, reproduce and maintain the oppression of women, but it does not originate there. It originates in the original experience of separation from the unified mother–infant dyad, and is reified and socially structured through the Oedipus complex. Change requires nothing less than a complete dismantling of gender.

My experience shows that the majority of professional carers, both male and female, feel trapped and often outraged by the perspective this book espouses. It effectively says that all the traditional ways of understanding women are redundant and – not to put too fine a point on it – that we have been getting it wrong. The basic tenet is that what we think of as femininity is a product of – and occasionally a protest against – masculinity. It is another way of saying that where men place the mother, in femininity, is in the gaps in ourselves. In the extreme – in particular in work with men who are violent towards women, in whom one can see these processes at work most clearly – it means that we take as mistaken almost everything they perceive about the victim on whom they inflict their violence. One gets into the habit of understanding the victim's behaviour as a response to abuse, and not in the least causative; to attempting to understand her as a hostage to terror with only her fear as a guide to survival. Most therapeutic models collude with cultural – that is, patriarchal – norms of heterosexual relationships which enshrine and reify male power and control over women.

It must also be said that this model can evoke despair in women. I do not believe that men are good for women, or good to them. Under pressure I would maintain that in terms of romantic stereotypes there are no good men. I believe that the abuse of women, even if it is simply the need to be in control without using violent sanctions, is an 'innate' characteristic of our masculinity. I am not surprised by feminist separatism even though, as a man, I find it discouraging. I have no doubt, either, that my thesis can seem inherently insulting to women. It places them in an extremely passive position. I can only say to such women, who point to their hard-won independence, paraphrasing what Freud used to say: 'you are different'. He went on to add that such women were more masculine than feminine. I would simply say that they have resisted men's attempts to tame them. Ultimately, also, I hope that such thinking will be empowering for women if it helps them to understand men and to lead more fulfilling and separate lives which are not dependent on the goodwill of men.

Such a way of thinking also gives a new dimension to individual psychotherapy. It provides a model for confronting men with their sexist and abusive behaviour from the premiss that they are responsible for it. The bottom line is that male abusiveness and violence, our power and control, are not negotiable currency. Any therapy which does not deal with these issues fails. The irony is that rather than undermining traditional perspectives and approaches, such an attitude actually seems to enhance work with men. With traditional male methods of acting out their power and control behaviour with women made more difficult (because they are subject to censure), the tendency is for the underlying issues to become more accessible, even though this may generate some rather intense moments between patient and therapist. Dealing with these moments is, in any case, the everyday stuff of psychotherapy. The modifications in technique required (mainly being willing to define abusive behaviour for what it is, and confront it) are minor, and are more than justified by the benefits which can ensue. I know of no stronger way of urging that therapists, of both sexes and all schools, should familiarize themselves with feminist thinking and commit their sexual politics to close self-examination.

Many feminists think that the oppression of women will continue for so long as women are the objects of men's sexual desire, and are dependent on men. At the extreme, this means that sexual politics is the cornerstone of the fight for liberation, and entails the encouragement of lesbianism as a political statement. The argument of this book leads naturally to this conclusion. Admittedly this is a minority view, but to some it may sound an attractive idea. The banal reality is that, for whatever reason, the vast majority of women would find the idea repugnant and sterile. That is hardly surprising, even though it is far from saying that the vast majority of women are happy with the limits imposed on them by male-defined sex roles. There may be little doubt that many women are happy to be women, and to fulfil their 'unique' role. What is required is that this unique role be recognized and suitably rewarded. Additionally, it should be possible, for women who are so inclined, to compete with men as equals and eschew their male-defined sex-determined behaviour. Sadly – and it seems to be increasingly true in Europe, as in the USA – men will not make it easy for woman to abjure her role as mother, even where equal opportunities are enshrined in legislation.

Despite the confusion and anxiety it evokes, feminism seems to offer an exciting opportunity to rethink our view of the world. My own experience is of discovering (rather late in the day, I confess) a new window on reality. My anxiety is that men will do with feminism what we have always done with women's issues: colonize them and make them ours. To some extent this book may be an example of this. One sees only too clearly what this means in work with men who are abusive towards women. There comes a point in the treatment and re-education process, if it is successful, when the perpetrator realizes that his violence is about his need to have power over his partner, and that he is violent when this power is challenged or threatened. If he decides to renounce violence and abusiveness, he comes up against the most difficult problem of all in the struggle against sexism: that of renouncing power. To assert that men's abusiveness derives from anger with women because they fail our expectations is simplistic. It has led many to think that if we simply confront these expectations, make them explicit and analyse them, the anger will dissipate. In my experience this is not entirely true, for the simple reason that many of these expectations are pre-verbal, even ineffable. At these levels we need to understand the profoundly deep roots of misogyny, and this involves going beyond simple behaviour and cognitive processes.

The stark reality is that men have this power. What does it mean to give it up? It is not, as men who attempt it discover, a once-and-for-all decision: it is a lifelong process. Although abusiveness is not an addiction, it shares many features of addictive behaviour, and renouncing it parallels the struggles of a reformed alcoholic. Every day has to begin with a commitment that this will be another day without drinking. So it is with sexism. Men's power over women cannot be given up; the best one can hope for is not to exercise it. Women, at best, have little influence over this. Change can be brought about only by men.

In 'Our own worst enemies: unconscious factors in female disadvantage' (1985), Jane Temperley cautions against:

> those feminists who berate men as the architects and perpetuators of the social inequality between the sexes who . . . *run the risk* of using the hysterical defence, the excuse and privilege of the subordinate, where guilt is projected and the illusion of innocence is maintained. (emphasis added)

She insists on the reciprocity of the system whereby men and women swap uncomfortable parts of themselves for mutual benefit. To my mind she not only runs the risk of denial, but actually denies the reality that women have no choice. Although I agree that many women do maintain the illusion of innocence in just this way, it is small consolation for the injustice of their social inequality and maltreatment. She goes on to say that 'some feminists may unconsciously unite in a shared hostility to the idea of good intercourse between what is different and incomplete in each sex'. This hostility derives, as she sees it, from the feminists' inability to come to terms with the parental couple united in creative sexual intercourse. This is rather rich when one considers how dangerous the family can be for women.

If we turn this thinking around, we conclude that a woman's hostility towards feminism is a product of her inability to resolve her oedipal idealization of her father, and her wish to have his babies. It is a travesty of the truth to attempt to interpret feminist women's anger or non-feminist women's passivity in this way: an attempt to discount and minimize which does not address the issue that female sexuality is structured by men. It is simply a sophisticated form of victim-blaming and a denial of any justified female anger with men. This kind of thinking reflects the double bind which some – admittedly orthodox – psychoanalytic thinking can put women into: either feminists are maintaining an illusion, or they are unable to come to terms with parental intercourse. You can't win. If you're not maintaining an illusion, you're angry with the united parental couple for excluding you from their pleasure. There is no room in this kind of thinking for genuine female anger. This criticism of Temperley's position is not a way of denying that women have an unconscious. It denies that whatever is innate can be known. The unconscious is structured like a language: it is largely learned.

The female unconscious is different from the male because it is predicated largely on the woman's relationship to the absent penis, whereas the man's is predicated on the fear of its absence. These anxieties derive from the fundamental significance of the phallus as a symbol in the structure of language, and not from any fundamental – that is, innate – female anxieties about not having one.

Nobody could possibly disagree that we should go on to 'encourage people to appreciate the possibility of interdependence, complementarity and creative union' (Temperley, 1985) and to renounce the possibility of satisfying a bottomless infantile desire. However, the task of releasing women from the yoke of men's hatred, and their oppressive and persecuting behaviour, requires rather more: it requires radical changes in our most fundamental institutions – politics, law, medicine, education. Language must be rethought. Discrimination against women must be outlawed and replaced by positive discrimination policies.

Violence against women must be treated as the serious crime it is. The state must provide for women to be free to leave abusive relationships without penalty and with appropriate protection. This would include appropriate welfare and housing benefits. Most of all, legislative assemblies must be representative of women. The lesson of history is that men will arrange society to suit themselves.

Even if such changes were to be instituted – and I doubt if they ever will – it is questionable how many women would take advantage of the opportunities they would provide. To the extent that the 'masochistic move' is not a free choice, many women would no doubt continue to make it.

The objective of such changes is to undermine the conflation between anatomical femaleness and culturally determined psychological femininity and sex-role stereotypes; to provide women with the opportunity for choice in those areas which at the moment are proscribed as a result of this conflation, and derive directly from men's excessive need to have power and control over them.

I have no reservations in concluding that the hatred of women and its central role in the formation of masculinity leads, seemingly inexorably, to the oppression of women and the establishment of linguistic and social structures which exclude and control them. Gender identity may not be innate, like physical attributes, but the inexorability of anatomical, psychological and cultural pressures makes it no less certain. The oppression of woman begins at birth, when she is assigned to her no-sex.

This is not an argument for passivity. Much good can come of struggling against misogyny and sexism. That struggle already exists on many different fronts. Feminists of all shades of opinion are fighting for equality with men and recognition of women's special needs. I am convinced that if change is ever to come about, more men are needed to identify with and publicize the plight of women. Just as marital therapy is ineffective and misleading when the man is battering his wife, so I believe that women will achieve equality only when men grant it to them. However, the contribution of feminism cannot be overvalued. Without the work of women, from Mary Wollstonecraft on, men would still be largely unaware of the power politics of gender. It is to feminists that we must look for a redefinition of gender roles. Equality for women does not simply mean having access to the same resources as men, although this would be a good beginning.

Change is required in the hearts of men; it will not do to say that women must like it or they would not put up with it. This is the rationalization of all victim blamers. Victims cannot be blamed for their powerlessness and passivity.

On the whole it seems that men have too much to lose and too little to gain by sharing power with women. This goes to the heart of what it means to be a man: that we assume control over women and are prepared to use violence to sustain it. Ultimately, even if men share access to power with women, the one thing that cannot be shared is control over who has control. Independent women may be able to retain their independence only by refusing partnership with men, unless they are fortunate enough to encounter one of the few who can be comfortable without control, and can tolerate and take responsibility for his primitive ambivalence and confusion.

Postscript: John

What happened to John, whose violence towards Jane began this book?

He came into an anti-abuse programme almost six years ago. Before this he had been battering Jane at least twice a week for five years. After he had been in the programme for a month, Jane left the refuge and went back to the family home. During the programme he battered her once – seriously. As a result, and after we had discussed it with Jane, he was informed that we would not feel safe working with him while he stayed at home. He agreed to leave until he was prepared to control his violence rather than Jane. He went home, by agreement with Jane, after five months.

To this day, although Jane still feels afraid of him sometimes, he has not been violent towards her. He describes himself as trying to rebuild the relationship from scratch, and as courting her. He does not believe he can trust himself enough to say that he will never be violent again. It is clear from Jane's reports that he is working hard to give up his need to control her and his controlling behaviour, and that major changes in their relationship have occurred which, she thinks, are to her benefit.

Bibliography

Place of publication is London unless otherwise stated.

Adams, D. (1982) 'The continuum of male controls over women', monograph. Boston, MA: Emerge.

—— (1988) 'Treatment models of men who batter: a pro-feminist analysis', in Bograd and Yllo, eds, pp. 176–99.

Aleksandrowicz, M. and D. (1976) 'Precursors of ego in neonates', *Journal of the American Academy of Child Psychiatry* 15: 257–68.

Amir, M. (1971) *Patterns in Forcible Rape*. Chicago: University of Chicago Press.

Andrews, D. (1987) 'Normal violence in the family', unpublished paper. New Hampshire Conference on Family Violence.

Ashworth, G. and Bonnerjea, L., eds (1985) *The Invisible Decade*. Aldershot: Gower.

Baker, P. (1991) 'Do we need men's centres?', *Achilles Heel*, Autumn: 14.

—— (1992) 'Heterosexuality and pornography', in Itzen, ed.

Baker, T. and Duncan, S. (1986) 'Child sexual abuse', in R. Meadow, ed. *Recent Advances in Paediatrics*. Edinburgh: Livingstone.

Bamberger, J. (1974) 'The myth of matriarchy: why men rule in primitive societies' in Rosaldo and Lamphere, eds, pp. 263–80.

Barkowski, M., Murch, M. and Walker, V. (1983) *Marital Violence: The Community Response*. Tavistock.

Barnet, S., Corder, F. and Jehu, D. (1990) 'Group treatment for women sex offenders against children', *Groupwork* 3: 191–203.

Barnett, C. *et al.* (1970) 'Neonatal separation: maternal side of interactional deprivation', *Paediatrics* 46: 197–205.

Barrett, M. (1980) *Women's Oppression Today*. Verso.

Barry, K. (1982) 'Sado-masochism: the new backlash to feminism', *Trivia* 1.

Beauvoir, S. de (1949) *The Second Sex*, H.M. Parshley, trans. Harmondsworth: Penguin, 1960.

Benjamin, J. (1990) *The Bonds of Love*. Virago.

Bettelheim, B. (1972) *The Uses of Enchantment*. Harmondsworth: Peregrine.

Bly, R. (1991) *Iron John: A Book About Men*. Dorset: Element.

Bograd, M. and Yllo, K., eds (1988) *Feminist Perspectives on Wife Abuse*. Sage.

Bolton, F.G. and Bolton, S.R. (1988) *Working with Violent Families*. Beverley Hills, CA: Sage.

Borland, M., ed. (1976) *Violence in the Family*. Manchester: Manchester University Press.

Bowlby, J. (1988) *A Secure Base*. Routledge.

Brannen, J. and Collard, J. (1982) *Marriage in Trouble*. Tavistock.

Brenner, C. (1974) *An Elementary Textbook of Psychoanalysis*. New York: IUP Doubleday.

Brownmiller, S. (1976) *Against Our Will: Men, Women and Rape*. Harmondsworth: Penguin.

Brunswick, M.R. (1940) 'The pre-oedipal phase of the libido development', reprinted in Fleiss, ed. (1948) pp. 231–52.

Burns, G. (1986) *Somebody's Husband, Somebody's Son*. Heinemann.

Carpenter, G. (1974) 'Mother's face and the newborn', *New Scientist* 61: 742.

Chapman, J.R. and Gates, M., eds (1978) *The Victimisation of Women*. Sage.

Chasseguet-Smirgel, J. (1976) 'Freud and female sexuality', *Int. J. Psycho-Anal.* 57: 275–86

Chesler, P. (1972) *Women and Madness*. New York: Avon.

Chodorow, N. (1978) *The Reproduction of Mothering*. Berkeley, CA: University of California Press.

—— (1989) *Feminism and Psychoanalytic Theory*. Cambridge: Polity.

CIBA Foundation (1984) *Child Sexual Abuse within the Family*. Tavistock/Routledge (updated 1988).

Connell, R. (1983) *Which Way Is Up?* Sydney: George Allen & Unwin.

Connell, R.W. (1987) *Gender and Power*. Cambridge: Polity.

Croll, E. (1983) *Chinese Women Since Mao*. Zen.

Cucchiari, S. (1981) 'The origins of gender hierarchy', in Ortner and Whitehead, eds, pp. 31–79.

Daly, M. (1979) *Gyn/Ecology: The Metaethics of Radical Feminism*. The Women's Press.

D'Andrade, R.G. (1966) 'Sex differences and cultural institutions', in Maccoby, ed., pp. 173–203.

Deschner, J. (1984) *The Hitting Habit: Anger Control for Battering Couples*. New York: Free Press.

Deutsch, H. (1924) 'The psychology of women in relation to the functions of reproduction', reprinted in Fleiss, ed. (1948), pp. 165–79.

—— (1930) 'The significance of masochism in the mental life of women', reprinted in Fleiss, ed. (1948), pp. 195–207.

Dinnerstein, D. (1976) *The Mermaid and the Minotaur*. New York: Harper & Row.

Dobash, E.R. and Dobash, R. (1978) 'Wives, the "appropriate" victims of marital violence', *Victimology* 2: 426–42.

—— (1980) *Violence Against Wives: A Case Against the Patriarchy*. Open Books.

Dobash, R. (1990) 'Suffering in Silence', Granada Television, 11 November.

Driver, E. and Droisen, A., eds (1989) *Child Sexual Abuse*. Macmillan.

Dubois, E.C., Kelly, G.P., Kennedy, E.L., Korsmeyer, C.W. and Robinson, L.S. (1987) *Feminist Scholarship: Kindling in the Groves of Academe*. Chicago: Illinois University Press.

Dworkin, A. (1981) *Pornography: Men Possessing Women*. The Women's Press.

Edelson, J.L. and Syers, M. (1989) 'The relative effectiveness of group treatments for men who batter', Monograph. Minnesota: Domestic Abuse Research Project.

Edwards, A. (1987) 'Male violence in feminist theory', in Hanmer and Maynard, eds, pp. 13–29.

Edwards, S. (1981) *Female Sexuality and the Law*. Oxford: Martin Robertson.

—— (1984) *Women on Trial*. Manchester: Manchester University Press.

——, ed. (1985) *Gender, Sex and the Law*. Croom Helm.

Engels, F. (1975) *Origin of the Family: Private Property and the State*, ed. Eleanor Leacock. New York: International.

Erikson, E. (1950) *Childhood and Society*. New York: Norton.

Everywoman (1988) *Pornography and Sexual Violence: Evidence of the Links*. Everywoman.

Fenichel, O. (1946) *The Psychoanalytic Theory of Neurosis*. Routledge & Kegan Paul.

Finkelhor, D. (1986) *A Sourcebook on Child Sexual Abuse*. Beverley Hills, CA: Sage.

—— and Yllo, K. (1985) *License to Rape: Sexual Abuse of Wives*. New York: Holt, Rinehart & Winston.

Firestone, S. (1971) *The Dialectic of Sex*. Paladin.

Fleiss, R., ed. (1948) *The Psychoanalytic Reader*. New York: International Universities Press.

Foucault, M. (1979) *The History of Sexuality*. Allen Lane.

Fowles, J. (1981) *Aristos*. Panther.

Frank, A. (1969) 'The unrememberable and the unforgettable: passive primal repression', *Psychoanal. Study Child* 18: 464–83.

Freidl, E. (1975) *Women and Men: An Anthropologist's View*. New York: Holt, Rinehart & Winston.

French, M. (1991) *The War Against Women*. Harmondsworth: Penguin.

Freud, A. (1981) 'A psychoanalyst's view of sexual abuse by parents', in Mralek and Kempe, eds, *Sexually Abused Children and Their Families*. Oxford: Pergamon.

Freud, S. (1895) 'Project for a scientific psychology', in James Strachey, ed. *The Standard Edition of the Complete Psychological Works of Sigmund Freud*, 24 vols. Hogarth, 1953–73, vol. 1, pp. 295–397.

—— (1900) *The Interpretation of Dreams. S.E.* 4 and 5.

—— (1901) *The Psychopathology of Everyday Life*, *S.E.* 6.

—— (1905) *Three Essays on the Theory of Sexuality. S.E.* 7, pp. 130–243.

—— (1907) *Delusions and Dreams in Jensen's 'Gradiva'. S.E.* 9, pp. 7–95.

—— (1909) 'Analysis of a phobia in a five-year-old boy'. *S.E.* 10, pp. 4–148.

—— (1910) 'A special type of choice of object made by men'. *S.E.* 11, pp. 163–75.

—— (1912a) 'On the universal tendency to debasement in the sphere of love'. *S.E.* 11, pp. 179–90.

—— (1912b) 'Contributions to a discussion on masturbation'. *S.E.* 12, pp. 243–54.

—— (1913) *Totem and Taboo. S.E.* 13, pp. 1–162.

—— (1914) 'On narcissism: an introduction'. *S.E.* 14, pp. 73–102.

—— (1915) 'The unconscious'. *S.E.*14, pp. 166–215.

—— (1916) The Archaic Features and Infantilism of Dreams. *S.E.* 15, pp. 199–212.

—— (1920) *Beyond the Pleasure Principle. S.E.* 18, pp. 7–64.

—— (1923) *The Ego and the Id. S.E.* 19, pp. 3–66.

—— (1924) 'The economic problem of masochism'. *S.E.* 19, pp. 159–70.

—— (1925a) The Dissolution of the Oedipus Complex. *S.E.* 19, pp. 173–9.

—— (1925b) 'Some psychical consequences of the anatomical distinction between the sexes'. *S.E.*19, pp. 248–58.

—— (1925c) 'On negation', *S.E.* 19, pp. 235–9.

—— (1930) *Civilization and its Discontents. S.E.*21, pp. 64–145.

—— (1932) Feminity. *S.E.* 22, pp. 112–35.

—— (1954) *The Origins of Psycho-Analysis: Letters to Wilhelm Fliess*, J. Strachey and E. Mosbacher, trans. M. Bonaparte, A. Freud and E. Kris, eds. New York: Basic Books.

—— and Breuer, J. (1893) *Studies on Hysteria. S.E.* 2.

Friday, N. (1977) *My Secret Garden: Women's Sexual Fantasies*. New York: Arrow.

—— (1980) *Men in Love*. New York: Arrow.

Frosh, S. (1989) *Psychoanalysis and Psychology: Minding the Gap*. Macmillan.

Fuss, D. (1989) *Essentially Speaking*. Routledge.

Gayford, J.J. (1975) 'Wife Battering: a preliminary survey of 100 cases', *British Medical Journal* 1 (5951): 194–7.

Gebhard, P., Gagnon, W., Pomeroy, W. and Christenson, C. (1965) *Sex Offenders: An Analysis of Types*. New York: Harper & Row.

Gilbert, L. and Webster, P. (1982) *Bound by Love*. Boston, MA: Beacon.

Gillespie, W.H. (1975) 'Woman and her discontents: a re-assessment of Freud's views on female sexuality', in Kohon, ed. (1986), pp. 344–61.

Glaser, D. and Frosh, S. (1988) *Child Sexual Abuse*. Macmillan.

Goldberg, H. (1976) *The Hazards of Being Male*. New York: Nash.

Goldstein, J., Freud, A. and Solnit, A. (1979) *Before the Best Interests of the Child*. New York: Free Press.

Graham, D.L.R., Rawlings, E. and Rimini, N. (1988) 'The Stockholm syndrome', in Bograd and Yllo, eds, pp. 217–34.

Greenson, R. (1964) 'On homosexuality and gender identity', in *Explorations in Psychoanalysis*. New York: International Universities Press (1978), pp. 191–8.

—— (1968) 'Disidentifying from the mother: its special importance for the boy', ibid., pp. 305–12.

Griffin, S. (1971) 'Rape: the all American crime'. *Ramparts* 10: 26–35.

Groth, A.N. and Birnbaum, H.J. (1979) *Men Who Rape, The Psychology of the Offender*. New York: Plenum.

Hadon, C. (1984) *Women and Tranquillisers*. Sheddon.

Hall, R. (1985) *Ask Any Woman: A London Enquiry into Rape and Sexual Assault*. Falling Wall Press.

Hanmer, J. (1978) 'Violence and the social control of women', in Littlejohn *et al. Power and the State*. Croom Helm.

—— and Maynard, M., eds (1987) *Women, Violence and Social Control*. Macmillan.

Harding, S. and Hintikka, M.B. (1983) *Discovering Reality*. Boston, MA: Reidl.

Hart, B. (1988) 'Safety for women', monograph. Pennsylvania Coalition Against Domestic Violence.

Hartman, E. (1869) *The Philosophy of the Unconscious*. Quoted in Freud *S.E.* VI.

Havelock Ellis, H. (1937) *The Psychology of Sex*. Heinemann.

Hawton, K. and Catalan, J. (1982) *Attempted Suicide: A Practical Guide to its Nature and Management*. Oxford: Oxford University Press.

Heaton, J. (1976) 'The place of theory in psychotherapy', *Jnl Brit. Soc. Phenomenology*, May, pp. 73–85.

Herman, J. (1981) *Father/Daughter Incest*. London: Harvard University Press.

Herman, N. (1988) *My Kleinian Home*. Free Association Books.

Hintikka, B.M. and Hintikka, J. (1983) 'How can language be sexist?', in Harding and Hintikka, eds, pp. 139–48.

Hite, S. (1981) *The Hite Report on Male Sexuality*. New York: Knopf.

—— (1987) *Women and Love*. Harmondsworth: Penguin.

Hoffman Baruch, E. and Serrano, L.J. (1990) *Women Analyse Women*. Hemel Hempstead: Harvester Wheatsheaf.

Hopper, E. (1991) 'The encapsulated psychosis', *Int. J. Psycho-Anal.* 72: 607–24.

Horley, S. (1991) *The Charm Syndrome*. Macmillan.

Horney, K. (1924) 'On the genesis of the castration complex in women', *Int. J. Psycho-Anal.* 5: 50–63.

—— (1926) 'The flight from womanhood', *Int. J. Psycho-Anal.* 7: 324–39.

—— (1933) 'The denial of the vagina', *Int. J. Psycho-Anal.* 14: 57–70.

Horsfall, J. (1991) *The Presence of the Past: Male Violence in the Family*. Allen & Unwin.

Hubbard, R. (1979) 'Have only men evolved?' in Hubbard *et al.*, eds *Women Looking at Biology Looking at Women*, Cambridge, MA: Schenkman, pp. 7–36.

Hunter, M. (1990) *Abused Boys*. New York: Fawcett Columbine.

Irigaray, L. (1985) *This Sex Which is Not One*. New York: Cornell.

Itzen, K., ed. (1992) *Pornography*. Oxford: OUP.

James, J. and Meyerling, J. (1979) 'Early sexual experience as a factor in prostitution', *Archives of Sexual Behaviour*, 7 (1): 31–42.

Jeffreys. S. (1990) *Anticlimax*. The Women's Press.

Johnson, N., ed. (1985) *Marital Violence*. Routledge and Kegan Paul.

Jones, E. (1933) 'The phallic phase', *Int. J. Psycho-Anal.* 14: 1–33.

Jouve, N. W. (1986) *The Streetcleaner: The Yorkshire Ripper Case on Trial*. Marion Boyars.

Judge, C.S. (1979) *The Book of American Rankings*. New York: Facts on File.

Jukes, A.E. (1988) 'Men who batter: a suitable case for treatment', Monograph. The Men's Centre.

—— (1990a) 'The Men's Centre programme', *Everyman* 2: 12–14.

—— (1990b) 'Domestic violence: making women safe', *Social Work Today*, June 1991: 14–17.

—— (1990c) 'Working with men who are violent to women', *British Association of Counselling Journal*, November 1991: 124–6.

—— (1993a) 'Violence, helplessness, vulnerability and male sexuality', *Free Associations* 29: forthcoming.

—— (1993b) 'Working with men who are helpless, vulnerable and violent', *Free Associations* 30: forthcoming.

Kaluzynska, E. (1980) 'Wiping the floor with theory: a survey of writings on housework', *Feminist Review* 6: 27–54.

Kelly, E. (1986) 'Women's experience of sexual violence', PhD thesis, University of Essex.

—— (1988a) 'The continuum of male violence', in Hanmer and Maynard, eds, pp. 46–60.

—— (1988b) *Surviving Sexual Violence*. Cambridge: Polity.

Kelly, E., Regan, L. and Burton, S. (1991) 'An exploratory study of sexual abuse in a sample of 16–21-year-olds'. Polytechnic of North London: Child Abuse Studies Unit.

Khan, M.R. (1979) *Alienation in Perversions*, International Psychoanalytic Library 108.

—— (1986) 'The concept of cumulative trauma', in Kohon, ed. (1986), pp. 117–35.

Kinsey, A.C., Pomeroy, W.B. and Martin, C.E. (1948) *Sexual Behaviour in The Human Male*. Philadelphia: W.B. Saunders.

—— (1953) *Sexual Behaviour in the Human Female*. Philadelphia: W. B. Saunders.

Kittay, E.F. (1984) 'Pornography and the erotics of domination', in C.C. Gould, ed. *Beyond Domination*. Totowa, NJ: Rowbotham & Allenheld, pp. 145–74.

Klaus, M. and Kennell, J. (1976) *Maternal/Infant Bonding*. St Louis, MO: Mosby.

Klein, D. (1979) 'Can the marriage be saved?', *Crime and Social Justice* 12.

Klein, M. (1935) 'A contribution to the psychogenesis of manic-depressive states', in *Love, Guilt and Reparation*. Hogarth, 1975, pp. 262–89.

—— (1952) 'The emotional life of the infant', in *Envy and Gratitude and Other Works*. Hogarth, 1975, pp. 61–93.

Kohon, G., ed. (1986) *The British School of Psychoanalysis: The Independent Tradition*. Free Association Books.

Koppel, G. (1985) 'Breaking the cycle of violence', *Guardian*, 23 September.

Kovel, J. (1981) *The Age of Desire: Case Histories of a Radical Psychoanalyst*. New York: Basic Books.

—— (1985) 'Sins of the fathers', *Free Associations* 1: 113–24.

Kreiner, C. (1991) Interview in *Achilles Heel* 12.

Kurian, G.T. (1984) *The New Book of World Rankings*. New York: Facts on File.

Lacan, J. (1957) 'The agency of the letter in the unconscious or reason since Freud', in *Ecrits*, pp. 146–78.

—— (1977) *The Four Fundamental Concepts of Psychoanalysis*. Hogarth.

—— (1980) *Ecrits: A Selection*, A. Sheridan, trans. Tavistock.

Lampl-de-Groot, J. (1928) 'The evolution of the Oedipus complex in women', reprinted in Fleiss, ed. (1948), pp. 180–94.

Lane, A. (1976) 'Women in society: a critique of Frederick Engels', in Bernice Carroll, ed. *Liberating Women's History: Theoretical and Critical Essays*. Chicago: University of Illinois Press, pp. 4–25.

Lawson, A. (1990) Institute of Family Therapy Conference, quoted in *Observer* 28 February, p. 60.

Leghorn, L. (1976) 'Social responses to battered women', paper delivered to Wisconsin Conference on Battered Women.

Lesbians Against Pornography (1984) 'A blow job for a man is a con job for women', *City Limits*, 16 March.

Lichtenberg, J. (1981) 'Implications for psychoanalytic theory of research on the neonate', *Int. Rev. Psycho-Anal.* 8: 35–52.

London Rape Crisis Centre (1984) *Sexual Violence: The Reality for Women*. Women's Press.

McAndrew, M. and Peers, J. (1981) *The New Soviet Woman*. Change International Reports.

Maccoby, E., ed. (1966) *The Development of Sex Differences*. Stanford, CA: Stanford University Press.

—— (1980) *Social Development: Psychological Growth and Parent/Child Relationship*. New York: Harcourt Brace.

—— and Jacklin, G. (1974) *The Psychology of Sex Differences*. Stanford, CA: Stanford University Press.

—— *et al.* eds (1958) *Readings in Social Psychology*. New York: Holt, Rinehart & Winston.

McDougall, J. (1990) *A Plea for a Measure of Abnormality*. Free Association Books.

McLean, S. and Graham, S.E. (1983) *Female Circumcision and Infibulation*. Minority Rights Group: Revised Report No. 47.

MacLeod, M. and Saraga, E. (1988) 'Challenging the orthodoxy: towards a feminist theory and practice', *Feminist Review* 28: 16–55.

McNickle Rose, V. and Randall, S. (1978) 'Where have all the rapists gone?', in Incavdi and Potteiger, eds *Violent Crime: Historical and Contemporary Issues*. Sage.

Mahler, M., Pine, F. and Bergmann, A. (1975) *The Psychological Birth of the Human Infant*. Hutchinson.

Mahony, P. (1985) *Schools for the Boys*. Hutchinson.

Malamuth, N. and Donnerstein, E. (1984) *Pornography and Sexual Aggression*. Orlando, FL: Academic Press.

Malcolm, J. (1983) 'Annals of scholarship: trouble in the archives – 1', *New Yorker*, 5 December (pp. 59–152); 'Trouble in the archives – 2', *New Yorker*, 12 December (pp. 60–119).

Masson, J. (1984) *The Assault on Truth*. Faber & Faber.

—— (1989) *Against Therapy*. Collins.

Masters, W.H. and Johnson, V.E. (1961) *Human Sexual Response*. Boston, MA: Little Brown.

Mathews, R. *et al.* (1989) *Female Sexual Offenders*. The Safer Society Press.

Meltzer, D. (1973) *Sexual States of Mind*. Perthshire: Clunie Press.

Miles, R. (1988) *The Women's History of the World*. Salem House.

Miller, A. (1979) *The Drama of the Gifted Child and the Search for the True Self*. Faber & Faber (1983).

—— (1980) *For Your Own Good: The Roots of Violence in Child-Rearing*. Virago (1987).

—— (1981) *Thou Shalt Not be Aware: Society's Betrayal of the Child*. Pluto (1986).

—— (1987) *The Drama of Being A Child and the Search for the True Self*. Virago (1987).

Millett, K. (1977) *Sexual Politics*. Virago.

Mitchell, J. (1986) 'The question of femininity and the theory of psychoanalysis', in Kohon, ed. pp. 381–98.

—— and Rose, J. eds (1982) *Feminine Sexuality: Jacques Lacan and the* école freudienne. Macmillan.

Moberley, E. (1987) *Psychogenesis*. Tavistock.

Molière (1665) *Don Juan*, in *The Miser and Other Plays*. Harmondsworth: Penguin Classics (1953).

Money, J., ed. (1965) 'Psychosexual differentiation', in *Sex Research: New Developments*. New York: Holt, Rinehart & Winston.

—— *et al.* (1957) 'Imprinting and the establishment of gender role. *Arch. Neurol. Psych*. 77: 333–6.

Morgan, D. (1985) *The Family, Politics, and Social Theory*. Routledge & Kegan Paul.

Mukhopadhyay, M. (1984) *Silver Shackles: Women and Development in India*. Oxford: Oxfam.

Nash, C.L. and West, D.J. (1985) 'Sexual molestation of young girls', in D.J. West. ed. *Sexual Victimisation*. Aldershot: Gower.

Oakley, A. (1981) *Subject Women*. Oxford: Martin Robertson.

Orbach, S. (1981) *Fat is a Feminist Issue*. Hamlyn.

—— and Eichenbaum, L. (1982) *Outside In, Inside Out*. Harmondsworth: Penguin.

Ortner, S.B. and Whitehead, H., eds (1981) *Sexual Meanings: The Cultural Construction of Gender and Sexuality*. Cambridge: Cambridge University Press.

Penfold, P.S. and Walker, G.A. (1984) *Women and the Psychiatric Paradox*. Milton Keynes: Open University Press.

Pepinster, K. (1991) 'Man handlers', *Time Out*, June, p. 16.

Pleck, J.H. (1979) 'Men's traditional attitudes towards women: conceptual issues in research', in J. Sherman and F. Denmark, eds *The Psychology of Women*. New York: Psychological Dimensions.

—— (1981) *The Myth of Masculinity*. Cambridge, MA: MIT Press.

—— and Sawyer, J., eds (1974) *Men and Masculinity*. Englewood Cliffs, NJ: Prentice Hall.

Rabkin, J. (1979) 'Epidemiology of forcible rape', *American Journal of Orthopsychiatry* 49(4): 634–47.

Radway, J.A. (1983) 'Women read the romance: the integration of text and context. *Feminist Studies* 9: 53–78.

Regan, J., Creighton, S. and Jones, D. (1984) 'Incidence of child sexual abuse'. NSPCC Information Briefing no. 2.

Reibstein, J. and Richards, M. (1991) *Sexual Arrangements: Marriage and Extramarital Affairs*. Heinemann.

Reich, A. (1956) *Psychoanalytic Contributions*. New York: International Universities Press.

Reich, W. (1933) *Character Analysis*. Vision Press.

Renvoize, J. (1978) *The Web of Violence: A Study of Family Violence*. Harmondsworth: Penguin.

Rich, A. (1976) *Of Woman Born*. New York: Norton.

—— (1980) 'Compulsory heterosexuality and lesbian existence', *Signs* 5(4): 631–60.

Rodgerson, G. and Wilson, E. (1991) *Pornography and Feminism: The Case Against Censorship*. Lawrence & Wishart.

Rogers, R.S. (1989) 'The social construction of childhood', in E. Ash, ed. *Child Abuse and Neglect*. Open University. Batsford.

Rohrbaugh, J.B. (1980) *Women: Psychology's Puzzle*. Sussex: Harvester.

Roper, M. and Tosh, J. (1991) *Manful Assertions: Masculinities in Britain since 1800*. Routledge.

Rosaldo, M.Z. and Lamphere, L., eds (1974) *Woman, Culture and Society*. Stanford, CA: Stanford University Press.

Rosenbaum, A. and O'Leary, K.D. (1981) 'Marital violence: characteristics of abusive couples', *Journal of Consulting and Clinical Psychology* 49: 49–63.

Rosenberg and Sutton (1972) *Sex and Identity*. Sage.

Roy, M. ed. (1977) *Battered Women: A Psychological Study of Domestic Violence*. New York: Van Nostrand Reinhold.

Rowan, J. (1990) *The Horned God*. Routledge.

Rubin, G. (1975) 'The traffic in women'; 'Notes on the political economy of sex', in R.R. Reiter, ed. *Towards an Anthropology of Women*. New York: Monthly Review Press, pp. 157–210.

Rubin, Z. and McNeil, E.B. (1983) *The Psychology of Being Human*. Harper & Row.

Russell, D. (1984) *Sexual Exploitation*. Beverly Hills: Sage.

—— and Van Den Ven, N., eds (1976) *Crimes Against Women*. Millbrae, CA: Les Femmes.

Sander, L. (1975) *Infant and Caretaking Environment: Explorations in Child Psychiatry*. ed. A.J. Anthony. New York: Plenum, pp. 129–66.

Schatzman, M. (1973) *Soul Murder*. Allen Lane.

Schechter, S. (1982) *Women and Male Violence: The Visions and Struggles of the Battered Women's Movement*. Boston, MA: South End Press.

Schlafly, P. (1977) *The Power of the Positive Woman*. New Rochelle, NY: Arlington House.

Scott, A. (1988) 'Feminism and the seductiveness of the "real event"', *Feminist Review* 28: 88–101.

Scully, D. and Marolla, J. (1984) 'Convicted rapists' vocabulary of motive: excuses and justifications', quoted in Kelly (1988b), p. 47.

Segal, H. (1973) *Introduction to the Work of Melanie Klein*. Hogarth.

Segal, L. (1987) *Is The Future Female?* Virago.

—— (1990) *Slow Motion: Changing Masculinities, Changing Men*. Virago.

—— and McIntosh, M., eds (1992) *Sex Exposed*. Virago.

Sharma, K. *et al.* (1984) *Women in Focus*. New Delhi: Sangam.

Sherfey, M.J. (1966) *The Nature and Evolution of Female Sexuality*. New York: Random House.

Shute, S. (1981) 'Sexist language and sexism', in Vetterling-Braggin, ed.

Smakowska, C. (1985) *Marital Problems and Family Violence*. NSPCC Information Briefing no. 7.

Snitow, A.B. (1979) 'Mass market romance: pornography for women is different', *Radical History Review* 20: 141–63.

Spender, D. (1980) *Man Made Language*. Routledge & Kegan Paul.

—— (1983) *Invisible Women*. Writers & Readers.

—— and Kline, S. (1989) *Reflecting Men at Twice Their Natural Size*. Glasgow: Fontana Collins.

Spitz, R. (1965) *The First Year of Life*. New York: International Universities Press.

Stanko, E. (1985) *Intimate Intrusions:Women's Experience of Male Violence*. Routledge & Kegan Paul.

Stoller, R.J. (1968) *Sex and Gender: The Development of Masculinity and Femininity*. vol. 1. Maresfield Reprints (1984).

—— (1975) *Perversion: The Erotic Form of Hatred*. Maresfield Reprint (1986).

Storr, A. (1965) *Sexual Deviation*. Heinemann.

Straus, M.A., Gelles, R. and Steinmetz, S.K. (1980) *Behind Closed Doors*. New York: Anchor.

Strouse, J. (1974) *Women and Analysis: Dialogues on Psychoanalytic Views of Femininity*. New York: Dell.

Temperley, J. (1985) 'Our own worst enemies: unconscious factors in female disadvantage', *Free Associations*, pilot issue.

Tempkin, J. (1987) *Rape and the Legal Process*. Sweet & Maxwell.

Thomas, W.I. (1907) *Sex and Society: Studies in the Psychology of Sex*.

Vetterling-Braggin, M. ed. (1981) *Sexist Language: A Modern Philosophical Analysis*. Totowa, NJ: Littlefield Adams.

Walker, L.E. (1978) 'Battered women and learned helplessness', *Victimology* 2: 525–34.

—— (1979) *The Battered Woman*. New York: Harper Colophon.

Walkowitz, J. (1982) 'Jack the Ripper and the myth of male violence', *Feminist Studies* 8(3): 570.

Ward, E. (1984) *Father-Daughter Rape*. The Women's Press.

Weaver, M.A. (1984) 'Women who pay with their life', *Sunday Times*, 12 February, p. 46.

Welldon, E. (1988) *Mother, Madonna, Whore*. Free Association Books.

Whitehead, A. (1976) 'Sexual antagonism in Hertfordshire', in D.L. Barker and S. Allen, eds *Dependence and Exploitation in Work and Marriage*. Longman.

Whitehead, G. (1991) Review in *Achilles Heel* 12, Autumn: 38.

Whiting *et al.* (1958) 'The function of male initiation ceremonies at puberty', in Maccoby *et al.* eds.

Williams, J. and Holmes, K. (1981) *The Second Assault: Rape and Public Attitudes*. Westport, CT: Greenwood.

Wilson, E. (1983) *What Is To Be Done About Violence Towards Women?* Harmondsworth: Penguin.

Winnicott, D. (1949) 'Mind in relation to the psyche-soma', reprinted in *Through Paediatrics to Psychoanalysis*. International Library Psychoanalysis 100, pp. 243–54.

—— (1960a) 'Ego distortion in terms of true and false self', in *The Maturational Processes and the Facilitating Environment*. International Library Psychoanalysis 64, pp. 140–52.

—— (1960b) 'The theory of the parent–infant relationship', ibid., pp. 37–55.

—— (1963a) 'Communicating and not communicating leading to a study of certain opposites', ibid., pp. 179–92.

—— (1963b) 'From dependence towards independence in the development of the individual', ibid., pp. 83–92.

Wollstonecraft, M. (1792) *A Vindication of the Rights of Woman*. Harmondsworth: Penguin, 1975.

Women: A World Report (1985) Methuen.

'World in Action' (1989) Granada Television Survey.

Wyre, R. (1988a) *Men, Women and Rape*. Oxford: Perry.

—— (1988b) *Working with Sexual Abuse*. Oxford: Perry.

INDEX

This first edition of
Why Men Hate Women
was finished in June 1993

The book was commissioned by Robert M. Young,
edited by Selina O'Grady and Ann Scott,
copy-edited by Gillian Beaumont,
proofread by Julia Henderson,
indexed by Linda English,
and produced by Ann Scott and Chase Production Services
for Free Association Books